THE Bible REVEALED

A 365-Day Guided
Journey Through God's Word

PHILIP YANCEY AND BRENDA QUINN

ZONDERVAN®

Titles by Philip Yancey

The Bible Jesus Read
The Bible Revealed (with Brenda Quinn)
Church: Why Bother?
Disappointment with God
Fearfully and Wonderfully: The Marvel of Bearing God's Image (with Dr. Paul Brand)
Finding God in Unexpected Places
The Gift of Pain (with Dr. Paul Brand)
Grace Notes: 366 Daily Inspirations from a Fellow Pilgrim
I Was Just Wondering
The Jesus I Never Knew
Prayer: Does It Make Any Difference?
The Question That Never Goes Away
Reaching for the Invisible God
Rumors of Another World
Soul Survivor: How Thirteen Unlikely Mentors Helped My Faith Survive the Church
The Student Bible (with Tim Stafford)
Undone: A Modern Rendering of John Donne's Devotions
Vanishing Grace: Bringing Good News to a Deeply Divided World
What Good Is God?: In Search of a Faith That Matters
What Went Wrong?: Russia's Lost Opportunity and the Path to Ukraine
What's So Amazing About Grace?
Where Is God When It Hurts?
Where the Light Fell: A Memoir

Titles by Brenda Quinn

The Bible Revealed (with Philip Yancey)
The Jesus I Never Knew: Study Guide
The Life with God Bible (Renovaré)
Reaching for the Invisible God: Study Guide
What's So Amazing About Grace?: Study Guide

ZONDERVAN

The Bible Revealed

© 2025 by Philip D. Yancey and Brenda Quinn

Published in Grand Rapids, Michigan, by Zondervan. Zondervan is a registered trademark of The Zondervan Corporation, L.L.C., a wholly owned subsidiary of HarperCollins Christian Publishing, Inc.

Requests for information should be addressed to customercare@harpercollins.com.

Content is revised and updated from *Meet the Bible*, by Philip Yancey and Brenda Quinn, ISBN 978-0-310-22776-2, copyright © 2000, Zondervan. Used by permission. The Philip Yancey portions of this book were previously published in the books *Discovering God* ©1989 (Zondervan) and *Guided Tour of the Bible* ©1989 (Zondervan).

Unless otherwise noted, Scripture quotations are from the Holy Bible, New International Version®, NIV®. Copyright © 1973, 1978, 1984, 2011 by Biblica, Inc.® Used by permission of Zondervan. All rights reserved worldwide. www.zondervan.com. The "NIV" and "New International Version" are trademarks registered in the United States Patent and Trademark Office by Biblica, Inc.®

Scripture quotations marked NRSV are from the New Revised Standard Version Bible. Copyright © 1989 National Council of the Churches of Christ in the United States of America. Used by permission. All rights reserved worldwide.

Scripture quotations marked TLV are from the Holy Scriptures, Tree of Life Version. Copyright © 2014, 2016 by the Tree of Life Bible Society. Used by permission of the Tree of Life Bible Society.

Any internet addresses (websites, blogs, etc.) and telephone numbers in this book are offered as a resource. They are not intended in any way to be or imply an endorsement by Zondervan, nor does Zondervan vouch for the content of these sites and numbers for the life of this book.

All rights reserved. No part of this publication may be reproduced, stored in a retrieval system, or transmitted in any form or by any means—electronic, mechanical, photocopy, recording, or any other—except for brief quotations in printed reviews, without the prior permission of the publisher.

Art direction: Gabriella Wikidal

Interior design: Lori Lynch

ISBN 978-0-310-46785-4 (HC)
ISBN 978-0-310-46783-0 (eBook)

Printed in Vietnam
25 26 27 28 29 SEV 10 9 8 7 6 5 4 3 2 1

Contents

A Note to Our Readers xvii

Part 1: Beginnings

Day 1 **Genesis 1:1–2:3** Creation 2
Day 2 **Genesis 2:1–25** Adam and Eve 3
Day 3 **Genesis 3:1–24** The Fall of Man 4
Day 4 **Genesis 4:1–24** Cain and Abel 5
Day 5 **Reflection** Did God Really Say . . . ? 6
Day 6 **Genesis 6:1–7:24** The Flood 7
Day 7 **Genesis 8:1–22** The Land Dries 8
Day 8 **Genesis 9:1–17** God's Covenant Rainbow 9
Day 9 **Genesis 11:1–9** The Tower of Babel 10
Day 10 **Reflection** God Becomes a Parent 11
Day 11 **Genesis 12:1–20** The Call of Abram 13
Day 12 **Genesis 13:1–18** Abram and Lot Separate 14
Day 13 **Genesis 15:1–21** God's Covenant with Abram 15
Day 14 **Genesis 16:1–16** Hagar and Ishmael 16
Day 15 **Genesis 18:1–15** The Three Visitors 17
Day 16 **Reflection** God Calls 18
Day 17 **Genesis 18:16–33** Abraham Pleads for Sodom 19
Day 18 **Genesis 19:1–29** Sodom and Gomorrah Destroyed 20
Day 19 **Genesis 21:1–21** Isaac's Birth 21
Day 20 **Genesis 22:1–19** Abraham Tested 22
Day 21 **Genesis 24:1–67** Isaac and Rebekah 23
Day 22 **Reflection** Beneath the Surface of Faith 24
Day 23 **Genesis 25:19–34** Jacob and Esau 25
Day 24 **Genesis 27:1–40** Jacob Gets Isaac's Blessing 26
Day 25 **Genesis 27:41–28:22** Jacob's Dream at Bethel 27
Day 26 **Genesis 29:1–30** Jacob Marries Leah and Rachel 28
Day 27 **Genesis 29:31–30:24** Jacob's Children 29
Day 28 **Reflection** God Shining from the Shadows 30
Day 29 **Genesis 31:1–21** Jacob Flees from Laban 31
Day 30 **Genesis 31:22–55** Laban Pursues Jacob 32

Day 31 Genesis 32:1–21 Jacob Prepares to Meet Esau 33
Day 32 Genesis 32:22–32 Jacob Wrestles with God 34
Day 33 Genesis 33:1–20 Jacob Reunites with Esau 35
Day 34 Genesis 35:1–15 Jacob Returns to Bethel 36
Day 35 Reflection Wrestling with God 37
Day 36 Genesis 37:1–36 Joseph's Dreams 38
Day 37 Genesis 39:1–23 Joseph and Potiphar's Wife 39
Day 38 Genesis 40:1–23 The Cupbearer and the Baker 40
Day 39 Genesis 41:1–57 Pharaoh's Dreams 41
Day 40 Reflection A Life Motto 42
Day 41 Genesis 42:1–26 Joseph's Brothers Go to Egypt 43
Day 42 Genesis 42:27–38 Joseph's Brothers Return to Canaan 44
Day 43 Genesis 43:1–34 Joseph's Brothers Return to Egypt 45
Day 44 Genesis 44:1–34 A Silver Cup in a Sack 46
Day 45 Genesis 45:1–46:34; 50:15–21 Joseph Makes Himself Known 47
Day 46 Reflection Why Forgive? 48

Part 2: Birthing a Nation

Day 47 Exodus 1:1–2:10 The Birth of Moses 50
Day 48 Exodus 3:1–22 Moses and the Burning Bush 51
Day 49 Exodus 4:1–17 Signs for Moses 52
Day 50 Exodus 7:14–8:15 The Plagues of Blood and Frogs 53
Day 51 Exodus 8:16–9:7 The Plagues of Gnats, Flies, and Livestock . . . 54
Day 52 Reflection Prayer of a Reluctant Servant 55
Day 53 Exodus 9:8–35 The Plagues of Boils and Hail 56
Day 54 Exodus 10:1–11:10 Plagues: Locusts, Darkness, and Death of Firstborn . . . 57
Day 55 Exodus 12:1–30 The Passover 58
Day 56 Exodus 12:31–42 The Exodus 59
Day 57 Exodus 13:17–14:31 Crossing the Red Sea 60
Day 58 Reflection Spiritual Amnesia 61
Day 59 Exodus 16:1–36 Manna from Heaven 62
Day 60 Exodus 18:1–27 Jethro Visits Moses 63
Day 61 Exodus 19:1–20:17 The Ten Commandments 64
Day 62 Exodus 32:1–35 The Golden Calf 65
Day 63 Reflection Traveling on God's Wings 66
Day 64 Leviticus 26:3–45 Reward for Obedience; Punishment for Disobedience . . 67
Day 65 Numbers 9:15–23 The Cloud Above the Tabernacle 68

Day 66 Numbers 11:4–23, 31–34 Quail from the Lord 69
Day 67 Numbers 12:1–16 Miriam and Aaron Oppose Moses 70
Day 68 Reflection God's Puzzling Ways. 71
Day 69 Numbers 13:1–33 Exploring Canaan 72
Day 70 Numbers 14:1–44 The People Rebel. 73
Day 71 Numbers 20:1–13; 21:4–9 Water from the Rock; The Bronze Snake 74
Day 72 Deuteronomy 1:1; 4:7–38 Obedience Commanded 75
Day 73 Deuteronomy 8:1–20 Do Not Forget the Lord 76
Day 74 Reflection A Jekyll-and-Hyde God? 77
Day 75 Joshua 2:1–24 Rahab and the Spies 79
Day 76 Joshua 3:1–4:24 Crossing the Jordan 80
Day 77 Joshua 5:13–6:27 The Fall of Jericho. 81
Day 78 Joshua 7:1–26 Achan's Sin 82
Day 79 Joshua 24:1–33 The Covenant Renewed at Shechem 83
Day 80 Reflection Choosing to Love God. 84
Day 81 Judges 4:1–24 Deborah 85
Day 82 Judges 6:1–40 Gideon. 86
Day 83 Judges 7:1–8:35 Gideon Defeats the Midianites 87
Day 84 Reflection Follow the Leader 88
Day 85 Judges 13:1–25 The Birth of Samson. 89
Day 86 Judges 14:1–20 Samson's Marriage. 90
Day 87 Judges 16:1–31 Samson and Delilah 91
Day 88 Reflection A Strong Need for God 92
Day 89 Ruth 1:1–22 Naomi and Ruth 93
Day 90 Ruth 2:1–23 Ruth Meets Boaz. 94
Day 91 Ruth 3:1–4:17 Boaz Marries Ruth 95
Day 92 Reflection The Looks of a Believer 96
Day 93 1 Samuel 1:1–28 The Birth of Samuel 97
Day 94 1 Samuel 2:18–21; 3:1–21 The Lord Calls Samuel 98
Day 95 1 Samuel 8:1–22 Israel Asks for a King 99
Day 96 1 Samuel 9:1–10:8 Samuel Anoints Saul. 100
Day 97 Reflection Passionate Prayer. 101
Day 98 1 Samuel 15:1–29 The Lord Rejects Saul as King 102
Day 99 1 Samuel 16:1–23 Samuel Anoints David 103
Day 100 Psalm 23:1–6 A Shepherd's Song 104
Day 101 1 Samuel 17:1–58 David and Goliath 105
Day 102 Psalm 19:1–14 Outdoor Lessons 106

Day 103 Reflection Fighting Giants 107
Day 104 1 Samuel 18:1–11; 19:1–24 Saul Tries to Kill David 108
Day 105 1 Samuel 20:1–42 David and Jonathan 109
Day 106 Psalm 27:1–14 Ups and Downs 110
Day 107 1 Samuel 24:1–22 David Spares Saul's Life 111
Day 108 1 Samuel 25:1–42 David, Nabal, and Abigail 112
Day 109 Reflection Taking Risks, Trusting God 113
Day 110 2 Samuel 6:1–23 King David Brings the Ark to Jerusalem 114
Day 111 1 Chronicles 17:1–27 God's Promise to David 115
Day 112 Psalm 103:1–22 The Goodness of God 116
Day 113 2 Samuel 11:1–27 David and Bathsheba 117
Day 114 Reflection Sin and God's Love Through the Eyes of an Unbeliever 118
Day 115 2 Samuel 12:1–25 Nathan Rebukes David 119
Day 116 Psalm 51:1–17 True Confession 120
Day 117 Psalm 139:1–24 David's Spiritual Secret 121
Day 118 Reflection Practicing His Presence 122
Day 119 1 Kings 1:28–30; 3:1–28 Solomon Asks for Wisdom 124
Day 120 1 Kings 6:1–38; 8:1–66 The Ark Brought to the Temple 125
Day 121 Psalm 84:1–12 More Than a Building 126
Day 122 1 Kings 10:1–13 The Queen of Sheba Visits Solomon 127
Day 123 1 Kings 10:23–11:13 Solomon's Splendor, Solomon's Wives 128
Day 124 Reflection Losing Sight of God 129
Day 125 Song of Songs 2:1–17 Uncommon Song 130
Day 126 Song of Songs 3:6–4:16 The Wedding 131
Day 127 Song of Songs 8:1–14 Maturing Marriage 132
Day 128 Reflection Loving God's Way 133
Day 129 Proverbs 4:1–27 Life Advice 135
Day 130 Proverbs 10:1–23 How to Read Proverbs 136
Day 131 Proverbs 3:1–35 Wisdom for Living 137
Day 132 Ecclesiastes 3:1–22 A Time for Everything 138
Day 133 Reflection Keys to Becoming Wise 139
Day 134 1 Kings 12:1–24 Israel Rebels Against Rehoboam 141

Part 3: The Northern Kingdom—Israel

Day 135 1 Kings 17:1–24 The Widow at Zarephath 144
Day 136 1 Kings 18:15–40 Elijah on Mount Carmel 145
Day 137 1 Kings 19:1–18 The Lord Appears to Elijah 146

Day 138 2 Kings 2:1–18 Elijah Taken Up to Heaven 147
Day 139 Reflection Hearing God's Voice 148
Day 140 2 Kings 4:1–36 The Widow's Oil; A Son Restored 150
Day 141 2 Kings 5:1–27 Naaman Healed of Leprosy 151
Day 142 2 Kings 6:8–23 Elisha and the Chariots of Fire. 152
Day 143 Reflection Greater Is God in Us 153
Day 144 Joel 2:1–32 Rend Your Heart 155
Day 145 Jonah 1:1–2:10 Jonah Flees from the Lord 156
Day 146 Jonah 3:1–4:11 Jonah Goes to Nineveh. 157
Day 147 Reflection Working with God 158
Day 148 Amos 4:1–13 Israel Has Not Returned to God 160
Day 149 Hosea 1:1–35 Hosea's Wife and Children 161
Day 150 Hosea 11:1–11 God's Love for Israel 162
Day 151 2 Kings 17:1–41 Israel Exiled Because of Sin. 163
Day 152 Reflection God's Love Story 164

Part 4: The Southern Kingdom—Judah

Day 153 2 Chronicles 20:1–30 Jehoshaphat Defeats Moab and Ammon 166
Day 154 Micah 6:1–16 The Lord's Case Against Israel 167
Day 155 2 Chronicles 30:1–27 Hezekiah Celebrates Passover 168
Day 156 Isaiah 6:1–13 Isaiah's Commission 169
Day 157 Isaiah 25:1–26:21 Praise to the Lord 170
Day 158 Reflection Ready to Be Used by God. 171
Day 159 2 Chronicles 32:1–31 Sennacherib Threatens Jerusalem. 173
Day 160 Nahum 1:1–15 The Lord's Anger Against Nineveh 174
Day 161 Zephaniah 3:1–20 The Future of Jerusalem. 175
Day 162 2 Kings 22:1–23:3 Josiah Renews the Covenant 176
Day 163 Reflection What Does It Take to Be Faithful? 177
Day 164 Jeremiah 2:1–37 Israel Forsakes God 179
Day 165 Jeremiah 15:1–21 Death, Famine, Sword 180
Day 166 Jeremiah 31:1–40 Restoration of Israel 181
Day 167 Jeremiah 38:1–28 Jeremiah Thrown into a Cistern 182
Day 168 Reflection Serving from a Sensitive Spirit 183
Day 169 Habakkuk 1:1–17 Habakkuk's Complaint. 185
Day 170 Lamentations 3:1–40 His Compassion Never Fails 186
Day 171 Obadiah 1–21 Your Deeds Will Return 187
Day 172 Reflection To Love or Leave Unbelievers? 188

Part 5: Starting Over—In Exile and Returning from Exile

Day 173 Ezekiel 1:1–28 The Living Creatures and the Glory of the Lord. 192
Day 174 Ezekiel 2:1–3:27 Ezekiel's Call 193
Day 175 Ezekiel 4:1–17 Siege of Jerusalem Symbolized 194
Day 176 Ezekiel 37:1–28 The Valley of Dry Bones 195
Day 177 Reflection God's Bizarre Ways of Showing Love 196
Day 178 Daniel 1:1–21 Daniel's Training in Babylon 198
Day 179 Daniel 2:1–23 Nebuchadnezzar's Dream 199
Day 180 Daniel 2:24–49 Daniel Interprets the Dream 200
Day 181 Daniel 3:1–29 The Image of Gold and the Blazing Furnace 201
Day 182 Daniel 5:1–30 The Writing on the Wall 202
Day 183 Daniel 6:1–26 Daniel in the Den of Lions 203
Day 184 Reflection An Excellent Example 204
Day 185 Ezra 3:1–4:5 Rebuilding the Altar 206
Day 186 Haggai 1:1–2:9 A Call to Build the House of the Lord 207
Day 187 Zechariah 8:1–23 The Lord Promises to Bless Jerusalem 208
Day 188 Nehemiah 1:1–2:20 Artaxerxes Sends Nehemiah to Jerusalem 209
Day 189 Nehemiah 7:33–8:18 Ezra Reads the Law 210
Day 190 Reflection Building God into Our Lives 211
Day 191 Esther 1:1–22 Queen Vashti Deposed 212
Day 192 Esther 2:1–23 Esther Made Queen 213
Day 193 Esther 3:1–4:17 Haman's Plot and Mordecai's Plan 214
Day 194 Esther 5:1–6:14 Esther's Request to the King 215
Day 195 Esther 7:1–8:17 Haman Impaled 216
Day 196 Reflection God's Strategic Ways 217
Day 197 Malachi 2:17–3:18 Airing Complaints 218

Part 6: Cries of Pain

Day 198 Job 1:1–2:10 Job Is Tested 220
Day 199 Job 38:1–41 The Lord Speaks 221
Day 200 Job 42:1–17 Job Is Restored 222
Day 201 Reflection Loving God Freely 223
Day 202 Isaiah 40:1–31 Comfort for God's People 224
Day 203 Isaiah 52:1–15 The Suffering Servant 225
Day 204 Isaiah 53:1–12 The Glory of the Servant 226
Day 205 Isaiah 55:1–13 Invitation to the Thirsty 227
Day 206 Reflection Jesus, Our Highest Choice, Our Greatest Promise 228

Part 7: A Surprising Messiah

Day 207 Luke 1:5–52 The Births of John the Baptist and Jesus Foretold 232
Day 208 Matthew 1:1–25 An Angel Appears to Joseph 233
Day 209 Luke 1:57–80 The Birth of John the Baptist 234
Day 210 Luke 2:1–40 The Birth of Jesus 235
Day 211 John 1:1–18 The Word Became Flesh 236
Day 212 Reflection Jesus, Our Picture of God 237
Day 213 Matthew 2:1–23 The Visit of the Magi, Travels to Egypt and Nazareth . . 239
Day 214 Luke 2:41–52; Matthew 3:1–12 The Boy Jesus at the Temple;
    John the Baptist Prepares the Way 240
Day 215 Mark 1:9–45 Jesus Is Baptized, Tempted, and Begins His Work 241
Day 216 Matthew 4:1–11 The Temptation of Jesus 242
Day 217 Reflection Jesus' Pattern of Restraint 243
Day 218 John 2:1–11 Jesus Changes Water to Wine 245
Day 219 John 3:1–21 Jesus Teaches Nicodemus 247
Day 220 John 4:1–42 Jesus Talks with a Samaritan Woman 248
Day 221 Luke 4:14–30 Jesus Rejected at Nazareth 249
Day 222 Reflection Jesus Came for All People 250
Day 223 Luke 5:1–11 The Calling of the First Disciples 252
Day 224 Mark 2:1–28 Jesus Meets Opposition 253
Day 225 Mark 3:1–35 Jesus Teaches and Heals 254
Day 226 Mark 4:1–41 Jesus Tells Parables, Calms the Storm 255
Day 227 Mark 5:1–43 Jesus Heals and Restores Life 256
Day 228 Reflection Jesus Desires to Touch and Heal 257
Day 229 Matthew 5:1–48 The Sermon on the Mount 259
Day 230 Matthew 6:1–34 The Sermon on the Mount, Part 2 260
Day 231 Matthew 7:1–29 The Sermon on the Mount, Part 3 261
Day 232 Reflection Seeing Through God's Eyes 262
Day 233 Matthew 11:25–30; Luke 11:1–13 Rest for the Weary; Jesus' Teaching
    on Prayer 264
Day 234 Matthew 13:24–58 Parable of the Weeds, Mustard Seed, and Others . . 265
Day 235 Mark 6:14–56 Two Kinds of Power: Jesus' and Herod's 266
Day 236 Luke 16:1–31 Parables: Shrewd Manager; The Rich Man and Lazarus . . 267
Day 237 Luke 12:13–48 Jesus Teaches on Money 268
Day 238 Reflection God's Loving Nature 269
Day 239 Luke 18:1–43 Jesus Teaches, Heals, and Welcomes the Children 271
Day 240 John 5:1–47 Healing at the Pool; Life Through the Son 272

Day 241 Matthew 20:1–16 Parable of the Workers in the Vineyard 273
Day 242 Matthew 25:1–30 Parable of the Ten Virgins and the Parable of the Talents. 274
Day 243 Reflection Obedience Is the Thing. 275
Day 244 Matthew 25:31–46 The Sheep and the Goats 277
Day 245 Luke 14:15–35 Parable of the Great Banquet; Cost of Being a Disciple. . 278

Part 8: Responses to Jesus

Day 246 Luke 15:1–10 The Parables of the Lost Sheep and the Lost Coin 280
Day 247 Luke 15:11–32 The Parable of the Lost Son (Prodigal) 281
Day 248 Luke 19:1–10 Zacchaeus the Tax Collector 282
Day 249 John 6:24–71 Jesus, the Bread of Life; Deserted by Many Disciples . . . 283
Day 250 John 8:2–11 The Woman Caught in Adultery 284
Day 251 Reflection Finding Jesus 285
Day 252 Mark 7:1–37 Jesus Goads Hypocrites; Heals Man and Young Girl 287
Day 253 Matthew 18:21–19:12 Jesus Teaches on Forgiveness; On Divorce. 288
Day 254 John 10:1–40 The Good Shepherd; His Sheep; The Unbelievers 289
Day 255 Mark 8:1–38 Jesus Feeds, Teaches, and Heals 290
Day 256 Mark 9:1–41 The Transfiguration; Jesus Heals and Teaches. 291
Day 257 Reflection Still Trying to Figure Jesus Out. 292
Day 258 Luke 10:1–24 Jesus Sends Out Seventy-Two Disciples 293
Day 259 Luke 10:25–37 The Parable of the Good Samaritan 294
Day 260 Luke 10:38–42 At the Home of Mary and Martha 295
Day 261 John 11:1–44 Jesus Raises Lazarus from the Dead. 296
Day 262 Mark 10:32–11:11 Jesus Predicts His Death; Heals; Enters Jerusalem . . . 297
Day 263 Reflection Waiting on God 298
Day 264 Mark 11:12–12:12 Jesus Clears the Temple and Teaches. 300
Day 265 Mark 12:13–44 The Law; Greatest Commandment; Widow's Offering. . 301
Day 266 Mark 13:1–37 Signs of the End of the Age 302
Day 267 Mark 14:1–31 Woman Anoints Jesus; The Last Supper 303
Day 268 Reflection Loving Jesus Extravagantly. 304

Part 9: Jesus' Final Hours

Day 269 John 13:1–17 Jesus Washes His Disciples' Feet 308
Day 270 John 14:1–31 Jesus Offers Comfort, The Father, The Holy Spirit 309
Day 271 John 15:1–16:4 The True Vine; The World; The Holy Spirit. 310
Day 272 John 16:5–33 The Spirit of Truth; Return of Joy 311
Day 273 John 17:1–26 Jesus Prays 312

Day 274 Reflection Abiding in Jesus 313
Day 275 Matthew 26:36–75 Jesus in Gethsemane; Arrested; Faces Sanhedrin. . . 314
Day 276 Matthew 27:1–31 Judas Hangs Himself; Jesus Before Pilate 315
Day 277 Mark 15:21–47 The Crucifixion, Death, and Burial of Jesus 316
Day 278 Matthew 27:62–28:15 The Resurrection 317
Day 279 John 20:1–31 Jesus' Resurrection and Appearances 318
Day 280 Luke 24:13–49 On the Road to Emmaus 319
Day 281 John 21:1–25 Jesus and the Miraculous Catch of Fish; Jesus
   Reinstates Peter 320
Day 282 Reflection Remembering Jesus' Death and Victory 321

Part 10: The Word Spreads

Day 283 Matthew 28:16–20; Acts 1:1–26 The Great Commission; Jesus Taken
   Up into Heaven. 324
Day 284 Acts 2:1–41 The Holy Spirit Comes at Pentecost 325
Day 285 Acts 3:1–26 Peter Heals a Beggar. 326
Day 286 Acts 4:1–31 Peter and John Before the Sanhedrin. 327
Day 287 Reflection The Gift of the Holy Spirit 328
Day 288 Acts 2:42–47; 4:32–37 The Fellowship of the Believers 330
Day 289 Acts 5:1–42 Ananias and Sapphira; The Apostles Persecuted 331
Day 290 Acts 6:8–8:3 The Stoning of Stephen 332
Day 291 Acts 8:26–40 Philip and the Ethiopian 333
Day 292 Reflection Living by the Spirit. 334
Day 293 Acts 9:1–31 Saul's Conversion 336
Day 294 Acts 10:1–48 Peter's Vision; Peter at Cornelius's House 337
Day 295 Acts 12:1–19 Peter's Miraculous Escape from Prison 338
Day 296 Galatians 3:1–4:7 Faith or Observance of the Law. 339
Day 297 Reflection Faith, the Only Way 340
Day 298 Acts 16:6–40 Lydia's Conversion; Paul and Silas in Prison. 342
Day 299 Philippians 2:1–30 Imitating Christ's Humility 343
Day 300 Acts 17:1–34 Paul in Thessalonica, Berea, and Athens 344
Day 301 Reflection Finding Common Ground for the Gospel 345
Day 302 1 Thessalonians 2:17–4:12 Living to Please God 346
Day 303 2 Thessalonians 2:1–3:13 Stand Firm 347
Day 304 Acts 18:1–28 Paul in Corinth 348
Day 305 1 Corinthians 12:1–13:13 One Body, Many Parts; Love 349
Day 306 Reflection What Is a Church? 350

Day 307 **1 Corinthians 15:3–57** The Resurrection of Christ and the Dead 352
Day 308 **2 Corinthians 4:1–5:10** Treasures in Jars of Clay. 353
Day 309 **2 Corinthians 5:11–6:2; 6:14–7:1** The Ministry of Reconciliation;
  Do Not Be Yoked with Unbelievers 354
Day 310 **2 Corinthians 9:6–15** Sowing Generously 355
Day 311 **2 Corinthians 11:16–12:10** Paul Boasts About His Sufferings,
  His Thorn. 356
Day 312 **Reflection** Living with Thorns 357

Part 11: Paul's Legacy

Day 313 **Romans 3:10–31** No One Is Righteous 360
Day 314 **Romans 7:1–25** Struggling with Sin 361
Day 315 **Romans 8:1–27** Life Through the Spirit 362
Day 316 **Reflection** How God Changes Us 363
Day 317 **Romans 5:1–11; 8:28–39** Peace and Joy; More Than Conquerors 365
Day 318 **Romans 12:1–21** Living Sacrifices; Love. 366
Day 319 **Romans 13:1–14** Submission to Authorities; Love. 367
Day 320 **Romans 14:1–15:13** The Weak and the Strong 368
Day 321 **Reflection** Spending Myself on God 369
Day 322 **Acts 25:23–26:32** Paul Before Agrippa. 371
Day 323 **Acts 27:1–44** Paul Sails for Rome; Shipwreck 372
Day 324 **Acts 28:1–31** Ashore on Malta; Arrival at Rome 373
Day 325 **Ephesians 1:15–2:13** Thanksgiving and Prayer; Made Alive in Christ . . 374
Day 326 **Ephesians 2:14–3:21** Paul the Preacher to the Gentiles; A Prayer 375
Day 327 **Ephesians 4:1–5:20** Unity in the Body of Christ; Living as Children
  of the Light 376
Day 328 **Reflection** Fixing Broken Love. 377
Day 329 **Ephesians 5:21–6:20** Submit to One Another; The Armor of God . . . 379
Day 330 **Colossians 1:1–2:5** The Supremacy of Christ, Son of God 380
Day 331 **Colossians 3:1–25** Rules for Holy Living 381
Day 332 **Reflection** Fighting a Spiritual War 382
Day 333 **Philemon 1–25** Paul's Plea for Onesimus. 384
Day 334 **Titus 2:1–3:8** Paul Instructs Titus: Tell People to Do Good 385
Day 335 **1 Timothy 1:1–3:8** Teaching on Church Issues, Worship, Leaders 386
Day 336 **Reflection** Finding a Family That Works. 387
Day 337 **1 Timothy 6:3–21** Love of Money 389
Day 338 **2 Timothy 1:1–18** Encouragement to Be Faithful. 390

Day 339 **2 Timothy 2:1–26** A Workman Approved by God 391
Day 340 **Reflection** Choosing to Run or Remain 392

Part 12: Vital Letters

Day 341 **Hebrews 2:1–3:6** Jesus Made Superior to Angels and Fully Human 396
Day 342 **Hebrews 10:19–39** A Call to Persevere 397
Day 343 **Hebrews 11:1–40** By Faith 398
Day 344 **Hebrews 12:1–28** God Disciplines His Sons 399
Day 345 **Reflection** The Radical Side of Faith 400
Day 346 **James 1:1–2:10** Test of Faith; Listen and Act; Show No Favoritism 402
Day 347 **James 2:14–3:18** Faith and Deeds, Taming the Tongue, and Wisdom . . 403
Day 348 **James 4:1–17** Submit Yourselves to God 404
Day 349 **James 5:1–20** Warning to Rich Oppressors; Patience in Suffering;
   The Prayer of Faith 405
Day 350 **Reflection** Grace and Works 406
Day 351 **1 Peter 1:1–2:3** Praise to God for a Living Hope; Be Holy 408
Day 352 **1 Peter 3:8–4:19** Suffering for Doing Good; Living for God 409
Day 353 **2 Peter 1:1–2:3** Making One's Calling and Election Sure 410
Day 354 **Reflection** Refined by Fire 411
Day 355 **Jude 1–25** Sin and Doom of the Ungodly; Persevere 412
Day 356 **1 John 3:1–24** Children of God; Love One Another 413
Day 357 **1 John 4:1–21** Test the Spirits; God's Love and Ours 414
Day 358 **1 John 5:1–15** Faith in the Son of God 415
Day 359 **2 John 1–13; 3 John 1–14** When to Be Hospitable 416
Day 360 **Reflection** The Song of the Bible 417
Day 361 **Revelation 1:1–20** One Like a Son of Man 419
Day 362 **Revelation 2:1–29** To the Churches in Ephesus, Smyrna, Pergamum,
   and Thyatira 420
Day 363 **Revelation 3:1–21** To the Churches in Sardis, Philadelphia, and Laodicea . . 421
Day 364 **Revelation 12:1–17** The Woman and the Dragon 422
Day 365 **Revelation 21:1–22:5** The New Jerusalem; The River of Life 423
Day 366 **Reflection** Confidence in the Future 424

Notes 427
About the Authors 430

A Note to Our Readers

Welcome to *The Bible Revealed*! You are embarking on an incredible journey with the world's all-time bestseller. No book has had a more profound impact on human history than the Bible. Two and a half billion people on the planet now identify as Christians[1], and together they look to the Bible for answers to life's deepest questions. Why are we here? What does God have in mind for planet earth? Can we truly get to know God personally?

Yet the Bible can be a daunting book, whether you are reading a single chapter or attempting to read from cover to cover. After all, it includes sixty-six different books by several dozen authors whose writing styles vary widely. To understand the individual parts, it helps to get an overview of the entire sweep of the Bible.

We feel privileged to serve as your guides, starting with the book of Genesis and continuing to the book of Revelation at the end. We've carefully chosen key passages from each book of the Bible as a kind of sampler, and our background notes and explanations piece together the story of God's relationship with people throughout history.

There are 366 readings in *The Bible Revealed*, one for each day of the year. The readings consist of either (1) a suggested Bible passage accompanied by comments about the passage, or (2) a personal Reflection by either of the editors, Philip Yancey or Brenda Quinn. The Reflections will offer thoughts about the previous few readings and also make practical applications to daily life.

Such an overview plan is no substitute for mastering the entire Bible, of course, but it may help lower barriers and point the way down a path for further study. Think of it as something like a guided tour through a great city or a national park. You won't get to see every site of interest, but you will learn the basic layout and may acquire a taste that will entice you to return again and again.

We have arranged the biblical material in rough chronological order. You will read the psalms attributed to David as you read about David's life, and the books attributed to the prophets as you read about their context. Portions from the Gospels, too, are interspersed, giving a composite picture of Jesus' life on earth; and Paul's letters are pegged to the record of his travels. This arrangement should help convey the Bible's "plot."

For the best experience, please **read the entire noted Bible passage first before reading each day's entry in *The Bible Revealed*.** Sometimes a portion of the selected passage is provided for you, but it's always best to read the entire referenced passage. If you don't have a Bible, search for a translation that is easy to understand. We recommend using a printed Bible that you can mark with a highlighter or add your own notes to. If you prefer, use a phone or computer to read Bible passages. (While online access may be the most convenient, be aware of the distractions it may introduce.) Audio listening also provides a good option.

We live in an age of diminishing attention spans. The amount of information continually available at our fingertips can pull our focus in several directions at once. Yet the Bible deserves our committed, sustained attention. Push through your tendency to lose momentum, and stay with it. You may miss days here or there. If so, simply continue reading day by day, with no pressure to finish in a year. As you persist, you will be rewarded in your journey with God's Word, from beginning to end.

We echo the psalmist's prayer: "I delight in your decrees; I will not neglect your word" (Psalm 119:16).

God's Story and Your Story

No doubt you approach the Bible with your own questions, perhaps wondering how you relate to Scripture or to God. Maybe you have a different religious tradition, or an unfavorable opinion of Christians, or some wounds that make it hard to consider the possibility of a loving God. You're not alone. Even if you don't believe in God, you are welcome here. Join us in exploring how the simple act of engaging with the Bible each day might provide a way forward. You may find that the story of Scripture is more your story than you ever could have imagined.

The Bible tells of people from long ago whose stories range from heartwarming to shocking. In the process we begin to see that the story of God and his people is our story, *your* story. We find ourselves over and over again in the pages of the Bible. God gave us this book to reveal himself and to reveal who we are as his beloved creation. Along the way, we learn how to relate to him.

We hope you will find yourself in the Bible and, as you do so, will enter a life with God that fills you and overflows into the world. The Bible is a gift from our God who speaks to us each time we open its cover and read.

So, let's begin!

Philip Yancey and *Brenda Quinn*

Free online resources to help you choose a Bible, explore Bible translations and alternate language Bibles, and access audio Bible options: Bible Gateway, Bible Hub, YouVersion.

PART 1

Beginnings

DAY 1

Creation
Genesis 1:1–2:3

As you begin Day 1, please read "A Note to Our Readers" on page xvii. Then, in your Bible, read from Genesis 1:1 through Genesis 2:3. After reading the passage, proceed by reading the comments below. Follow this pattern each day.

Everything, truly everything, begins here. The story of the Bible—more, the history of the universe—starts with the simple statement "In the beginning God created," and the rest of the chapter fills in what he created: stars, oceans, plants, birds, fish, mammals, and, finally, man and woman.

Genesis 1 says little about the processes God used in creation; you'll find no explanations of DNA or the scientific principles behind creation. But the opening chapter of the Bible does insist on two facts:

Creation was God's work. "And God said . . . And God said . . . And God said . . ."—the phrase beats in cadence all the way through the chapter, which mentions the word *God* thirty times. And in this first chapter, the very first glimpse we have of God is as an artist. Butterflies, waterfalls, bottlenose dolphins, praying mantises, kangaroos—they were all God's idea. This entire magnificent world we live in is the product of God's creative work. All that follows in the Bible reinforces the message of Genesis 1: Behind all of history, there is God.

Creation was good. Another sentence tolls softly, like a bell, throughout this chapter: "And God saw that it was good." In our day, we hear alarming reports about nature: toxic plastics, polluted oceans, vanishing species, climate change, the destruction of rainforests. Much has changed, much has been spoiled since that first moment of creation. Genesis 1 describes the world as God wanted it, before any spoiling. Whatever beauty we sense in nature today is a faint echo of that pristine state.

Captain Frank Borman, one of America's Apollo astronauts, read from this chapter of Genesis on a telecast from outer space on Christmas Eve 1968. As he gazed out of his window, he saw Earth as a brightly colored ball hanging alone in the darkness of space. It looked at once awesomely beautiful and terribly fragile. It looked like the view from Genesis 1.

—PY

Daily Contemplation

When was the last time you really noticed the beauty of the natural world? What do you notice today?

DAY 2

Adam and Eve
Genesis 2:4–25

After presenting the cosmic view in chapter 1, Genesis repeats the story of creation, narrowing the focus to human beings. We alone, of all God's works, are made "in God's image." Over the years people have disagreed on what, exactly, that phrase "image of God" means. Is it immortality? Intelligence? Creativity? Relationship? Perhaps the best way to understand is to think of "the image of God" as a mirror. God created us so that when he looked upon us, he would see reflected something of himself.

Nothing else God created reflects that same likeness to God. Alone of all creation, human beings received the very breath of life from God. Genesis declares that human beings, in God's eyes, possess a value far beyond other living things. Similarly, humans have value that can never be equaled even by today's increasingly powerful computers, no matter how intelligent and lifelike they may be.

Genesis 2 shows human history just getting underway. Marriage begins here: Even in a state of perfection, Adam feels loneliness and desire, and God provides woman. From then on, marriage takes priority over all other relationships. Work begins here too: Adam is given authority over the animals and plants. Ever since, humans have had a kind of mastery, or "stewardship," over the rest of creation.

Only the slightest hint of foreboding clouds this blissful scene of Paradise. It appears in verse 17, in the form of a single negative command from God. Adam enjoys perfect freedom with one small exception—a test of obedience.

Throughout history, artists have tried to recreate in words and images what a perfect world would look like, a world of love and beauty, one without guilt or suffering or shame. Genesis 1–2 describes such a world. For a time in Genesis, peace reigns. When God looks at all he has created, he pays humanity its highest compliment. "Very good," he pronounces. Creation is now complete.

—PY

Daily Contemplation

Think about a close friend or family member. In what way does this person reflect God? Does some quality or personality trait speak of what God must be like?

DAY 3

The Fall of Man
Genesis 3:1–24

The "fall of man," theologians call it, but really it is more like a crash. Adam and Eve have everything a person could want in Paradise, and yet still a thought nags them: *Are we somehow missing out? Is God keeping something from us?* Like every human being who has ever lived, they cannot resist the temptation to reach for what lies beyond them.

Genesis gives few details about that first sin. Only one thing matters: God labeled one tree, just one, off-limits. Many people mistakenly assume sex is involved, but in fact something far more basic is at stake. The real issue is *who will set the rules*—the humans or God? Adam and Eve decide in favor of themselves, and the world has never been the same.

Adam and Eve react to their sin as anyone reacts to sin. They rationalize, explain themselves, and look for someone else to take the blame. They hide from each other, sensing for the first time a feeling of shame over their nakedness. Perhaps the greatest change of all, however, occurs in their relationship with God. Previously they walked and talked with God in the Garden as a friend. Now, when they hear his approach, they hide.

Genesis 3 tells of other profound changes that affect the world when the creatures choose against their Creator. Suffering multiplies, work becomes harder, and a new word, *death*, enters human vocabulary. Perfection has been permanently spoiled.

The underlying message of Genesis goes against some common assumptions about human history. According to these chapters, the world and humanity have not been gradually evolving toward a better state. Long ago, we wrecked against the rocks of our own pride and stubbornness. We're still bearing the consequences: All wars, all violence, all broken relationships, all grief and sadness trace back to that one monumental day in the Garden of Eden.

—PY

Daily Contemplation

Have you felt hemmed in or stifled by any of God's commands? How have you responded to this feeling?

DAY 4

Cain and Abel
Genesis 4:1-24

Creation, the origins of man and woman, a fall into sin—in three chapters Genesis has set the stage for human history, and now that history begins to play itself out. The first childbirth—imagine the shock!—the first formal worship of God, the first division of labor, the first extended families, and cities, and signs of culture all appear in chapter 4. But one "first" overshadows all the others: the first death of a human being, a death by murder.

It takes just one generation for sin to enter the world; by the second generation, people are already killing each other. The malignant results of the Fall spread that quickly. Cain offers a sacrifice to God with a poor attitude and then kills his brother when he learns God is more pleased with Abel's offering (see also Hebrews 11:4). God steps in once again with a custom-designed punishment: Cain must bear a mark of shame the rest of his life. The slide continues, though, for a few generations later a man named Lamech, a descendant of Cain, will brag about his own murders.

Not all the news is bad. Civilization progresses rather quickly, with some people learning agriculture, some choosing to work with tools of bronze and iron, and some discovering music and the arts. In this way, human beings begin to fulfill the role assigned to them by God to be masters over the created world. But despite these advances, history is sliding along another track as well. Every person who follows Adam and Eve faces the same choice of whether or not to obey God's word. And, with numbing monotony, all make a choice similar to that of their original parents. The next few chapters tell of an ever-worsening spiral of rebellion and evil.

—PY

Daily Contemplation

Look at Cain's response when God confronts him. What do you think you would say if God appeared in person to confront you about your sin?

DAY 5

Did God Really Say . . . ?
Reflection

The Bible is God's great storybook, full of the tales of men and women who lived on earth, walked with God, experienced his love, and yet struggled in believing what he said. We see this pattern beginning right away in Genesis. God crafts a magnificent world and gives it to man and woman. Yet Adam and Eve, discontent, fall right into Satan's alluring trap.

"Did God really say . . . ?" Every person who has lived since Adam and Eve has been tempted by Satan with these words. Just as the Serpent coaxed Eve with this question in Genesis 3:1, Satan uses similar reasoning with us as he tempts us to water down God's words and walk beyond his loving protection. Such reasoning can appear so sensible, so innocently self-assuring. We think we know what we need, and rather than asking of God, "Did you really say . . . ?" we feel the urge to move ahead on our own, rationalizing, "God did not *really* say . . ."

Eventually we regret ignoring God's warning and, like Adam and Eve, may suffer consequences that shape our future. If we are wise, in time we develop a good ear for distinguishing between God's voice and deceptive substitutes. The glittering promises that once appeared so sensible and hopeful lose their appeal. Only God's promises stand worthy of trust.

Although the Bible doesn't speak in specifics about every choice we must make, God's Word and a relationship with God himself suffice to help us choose His way. We can trust that he will never deceive us, mislead us, or abandon us. This is his promise in Isaiah 41:10: "Do not fear, for I am with you; do not be dismayed, for I am your God. I will strengthen you and help you; I will uphold you with my righteous right hand."

—BQ

Daily Contemplation

Our God, who created an earth full of wonder, who crafted the intricately beautiful human person, cares deeply and intimately about you. How have you come to know this? Spend a few moments talking with him. Tell him, "God, I want to hear what you really say . . ."

DAY 6

The Flood
Genesis 6:1–7:24

The LORD saw how great the wickedness of the human race had become on the earth, and that every inclination of the thoughts of the human heart was only evil all the time. The LORD regretted that he had made human beings on the earth, and his heart was deeply troubled. So the LORD said, "I will wipe from the face of the earth the human race I have created—and with them the animals, the birds and the creatures that move along the ground—for I regret that I have made them." But Noah found favor in the eyes of the LORD. (Genesis 6:5–8)

God can no longer tolerate the violence that has already spread across the world. It seems that the human experiment has failed. God, who has taken such pride in his creation, is now ready to destroy it.

Legends of a great flood exist in the records of different cultures in the Middle East, Asia, and South America. One Babylonian document (*The Epic of Gilgamesh*) has many parallels to the account in this chapter. But Genesis presents the Flood not merely as an accident of geography or climate; it is an act of God to destroy all humans who have turned their backs on him. Yet Noah's ark—a huge, ungainly boat riding out the storm—stands as a symbol of God's mercy. God has resolved to give earth a second chance.

Genesis underscores one message above all: The first human beings on earth made a mess of things. Their rebellion brought about the downfall of all creation. But God spares Noah and his family—eight people who will birth future generations and carry on the story of God's undying love for his people.

—PY

--- *Daily Contemplation* ---

Many people feel that good and evil, right and wrong, must be defined by each individual. Do you agree?

DAY 7

The Land Dries
Genesis 8:1–22

By the twenty-seventh day of the second month the earth was completely dry. Then God said to Noah, "Come out of the ark, you and your wife and your sons and their wives. Bring out every kind of living creature that is with you—the birds, the animals, and all the creatures that move along the ground—so they can multiply on the earth and be fruitful and increase in number on it." (Genesis 8:14–17)

The gloomy tone of Genesis 7 brightens almost immediately. Genesis 8 tells of Noah and his family landing on a cleansed earth that is bringing forth new life. All the people who have so grievously offended God have died off. For the first time in years, human beings seek to please God: In his first act on land, Noah makes an offering of thanksgiving.

Noah has reason to be thankful, for God took good care of him and his family as the unthinkable happened to all those they had known and lived with. Noah became the first person to trust a plan of God's that looked absurd at the time, and yet he came out on the other side with a renewed respect and a deepened love for God.

Think of the ridicule Noah must have endured as he built an enormous boat and turned it into a zoo. Like Noah, many men and women throughout subsequent generations will have to decide whether to obey God in actions that seem senseless. Many, after obeying, will give thanks just as Noah did, realizing anew that although we may not understand God's ways, we can trust and follow him in confidence. He's known to be dependable—and full of good surprises.

—BQ

Daily Contemplation

What difficult time in your life can you look back on now with thankfulness to God for his awareness of your needs?

DAY 8

God's Covenant Rainbow
Genesis 9:1–17

And God said, "This is the sign of the covenant I am making between me and you and every living creature with you, a covenant for all generations to come: I have set my rainbow in the clouds, and it will be the sign of the covenant between me and the earth. Whenever I bring clouds over the earth and the rainbow appears in the clouds, I will remember my covenant between me and you and all living creatures of every kind. Never again will the waters become a flood to destroy all life." (Genesis 9:12–15)

God shows his pleasure by making a solemn promise to Noah, the first of several covenants in the Bible. The terms of the covenant reveal how deeply the Fall has affected all of creation. Humankind has cast a shadow across all nature, a shadow of fear and dread that will continue to spread throughout the animal kingdom. God's covenant recognizes certain sad adjustments to the original design of the world, taking for granted that human beings will continue to kill not only the animals but also each other.

Despite these adjustments, God promises that regardless of what might happen, never again will he destroy life on such a massive scale. He vows in effect to find another way to deal with the rebellion and violence of humanity, "though every inclination of the human heart is evil from childhood" (Genesis 8:21).

An appropriate symbol—the rainbow—marks this first recorded covenant by God. Before he dies, even Noah will need this reminder of God's covenant in the rainbow. The last glimpse Genesis gives of Noah (9:20–29) shows him sprawled in his tent, drunk and naked. Despite Noah's remarkable story as a man who walks radically with God, Noah also makes a mistake. He fails God and finds himself in need of God's mercy.

—PY

Daily Contemplation

How do you react to those in your life who make mistakes and treat you wrongly?

DAY 9

The Tower of Babel
Genesis 11:1–9

Now the whole world had one language and a common speech. . . . They said, "Come, let us build ourselves a city, with a tower that reaches to the heavens, so that we may make a name for ourselves; otherwise we will be scattered over the face of the whole earth." But the LORD came down to see the city and the tower the people were building. The LORD said, "If as one people speaking the same language they have begun to do this, then nothing they plan to do will be impossible for them. Come, let us go down and confuse their language so they will not understand each other." So the LORD scattered them from there over all the earth, and they stopped building the city. That is why it was called Babel—because there the LORD confused the language of the whole world. From there the LORD scattered them over the face of the whole earth. (Genesis 11:1, 4–9)

Human civilization undergoes another significant change after plans for the Tower of Babel collapse. While attempting to take destiny into their own hands, the people of the world learn they cannot overcome God. Although they think they are all-powerful, they learn that God's ways will prevail and that humans are ultimately incapable of determining their own future.

God actually does the people a favor by confusing their language and causing them to scatter throughout the earth. In this way he separates them from each other and causes them once again to realize their need for him. We catch another glimpse of a God who loves people too much to let them stray outside the realm of his love and toward their own utter destruction.

—BQ

Daily Contemplation

Has God ever revealed his great love for you by putting something in your life to show you that you needed him?

DAY 10

God Becomes a Parent
Reflection

If I (Philip) had to reduce the "plot" of Genesis to one sentence, it would be something like this: God learns how to be a parent.* The disruption in Eden changed the world forever, destroying the intimacy Adam and Eve had known with God. In a kind of warm-up to history, God and human beings had to get used to each other. The humans set the pace by breaking all the rules, and God responded with individualized punishments. What did it feel like to be God? What does it feel like to be the parent of a two-year-old?

No one could accuse God of being shy to intervene in the early days. He seems a close, even hovering, parent. When Adam sins, God meets with him in person, explaining that all creation will have to adjust to the choice Adam has made. Just one generation later, a new kind of horror—murder—appears on earth. "What have you done?" God demands of Cain. "Listen! Your brother's blood cries out to me from the ground" (Genesis 4:10). Once again God meets with the culprit and custom-designs a punishment.

The state of the earth and, indeed, the entire human race deteriorates toward a point of crisis that the Bible sums up in the most poignant sentence ever written: "The Lord regretted that he had made human beings on the earth, and his heart was deeply troubled" (6:6). Behind that one statement stands all the shock and grief God feels as a parent.

What human parent has not experienced at least a pang of such remorse? A teenage son tears away in a fit of rebellion. "I hate you!" he cries, fumbling for words that will cause the most pain. He seems bent on twisting a knife in the belly of his parents. That rejection is what God experiences, not just from one child but from the entire human race. As a result, what God has created, God destroys. All the joy of Genesis 1 vanishes under the churning waters of the Flood.

But here is Noah, that one man of faith who "walked with God." After the remorse expressed in Genesis 3–7, you can almost hear God sigh with relief as Noah, in his first act back on land, worships the God who has saved him. *At last, someone to build on.* (Years later, in a message to Ezekiel, God will mention Noah as one of his three most righteous followers.) With the whole planet freshly scrubbed and sprouting life anew, God agrees to a covenant, or contract, that binds him not just to Noah but to every living creature. The covenant promises one thing only: that God will never again destroy all creation.

11

Even in that promise, God limits himself. He, the sworn enemy of all evil in the universe, pledges to endure wickedness on this planet for a time—or, rather, to solve it through some means other than annihilation. Like the parent of a runaway teenager, he forces himself into the role of the Waiting Father (as Jesus' story of the Prodigal Son expresses so eloquently). Before long another mass rebellion, at a place called Babel, tests God's resolve, and he keeps his promise not to destroy.

In earliest history, then, God acts so plainly that no one can grouse about his hiddenness or silence. Yet these early interventions share one important feature: Each is a punishment, a response, to human rebellion. If it is God's intention to have a mature relationship with free human beings, he certainly meets with a lot of rude setbacks. How can he ever relate to his creation as adults when they keep behaving like children?

Soon, with the coming of Abraham, God will set into motion a new plan for human history. Rather than trying to restore the whole earth at once, God will begin with a pioneer settlement, a new race set apart from all others.[2]

—PY

*A phrase like "God learns" may seem strange because we normally think of learning as a mental process, moving in sequence from a state of not knowing to a state of knowing. God, of course, is not bound by time or ignorance. He "learns" in the sense of taking on new experiences, such as the creation of free human beings. Using the word in a similar sense, Hebrews says that Jesus "learned obedience from what he suffered."

Daily Contemplation

In what ways have you responded to God as a rebellious child? Are you, like Noah, walking with God and following his guidance? Or are you, like the people of Babel, building your own methods for handling life?

DAY 11

The Call of Abram
Genesis 12:1–20

The LORD had said to Abram, "Go from your country, your people and your father's household to the land I will show you.
"I will make you into a great nation,
and I will bless you;
I will make your name great,
and you will be a blessing.
I will bless those who bless you,
and whoever curses you I will curse;
and all peoples on earth
will be blessed through you."
So Abram went, as the LORD had told him. (Genesis 12:1–4a)

Middle-aged and prospering financially, Abram suddenly hears a call from God to leave his comfortable life in the land of his fathers. He has no reason to leave home except that God tells him to go. Although Abram can't see the big picture at the time, God has plans to make him the father of God's chosen people, Israel. Abram will found a nation, and it all begins with these words: "Go . . . to the land I will show you."

Probably more than any other person in the Bible, Abram characterizes faith. Because Abram makes himself available to be used by God, a nation is born that will become the model for God's love relationship with all people. God has a plan for Abram. He asks Abram to take the first step, promising in turn to bless him and make him a blessing to others.

Abram leaves his fertile, prosperous homeland to journey by faith through a parched land of famine. He falters along the way, even lying about his wife in Egypt to protect himself. Early in Abram's story this great man of faith does slip, yet God remains faithful to his word and doesn't let Abram's mistake harm his larger plan.

—BQ

Daily Contemplation

Is God nudging you to step beyond your comfort zone in any way today?

DAY 12

Abram and Lot Separate
Genesis 13:1–18

Now Lot, who was moving about with Abram, also had flocks and herds and tents. But the land could not support them while they stayed together, for their possessions were so great that they were not able to stay together. And quarreling arose between Abram's herders and Lot's. . . . So Abram said to Lot, "Let's not have any quarreling between you and me, or between your herders and mine, for we are close relatives. Is not the whole land before you? Let's part company. If you go to the left, I'll go to the right; if you go to the right, I'll go to the left." . . . So Lot chose for himself the whole plain of the Jordan and set out toward the east. The two men parted company: Abram lived in the land of Canaan, while Lot lived among the cities of the plain and pitched his tents near Sodom. (Genesis 13:5–9, 11–12)

Like children who must decide who will get which piece of chocolate cake, Abram and Lot find they must part ways, with each taking for himself a portion of the land. But Abram isn't childish as he considers the situation. Rather than hurriedly claiming what might seem best, he generously lets his nephew Lot choose first. As any child would do, Lot takes what looks most appealing to him at the moment. He chooses selfishly and gets more than he bargained for. His choice of land will later prove calamitous for him and his family.

Abram has learned that he isn't responsible for bringing about God's promise. He is content to give up control and let God handle whatever situation arises. This story is a beautiful tribute to Abram's outlook of faith. By resting in God's hands, Abram allows God to work out his plan without interference.

—BQ

Daily Contemplation

What are your needs today? Can you give them up to God and trust him to provide for you?

DAY 13

God's Covenant with Abram
Genesis 15:1–21

Many times already in Genesis God has intervened directly in human history but almost always for the sake of punishment—in the days of Adam, Cain, and Noah, and at Babel. After scanning these centuries of dismal failure, Genesis changes dramatically at chapter 12. It leaves the big picture of world history and settles on one lonely individual: not a great king or a wealthy landowner but a childless nomad named Abram.

It's almost impossible to exaggerate the importance of Abraham (Abram's later name given to him by God in Genesis 17:5) in the Bible. To the Jews he is the father of a nation, but to all Christians he represents far more. The Bible treats him as a singular man of faith whose relationship to God was so close that for many centuries God was known as "the God of Abraham."

In effect, God in Abram's day is narrowing the scope of divine activity on earth by separating out one group of people with whom to have a unique relationship. They will be set apart from other men and women as God's peculiar treasures, his kingdom of priests. This special group will, by example, teach the rest of the world the advantages of loving and serving God. And Abram is the father of this new humanity.

Dozens of other passages in the Old Testament set forth the details of God's covenant, or contract, with his chosen people. (The word *testament* means "covenant.") Genesis 15 is the first to spell out the terms of this covenant.

Here is what God promises to Abram. First, *a new land to live in*. Trusting God, Abraham travels hundreds of miles toward Canaan (KAY-nuhn). Second, *a large and prosperous family*. Obsessed with this dream, Abram will face a severe test of faith when its fulfillment seems long in coming. Third, *a great nation*. It takes many centuries after Abram for this promise to come true, but finally, in the days of David and Solomon, the Hebrews become a nation. Fourth and finally, *a blessing to the whole world*. From the beginning, God makes clear that he has chosen the Hebrew people not as an end but as a means to the end goal of reaching other nations.*

—PY

*You will begin to see the terms *Hebrew*, *Israelite*, and *Jew* used interchangeably. Each refers to the group of God's chosen people who will remain the focus of most of the Old Testament.

Daily Contemplation

God chose you to be his beloved child. Is it hard for you to envision him loving you this way?

DAY 14

Hagar and Ishmael
Genesis 16:1–16

> Now Sarai, Abram's wife, had borne him no children. But she had an Egyptian slave named Hagar; so she said to Abram, "The LORD has kept me from having children. Go, sleep with my slave; perhaps I can build a family through her." Abram agreed to what Sarai said. So after Abram had been living in Canaan ten years, Sarai his wife took her Egyptian slave Hagar and gave her to her husband to be his wife. He slept with Hagar, and she conceived. When she knew she was pregnant, she began to despise her mistress. . . . So Hagar bore Abram a son, and Abram gave the name Ishmael to the son she had borne. (Genesis 16:1–4, 15)

Once again Abram and his wife, Sarai (SAY-ri), wander from their walk of faith. When the child that God promised is delayed in coming, they decide to take matters into their own hands and find another way to fulfill the promise. Problems begin as soon as they act, however. Sarai and Hagar (HAY-gahr) begin to hate each other. Abram and Sarai's marriage reels from blame and jealousy. And a child is on the way whose descendants will carry hostility toward God's people for many generations.

The story of Sarai, Abram, Hagar, and Ishmael (ISH-may-uhl) declares that God hears and God sees even when to us he seems absent (Genesis 16:11, 13). He reminds those he loves that they can trust his word and wait for its fulfillment. God knows the difficulties in waiting. Our sorrows matter to him. He hears our cries and sees our troubles. Still, he asks us to wait patiently, because he *will* bring about what he has promised.

—BQ

Daily Contemplation

What are you waiting for? How are you doing in your waiting?

DAY 15

The Three Visitors
Genesis 18:1–15

The LORD appeared to Abraham near the great trees of Mamre. . . Abraham looked up and saw three men standing nearby. When he saw them, he hurried from the entrance of his tent to meet them and bowed low to the ground. . . . Then one of them said, "I will surely return to you about this time next year, and Sarah your wife will have a son." . . . So Sarah laughed to herself as she thought, "After I am worn out and my lord is old, will I now have this pleasure?" Then the LORD said to Abraham, "Why did Sarah laugh and say, 'Will I really have a child, now that I am old?' Is anything too hard for the LORD?" (Genesis 18:1–2, 10, 12–14)

Before this chapter begins, Ishmael has reached age thirteen, and God has changed Abram's and Sarai's names. In doing so, God is preparing to provide the promised child to this chosen couple, and the changes in name are one more step in the fulfillment of the promise. The name Abram, meaning "exalted father," looks back to Abram's royal lineage. His new name, Abraham, meaning "father of a multitude," looks ahead to his many descendants. Sarai's new name, Sarah, meaning "princess," is a fitting title for one who will produce kings.

Soon after, the Angel of the Lord and two other angels visit Abraham. This visit of God in person represents an intimate reminder of the close and ongoing relationship that God and Abraham share. Yet despite the many times God has confirmed his promise to Abraham, Sarah laughs when she hears about the son who will arrive in the next year. The prospect of pregnancy seems absurd to a woman in her nineties. But once again we learn that what is impossible for humans is possible for God. His promises are no laughing matter.

—BQ

Daily Contemplation

Is God asking you to believe one of his promises? Is your attitude one of laughter or one of belief?

DAY 16

God Calls
Reflection

Abraham's story tells us a lot about how fickle people are. One day content with what we have, the next day we want something *now*. One day filled with hope, the next day we wallow in despair. Abraham earned a reputation as a man of great faith, yet clearly he faltered a few times. Though he believed God, his own doubts and fears crept in at times to obscure his faith.

As we look at Abraham's stellar acts of faith—and there are more coming in the next chapters—we'll see that it is God who ultimately proves faithful. When God saves us, he calls us to a plan that uniquely fits us. As with Abraham, God is consistent in gradually unfolding his call in our lives, both during those times when we trust him and even in those times when we don't.

Sometimes, like Abraham, we may feel God has forgotten us. His provision will seem long in coming, and we may doubt whether he will ever provide. Yet, as we'll see in Abraham's life, God's plans are not vague. No matter how things look, he has not tired of us and moved on. At times he works slowly and quietly, at others quickly and unmistakably. Never, though, does he abandon us.

Abraham's story is really God's story. We learn that people will waver and fail but God will not. God reminds us again and again, in a voice that is creative and eloquent and clear, that he loves us, has a purpose for us, and will not let go of us. As we recall the story of God and Abraham today, we have the privilege of believing even more deeply than Abraham was able to, because we have seen God prove that he will finish what he started. We have seen that he can do the impossible. What was true for Abraham is equally true for us.

—BQ

Daily Contemplation

Do you have a sense of what God is calling you to in your life? Ask God to help you keep believing in his plan and pray for its fulfillment. If you're not sure how God is calling you, ask him to speak. Believe that he has a plan and wait for him to reveal it to you.

DAY 17

Abraham Pleads for Sodom
Genesis 18:16–33

Then the LORD said, "The outcry against Sodom and Gomorrah is so great and their sin so grievous that I will go down and see if what they have done is as bad as the outcry that has reached me. If not, I will know." The men turned away and went toward Sodom, but Abraham remained standing before the LORD. Then Abraham approached him and said: "Will you sweep away the righteous with the wicked? What if there are fifty righteous people in the city? Will you really sweep it away and not spare the place for the sake of the fifty righteous people in it? Far be it from you to do such a thing—to kill the righteous with the wicked, treating the righteous and the wicked alike. Far be it from you! Will not the Judge of all the earth do right?" The LORD said, "If I find fifty righteous people in the city of Sodom, I will spare the whole place for their sake." (Genesis 18:20–26)

We learn more here about Abraham's character. In genuine humility and reverence, he pleads with God to save all the people in Sodom (SAH-dum) and Gomorrah (guh-MOR-uh), both the righteous and the wicked, for the sake of the righteous.

Abraham feels compassion toward those who love God and face destruction. His compassion makes him bold in coming before God on behalf of these people in need. Not only does Abraham faithfully guide his own household in God's ways; he looks beyond his family to care about others, including the family of his nephew Lot, now living within Sodom (see Genesis 13). Abraham understands that sometimes the wicked must be spared with the righteous, so he entreats God to delay his punishment and spare all the people for a time.

—BQ

Daily Contemplation

Who is in need of your prayers today?

DAY 18

Sodom and Gomorrah Destroyed
Genesis 19:1–29

Like a photo negative, this chapter shows by contrast what Abraham is up against in his efforts to found a new and godly nation. His own nephew lives in the city of Sodom, a sordid place that looks on visiting strangers—angels, as it turns out—as prime targets for gang rape. Sexual violence is just one of Sodom's problems; Ezekiel 16:49 says that Sodom was "arrogant, overfed and unconcerned; they did not help the poor and needy."

In the midst of this story, we also see Lot's true character. Although he opposes some of the evil of Sodom, he has been drawn into its allure. His hypocrisy becomes evident when he takes hospitality much too far, offering his own daughters in exchange for the protection of his guests. Clearly, the hearts of Lot and the rest of his family have been colored by their time in Sodom.

God's patience with Sodom and Gomorrah finally runs out. Once more God steps in with direct punishment, not to destroy the whole world but to wipe out two centers of evil. In typical style, the Bible doesn't bother with scientific explanations of the destruction. Was it a volcanic eruption? An earthquake? The Bible does not say, and the area, now possibly at the bottom of the Dead Sea, cannot easily be investigated. Genesis stresses not how it happened but why.

According to this chapter, Lot does not learn a lesson from Sodom. Later in the chapter, in a drunken state, he commits incest with his daughters, producing two family lines that will be traditional enemies of Abraham's family, the Jews.

Jesus later uses the account of Sodom and Gomorrah as a warning to people who see his miracles but ignore them (Matthew 11). God may not always intervene so spectacularly, but this story serves as a warning that his tolerance for evil has a limit.

—PY

Daily Contemplation

What practices common to our society do you think God considers intolerable?

DAY 19

Isaac's Birth
Genesis 21:1–21

> Now the LORD was gracious to Sarah as he had said, and the LORD did for Sarah what he had promised. Sarah became pregnant and bore a son to Abraham in his old age, at the very time God had promised him. Abraham gave the name Isaac to the son Sarah bore him. . . . Sarah said, "God has brought me laughter, and everyone who hears about this will laugh with me." And she added, "Who would have said to Abraham that Sarah would nurse children? Yet I have borne him a son in his old age." (Genesis 21:1–3, 6–7)

Paul, writer of the New Testament letter of Galatians (guh-LAY-shuns), discusses the deep significance of this story of Abraham and his family (Galatians 4:21–31). Paul uses the story to illustrate how Christ's coming has changed our lives. Ishmael was born of the flesh "by the slave woman," a by-product of Abraham's impatience and human effort. In contrast, Isaac was born as the result of God's promise; a gift of grace in Abraham's old age, Isaac became heir to the nation God would build. According to Paul, Ishmael represents the Old Testament time when people could be saved only by following God's law. Isaac represents the coming of Jesus, God's Promised One, the Savior.

For those who belong to Jesus, we also have become, like him, God's sons and daughters. We, too, are children of the promise. We place our hope in Jesus. Because he loved us and died for us, we have been set free from the burden of needing to save ourselves by being good enough.

—BQ

Daily Contemplation

In God's eyes you are a child he has wanted and specially planned for. How does this make you feel toward God?

DAY 20

Abraham Tested
Genesis 22:1–19

Once more Abraham's faith faces a test. Although God has shown Abraham his overall plan for the future in spectacular fashion, the outworking of that plan has included many bumps and pitfalls.

What does God want? He wants faith, the Bible says, which means complete trust against all odds, and Abraham finally learns that lesson. Abraham and Sarah will never live to see their descendants multiply to become as numerous as the stars in the sky. But they have one beloved son, whom they name Isaac, meaning "laughter," as if to remind them of the very absurdity, the miracle, of childbirth at their ages.

Now God presents a final test of faith, a trial so severe that it makes the others seem like kindergarten games. The Bible makes clear that God never intends to let Abraham go through with his plan of child sacrifice. (Years later, when the Israelites actually commit infant sacrifice, God will call it "something I did not command or mention, nor did it enter my mind" [Jeremiah 19:5].) All along, God had planned to provide another sacrifice, a ram caught by its horns nearby. But Abraham does not know these things as he climbs the steep mountain with his only son. (Later, this same mountain, Moriah, will become home to Jerusalem, the place where God will provide his only Son as the final sacrifice for all people.)

Too many times Abraham has doubted God—this time he will obey no matter what. It has taken more than a hundred years, but Abraham finally has learned to trust. Ever since, he's been known as a man of great faith.

—PY

Daily Contemplation

Have you ever had a "Mount Moriah experience" in which you faced extreme circumstances and needed to have great faith in God? How has God been teaching you that you can trust him?

DAY 21

Isaac and Rebekah
Genesis 24:1–67

Abraham was now very old, and the LORD had blessed him in every way. He said to the senior servant in his household, the one in charge of all that he had, "Put your hand under my thigh. I want you to swear by the LORD, the God of heaven and the God of earth, that you will not get a wife for my son from the daughters of the Canaanites, among whom I am living, but will go to my country and my own relatives and get a wife for my son Isaac." . . . Isaac brought her into the tent of his mother Sarah, and he married Rebekah. So she became his wife, and he loved her; and Isaac was comforted after his mother's death. (Genesis 24:1–4, 67)

This story involves no words from God, no miracle, and no prophecy, but throughout the story the Bible makes clear God's intimate involvement in every aspect of bringing Isaac and Rebekah together. The events of the story testify to God's loving care in the lives of those who follow him. In its original Hebrew, the passage contains the word *hesed*, used several times to convey the "loyal love" shown by God and also by God's people, who cooperated in love and reverence with his plan.

God's *hesed* shows itself in the details of Isaac's life, and we can be confident that God's *hesed* goes with us too. Not only will God carry out his good plan, but he will loyally and lovingly orchestrate circumstances along the way if we walk with him in faith.

—BQ

Daily Contemplation

How have you seen God acting out his *hesed* in your life this week?

DAY 22

Beneath the Surface of Faith
Reflection

What comes to mind when you think of a person of great faith—a person like Abraham? You might think of someone who is strong in a quiet way, someone sure of his or her beliefs about God and of the relationship he or she has with God. You might think of someone who doesn't get ruffled too easily, who seems capable of handling anything.

Abraham fits the image. Yet he also proves that what we see on the surface is only part of the picture. Underneath, in any person of faith, we likely will find vivid images of struggles and sorrows and challenges that have consumed heart and strength. For instance, Abraham's record of difficulty began when he agreed to follow God to a foreign place. Soon he met challenges with his nephew Lot and then puzzled over the barrenness of his marriage. A second wife and a child brought new layers of hardship. Finally, Abraham underwent the ultimate test with God's command to sacrifice his long-awaited son.

Abraham earned his reputation through the real, life-shaking struggles he encountered. His faith grew in the soil of tough times as he watched God move and direct in loving, unexpected ways.

Do you want to be a person of faith if it means learning to trust through difficult days? Perhaps a better question is, can you learn to trust a God who is there for you in your struggles? As you cope with hard times, you, together with God, are writing a life story. The way you respond to struggles and to God will determine that story's outcome. Are you becoming a strong person of faith who, when others probe beneath the surface, can tell of God's triumph through your tough times?

—BQ

Daily Contemplation

Come to God now and talk to him about a struggle you are experiencing. Later in life, how would you like to look back on the way you coped with this difficulty? Give it to God and pray for help in being obedient. Then wait as God turns your struggle into triumph.

DAY 23

Jacob and Esau
Genesis 25:19–34

"Two nations are in your womb,
and two peoples from within you will be separated;
one people will be stronger than the other,
and the older will serve the younger." (Genesis 25:23)

God's promise of the birth of a nation moves forward here with the birth of twin boys to Rebekah and Isaac. Already conflict within Rebekah's womb foreshadows the future for the nations to come from Jacob and Esau (EE-saw). The Israelites, descending from Jacob, and the Edomites, descending from Esau, will fight continuously in the coming decades.

As the two boys are born and grow, God's preference for Jacob over Esau becomes clear. Although Esau, the firstborn, is entitled to the bulk of his father's inheritance, Jacob, by scheming and trickery, foils the law of his day. Early in their story we see them model two ways of handling things of great spiritual importance. Esau, who by tradition would have inherited headship over Isaac's family, "despised his birthright" (Genesis 25:34). He treats this first of God's family blessings with contempt, seeing no great value in the spiritual inheritance due him. Esau, anxious to satisfy his immediate physical appetite, openly reveals a lack of any spiritual hunger.

Jacob, in contrast to his brother, has a great craving for spiritual blessing. But he chooses human tactics of craft and manipulation to pursue his ambition. Although he wants the right things, Jacob wants them in order to serve himself. He focuses on his own gain rather than on God's. Later God will teach Jacob what it means to be a servant used for his higher purposes.

—BQ

Daily Contemplation

Are you more like Esau, focused on fulfilling immediate desires in the here and now, or are you like Jacob, focused on pursuing lasting and spiritual gain? Are you seeking spiritual things through God's help or through your own efforts?

DAY 24

Jacob Gets Isaac's Blessing
Genesis 27:1–40

> After this, his brother came out, with his hand grasping Esau's heel; so he was named Jacob. Isaac was sixty years old when Rebekah gave birth to them. (Genesis 25:26)

If Abraham is renowned for faith, his grandson Jacob is renowned for treachery. Jacob was born with one hand grasping the heel of his twin brother who preceded him, and his parents memorialized that scene by giving him a name meaning "he grasps the heel," or "he deceives" (Genesis 25:26).

In ancient times, the oldest son had two clear advantages: He would receive the family birthright and the father's blessing. The *birthright*, like an inheritance document, granted the right to be in charge of the family and its property. Jacob has already taken the birthright from Esau by striking a bargain for food.

For most people of that day, the *blessing* represented a kind of magical power that conveyed prosperity from one generation to another; for Isaac, it represents far more. He is transferring to his son the covenant blessing passed down from his father Abraham, a blessing that will one day produce a whole nation of God's favored people. This chapter records one of Jacob's most elaborate tricks: a ruse to get from his tottery father the blessing that rightfully belongs to his elder brother.

As you read these stories, you might find your sympathies leaning toward poor Esau, who gets tricked out of his blessing and sells his birthright for a hot meal. But the Bible comes down clearly on the side of Jacob. Esau is blamed for "despising his birthright" (Genesis 25:34; Hebrews 12:16).

Jacob, willing to lie, cheat, and steal to get in on God's blessing, would have flunked anyone's morality test (Genesis surely does not commend these tricks—Jacob has to pay dearly for them, as we will read later on). Yet his life offers up an important lesson: God can deal with anyone, no matter how flawed, who passionately pursues him. The story of Jacob gives hope to imperfect people everywhere.

—PY

Daily Contemplation

In Old Testament times, names like Isaac ("laughter") or Jacob ("grasper") carried great significance. Do you know what your name means? Does the description fit you? If not, what kind of description would fit you better?

DAY 25

Jacob's Dream at Bethel
Genesis 27:41–28:22

> Jacob . . . stopped for the night . . . and lay down to sleep. He had a dream in which he saw a stairway resting on the earth, with its top reaching to heaven, and the angels of God were ascending and descending on it. There above it stood the LORD, and he said: "I am the LORD, the God of your father Abraham and the God of Isaac. I will give you and your descendants the land on which you are lying. Your descendants will be like the dust of the earth. . . . All peoples on earth will be blessed through you and your offspring. I am with you and will watch over you wherever you go, and I will bring you back to this land. I will not leave you until I have done what I have promised you." (Genesis 28:10–15)

Jacob and Rebekah, by scheming, won the birthright and blessing for Jacob. But in doing so, they won for themselves something God would have given Jacob anyway and lost much in the process. Now, as a consequence of Jacob's deception, he must flee his home to avoid his brother's wrath. Jacob will have difficult years ahead, and Rebekah will never see him again.

Despite Jacob's selfish ways, God provides him a vision at Bethel (BETH-uhl) to reassure him that God will go with him and will fulfill his promises to Abraham, Isaac, and now to Jacob. Jacob's response establishes a pattern that Jews and believers since have followed as a response to God's faithfulness and grace.

Prior to this vision, Jacob viewed God as belonging to his fathers. Now, for the first time, Jacob considers that "the LORD will be my God" (Genesis 28:21). Jacob also recognizes at Bethel that all he has belongs to God. He pledges to give back 10 percent of his belongings and in this way bless God and others.

Jacob is so moved by God's word to him at Bethel that he sets stones in place to memorialize his visitation from God. He thus creates a tradition for believers, affirming the importance of memorials: physical reminders of God's work in our lives. When we make these memorials—perhaps planting a tree, creating a wall hanging, or keeping a journal—we create a tangible memory of God's presence and personal care for us.

—BQ

Daily Contemplation

Can you recall a time when God made one of his promises very clear to you? What kind of memorial have you made to commemorate this promise?

DAY 26

Jacob Marries Leah and Rachel
Genesis 29:1–30

> Now Laban had two daughters; the name of the older was Leah, and the name of the younger was Rachel. Leah had weak eyes, but Rachel had a lovely figure and was beautiful. Jacob was in love with Rachel and said, "I'll work for you seven years in return for your younger daughter Rachel." ... Then Jacob said to Laban, "Give me my wife. My time is completed, and I want to make love to her." So Laban brought together all the people of the place and gave a feast. But when evening came, he took his daughter Leah and brought her to Jacob ... When morning came, there was Leah! So Jacob said to Laban, "What is this you have done to me? I served you for Rachel, didn't I? Why have you deceived me?" (Genesis 29:16–18, 21–23, 25)

It is said "what goes around comes around." Jacob waited only seven years to experience the justice reflected in this statement. After deceiving his father and taking by trickery what didn't belong to him, Jacob himself is tricked into taking as a wife someone he doesn't want. If he had waited on God to provide, Jacob could have received the birthright and blessing through God's provision; he might also have wed Rachel right away without hurting Leah in the process. Instead, Jacob's selfishness and lack of trust bring about painful consequences. God doesn't leave Jacob, but he teaches him a lesson by allowing him to be a victim of duplicity in his own life.

This passage does show that Jacob has grown, however. Able to accept the circumstances and finish what he's begun, Jacob yields to God's discipline through the hand of Laban (LAY-buhn). As he does so, he learns to look to God for help, rather than his own conniving.

—BQ

Daily Contemplation

What circumstances in your life are difficult? Have you brought any of them upon yourself? How are you looking to God to take you through them?

DAY 27

Jacob's Children
Genesis 29:31–30:24

> When the LORD saw that Leah was not loved, he enabled her to conceive, but Rachel remained childless. Leah became pregnant and gave birth to a son. She named him Reuben, for she said, "It is because the LORD has seen my misery. Surely my husband will love me now." . . . Then God remembered Rachel; he listened to her and enabled her to conceive. She became pregnant and gave birth to a son and said, "God has taken away my disgrace." She named him Joseph, and said, "May the LORD add to me another son." (Genesis 29:31–32; 30:22–24)

Earlier chapters of Genesis told the stories of both Sarah's and Rebekah's struggle with barrenness. Rachel's story reiterates God's power as Lifegiver, opener of the womb. Neither maidservants nor mandrakes, superstitiously thought to induce pregnancy, could alter a woman's barren state. God, however, bestows fertility to all these women, and they learn to direct their hopes and prayers to him.

God also shows his great love and compassion for those who are unloved. Jacob clearly cares more deeply for Rachel than for Leah, and despite Leah's hopes to change his affections through having children, she will live the rest of her life in Rachel's shadow. Yet God cares about Leah's pain and blesses her with many sons. He exalts her by making her the first of Jacob's wives to bear him a child (Reuben) and gives her five more sons as well as Jacob's only daughter, Dinah.

The twelve sons of Jacob (from four different women) will go on to be the forefathers and namesakes of the twelve tribes of Israel. Jesus, the Messiah, will descend from the tribe of Judah, from the lineage of Leah. Just as Leah was rejected by Jacob but loved by God and blessed with children, so too her descendent Jesus would be rejected by humanity but loved dearly by God.

—BQ

Daily Contemplation

When have you felt unloved? How has God shown a deep love for you in the midst of your pain?

DAY 28

God Shining from the Shadows
Reflection

Genesis paints a rather unflattering portrait of the third of Israel's patriarchs, or fathers. Although the first patriarchs, Abraham and Isaac, were human and made some mistakes, Jacob tops them both.

As a young man, greedy and conniving, he takes advantage of his brother and then deceives his dying father. Jacob must go on the run to escape his brother's anger; later he neglects one of his two wives, fueling the rivalry between them. Jacob hardly models for us the "spiritual giant" we would like to envision when we think of the renowned fathers of our faith.

As we look at the panorama of Jacob's life to this point, however, we see again that the story is really about God, not Jacob. Looming in the background of Jacob's early treachery, we see a God who has higher purposes, who works out his plan despite Jacob's insistence on doing it himself. As Jacob flees, we glimpse God in the shadows before him and surrounding him, even appearing in a dream to bring comfort, reminding Jacob of the promises God still intends to keep. Then, as Jacob marries not one wife but two, we see God filling in the gaps, giving love where love is lacking.

Across the canvas of Jacob's life, we see God building a nation through an inadequate man, an unloved woman, and a woman who long felt abandoned by God. God doesn't need perfect people to do the things he has planned. With supreme irony, he chooses a flawed, self-centered man to carry on the lifeline of a nation that will eventually produce the perfect Messiah, who will offer a way for all sinful people to come back to God.

Jacob's mural looks a lot like our own. Each believer is chosen by God, and once we are chosen, nothing can change God's love for us. No mistake, no matter how big, can alter the way God cares for us. And like Jacob, as we walk with God and listen to him, we gradually find our hearts and our wills looking more like God's own.

—BQ

Daily Contemplation

What mistakes seem to dominate the mural of your life? Are these mistakes keeping you at a distance from God? If you've never confessed your mistakes to God, do it now, asking for forgiveness. Know that God hears and forgives. He is already near to you and loving you.

DAY 29

Jacob Flees from Laban
Genesis 31:1–21

Jacob heard that Laban's sons were saying, "Jacob has taken everything our father owned and has gained all this wealth from what belonged to our father." And Jacob noticed that Laban's attitude toward him was not what it had been. Then the LORD said to Jacob, "Go back to the land of your fathers and to your relatives, and I will be with you." . . . Then Jacob put his children and his wives on camels, and he drove all his livestock ahead of him, along with all the goods he had accumulated in Paddan Aram, to go to his father Isaac in the land of Canaan. (Genesis 31:1–3, 17–18)

God finally calls Jacob back to his own land. Jacob leaves Laban for some of the same reasons he originally left his homeland—he flees to escape the animosity directed toward him, this time from Laban and his sons. Jacob has good reason to leave, for he and his wives have been cheated by Laban (Genesis 31:4–9). But more importantly, it is God's time for Jacob to return home.

A wordplay in the original Hebrew text stresses that while Jacob "stole away," Rachel stole the gods of her father (Genesis 31:19–20). Jacob's dishonesty now spreads to his wife. In ancient days the possession of a family's gods was often tied to the rights of inheritance. Perhaps in taking the gods, Rachel wants to ensure that her family will inherit Laban's estate. In any case, Laban will pursue Jacob and his family, seeking to discover why they secretly left, absconding with the idols he relies on for protection.

—BQ

Daily Contemplation

Where do you turn for protection? Are you inclined, like Jacob, to turn to your own ways of protecting yourself? Or do you, like Laban and Rachel, turn to things in your life for protection? How often do you ask God to protect you?

DAY 30

Laban Pursues Jacob
Genesis 31:22–55

Laban answered Jacob, "The women are my daughters, the children are my children, and the flocks are my flocks. All you see is mine. Yet what can I do today about these daughters of mine, or about the children they have borne? Come now, let's make a covenant, you and I, and let it serve as a witness between us." (Genesis 31:43–44)

Just as Jacob had done to his own father, Rachel now lies to her father once Laban overtakes Jacob's caravan, and she successfully deceives him. She lies in order to protect the useless gods she stole from him and an inheritance she will never need. Jacob's character flaw of deception is carried on by his new family. For his part, Laban, having cheated his daughters and Jacob, now seems most concerned for his own safety, and he proposes a treaty to prevent future conflicts.

In this chapter, God speaks separately to Jacob and Laban to bring about their separation. Despite the selfish ways of both men, God protects Jacob from Laban's animosity and ensures that Jacob will reach his homeland safely. Jacob's journey will become a model for Israel later when the nation is led out of captivity in Egypt back to Jacob's homeland of Canaan. God will deliver and protect the nation of Israel despite its imperfections, just as he is doing for Jacob.

The Israelites and eventually modern-day generations of believers will repeat again and again a pattern similar to Jacob's. Rather than trusting in God's ways, we follow our own ways and seek what we want by our own methods. We will suffer consequences; nevertheless, we will find that despite our selfish wanderings, God never leaves us.

—BQ

Daily Contemplation

Do you reflect any character qualities of your family? What qualities are you passing on to others?

DAY 31

Jacob Prepares to Meet Esau
Genesis 32:1–21

Jacob sent messengers ahead of him to his brother Esau in the land of Seir, the country of Edom.... When the messengers returned to Jacob, they said, "We went to your brother Esau, and now he is coming to meet you, and four hundred men are with him."... Then Jacob prayed, "O God of my father Abraham, God of my father Isaac, LORD, you who said to me, 'Go back to your country and your relatives, and I will make you prosper,' I am unworthy of all the kindness and faithfulness you have shown your servant. I had only my staff when I crossed this Jordan, but now I have become two camps. Save me, I pray, from the hand of my brother Esau, for I am afraid he will come and attack me, and also the mothers with their children. But you have said, 'I will surely make you prosper and will make your descendants like the sand of the sea, which cannot be counted.'" (Genesis 32:3, 6, 9–12)

Jacob's deceptions have marked him as an untrustworthy, dishonest man. But in this passage we see once more that despite Jacob's character flaws, God is ultimately in charge of his future. We also glimpse a place of honesty deep inside Jacob. He knows he is "unworthy of all the kindness and faithfulness" God has shown him (Genesis 32:10). Coming home and facing pain from the past, Jacob must reach to the core of himself and his relationship with God to find the answers to his crisis.

Jacob's prayer is the prayer of every believer in a fearful situation: "Save me, I pray . . . for I am afraid" (Genesis 32:11). This is the honesty God awaits, the prayer that implores God to do for us better than we could do for ourselves.

—BQ

Daily Contemplation

What are you afraid of today? Have you talked to God about your fear?

DAY 32

Jacob Wrestles with God
Genesis 32:22–32

> So Jacob was left alone, and a man wrestled with him till daybreak. When the man saw that he could not overpower him, he touched the socket of Jacob's hip so that his hip was wrenched as he wrestled with the man. (Genesis 32:24–25)

In Romans 9, the apostle Paul uses Jacob as an example of God's grace. Why would God use a cheating rascal like Jacob to carry out his plan of building a holy nation? "I will have mercy on whom I have mercy, and I will have compassion on whom I have compassion" (Romans 9:15; quoted from Exodus 33:19) is God's answer. Paul, who had spent the first part of his life fighting against God's will, came to love the word *grace*—meaning "an undeserved gift"—because God loved him nonetheless.

Two scenes in Jacob's life especially show grace at work. At two critical moments, just as Jacob is about to lose heart, God meets him in dramatic personal encounters.

The first time, Jacob was crossing a desert alone as a fugitive (Genesis 28). Having cheated his brother out of the family birthright, he was running away from Esau and his murderous threats. Yet God came to him with bright promises, not the reproaches he deserved. Jacob had not sought God; rather, God sought him. At that tender moment, God confirmed that all the blessings he had promised Abraham would apply to Jacob, the disgraced runaway.

The next encounter occurs several decades later, the night before Jacob plans to attempt reconciliation with Esau. In the intervening years, Jacob has learned many hard lessons, but as he thinks about the rendezvous he trembles in fear. After pleading with God to keep his promises, he receives in response a supernatural encounter as strange as any in the Bible. Jacob the grasper has met a worthy opponent at last: He wrestles with God himself. After this strange night, Jacob will always walk with a limp, a permanent reminder of the struggle.

Along the way, Jacob gains a new name, "Israel," a name that puts the final seal of God's grace on him. Jacob the cheat becomes the namesake of God's chosen people, the Israelites—or, "God-wrestlers."

—PY

Daily Contemplation

Not many people have such dramatic encounters with God. How has God met you at a time of need?

DAY 33

Jacob Reunites with Esau
Genesis 33:1–20

> Jacob looked up and there was Esau, coming with his four hundred men; so he divided the children among Leah, Rachel and the two female servants. He put the female servants and their children in front, Leah and her children next, and Rachel and Joseph in the rear. He himself went on ahead and bowed down to the ground seven times as he approached his brother. But Esau ran to meet Jacob and embraced him; he threw his arms around his neck and kissed him. And they wept.
> (Genesis 33:1–4)

God answers Jacob's prayer for help in a way beyond Jacob's imagining. Not only does Esau not harm his brother; he runs with open arms to embrace him. God has changed the hearts of both brothers: Esau now wants reconciliation more than revenge, and Jacob has gained humility and generosity in his time away from Esau.

In this long-awaited meeting, Jacob gets a clearer picture of the face of God than he has ever seen before. For so long Jacob wrestled with God, insisting on his own way in the course of his life. In a final wrestling match, God showed Jacob his power and once again bestowed blessing (Genesis 32:22–32). Now, as Jacob limps home to a sibling who should hate him, he instead sees God in the face of this weeping, eager brother.

God will give believers this same picture of himself several times throughout the Bible. One who should be angry and finished with forgiveness, such as Esau, instead welcomes back another who deserves reproach. These scenes of grace demonstrate God's unrelenting love for us, his children. May we, like Jacob, have the eyes to see.

—BQ

--- *Daily Contemplation* ---

When has God shown you himself through the unexpected love of another person?

DAY 34

Jacob Returns to Bethel
Genesis 35:1–15

Then God said to Jacob, "Go up to Bethel and settle there, and build an altar there to God, who appeared to you when you were fleeing from your brother Esau." So Jacob said to his household and to all who were with him, "Get rid of the foreign gods you have with you, and purify yourselves and change your clothes. Then come, let us go up to Bethel, where I will build an altar to God, who answered me in the day of my distress and who has been with me wherever I have gone." (Genesis 35:1–3)

Jacob has come full circle. He has made mistakes, gone his own way, suffered due to his actions, and experienced God's guiding grace time and again. Now he returns to a familiar place of safety for the continued growth of the nation God has promised.

God calls Jacob back to Bethel so that Jacob can recall the journey he has traveled and remember God's role in his life. After all Jacob has seen and experienced, he must pass on to his family the heritage of a God who has shown himself true and faithful.

As Jacob begins the journey, he recalls the vows he made to God at Bethel many years ago. He remembers the loyalty he promised God, and yet his family now allows idols to share a place with God. They must rid themselves of these objects of trust and attention. They must become pure before entering a place dedicated to the Lord.

Once again God speaks to Jacob at Bethel, underscoring that he will fulfill what he has promised. Although Jacob has not always been faithful, God has remained faithful to him. God's promise at Bethel has not changed.

—BQ

Daily Contemplation

Where are you in your journey with God? Are you insisting on your own way? Are you experiencing God's grace? Are you seeing some of God's promises fulfilled?

DAY 35

Wrestling with God
Reflection

What are we to make of ancient Bible stories about a man who went around lying to people and then spent a dark night wrestling on a riverbank with a figure who turned out to be God? We find in these accounts striking truths about the love of God for even the most undeserving of people. We also learn something about the process of living alongside our God, who has a plan for our lives and the power to implement it.

The image of wrestling fits well with the relationship many of us have with God throughout our lives. Like Jacob, we get acquainted with God and make tentative pledges to follow him. Then we carry on with life, doing whatever seems right at the moment to clear the path we've chosen for ourselves. We may consult God occasionally, sometimes in sincerity and sometimes simply going through the motions. But then we charge ahead again like strong-willed children, insisting on doing things our way. We struggle with God again and again, often failing to recognize the nature of the loving God with whom we're wrestling. If only we could more fully realize the perfect plan God has for us, then maybe we would give up this foolhardy fight.

God will not force himself on us. He will let the struggle go on if we insist. Finally, if we are truly blessed, he may touch us on the hip and reveal to us the truth of our weakness. Then we realize that God has always been the winner. And we know that only when God wins can we win too. That first shy act of acquaintance with God, those first tentative pledges we made, may have been weak, but they set in motion God's loving act of replacing our weakness with his strength.

We may wrestle with God for a while, but in time we'll stop the struggle and say to God, as Jacob did, "I will not let you go" (Genesis 32:26). We'll echo the words of the apostle Paul from later in the Bible: "When I am weak, then I am strong" (2 Corinthians 12:10).

—BQ

Daily Contemplation

Are you wrestling with God? What are you trying to achieve? Ask God to help you understand yourself and what lies at the heart of your desires. Ask God to help you trust his plan and rely on his strength.

DAY 36

Joseph's Dreams
Genesis 37:1–36

> Joseph had a dream, and when he told it to his brothers, they hated him all the more. He said to them, "Listen to this dream I had: We were binding sheaves of grain out in the field when suddenly my sheaf rose and stood upright, while your sheaves gathered around mine and bowed down to it." (Genesis 37:5–7)

Nobody fights like brothers and sisters—family closeness seems to rub salt in the wounds of relationships. Genesis tells of several fierce sibling rivalries: Cain and Abel, Isaac and his half-brother Ishmael, Jacob and Esau, Leah and Rachel. In this concluding story, Joseph's story, eleven brothers line up against one.

The pace of Genesis slows down when it gets to Joseph, with the book devoting far more attention to his life story than anyone else's. Little wonder—Joseph lived one of the greatest adventure stories of history. A stowaway slave and condemned prisoner, he rose to become the number-two ruler of Egypt, then the greatest empire on earth. The saga begins with the near-tragic event recorded in this chapter.

As his father's acknowledged favorite, Joseph seems curiously insensitive to the potential of his brothers' jealousy. He flaunts his status by relating two dreams of his family bowing down to him. At the least, he alienates his brothers so strongly that they decide to take revenge.

The brothers' first plan involves murder. As a last-second thought, they sell Joseph instead to traveling merchants on their way to Egypt. Neither the brothers nor Joseph's grieving father, Jacob—who swallows their story of a wild animal attack—ever expect to see him again. God, however, has other plans. Joseph's strange dreams, which got him into so much trouble at home, will prove to be his salvation in the faraway land of Egypt.

—PY

Daily Contemplation

Have you ever experienced God bringing good out of what at first seemed like a disaster?

DAY 37

Joseph and Potiphar's Wife
Genesis 39:1–23

> Now Joseph was well-built and handsome, and after a while his master's wife took notice of Joseph and said, "Come to bed with me!" But he refused. . . . "How then could I do such a wicked thing and sin against God?" (Genesis 39:6; 9)

This story begins and ends with the words "the Lord was with Joseph." Throughout the story we are told many times that God's hand is on Joseph in every situation. Clearly, it is God's hand that turns the heart of Potiphar (PAHT-ih-fuhr), the Egyptian official who becomes Joseph's master, toward Joseph. God's hand allows Joseph to prosper in all he does as a servant. Even when he is in prison following the false accusations of Potiphar's wife, it is God's hand that causes Joseph to find favor with the warden. Without a doubt, God is watching over Joseph and fashioning good out of unfortunate circumstances.

Only in the incident with Potiphar's wife do we find a seeming absence of God's hand at work. Did he leave Joseph for a few hours that morning? Did he decide to test Joseph's obedience? Genesis doesn't tell us why God again allowed someone to mistreat and betray Joseph, but it does make clear that God was watching over him.

Through all his trials, Joseph remains faithful, refusing to give in to a short-lived pleasure that would dishonor God. In prison God reassures Joseph that he is near, showing kindness and making the situation bearable. He continues to bring Joseph success despite his captivity.

God has a big plan for Joseph. Although Joseph can't see how it will happen during his days as a servant and prisoner, he will become God's tool for helping the Israelites. Joseph has shown that he can resist temptation and wait for God to bless him. His servanthood and captivity won't be wasted. They will position him for the greater work God has planned.

—BQ

Daily Contemplation

Is a temptation calling to you, offering a chance for immediate gratification? Will giving in to temptation dishonor God and hinder his bigger plan for you?

DAY 38

The Cupbearer and the Baker
Genesis 40:1–23

Pharaoh was angry with his two officials, the chief cupbearer and the chief baker, and put them in custody in the house of the captain of the guard, in the same prison where Joseph was confined . . . each of the two men—the cupbearer and the baker of the king of Egypt, who were being held in prison—had a dream the same night, and each dream had a meaning of its own. When Joseph came to them the next morning, he saw that they were dejected. So he asked Pharaoh's officials who were in custody with him in his master's house, "Why do you look so sad today?" "We both had dreams," they answered, "but there is no one to interpret them." Then Joseph said to them, "Do not interpretations belong to God? Tell me your dreams." (Genesis 40:2–3, 5–8)

God again uses dreams to speak to Joseph about what lies in store for the future. Although the dreams of the cupbearer and the baker don't directly involve Joseph, God uses the fulfillment of the prophecies in these dreams to show Joseph that indeed God has given him the gift of interpreting dreams. Just as God brings about the events Joseph predicted for his fellow prisoners, God will in the same way bring about the future predicted in Joseph's own dreams.

The cupbearer, seemingly Joseph's ticket out of prison, lets him down by promptly forgetting Joseph once released (Genesis 40:23). God, however, does not forget him. God's dream for Joseph stays alive and well. Though things look dim in the confines of the dungeon, God's plan will prove unbounded.

—BQ

Daily Contemplation

What situation in your life is looking grim today? How can you look at your situation through God's eyes?

DAY 39

Pharaoh's Dreams
Genesis 41:1–57

Genesis provides a fascinating look at a variety of ways in which God gave guidance to his people. Sometimes, as with Abraham, he would appear spectacularly and in person or send angelic messengers. For other people, like Jacob, the guidance came in more mysterious forms, such as a late-night wrestling match or the image of a ladder reaching into heaven. For Joseph, God's guidance is indirect and probably quite mystifying.

God communicates to Joseph through dreams, including weird dreams he hears about from such dubious sources as jail mates and a despotic Egyptian pharaoh (FAIR-oh). Yet because God reveals to Joseph the proper meaning of these dreams, Joseph eventually rises to prominence. Egyptians of that day were fascinated by dreams (archaeologists have unearthed lengthy textbooks on dream interpretations), and Joseph the dream interpreter soon finds himself at the top of Pharoah's government.

In Joseph's time, God mostly works behind the scenes. In fact, on the surface it often seems that Joseph gets the exact opposite of what he deserves. He explains a dream to his brothers, and they throw him in a cistern (Genesis 37). He resists a sexual advance and lands in an Egyptian prison (Genesis 39). He interprets another dream to save a cellmate's life, and the cellmate forgets about him (Genesis 40).

Yet—and perhaps this is why Genesis devotes so much space to him—Joseph never stops trusting God. Joseph comes to see God's hand in the tragedies of his life. Being sold into slavery, for example, eventually turns out for good. It leads him into a powerful new career, and soon he will have the opportunity to save his own family from starvation.

—PY

Daily Contemplation

If God has an important message for you, how does he get it across?

DAY 40

A Life Motto
Reflection

Life isn't fair.

How many times have you been chided by those words in the face of an injustice you've encountered? How many times have you muttered them to yourself while pondering yet another unfair burden? Many of us learn this life motto at an early age. We realize as children that life just doesn't unfold in the way we'd prefer. As time moves on, we see the motto reconfirmed in numerous ways. Eventually we grow hardened. Why hope for anything better?

We expect to turn to the Bible and find a solution to the unfairness of life. Surely, life with God must clear up the inequities of a godless world. Yet here in Joseph's story, as in many earlier stories, life isn't fair, despite God's presence.

In a world like Joseph's and ours, where God has not yet destroyed evil finally and completely, life will remain unfair. But the reality for God's followers doesn't stop there. A believer's understanding of life goes far beyond a focus on fairness. It settles on God and his goodness. Life may not have been fair to Joseph, but God was abundantly good to him. In the midst of each unfair turn of events, each long night of heartache, God worked things for the good of this man he loved.

Julian of Norwich, a Benedictine nun in England who lived in a time of social unrest and fear of the Black Plague and who herself suffered a serious illness at a young age, penned the following words: "Just as our flesh is covered by clothing, . . . so are we, soul and body, covered and enclosed by the goodness of God. Yet the clothing and the flesh will pass away, but the goodness of God will always remain and will remain closer to us than our own flesh."[3]

Life isn't fair, but God is good.

—BQ

Daily Contemplation

What struggle are you facing today that seems to be another instance of unfairness? Come to God and talk about the anger you feel. Tell him of the ache in your heart. Ask for a clear view of his goodness in your life.

DAY 41

Joseph's Brothers Go to Egypt
Genesis 42:1–26

> Then ten of Joseph's brothers went down to buy grain from Egypt. . . . when Joseph's brothers arrived, they bowed down to him with their faces to the ground. As soon as Joseph saw his brothers, he recognized them, but he pretended to be a stranger and spoke harshly to them. "Where do you come from?" he asked. "From the land of Canaan," they replied, "to buy food." Although Joseph recognized his brothers, they did not recognize him. (Genesis 42:3, 6–8)

Finally, after at least twenty years apart, Joseph and his brothers reunite—in a way. He recognizes them, but they cannot see past his adopted Egyptian identity. Joseph is flooded with mixed emotions. He remembers the dreams he had many years ago, and as he remembers, the urge for revenge surges up. Once the victim of their cruelty, now he controls their fate.

As Joseph's brothers are brought into a position of vulnerability, their guilt comes to light. Even though they don't recognize this governor as their brother, at last they sense they will have to pay consequences for their actions. Just as the Bible reveals the injustices of life, it also confirms that in the end people often reap what they sow. Whatever suffering may lie ahead for the brothers stands justified. They deserve to pay for what they've done.

The true character of Joseph now begins to shine. He has spent many days and nights questioning the course his life has taken. Now, as the brothers question their future, Joseph finally sees that God has brought him to a place where he can save his family from death.

After breaking down weeping, Joseph gives himself time to collect his thoughts by sending nine of the brothers home for Benjamin. Now he will see his best-loved brother, and he will have time to consider this turn of events. His brothers also will have time to reckon with their wrongs.

—BQ

Daily Contemplation

When have you reaped the consequences of your actions?

DAY 42

Joseph's Brothers Return to Canaan
Genesis 42:27–38

At the place where they stopped for the night one of them opened his sack to get feed for his donkey, and he saw his silver in the mouth of his sack. "My silver has been returned," he said to his brothers. "Here it is in my sack." Their hearts sank and they turned to each other trembling and said, "What is this that God has done to us?" When they came to their father Jacob in the land of Canaan, they told him all that had happened to them. They said, "The man who is lord over the land spoke harshly to us and treated us as though we were spying on the land. . . . Then the man who is lord over the land said to us, 'This is how I will know whether you are honest men: Leave one of your brothers here with me, and take food for your starving households and go. But bring your youngest brother to me so I will know that you are not spies but honest men.'" (Genesis 40:27–30, 33–34)

God uses Joseph's desire to see Benjamin as a tool to help bring about repentant hearts in his brothers. By placing silver back in their grain sacks, Joseph frames them to appear as dishonest spies. To the brothers, it seems God is acting deliberately to punish them.

In truth, God is sovereignly caring for Jacob's family, preserving them during a time of widespread famine. Through Joseph he brings them to the land of Egypt, where the Israelites will live for four hundred years and grow into a great nation. As they enter Egypt, their hearts must turn toward God. They must become humble before him and remember his ways. Although for a time the brothers are afraid, God is guiding their hearts back to a place of oneness with him.

—BQ

Daily Contemplation

Has fear ever turned you to God? Did God bring good out of your fear?

DAY 43

Joseph's Brothers Return to Egypt
Genesis 43:1–34

> Now the famine was still severe in the land. So when they had eaten all the grain they had brought from Egypt, their father said to them, "Go back and buy us a little more food." But Judah said to him, "The man warned us solemnly, 'You will not see my face again unless your brother is with you.'" . . . So the men took the gifts and double the amount of silver, and Benjamin also. They hurried down to Egypt and presented themselves to Joseph. When Joseph saw Benjamin with them, he said to the steward of his house, "Take these men to my house, slaughter an animal and prepare a meal; they are to eat with me at noon." (Genesis 43:1–3, 15–16)

Once again Jacob's sons must travel to Egypt. Some time has passed, and they have used all the grain they bought from Joseph. Despite his misgivings, Jacob can no longer put off his decision. He must risk the life of Benjamin or lose all his family to starvation.

When the brothers arrive and are invited to dinner with Joseph, they try to explain to Joseph's steward about the silver. The steward's reply brings into focus their whole experience in Egypt. "Don't be afraid. Your God, the God of your father, has given you treasure in your sacks" (Genesis 43:23).

Joseph's brothers soon will learn that they have come to Egypt for much more than grain. They are to be reunited with their brother. They will receive a new home, and in this place they will grow into a treasured nation belonging to God. The silver that seemed to be a setup serves as a symbol of a people treasured by God, hidden in his hand amid the multitudes of a foreign land.

—BQ

Daily Contemplation

What are you afraid of today? Might treasure be hidden within the thing you fear?

DAY 44

A Silver Cup in a Sack
Genesis 44:1–34

Now Joseph gave these instructions to the steward of his house: "Fill the men's sacks with as much food as they can carry, and put each man's silver in the mouth of his sack. Then put my cup, the silver one, in the mouth of the youngest one's sack, along with the silver for his grain." . . . Joseph was still in the house when Judah and his brothers came in, and they threw themselves to the ground before him. Joseph said to them, "What is this you have done?" . . . "What can we say to my lord?" Judah replied. "What can we say? How can we prove our innocence? God has uncovered your servants' guilt. . . . Your servant guaranteed the boy's safety to my father. I said, 'If I do not bring him back to you, I will bear the blame before you, my father, all my life!' Now then, please let your servant remain here as my lord's slave in place of the boy, and let the boy return with his brothers." (Genesis 44:1–2, 14–16, 32–33)

Despite being reassured that they will not suffer for the silver in their sacks, Joseph's brothers must again face accusation for stealing—this time with the main suspicion resting on Benjamin. Joseph orchestrates this final trial to test his brothers' recognition of evil. If they show compassion for Benjamin and for their father, they will prove they have repented of their sin against Joseph. Then they can take part in the fulfillment of God's promises.

The brothers pass the test. Judah admits, "God has uncovered your servants' guilt." Rather than simply resigning himself to Benjamin's loss and returning home, Judah offers himself as Joseph's slave. He cares more about his father's well-being than about his own. When this becomes evident, Joseph stands ready to forgive and prepares to reveal his identity.

—BQ

--- *Daily Contemplation* ---

Are you learning from past mistakes?

DAY 45

Joseph Makes Himself Known
Genesis 45:1–46:34; 50:15–21

For nearly *two years* Joseph has conducted a series of elaborate tests, demanding things from his brothers, playing tricks on them, and accusing them. All these games provoke confusion and fear in his brothers, as well as flashbacks of guilt over their treatment of him years before.

Yet the drama also exacts an emotional toll on Joseph. Five times he has broken into tears, once with cries loud enough to be heard in the next room. Joseph is feeling the awful strain of forgiveness. Finally, the brothers discover the stunning truth: The teenager they once sold as a slave, and nearly killed, is now the second-ranking imperial official of Egypt. He holds their fate in his hands.

Joseph, however, has no interest in revenge. Ready at last to forgive, he understands now that "you intended to harm me, but God intended it for good to accomplish what is now being done, the saving of many lives" (Genesis 50:20). Seeing his difficult years as part of God's big picture, Joseph is free to let go of his anger. The brothers' reconciliation thus opens the way for the children of Israel to become one family of twelve tribes, a single nation.

The old man Jacob, back home in Canaan, hardly knows what to believe when he hears the news about his "dead" son. But, spurred on by one last personal revelation from God, he too heads for Egypt.

A large family, a nation, a land—God promised all these to Abraham and to Isaac and to Jacob. As Genesis closes, only the first of the promises has come true: Jacob's twelve sons have produced a flock of children. The Bible makes plain that these brothers are no more holy than any other sons—after all, consider their treatment of Joseph. But from this starting point God will build his nation.

—PY

Daily Contemplation

What makes it so hard for us to forgive others?

DAY 46

Why Forgive?
Reflection

The scandal of forgiveness confronts anyone who agrees to a moral ceasefire just because someone says, "I'm sorry." When I (Philip) feel wronged, I can contrive a hundred reasons against forgiveness. *He needs to learn a lesson. I'll let her stew for a while; it'll do her good. It's not up to me to make the first move.* When I finally soften to the point of granting forgiveness, it feels like a capitulation, a leap from hard logic to mushy sentiment.

Why do any of us, believer and unbeliever alike, choose this unnatural act? I can identify at least three pragmatic reasons.

First, forgiveness alone can halt the cycle of blame and pain, breaking the chain of ungrace. In the New Testament the most common Greek word for forgiveness (*aphiēmi*) means, literally, "to release, to hurl away, to free yourself." If we do not transcend nature, we remain bound to the people we cannot forgive, held in their vise grip. This principle applies even when one party is wholly innocent and the other wholly to blame, for the innocent party will bear the wound until they can find a way to release it—and forgiveness is the only way.

The second great power of forgiveness is that it can loosen the stranglehold of guilt in the perpetrator. Magnanimous forgiveness allows the possibility of transformation in the guilty party. Lewis Smedes cautions that forgiveness is not the same as pardon: You may forgive one who wronged you and still insist on a just punishment for that wrong. If you can bring yourself to the point of forgiveness, though, you will release its healing power both in you and in the person who wronged you.[4]

Forgiveness breaks the cycle of blame and loosens the stranglehold of guilt. It accomplishes these two things through a third: a remarkable linkage that places the forgiver on the same side as the party who did the wrong. Through it we realize we are not as different from the wrongdoer as we would like to think. "I also am other than what I imagine myself to be. To know this is forgiveness," said Simone Weil.[5]

Somehow God had to come to terms with these creatures he desperately wanted to love—but how? On earth, living among us, he learned what it was like. He put himself on our side.

—PY

Daily Contemplation

Is there someone in your life whom you have been unable to forgive? Ask God to guide you in how to go about forgiving. And thank him for all he has forgiven you.

PART 2

Birthing a Nation

DAY 47

The Birth of Moses
Exodus 1:1–2:10

> Now Joseph and all his brothers and all that generation died, but the Israelites were exceedingly fruitful; they multiplied greatly, increased in numbers and became so numerous that the land was filled with them. . . . Then Pharaoh gave this order to all his people: "Every Hebrew boy that is born you must throw into the Nile, but let every girl live." . . . Now a man of the tribe of Levi married a Levite woman, and she became pregnant and gave birth to a son. When she saw that he was a fine child, she hid him for three months. But when she could hide him no longer, she got a papyrus basket for him and coated it with tar and pitch. Then she placed the child in it and put it among the reeds along the bank of the Nile. (Exodus 1:6–7, 22; 2:1–3)

Generations have been born and have died since Jacob's family entered Egypt. In this time, a few hundred years in all, the Israelites have grown into a multitude of people. Though they are prospering in Egypt, this is not to be their home. As tension builds between the Egyptians and Israelites, God prepares his people to leave.

The Egyptians have become ever more severe in their treatment of the Hebrew people. Now God raises up the man he has chosen to deliver his people: Moses. Unlike many other Hebrew boys who are thrown in the Nile River to die, he is placed in the river only to be saved by the family of Pharaoh himself. Moses is nurtured by his own Hebrew mother and then raised as an Egyptian child, in the process becoming highly educated and learning to speak fluently both Egyptian and Hebrew. In this unexpected way, God appropriately prepares the one he has chosen to carry out his plan.

—BQ

Daily Contemplation

In what ways has God prepared you?

DAY 48

Moses and the Burning Bush
Exodus 3:1–22

> The angel of the LORD appeared to him in flames of fire from within a bush. . . . "I am sending you to Pharoah to bring my people the Israelites out of Egypt." (Exodus 3:2, 10)

Jacob's family has grown into a great, swarming tribe. God's plan is slowly progressing but with one major hitch: The Hebrews now toil as slaves under a hostile pharaoh.

God's promises to Abraham, Isaac, and Jacob have been passed down to each new generation, but who believes in the covenant anymore? Daily, the Israelites feel the whips of Egyptian taskmasters. As for the vaunted Promised Land, it lies to the east somewhere, carved up under the dominion of a dozen different kings.

At last God has had enough. "I have indeed seen the misery of my people in Egypt," God says. "Now you will see what I will do." The chapters that follow record the most impressive display of God's power unleashed on earth since creation.

First, God needs to designate a leader, and for that job he has selected Moses, a choice rich with irony. It took forty years in Egypt and then forty years in the desert to prepare Moses for this leadership role. God's announcement, or "call," is an encounter Moses will never forget: a fiery bush, a voice from nowhere, God introducing himself by name. That introduction—"I am the God of Abraham, Isaac, and Jacob"—draws a connection to all the promises that have gone before. And now the time for action has arrived. Moses is God's handpicked choice to lead the mob from slavery in Egypt to freedom in the Promised Land.

As this chapter shows, Moses is far from an eager recruit. Yet his own resistance to God's plan is minor compared with that put up by the Israelites . . . and the Egyptians.

—PY

Daily Contemplation

How has God gotten your attention to let you know of a job he had for you?

DAY 49

Signs for Moses
Exodus 4:1–17

Moses answered, "What if they do not believe me or listen to me and say, 'The LORD did not appear to you'?" Then the LORD said to him, "What is that in your hand?" "A staff," he replied. The LORD said, "Throw it on the ground." Moses threw it on the ground and it became a snake . . . . "This," said the LORD, "is so that they may believe that the LORD, the God of their fathers—the God of Abraham, the God of Isaac and the God of Jacob—has appeared to you." (Genesis 4:1–3, 5)

Moses has received a big assignment from God—a job that feels impossible. As Moses continues to talk with God at the burning bush, he shrinks back from the prospect of such an enormous leadership role. For years he has lived as a reclusive shepherd, overseeing animals and keeping company with the land. Now God is asking him to confront Pharaoh with a list of demands and then shepherd masses of Hebrew people out of the land of Egypt.

God understands Moses' initial fears and gives him three miraculous signs to help the people believe him. When Moses again doubts his abilities and asks God to find someone else, God becomes angry. Now Moses is displaying a disobedient heart. He may not feel qualified or confident, but if God has chosen him, surely God will give him the ability to do the job. Yet Moses still can't believe, and God must select Aaron as Moses' spokesperson. That accommodation, enough to calm Moses now, will later prove to be a decidedly mixed blessing.

Here on Mount Horeb (HOR-eb) God calls Moses to lead the Israelites into their next phase of life as God's people. Later Moses will again stand on this mountain as God relays the Ten Commandments—the law that will govern this nation.

—BQ

Daily Contemplation

What job has God recently asked you to do? In what ways do you feel like the wrong person for the job? Can God equip you anyway?

DAY 50

The Plagues of Blood and Frogs
Exodus 7:14–8:15

> Then the LORD said to Moses, "Pharaoh's heart is unyielding; he refuses to let the people go. Go to Pharaoh in the morning as he goes out to the river.... Then say to him, 'The LORD, the God of the Hebrews, has sent me to say to you: Let my people go... By this you will know that I am the LORD: With the staff that is in my hand I will strike the water of the Nile, and it will be changed into blood. The fish in the Nile will die, and the river will stink; the Egyptians will not be able to drink its water.'"
> (Exodus 7:14–18)

Moses and Aaron have gone to Pharaoh to ask for the release of the Israelites, but as God foretold, Pharaoh does not consent. Instead, he makes life harder for the people by increasing their workload. God begins a series of ten plagues on Egypt that within a year will wear down Pharaoh's resistance and bring about the release of the Israelite people.

God first turns the water in the Nile to blood. Some Bible scholars believe that the water did not literally become blood; rather, the Nile was flooded as large quantities of red soil washed down from Ethiopia, causing the water to run as red as blood. Whatever his method, God miraculously brings about the conditions that create plagues designed to change Pharaoh's heart.

In the second plague frogs descend upon the people of Egypt, invading their kitchens and bedrooms and even crawling on their bodies. If this plague was God's intensification of a natural event, the frogs, which were abundant in the Nile, probably left the river because of the dead fish and polluted water. Pharaoh becomes bothered enough to promise the people's release if Moses prays to God for relief. But when the frogs die, Pharaoh reneges on his promise.

—BQ

Daily Contemplation

When have you seen God move through an event to change a person's heart?

DAY 51

The Plagues of Gnats, Flies, and Livestock
Exodus 8:16–9:7

Then the LORD said to Moses, "Go to Pharaoh and say to him, 'This is what the LORD, the God of the Hebrews, says: "Let my people go, so that they may worship me." If you refuse to let them go and continue to hold them back, the hand of the LORD will bring a terrible plague on your livestock in the field—on your horses, donkeys and camels and on your cattle, sheep and goats. But the LORD will make a distinction between the livestock of Israel and that of Egypt, so that no animal belonging to the Israelites will die.'" . . . Pharaoh investigated and found that not even one of the animals of the Israelites had died. Yet his heart was unyielding and he would not let the people go. (Exodus 9:1–4, 7)

Now God allows gnats and flies to plague the Egyptian people. The gnats may have bred in the flooded fields of Egypt, and the flies on the wet banks of the receding Nile. It's likely that the flies were a type that when full-grown would bite both animals and people. As with the frogs, Pharaoh hates the flies so much that he again promises to let the people go. But when the flies vanish, he backs down on his promise.

Next God brings a plague on all the livestock belonging to the Egyptians and left out in the fields. God spares the livestock belonging to the Israelites. The flies of the earlier plague may have carried the anthrax bacteria that originated in the algae-infested Nile. Flies carrying these bacteria could easily infect livestock. Not only does this plague hurt the Egyptians economically; it also insults some of their deities. The bull and cow are considered sacred, representing Egyptian gods and goddesses. Yet despite his loss, Pharaoh remains unyielding.

—BQ

---------- *Daily Contemplation* ----------

Do you consider yourself a cooperative or stubborn person?

DAY 52

Prayer of a Reluctant Servant
Reflection

Dear God,
I've got to make a decision soon. I (Brenda) can't believe I'm even considering doing this. It's a big commitment, a huge change for me. And I'm not even sure it fits me. *Who am I, that I should go* and take this step? Of all people, why did you choose me? I really don't know if I can handle the task.

Let's imagine I say yes. How do I begin? I can't just waltz in there and assume command, as if everyone already trusts me. *What shall I tell them?* They might not accept me. Maybe they won't like me. I can't do this without their support. *What if they don't believe me?* What if they think I'm not qualified, or worse, don't want my help? I can't take being rejected, God. You know how fragile my ego is.

I can't picture myself doing this. I'm not cut out for it. *I have never been eloquent.* It's not in my nature. Why can't I stick to what I've been doing and not embarrass you or anyone else?

The more I think about it, the colder my feet get. I can't do this. It scares me, and I certainly don't need more fear in my life. I don't have what it takes for this one, God. *O Lord, please send someone else to do it.* Surely you have an alternate who will do a better job than I could ever do . . .

You're still asking me to do it. I can't shake the sense that you're serious. You really want *me*, don't you? Forgive my arguments, Lord. I'm learning that you have a much higher view of me than I do. Thanks for your confidence. I guess we both know who's really going to get it done. I'm going to need your help, God. Yes, I'm definitely going to need your help.
Amen.

—BQ

Daily Contemplation

Is God calling you to a job for which you still feel unqualified? Tell God why you are struggling and ask him to calm your fears. If you need to know whether God has really called you, ask him to make it clear. Then pray for a willing spirit.

DAY 53

The Plagues of Boils and Hail
Exodus 9:8–35

> Then the LORD said to Moses and Aaron, "Take handfuls of soot from a furnace and have Moses toss it into the air in the presence of Pharaoh. It will become fine dust over the whole land of Egypt, and festering boils will break out on people and animals throughout the land." So they took soot from a furnace and stood before Pharaoh. Moses tossed it into the air, and festering boils broke out on people and animals. The magicians could not stand before Moses because of the boils that were on them and on all the Egyptians. But the LORD hardened Pharaoh's heart and he would not listen to Moses and Aaron, just as the LORD had said to Moses. (Exodus 9:8–12)

The plague of boils is the first to directly afflict the bodies of the Egyptian people. The plague hits with no warning, incapacitating even the magicians. (The boils may have resulted from a skin anthrax similar to what plagued the livestock earlier.) Only Pharaoh remains stubbornly unmoved.

God deals with Pharaoh's hardness in the next plague, telling Moses to warn Pharaoh and the people about the coming of the worst hailstorm in the history of Egypt. God mercifully cautions any who will listen and act to save their own lives and the lives of their slaves and animals. Speaking to Pharaoh, God teaches about his sovereignty. The apostle Paul quotes Exodus 9:16 in Romans 9:17 as he discusses God's freedom in using people for his purposes: "I raised you up for this very purpose, that I might display my power in you and that my name might be proclaimed in all the earth." Rather than obliterating Pharaoh and the land of Egypt, which he could easily do, God chooses to display his own power to many people through Pharaoh's hardened heart.

—BQ

Daily Contemplation

When have you sensed God's power through an event of nature?

DAY 54

Plagues: Locusts, Darkness, and Death of Firstborn
Exodus 10:1–11:10

To liberate the Israelite slaves, God stages a cosmic showdown known as the Ten Plagues, a showdown so dramatic that in modern times it strains the limits of Hollywood special effects crews just to depict it on-screen. A nation is aborning, and the task of uprooting the Israelites from Egypt calls for outside intervention.

First, the Israelites themselves have to be convinced of God's power. Somehow God has to demonstrate that he has not forgotten his chosen people, even though he has seemed silent and unconcerned. Then, too, Egypt needs convincing: No empire will let thousands of valuable slaves walk away free. Exodus asserts more than a dozen times that the plagues are given so that the Israelites and Egyptians will recognize the power of Israel's God.

An even more basic issue is at stake: God's personal credibility. Is he just one more tribal god, like the ones the Egyptians worship? The plagues are, in effect, God's open warfare against the false gods of Egypt. God declares as much: "I will bring judgment on all the gods of Egypt" (Exodus 12:12). Some scholars see each plague as a targeted attack against a specific Egyptian idol. Thus, the plague on the Nile River countered the Egyptians' river god; the plague of flies, the sacred fly; the plague of darkness, the sun god Ra; and the plague on livestock, the sacred bull.

In the end, the plagues will work so effectively that thousands of slaves will leave unhindered, with the wealth of Egypt showered upon them as farewell gifts. "I am the God who brought you out of Egypt," God will remind the Israelites again and again whenever they are tempted to doubt his power or concern for them.

—PY

Daily Contemplation

If God declared war on the "gods" of our modern society, what would they be?

DAY 55

The Passover
Exodus 12:1–30

"Take some of the blood and put it on the sides and tops of the doorframes of the houses where they eat the lambs. . . . I will pass through Egypt and strike down every firstborn of both people and animals, and I will bring judgment on all the gods of Egypt. I am the LORD. The blood will be a sign for you on the houses where you are, and when I see the blood, I will pass over you. No destructive plague will touch you when I strike Egypt." (Exodus 12:7, 12–13)

Life in Egypt had been hellish. For centuries the Israelites were held captive to people who oppressed them and who worshiped false, powerless gods. Finally, the time for rescue has come. In the final plague, the plague of the deaths of the firstborn, God shows the Egyptians once and for all that he is the one true God. He spares the Israelites because he's chosen them as his own and because they use the blood of a lamb to signal they belong to him.

The story may sound vaguely familiar, not because you've heard it before but because it sets the stage for the central story of the Bible: the story of Jesus Christ, the Lamb slain to save the lives of those who love God, rescuing them out of a sinful world. Here in the Old Testament the Israelites are the people God has chosen for himself, the ones he singles out to save. As the story of God's presence with his people continues through the Bible, the group of chosen people will extend beyond this ethnic group of Jews to encompass all who follow Jesus.

Now we, as believers, share in the Passover story. Like the Israelites in Egypt, we know we're not at home in this world of pain and suffering. But we are ready to journey with God. Our hope is in the sacrifice Jesus made for us, and we're waiting to be with him always in the Promised Land of a restored earth.

—BQ

Daily Contemplation

What is your life like now compared with life "in Egypt," before you knew Jesus?

DAY 56

The Exodus
Exodus 12:31–42

During the night Pharaoh summoned Moses and Aaron and said, "Up! Leave my people, you and the Israelites! Go, worship the LORD as you have requested. Take your flocks and herds, as you have said, and go. And also bless me." . . . So the people took their dough before the yeast was added, and carried it on their shoulders in kneading troughs wrapped in clothing. The Israelites did as Moses instructed and asked the Egyptians for articles of silver and gold and for clothing. The LORD had made the Egyptians favorably disposed toward the people, and they gave them what they asked for; so they plundered the Egyptians. (Exodus 12:31–33, 34–36)

The journey has begun. For nearly a year the Israelites watched one plague after another besiege the Egyptian people, only to leave Pharaoh as hard-hearted as ever. Freedom seemed improbable for a long time; God's promises were clouded by the daunting circumstances. Suddenly Pharaoh is forcing the Israelites out of Egypt faster than they can go.

Everything changes, literally overnight. The man considered a god by his people orders the Israelites to leave, taking all their belongings with them. Pharaoh even asks for a blessing. As they go, the Israelites find their Egyptian neighbors only too willing to bestow going-away gifts of silver, gold, and clothing—a turn of events too good to be true.

Within hours this vast nation is heading to the desert. They discover that God will do what he says despite the odds against it. Unfortunately, the people will forget this lesson many times in the desert and even after they've reached the Promised Land. They will lose sight of a lesson that future believers will also struggle to embrace.

—BQ

Daily Contemplation

What circumstances are clouding your view of the plan God has for you?

DAY 57

Crossing the Red Sea
Exodus 13:17–14:31

It doesn't take long for Pharaoh and the Egyptians to second-guess their decision to release the slaves. Soon a glittering army of chariots and horsemen is charging after the defenseless Israelites.

Nor does it take long for the Israelites to second-guess their decision to leave. At the first sight of Pharaoh's army, they quake in fear and accuse Moses of leading them to certain destruction in the desert.

As this passage tells it, the Israelites' final confrontation with Egypt is divinely stage-managed to make a point for all time: God himself, no one else, is responsible for the Israelites' liberation. More than anything, the account of the Exodus underscores this one indisputable fact. No Israelite armies stand against the mighty Egyptians. At the last possible minute, God arranges a spectacular rescue operation and an equally spectacular defeat of the Egyptian army. The freed captives can only respond with humility and praise; there is no room for pride. For them, independence from Egypt means dependence on God.

That pattern of depending on God will continue all through the Exodus. When the wilderness wanderers run out of water, God provides. When food supplies fail, God provides. When raiders attack, God provides. In fact, the book of Exodus shows a greater proportion of miracles—direct supernatural acts of God—than any other part of the Bible except the Gospels. The psalmists will never tire of celebrating these events in music, and the prophets will later hearken back to the days of the Exodus to stir the conscience of their nation. The great miracle of the Red Sea sets the tone for a national history that is from beginning to end an active movement of God.

—PY

Daily Contemplation

Has God ever parted a "Red Sea" in your life, to rescue you from something that would have been harmful?

DAY 58

Spiritual Amnesia
Reflection

Now that you've read about the beginning of creation and become acquainted with the founding characters in God's story with his people, how much do you remember about the ways in which God makes his will possible in their lives?

Your recollections should include the Flood, when God saved only one family on a boat and then through them repopulated the earth. Abraham and Sarah, a couple who'd been infertile and were too old to conceive, gave birth to a son, Isaac, whose life was spared by an order from God. Twin brothers, Jacob and Esau, reunited with weeping and gifts after living apart for years due to rivalry and deception. Joseph, a son of Jacob, survived enslavement and became the wealthy governor of Egypt. Moses, a captive Hebrew who'd been raised an Egyptian, watched God rain destruction in the form of plagues and then saw God part the waters of the sea to provide an escape route.

In all these ways God kept his promises, never failing to surprise his people in working out his plans. Those coming after Moses will remember God's doings. King David finds the memories of God's acts comforting, and he declares to God, "You remain the same" (Psalm 102:27). The writer of Hebrews affirms, "Jesus Christ is the same yesterday and today and forever" (Hebrews 13:8). The God we've watched in the Bible so far is the same God the first Christians knew two thousand years ago and the same God we know today.

Why, then, don't believers do a better job of trusting? The Israelites sometimes remembered God's many feats, but sometimes they forgot. The early church remembered, too, but sometimes their memory lapsed. Believers throughout the ages have exhibited a sort of selective memory, recalling God's power and then letting fears block that memory. It's spiritual amnesia, usually resulting from a hard knock by the world. As many Christians before us have discovered, the surest cure for forgetfulness is to return to the beginning and remind ourselves of God's track record.

How's your memory?

—BQ

Daily Contemplation

Spend a few moments thinking about the ways in which God has rescued you in the past. Do you need rescuing now? Thank God for the ways in which he has already come through for you, and tell him you need him now.

DAY 59

Manna from Heaven
Exodus 16:1–36

In the desert the whole community grumbled against Moses and Aaron. The Israelites said to them, "If only we had died by the LORD's hand in Egypt! There we sat around pots of meat and ate all the food we wanted, but you have brought us out into this desert to starve this entire assembly to death." Then the LORD said to Moses, "I will rain down bread from heaven for you. The people are to go out each day and gather enough for that day. In this way I will test them and see whether they will follow my instructions. On the sixth day they are to prepare what they bring in, and that is to be twice as much as they gather on the other days." (Exodus 16:2–5)

Only weeks after they walk through a parted Red Sea and watch their Egyptian pursuers drown in the waters, the Israelites are already complaining about the death they feel is imminent. Out of food, they feel certain they'll starve. Not only does God provide an immediate and lasting food supply; he puts the Israelites on a schedule that gives them a day each week to rest and eat leftovers.

Again in this passage we see reflections of future Bible events. God provides for the Israelites in the desert by showering them with manna each morning. Jesus will teach the disciples to ask for similar provision by praying, "Give us today our daily bread" (Matthew 6:11). More importantly, Jesus will call himself "the living bread that came down from heaven" (John 6:51). Not only does God provide for our immediate physical needs; he has given us Jesus to care daily for our spirits and give us life that will last forever.

—BQ

Daily Contemplation

What kind of "manna" do you need God to provide in the coming days?

DAY 60

Jethro Visits Moses
Exodus 18:1–27

Jethro, Moses' father-in-law, together with Moses' sons and wife, came to him in the wilderness, where he was camped near the mountain of God. . . . The next day Moses took his seat to serve as judge for the people, and they stood around him from morning till evening. When his father-in-law saw all that Moses was doing for the people, he said, "What is this you are doing for the people? Why do you alone sit as judge, while all these people stand around you from morning till evening?" Moses answered him, "Because the people come to me to seek God's will. Whenever they have a dispute, it is brought to me, and I decide between the parties and inform them of God's decrees and instructions." Moses' father-in-law replied, "What you are doing is not good. You and these people who come to you will only wear yourselves out. . . . Select capable men from all the people . . . Have them serve as judges for the people at all times, but have them bring every difficult case to you; the simple cases they can decide themselves. That will make your load lighter, because they will share it with you." (Exodus 18:5, 13–18, 21–22)

Moses' father-in-law, Jethro, becomes the first advisor to perceive the value in delegation. God has given Moses the job of representing the people before God and teaching them how to live. But clearly Moses, who feels he must carry out his job from beginning to end and do it all himself, needs help. God brings somebody in from the outside to let him know he'll soon wear out. God wants to spread the work to others and keep Moses fresh for other leadership tasks.

—BQ

Daily Contemplation

Are you doing too much? Which responsibilities has God clearly given you? Which might you need to release to someone else?

DAY 61

The Ten Commandments
Exodus 19:1–20:17

Nearly everyone has heard of the Ten Commandments. For most of us, they represent a central core of morality, "the basics" that God requires. But for the Israelites in the desert, the Ten Commandments represent far more—nothing less than a major breakthrough. The nations around them, who worshiped many different gods, lived in constant fear of the gods' unpredictability. Who could tell what might anger or please them? But now God himself, Maker of the universe, is giving the Israelites a binding treaty signed with his own hand. They will always know exactly what God requires and where they stand before him.

God holds before them some wonderful guarantees: prosperity, abundant crops, victorious armies, immunity from health problems. In effect, God agrees to remove most of the problems people face in daily existence. In exchange, he asks that the Israelites obey the rules outlined in this and the next few chapters. God's original covenant with Abraham he now makes formal and applies it to a whole nation. (This middle part of Exodus is known as the "Book of the Covenant," for it contains the essence of the Israelites' treaty with God.)

"Although the whole earth is mine, you will be for me a kingdom of priests and a holy nation," God says (Exodus 19:5–6). He wants a nation like no other, a model society centered around a commitment to him. All the Israelites wait in anticipation as Moses climbs a dark, smoky mountain to meet with God. No one present could miss the significance of this meeting: It is marked by thunder and lightning and a loud, piercing trumpet blast and fire. The ground itself shakes, as in an earthquake.

Out of this meeting on Mount Sinai (SIE-nie) come the rules summarized here. The Bible fills in more details of the treaty, but these Ten Commandments express the kind of behavior God wants from his people. It is a day of wild hope. "We will do everything the LORD has said," the people all promise with a shout (19:8).

—PY

Daily Contemplation

What would some of the Ten Commandments say if worded positively (reading, "You shall . . ." rather than, "You shall not . . .")?

DAY 62

The Golden Calf
Exodus 32:1–35

The bright hope of Exodus 20 dies abruptly in Exodus 32; there is no more jarring contrast in all the Bible. For forty days Moses visits with God on Mount Sinai, receiving the terms of the covenant, or treaty, that will open up an unprecedented closeness between God and human beings. But what happens down below, at the foot of the mountain, almost defies belief.

The Israelites—the very people who saw the Ten Plagues of Egypt, who crossed the Red Sea on dry ground, who are digesting the miracle of manna in their stomachs at this moment—are the same people who, out of boredom or impatience or rebellion or jealousy or some such mortal urge, apparently forget all about their God. By the time Moses descends from Sinai, the Israelites, God's people, are dancing like pagans around a golden statue.

Moses is so angry that he hurls to the ground the tablets of stone signed by God himself. God is so angry that he nearly destroys the whole insolent nation.

This chapter has many parallels with the story of the very first human rebellion in Genesis 3. Both times, people favored by God fail to trust him and strike out instead against his clear command. Both times, the rebels devise elaborate rationalizations to explain their behavior. Both times, they forfeit special privileges and suffer harsh punishment.

It appears, for a moment, that something new in the history of humanity will take place among the Israelites: an entire nation devoted to following God. Instead, the same old story replays itself. No matter what terms God comes up with, people find ways to break them.

Only one ray of hope shines out of this dark scene. Moses, the stuttering, reluctant leader, seems to grow into his position at last. His eloquent prayers are answered, and God grants the Israelites yet another chance.

—PY

Daily Contemplation

Why do you think the Israelites rebelled? Have you ever rebelled for a similar reason?

DAY 63

Traveling on God's Wings
Reflection

In their first weeks growing up together as a liberated nation, the Israelites have experienced God's care—not only as Lord and Deliverer but also as a loving Parent. In their first stories of desert sojourn, God has also given us a lesson in parenting and being parented.

God first met the Israelites' most basic need for food, ensuring that they would have something to eat every day and feel satisfied. Next God gave them guidance. As any parent advises a child—"Don't lift that. It's too heavy for you. I'll help."—God advised Moses and the people as to how they could work best together without wearing out. After securing their physical and emotional needs, God led the people on to the next stage of maturity, introducing a set of rules to govern the household. Without rules these children would remain aimless, but with a clear set of directives they could become grounded people fit for serving God.

As God cared for the Israelites, he cares for us, his children, today. He gives us food to keep us going. He guides us day-to-day in handling our lives. And as we make choices, we turn to God's rules as a foundation for our behavior. Like typical children, we need rules to feel loved. We need a Parent who knows better than we do what is good for us.

God may come off a bit harsh and demanding in much of Exodus, but occasionally we get a glimpse of the poetry of his heart, the tenderness he feels for his people. As he prepares to give Moses the Ten Commandments, God says, "You yourselves have seen what I did to Egypt, and how I carried you on eagles' wings and brought you to myself" (Exodus 19:4).

God speaks not as a distant, bellowing old man. Rather, he likens himself to a mother eagle teaching her young to fly by soaring beneath, with wings spread to catch the faltering eaglet. He doesn't leave his children in a barren place to help themselves while calling from afar with pointless admonitions. Rather, he flies only inches underneath, offering his people security and rest.

—BQ

Daily Contemplation

Consider the ways in which God has been a truly loving Parent to you. Can you feel him near, wings spread to lift you when you fall? Thank him now for knowing your needs and for meeting them. Thank him for loving you tenderly and rightly.

DAY 64

Reward for Obedience; Punishment for Disobedience
Leviticus 26:3–45

Leviticus seems very strange to the modern world, so strange that readers intending to read the entire Bible often get bogged down in this book. Unlike most of the Bible, it has few stories or personalities and no poetry. It's a book of laws crammed full of detailed rules and procedures.

Many of these individual rules, appropriate to God's goal of calling out a "separate" people, were changed in the New Testament. Yet a study of such laws can prove rewarding, for they express God's priorities on subjects such as care for the land, concern for the poor, and abuses of family and neighbors.

Although the Old Testament laws recorded in Leviticus, Exodus, Numbers, and Deuteronomy may seem long-winded, keep them in perspective. These laws—just over six hundred in all—comprise the entire set of regulations for a nation, as far as we know. (Most modern cities have more traffic laws!) And they are brief and clear. You don't have to go to law school to understand them.

The variety of the laws shows that God involves himself in every aspect of the Israelites' lives. Laws against witchcraft are mixed in with laws concerning improper haircuts, tattoos, and prostitution. God is advancing his plan for the Israelites by carving out a separate culture. After four centuries in Egypt, the recently freed slaves, more Egyptian than anything else, need a comprehensive makeover. That is exactly what God gives them. Many of the laws seem designed primarily to keep the Israelites "different" from their pagan neighbors.

The Israelites in this Old Testament time are a unique people, unlike any other nation on earth, called by God to demonstrate holiness and purity to people around them. The reward for obeying the laws will make the Israelites the envy of the world. And if they disobey? God spells out in frightening detail the punishments they can then expect.

—PY

Daily Contemplation

Everybody has a code to live by. Where do you get yours?

DAY 65

The Cloud Above the Tabernacle
Numbers 9:15–23

On the day the tabernacle, the tent of the covenant law, was set up, the cloud covered it. From evening till morning the cloud above the tabernacle looked like fire. That is how it continued to be; the cloud covered it, and at night it looked like fire. Whenever the cloud lifted from above the tent, the Israelites set out; wherever the cloud settled, the Israelites encamped. At the LORD's command the Israelites set out, and at his command they encamped. . . . Sometimes the cloud was over the tabernacle only a few days; at the LORD's command they would encamp, and then at his command they would set out. Sometimes the cloud stayed only from evening till morning, and when it lifted in the morning, they set out. Whether by day or by night, whenever the cloud lifted, they set out. Whether the cloud stayed over the tabernacle for two days or a month or a year, the Israelites would remain in camp and not set out; but when it lifted, they would set out. At the LORD's command they encamped, and at the LORD's command they set out. They obeyed the LORD's order, in accordance with his command through Moses. (Numbers 9:15–18, 20–23)

God makes his presence obvious to the people every day in the wilderness through the visible symbol of a cloud. They have no doubt as to whether God is with them and directing their journey. Although God is unpredictable, sometimes stopping them only for a short time before moving them on and sometimes keeping them encamped for weeks or months, God remains continually present, a companion in their daily life and travels.

The Israelite people have no reason to doubt God's care. Each day they eat manna from God and are covered by the cloud of his guidance. But soon they will again falter in faith and gratitude.

—BQ

Daily Contemplation

What reminds you that God is present with you each day?

DAY 66

Quail from the Lord
Numbers 11:4–23, 31–34

> Now a wind went out from the LORD and drove quail in from the sea. It scattered them up to two cubits deep all around the camp, as far as a day's walk in any direction. All that day and night and all the next day the people went out and gathered quail. . . . But while the meat was still between their teeth and before it could be consumed, the anger of the LORD burned against the people, and he struck them with a severe plague. (Numbers 11:31–33)

The book of Numbers covers a journey through the desert that should have lasted about two weeks but instead lasted forty years. When they first crossed into the Sinai Peninsula, the Israelites were bursting with a spirit of hope and adventure. Free at last from the chains of slavery, they headed toward the Promised Land. But the weeks, months, and then years of wandering in a hostile desert soon wore down all positive feelings.

With relentless honesty, Numbers tells what happens to change a short excursion into a forty-year detour. Petty things seem to bother the Israelites most, as their constant complaints about food indicate. With a few exceptions, they eat the same thing every day: *manna* (meaning literally, "What is it?"), which appears like dew on the ground each morning. A monotonous diet may seem a trivial exchange for freedom from slavery, but read their grumbling for yourself in this chapter.

The rebellion portrayed here typifies the whole journey. And the more childishly the people act, the more their leaders are forced to respond like stern parents. Moses and God take turns getting exasperated by the Israelites' constant whining.

True, conditions are rigorous: facing a constant threat from enemy armies, the tribes have to march under a broiling sun through a desert region oppressed by snakes, scorpions, and constant drought. But the underlying issue is a simple test of faith: Will they trust God to see them through such hard circumstances? Will they follow the terms of the covenant he has signed with them and depend on his promised protection?

—PY

Daily Contemplation

Do you ever grumble against God? If so, what tends to trigger the complaining?

DAY 67

Miriam and Aaron Oppose Moses
Numbers 12:1–16

Then the Lord came down in a pillar of cloud; he stood at the entrance to the tent and summoned Aaron and Miriam. When the two of them stepped forward, he said, "Listen to my words:

"When there is a prophet among you,
    I, the Lord, reveal myself to them in visions,
    I speak to them in dreams.
But this is not true of my servant Moses;
    he is faithful in all my house.
With him I speak face to face,
    clearly and not in riddles;
    he sees the form of the Lord.
Why then were you not afraid
    to speak against my servant Moses?"

The anger of the Lord burned against them, and he left them. When the cloud lifted from above the tent, Miriam's skin was leprous—it became as white as snow. (Numbers 12:5–10)

Miriam and Aaron envy their brother Moses, who has been chosen to hear God's voice in a way no other person could. God acted sovereignly and selected one man as his primary representative to the Israelites as they travel through the desert to the Promised Land. God also chose both Miriam and Aaron as leaders, yet despite Moses' humility they feel resentful of their sibling.

This brother and sister, compelled to compare themselves with Moses, are exhibiting traits common to imperfect human nature. Seeing Moses to have something from God that they don't, they become jealous and critical. But this human nature can't be allowed to take hold. God is blessing all the people through Moses, and God will not tolerate anyone who questions his choice of caring for them.

—BQ

--- *Daily Contemplation* ---

Is God asking you to respect someone he has placed in a position of authority?

DAY 68

God's Puzzling Ways
Reflection

Jigsaw puzzles bother me. I (Brenda) never seem able to fit the pieces together and find myself more annoyed than amused by this pastime.

Puzzles have taught me something about my life, though. God sees each part of our lives as a puzzle piece in the larger picture of a life that belongs to him and is being made ready for his purpose. God doesn't desire for us to stray from him and suffer, but even if that happens, when we come to him with a humble heart, he works our experiences into the artistry of what he has already begun.

Unfortunately, we tend to hold a small piece of jigsaw puzzle in our hands, see the dark, unattractive piece as a symbol of the whole picture, and react the way the Israelites did: "God, we're sick of this dusty old desert. If we were in Egypt, we'd have a banquet at every meal rather than this insufferable manna." But listen to the Israelites before they left Egypt: "God, we're so tired of living under the thumb of these pagan Egyptians. Can't you do something to give us our freedom? Nothing about our lives here is good."

In short, the Israelites didn't like either piece of the puzzle. Worse, they refused to see these odd-shaped events as small parts of a bigger picture God was creating for their nation. If only they had looked back at God's promises and forward to the certain fulfillment of them. If only they had clung to the certainty that their difficult circumstances were temporary, bringing them one step closer to the fullness of God's plan. Listen to how their voices might have sounded: "God, we long to be freed to live as your people in a land of our own. You've increased our numbers and saved us from famine. Thanks for the good future you've promised us." And then: "Lord, this desert trip isn't always easy. We yearn to be settled in a place with good food and water. But we are free! You are feeding and protecting us, and soon you'll bring us home."

I may not enjoy puzzles, but I'm learning that if I can take my eyes off that pesky piece that doesn't seem to fit and look at the half-finished picture, I'll see that God is fitting together something beautiful.

—BQ

Daily Contemplation

Are you focusing on the specifics of your circumstances or on the bigger picture God has for your life? Ask God to help you take a step back and see things from his perspective, with your present challenges as part of his greater purpose for you.

DAY 69

Exploring Canaan
Numbers 13:1–33

The LORD said to Moses, "Send some men to explore the land of Canaan, which I am giving to the Israelites." . . . They gave Moses this account: "We went into the land to which you sent us, and it does flow with milk and honey! Here is its fruit. But the people who live there are powerful, and the cities are fortified and very large." . . . Then Caleb silenced the people before Moses and said, "We should go up and take possession of the land, for we can certainly do it." (Numbers 13:1–2, 27–28, 30)

Finally, the Israelites approach the borders of the Promised Land. Canaan is inhabited by powerful groups of people who seem to have firm control of the land. Although the Israelites are ready to take possession of their homeland, the spies take one look at their opponents and wilt. It seems impossible to overcome these tribes so established and confident. In scouting out the land, the spies see Canaan and themselves only through their own limited vision.

One spy, Caleb, chooses to see Canaan through the eyes of a believer. When he looks at the land, rather than seeing strong people, he sees a God who saved Noah's family in a worldwide flood, One who saved Jacob's family from widespread famine, One who plagued Egypt until Pharaoh released the Israelites, One who parted the Red Sea to save the Israelites and drown the Egyptians, One who provided water and manna to people wandering in the desert. To Caleb, no people or cities can pose even the smallest threat to God's power.

Caleb knows that God's promise far outweighs the threat of any form of earthly power. No matter how unlikely God's way seems to those who look with this world's eyes, God will do what he has set out to do.

—BQ

―――――― *Daily Contemplation* ――――――

What situation do you need to see through God's eyes rather than your own?

DAY 70

The People Rebel
Numbers 14:1–44

Most ancient histories record the heroic exploits of mighty warriors and unblemished leaders. The Bible, however, gives a strikingly different picture, as seen in the brutal realism of Numbers. On a dozen different occasions, the Israelites lash out in despair or rise up in rebellion, plotting against their leaders and denouncing God. The spirit of revolt spreads to the priests, to the military, to Moses' family, and ultimately to Moses himself.

This chapter recounts the pivotal event of Numbers, the most decisive event since the Exodus from Egypt. The Israelites are poised on the very border of the Promised Land. If they simply trust God, they can leave the torturous desert and walk into a land abundant with food and water.

Yet despite the miracles God has already performed on their behalf, the Israelites choose to distrust him once again. Cowed by a military scouting report of potential opposition, they loudly bemoan the original decision to leave Egypt. In open mutiny, they even conspire to stone Moses and his brother Aaron.

The real object of revolt, the Israelites' God, feels spurned, like a cast-off lover. Convinced at last that this band of renegades is unprepared for conquest of the Promised Land, he postpones all plans. The covenant promise of a new nation in a new land will have to wait, at least until all the adults of the grumbling generation have died off. And that's why, out of the many thousands who left Egypt, only two adults, Joshua and Caleb, survive to enter the Promised Land.

The Israelites have lost faith not only in themselves but in their God. The apostle Paul points out that these failures "happened to them as examples and were written down as warnings for us, on whom the culmination of the ages has come. So, if you think you are standing firm, be careful that you don't fall!" (1 Corinthians 10:11–12).

—PY

Daily Contemplation

What "giants" cause you fear? How do you respond?

DAY 71

Water from the Rock; The Bronze Snake
Numbers 20:1–13; 21:4–9

> Now there was no water for the community, and the people gathered in opposition to Moses and Aaron.... Moses said to them, "Listen, you rebels, must we bring you water out of this rock?" Then Moses raised his arm and struck the rock twice with his staff. Water gushed out.... But the LORD said to Moses and Aaron, "Because you did not trust in me enough to honor me as holy in the sight of the Israelites, you will not bring this community into the land I give them." (Numbers 20:2, 10–12)

Once again the people become irritated by their living conditions in the desert. Although they have seen God provide for them many times, they fall into an attitude of complaining. Moses and Aaron have endured the complaints and distrust for forty years now. They know it is nearly time to enter Canaan. Yet in these stories the people's grumbling reaches an all-time high. Fed up, Moses loses his temper and reacts in anger toward the Israelites and in disrespect toward God.

Later, the Bible tells us that "from everyone who has been given much, much will be demanded; and from the one who has been entrusted with much, much more will be asked" (Luke 12:48). Moses and Aaron hold great positions of responsibility, and because they act in front of the people with disrespect for God, calling attention to themselves, God denies them entrance to the Promised Land.

In an offense toward God that is just as serious, the people express contempt for the manna he has provided. Crying out "We detest this miserable food!" the Israelites thumb their noses at God's grace. By his holy nature, God must punish their disdain.

The Gospel of John compares the incident with the bronze snake to the salvation of Jesus. "Just as Moses lifted up the snake in the wilderness, so the Son of Man must be lifted up, that everyone who believes may have eternal life in him" (John 3:14–15).

—BQ

Daily Contemplation

What responsibilities has God given you?

DAY 72

Obedience Commanded
Deuteronomy 1:1; 4:7–38

Four decades after the Exodus, the Israelites stand at the edge of the Promised Land, spiritually and physically seasoned by their wilderness wanderings. Egypt is a faint memory from childhood. With the older generation of doubters and grumblers now dead and buried, a new generation chafes to march in and claim the land.

There at the border, the old man Moses delivers three speeches that, for their length and emotional power, have no equal in the Bible. It is his last chance to advise and inspire the people he has led for forty tumultuous years. Passionately, deliberately, tearfully, he reviews their history step by step, occasionally flaring up at a painful memory but more often pouring out the anguished love of a doting parent. An undercurrent of sadness runs through the speeches, for Moses has learned he will not join the triumph of entering Canaan.

Moses' longest speech reiterates all the laws that the Israelites have agreed to keep as their part of the covenant. Moses also recalls the hallmark day when God delivered the covenant on Mount Sinai. He remembers aloud the black clouds and deep darkness and blazing fire. *You saw no shape or form of God on that day*, he reminds them. God's presence cannot be reduced to any mere image. Moses' central message: *Never forget the lessons you learned in the desert.*

Besides all the warnings, Moses is giving a kind of pep talk, a final challenge for the Israelites to recognize their unique calling as a nation. If they follow God's laws, all the lavish benefits of the covenant will be theirs. More, every other nation will look to them and want to know their God. Moses seems incurably astonished at all God has done for him and the other Israelites, and this speech represents his last chance to communicate that sense of wonder and thanksgiving.

—PY

Daily Contemplation

What are you learning now from God that will become a part of your testimony with him?

DAY 73

Do Not Forget the Lord
Deuteronomy 8:1–20

Aleksandr Solzhenitsyn, the Nobel laureate Russian author, says that he first learned to pray in a Siberian concentration camp. He turned to prayer because he had no other hope. Before his arrest, when things were going well, he had seldom given God a thought.[6]

Similarly, Moses felt the Israelites had learned the habit of depending on God in the Sinai wilderness, where they had no choice; they needed his intervention each day just to eat and drink. But now, on the banks of the Jordan River, they are about to face a more difficult test of faith. After they enter the land of plenty, will they soon forget the God who has given it to them?

Desert-bred, the Israelites know little about the seductions of other cultures: the alluring sensuality, the exotic religions, the glittering wealth. Now they are preparing to march into a region known for these enticements, and Moses seems to fear the coming prosperity far more than the rigors of the desert. In the beautiful land, the Promised Land, the Israelites might put God behind them and credit themselves for their success.

"Remember!" Moses keeps urging. Remember the days of slavery in Egypt, and God's acts of liberation. Remember the trials of the vast and desolate desert, and God's faithfulness there. Remember your special calling as God's peculiar treasures.

Moses has good reason for concern, for God, who can see the future, has told him plainly what will happen: "When I have brought them into the land flowing with milk and honey, the land I promised on oath to their ancestors, and when they eat their fill and thrive, they will turn to other gods and worship them, rejecting me and breaking my covenant" (Deuteronomy 31:20). As the books following Deuteronomy relate, all Moses' fears come true.

Ironically, as Deuteronomy shows, success often makes it harder to depend on God. The Israelites prove less faithful to God after they move into the Promised Land. There is a grave danger in finally getting what you want.

—PY

---------- *Daily Contemplation* ----------

Do you think most about God when things are going well or when you are in trouble?

DAY 74

A Jekyll-and-Hyde God?
Reflection

Some of God's harshest words to the Israelite people are spoken in the last passages from Deuteronomy: "The Lord your God is a consuming fire, a jealous God" (4:24). "Like the nations the Lord destroyed before you, so you will be destroyed for not obeying the Lord your God" (8:20). Yet in the same passages we find words of unmistakable tenderness and compassion: "The Lord your God is a merciful God; he will not abandon or destroy you or forget the covenant with your ancestors, which he confirmed to them by oath" (4:31).

One minute God is warning the people of the doom that awaits them if they stray from him, and the next he is welcoming them back and reassuring them of his love. To the Israelites, God's alternating voices surely seem confusing. Who, really, is this God they serve? What is his true nature?

As we take a long look at God while reading through the Old Testament, we too may wonder about this God. We know him as One who forgives us and welcomes us into his family in love. We know him as caring and merciful. But in the Old Testament we see glimpses of a stern, unbending Power who speaks to his people in no uncertain terms about actions and consequences. God is demanding and blunt. Still, a few breaths later he gushes in willingness to forgive once more. Do we worship a Jekyll and Hyde? Is even God unsettled as to how to handle these unreliable children of his? Should we expect the same treatment from him today?

It is crucial that we, as believers, gain a right understanding of God's nature. Then we can see the big picture of God and his dealings with humanity. Then we can let go of the confusion that practically begs an explanation throughout the Old Testament.

God, in his holiness, can be compared to water—pure and life-giving. Jesus used this comparison, describing his gift of eternal life as "living water." Humans, though, are marred by sin, which is like oil, a substance incompatible with water. Try to clean oil from a stovetop with a cloth and water, and the oil only smears. When oil spills in the ocean, it holds together and continues to float atop the water. Oil and water don't mix, no matter how hard one may try.

This is a picture of God and sinful people. God's character is wholly incompatible with sin. Regardless of how he feels about people who are sinners, God's nature keeps him irreversibly separated from anyone with sin. Despite his compassion and mercy, he is incapable of compromising his nature. God's love flows freely, but when his people are unfaithful and disobedient, he must cast them away.

Extend the metaphor to Jesus. He is like soap. Water and oil will never mix, but soap is one substance that can allow water to interact effectively with oil. It cleans and dissolves oil. Only through Jesus' death for all sinners—his blood shed for us—was God able to cleanse away sin and draw people close to him.

God's holiness doesn't change, nor does his incompatibility with sin. But with those who have come to him through the saving gift of Christ, he can freely love and forgive and walk in relationship without threats or punishment, despite the fact that we continue to sin. God still desires holiness in his people. He still calls for respect and loyalty. But he gives his Spirit to make it possible to fulfill his demands and his grace to cover our failure. Through Jesus, God remains fully true to himself and fully true to the love he has always possessed for his people.

—BQ

Daily Contemplation

Has knowing Jesus changed your understanding of God and your relationship with him? Pray that in the areas in which your view of God is inappropriately stern and demanding, he will reveal the fullness of himself in his love and mercy.

DAY 75

Rahab and the Spies
Joshua 2:1–24

Often, as we have seen in the books of Exodus, Numbers, and Deuteronomy, the Israelites offer examples of what *not* to do. But the Old Testament does contain a few bright spots of hope, with the book of Joshua representing one of the brightest.

Joshua's opening scene replays an earlier scene. After listening to Moses' swan song speeches, the refugees amass again beside the Jordan River for a test of courage and faith. Are they ready to cross into the Promised Land? Forty years before, their forebearers had panicked in fear. Now, without their legendary leader, Moses, would the Israelites panic again? They have no chariots or even horses, only primitive arms, an untested new leader, and the promise of God's protection.

An entirely new spirit characterizes this group, however, and the spy story in Joshua 2 expresses the difference clearly. Forty years ago, sparking a revolt among the Israelites, only two of the twelve spies held out any optimism. But the older generation with its fearful mentality has died off, and the new generation is now led by one of the original optimistic spies, Joshua.

This time, Joshua handpicks his own scouts, and the report they bring back makes a sharp contrast with the spy report in Numbers 13:31–33. The new scouts conclude that God has given the land of Canaan into the Israelites' hands, that all the people are fearful of the Israelites. Thus Joshua begins as a good-news book, a welcome relief from the discouragement of Numbers and the fatalism of Deuteronomy. What a difference forty years has made!

The heroine of this chapter, Rahab (RAY-hab) the pagan prostitute, becomes a favorite figure in Jewish stories and is esteemed by Bible writers as well (see Hebrews 11:31 and James 2:25). She proves that God honors true faith from anyone, regardless of race or religious background. In fact, Rahab, survivor of Jericho, becomes a direct ancestress of Jesus.

—PY

Daily Contemplation

When you confront obstacles, are you more likely to see them as problems or opportunities?

DAY 76

Crossing the Jordan
Joshua 3:1–4:24

> So when the people broke camp to cross the Jordan, the priests carrying the ark of the covenant went ahead of them . . . Yet as soon as the priests who carried the ark reached the Jordan and their feet touched the water's edge, the water from upstream stopped flowing. . . . So the people crossed over opposite Jericho. The priests who carried the ark of the covenant of the LORD stopped in the middle of the Jordan and stood on dry ground, while all Israel passed by until the whole nation had completed the crossing on dry ground. (Joshua 3:14–17)

The day has come to set forth into the Promised Land. As he did in the parting of the Red Sea, God shows the people that a body of water is no obstacle. He stops up the Jordan River and dries the land, instructing the Israelites to follow behind the ark of the covenant as they cross over into Canaan.

The ark, kept in the tabernacle and regarded as the most sacred of furnishings, signifies the Lord's throne. In following the ark of the covenant across the Jordan River, the Israelites sense God himself leading them into the land he has promised. They must follow at a distance, observing a holy respect for the God that the ark represents.

Once everyone has crossed, God determines that his people will not forget what he has done for them once again. He knows that, like the story of the Red Sea, this story will be repeated for many generations to come. Not only will the people tell the story, but they will have a visible reminder of this momentous day whenever they look at the stone memorial erected by each of the twelve tribes.

God knows human nature, as demonstrated in the actions of his people during the last decades. He knows they are quick to forget his faithfulness and see life rather through their own eyes. He instructs Joshua to help them remember.

—BQ

Daily Contemplation

What memorials or reminders help you recall what God has done for you?

DAY 77

The Fall of Jericho
Joshua 5:13–6:27

The Israelites' abysmal failures in the Sinai Desert can be traced back to a simple matter of disobedience. Despite unmistakable divine guidance, they insisted on choosing their own way over God's. Will the new generation respond any differently? Once they have crossed into Canaan, God tests the Israelites' new resolve to follow him, and it surely strains their faith to new limits.

As for the residents of Canaan, who have long heard about the Israelites' plan to conquer the Promised Land, they brace for the worst. Citizens of Jericho, the first city in the invaders' path, barricade themselves behind stone walls and await the feared onslaught. But how do the vaunted Israelites spend their first week in Canaan? They build a stone monument to God, perform circumcision rituals, and hold a Passover celebration—not the sort of behavior you'd expect from a conquering army.

The incidents recorded in Joshua seem specially selected to strike home the point that God, and no one else, is in charge. Just before the battle of Jericho, a supernatural visitor appears to Joshua to remind him of the true commander of this military campaign. And the bizarre tactics of the Israelites in besieging Jericho leave no doubt who is really in charge. An army could hardly take credit for victory when all it does is march around in circles and shout.

Jericho was probably a center for the worship of the moon god in Canaan, and so the destruction of that city—like the ten plagues on Egypt—symbolically announces an open warfare between the God of the Israelites and the region's pagan gods. Although measures against the Canaanites may seem harsh, the Bible makes clear that the Canaanites have forfeited their right to the land. As Moses tells the Israelites, "It is not because of your righteousness or your integrity that you are going in to take possession of their land; but on account of the wickedness of these nations, the LORD your God will drive them out before you" (Deuteronomy 9:5). And, as the story of Rahab shows, Canaanites who turned to God were spared.

—PY

Daily Contemplation

Do you ever feel foolish or strange when following what you are convinced is God's plan for you?

DAY 78

Achan's Sin
Joshua 7:1–26

The Bible does not record history for its own sake. Rather, it selects and highlights certain events that yield practical and spiritual lessons. For example, the book of Joshua, which spans a period of approximately seven years, devotes only a few sentences to some extensive military campaigns. But other key events, such as the fall of Jericho, get detailed coverage. That battle establishes an important pattern: The Israelites will succeed only if they rely on God, not military might.

Perhaps inevitably, the Israelites get cocky after Jericho. Since they have conquered a fortified city without firing an arrow, the next target, the puny town of Ai (AY-ie), poses no threat at all. A few thousand soldiers stroll toward Ai. A short time later those same soldiers—minus their dead and wounded—are scrambling for home, thoroughly routed.

Clearly, the juxtaposition of these two stories, Jericho and Ai, is meant to convey a lesson. If the Israelites obey God and place their trust in him, no challenge is too great to overcome. On the other hand, if they insist on their own way, no obstacle is too small to trip them up.

Significantly, Ai stood near the original site where God had appeared to Abraham and revealed the covenant centuries before. A humiliating defeat in that place shakes Joshua to the core. He dissolves in fright, earning God's stern rebuke in Joshua 7:10: "Stand up! What are you doing down on your face?" Soon Joshua learns the real reason for his army's defeat: an act of looting and deception by Achan, one of his soldiers.

Without God's protection, Joshua realizes, the Israelites are hopelessly vulnerable. After the painful lesson of Ai, he goes back to the basics. The public exposure of Achan's sin underscores the need to follow God's orders scrupulously, even in the earthly matter of warfare. God will not tolerate any of the lying or looting typical of invading armies.

—PY

Daily Contemplation

Why would such a seemingly "little" sin, such as Achan's deceit, have such major consequences?

DAY 79

The Covenant Renewed at Shechem
Joshua 24:1–33

At the end of his life, Joshua, much like Moses before him, stands before the Israelites to deliver a farewell address. Things have gone well under his leadership. The Bible gives the remarkable assessment: "Israel served the LORD throughout the lifetime of Joshua" (Joshua 24:31). And now Joshua uses his final speech to review all that God has done and to remind the people of their obligations under the covenant with God.

"I gave you a land on which you did not toil and cities you did not build"—at every point, Joshua emphasizes that God is the sole source of their success. He called out Abraham and blessed him with children, delivered the Israelites from slavery in Egypt, and carried them across the desert. And in Joshua's own lifetime he fulfills one more promise of the covenant: He gives them the Promised Land. It is theirs to live in.

"Choose for yourselves this day whom you will serve," Joshua challenges his listeners in the stirring climax to his speech. All the people present swear their allegiance to God, the God who has kept his covenant with them. Joshua solemnly ratifies the covenant and sends the people away, then quietly prepares to die.

The book of Joshua ends with an act of deep symbolism: The Israelites finally bury the remains of Joseph. For four centuries those remains lay preserved in Egypt in anticipation of the Israelites' return to their homeland. During the forty years of wilderness wanderings, the tribes have carried Joseph's bones as a treasured reminder of their past. Now, at last, Abraham's descendants have come home, and even the dead can rest in peace.

—PY

Daily Contemplation

When you experience success, whom do you tend to credit—yourself or God?

DAY 80

Choosing to Love God
Reflection

"Choose for yourselves this day whom you will serve." Joshua posed this challenge to the Israelites when he was nearing death. He hoped they would choose God and hold to their choice in the days ahead. Joshua knew well that a choice made today wouldn't ensure the future. The choice would have to be made each day, or it would stand no chance of enduring.

Psychologists Gary Smalley and John Trent coined the phrase "Love is a decision" in their writing about marriage: "Contrary to popular belief, love is actually a reflection of how much we 'honor' another person—for at its core genuine love is a decision, not a feeling."[7] For love in a marriage to survive, husband and wife must decide to love and honor each other every day, regardless of how they feel at any particular moment. This concept is expressed in the traditional wedding vow: "To have and to hold, from this day forward, for better, for worse, for richer, for poorer, in sickness and in health, to love and to cherish, till death do us part." Two people pledge—choose—to love one another for a lifetime, regardless of circumstances.

In their marriage to God, the Israelites have often had to choose whether or not to serve him. Rahab, though not originally an Israelite, chose God over her people. The Israelites, on the edge of the Promised Land, decided to step out into the Jordan riverbed. And they chose to honor God when they conquered Jericho.

One man, however, made a wrong choice. When faced with the enticing goods of the world, Achan chose them over God. He couldn't resist keeping for himself a robe, silver, and gold rather than turning them in with the rest of the plunder of Jericho.

Several times in both the Old and New Testaments, God refers to his people and the Christian church as the bride of Christ. Believers have entered into a marriage-like relationship with God. Just as in human marriages, we will only make the pledge last if we choose daily to honor God no matter what our feelings tempt us to do. We'll stay true to God only if our love becomes a decision.

Whom will you love today?

—BQ

Daily Contemplation

In your love relationship with God, how are you feeling? Talk to God and ask him to help you choose to love him despite your feelings.

DAY 81

Deborah
Judges 4:1–24

> Now Deborah, a prophet, the wife of Lappidoth, was leading Israel at that time. She held court under the Palm of Deborah between Ramah and Bethel in the hill country of Ephraim, and the Israelites went up to her to have their disputes decided. She sent for Barak son of Abinoam from Kedesh in Naphtali and said to him, "The LORD, the God of Israel, commands you: 'Go, take with you ten thousand men of Naphtali and Zebulun and lead them up to Mount Tabor. I will lead Sisera, the commander of Jabin's army, with his chariots and his troops to the Kishon River and give him into your hands.'" Barak said to her, "If you go with me, I will go; but if you don't go with me, I won't go." "Certainly I will go with you," said Deborah. "But because of the course you are taking, the honor will not be yours, for the LORD will deliver Sisera into the hands of a woman." So Deborah went with Barak to Kedesh. (Judges 4:4–9)

About two hundred years have passed since God delivered the Israelites from Egypt. They have strayed from God since entering Canaan, and he has given them into the hands of the Canaanites as punishment. But God hears their cries. He uses Deborah, a prophetess, judge, and "mother in Israel" (Judges 5:7), to defeat the Canaanites.

Deborah stands out as the only woman to hold a place among the twelve judges who serve Israel during their time in the Promised Land. Although she lives in a patriarchal culture, this woman possesses a prophetic gift and strong moral character. God chooses her to lead the people. Nijay Gupta, professor and author on the topic of biblical women in leadership, writes, "If we look at the judges as a whole, especially Gideon and Samson, it is clear that they were not chosen for their virtue or strong faith. In fact, Deborah appears to be the most faithful, the most prophetically tuned into God, and the wisest of them all."[8]

Because Deborah walks closely with God and exhibits faith in him, God enables her to overcome the limitations imposed on women in her society and carry out the role he has appointed for her, leading Israel to forty years of peace in the land.

—BQ

Daily Contemplation

Do you feel God has asked you to do something atypical?

DAY 82

Gideon
Judges 6:1–40

The good-news tone of Joshua has soured abruptly in Judges. After an initial spurt of enthusiasm, the Israelites stray very far from the way God has pointed them. Ignoring Joshua's orders to clear the land, they settle in among the pagan occupants instead. These new neighbors practice an exotic religion that includes sex orgies and child sacrifice as a regular part of worship.

Just one generation later, the Israelites have lost their sense of national identity and have forgotten all about their parents' ringing vows to honor the covenant. They too are worshiping the idol Baal (BAY-uhl). Having violated virtually every moral standard, the nation slides toward chaos. The last verse of Judges sums up the scene: "Everyone did as they saw fit" (Judges 21:25).

The Israelites are suffering from a leadership crisis of huge dimensions. For eighty years they have followed Moses and Joshua, two outstanding leaders who proved impossible to replace. When the twelve tribes splinter apart and retreat into separate territories, God turns to more regional leaders called judges. The term may be misleading; these are people renowned not for court cases but for their military campaigns against foreign invaders. (Today these "judges" might be called guerrillas or freedom fighters.)

Some judges, such as Deborah and Gideon, the hero of this chapter, emerge as models of courage and faith. And yet a close look at the life of Gideon shows the material God must work with. His family and village worship Baal, not the Lord. In the face of God's clear direction, Gideon sputters, demands repeated proofs, uses delaying tactics, and worships at night to avoid detection. He is subject to paralyzing fears, even on the eve of battle. But God, knowing Gideon's potential, step-by-step brings him to the point of courage.

—PY

Daily Contemplation

How has God given you clear guidance when you've needed it?

DAY 83

Gideon Defeats the Midianites
Judges 7:1–8:35

Joshua won the battle of Jericho by following orders that defied all orthodox military tactics. Similarly, when the time comes for Gideon to strike a decisive blow for the Israelites, God gives instructions that would daunt a seasoned general, much less a greenhorn like Gideon. He reduces the size of Gideon's army from thirty-two thousand to three hundred men, so as to leave no doubt it is he, God of the Hebrews, who will fight this battle.

In Gideon's days the Israelites live at the mercy of marauding tribes of Bedouins, who help themselves to the produce and wealth of the local farmers. But by following God's commands, Gideon leads a great victory and frees his people from oppression.

Gideon's against-all-odds victory shows a pattern that is repeated throughout the book of Judges. At a time when women are regarded as second-class citizens, God chooses Deborah to lead. Jephthah, another judge, leads a gang of outlaws before God chooses him. In fact, this pattern appears throughout the entire Bible. God does not seek the people most outwardly capable, nor the most naturally "good." He works with unlikely material so that everyone can see the glory is his and his alone.

The apostle Paul marveled over this principle more than a thousand years later, writing, "Brothers and sisters, think of what you were when you were called. Not many of you were wise by human standards; not many were influential; not many were of noble birth. But God chose the foolish things of the world to shame the wise; God chose the weak things of the world to shame the strong. . . . Therefore, as it is written: 'Let the one who boasts boast in the Lord'" (1 Corinthians 1:26–27, 31).

—PY

Daily Contemplation

Is God using you in any unlikely ways, considering your background or abilities?

DAY 84

Follow the Leader
Reflection

You probably played the game "Follow the Leader" as a child. Kids mimick the antics of the one in front until someone new becomes the leader.

This childhood game is not far removed from real life. Whether we realize it or not, we are much the product of the leaders we have followed. Your parents, teachers, coaches, instructors, clergy, and peers have contributed to your life more than you may know, because they have been your up-close models of living.

Deborah and Gideon performed this role for their people. God picked these two as leaders and gave them a vision for freeing the people from Canaanite oppression and for restoring them once again to himself. God knew how childlike the Israelites were in their tendency to imitate the ones they followed, so in his grace he raised up two leaders who would again turn the eyes of the people to himself.

John Maxwell, of the Maxwell Leadership development institute, writes, "The focus of vision must be on the leader—like leader, like people. Followers find the leader and then the vision. Leaders find the vision and then the people."[9] Maxwell confirms what we find in Judges: With God-focused leaders, people will adopt a vision for God's ways; without God-focused leaders, people will adopt the ways of the self-focused leaders around them, just as Israel did when Deborah and Gideon died.

In looking at the long history of Israel in the Old Testament, we find that their times away from God lasted longer and were more severe in the absence of God-centered leaders. A good leader is hard to find. For this reason, the Bible speaks often about the importance of leadership.

"Remember your leaders, who spoke the word of God to you. Consider the outcome of their way of life and imitate their faith" (Hebrews 13:7).

"Have confidence in your leaders and submit to their authority, because they keep watch over you as those who must give an account" (Hebrews 13:17).

"Start children off on the way they should go, and even when they are old they will not turn from it" (Proverbs 22:6).

When we lead, may we do it in reverence of God and only through his guidance. When we follow, may we seek God's leaders as our models and pray for them. And may God through his Spirit be our most respected leader.

—BQ

Daily Contemplation

Thank God for those he has used to mold you in life-giving ways. Pray for God's help in areas in which you are currently leading.

DAY 85

The Birth of Samson
Judges 13:1–25

> A certain man of Zorah, named Manoah, from the clan of the Danites, had a wife who was childless, unable to give birth. The angel of the LORD appeared to her and said, "You are barren and childless, but you are going to become pregnant and give birth to a son. Now see to it that you drink no wine or other fermented drink and that you do not eat anything unclean. You will become pregnant and have a son whose head is never to be touched by a razor because the boy is to be a Nazirite, dedicated to God from the womb. He will take the lead in delivering Israel from the hands of the Philistines." . . . The woman gave birth to a boy and named him Samson. He grew and the LORD blessed him, and the Spirit of the LORD began to stir him while he was in Mahaneh Dan, between Zorah and Eshtaol. (Judges 13:2–5, 24–25)

In a familiar biblical plotline, an instance of barrenness leads to the God-appointed birth of a child who will serve in an important way. God raises up Samson as another judge over the people of Israel. Samson will lead in a very different way from both Deborah and Gideon. He will be a sort of lone ranger, distracting the Philistines (fih-LIS-tins) from their conquest of Israelite territory rather than leading the people in a military overthrow, as other judges have done. Samson's character qualities are different from those of Deborah and Gideon as well. He demonstrates again that God uses people with an odd mixture of strengths and weaknesses.

—BQ

Daily Contemplation

Has God ever surprised you with the kind of person he used in your life?

DAY 86

Samson's Marriage
Judges 14:1–20

Samson went down to Timnah and saw there a young Philistine woman. When he returned, he said to his father and mother, "I have seen a Philistine woman in Timnah; now get her for me as my wife." His father and mother replied, "Isn't there an acceptable woman among your relatives or among all our people? Must you go to the uncircumcised Philistines to get a wife?" But Samson said to his father, "Get her for me. She's the right one for me." (His parents did not know that this was from the LORD, who was seeking an occasion to confront the Philistines; for at that time they were ruling over Israel.) (Judges 14:1–4)

Samson stubbornly determines to marry a Philistine woman despite being forbidden by Mosaic law to marry any non-Israelite. Although his parents object, they do not forbid the marriage. Not only is Samson gifted with unusual physical strength, he also possesses a strong will. Yet just as God has given him physical strength to subdue the Philistines, God will use Samson's strong will for his own purposes. Although he disapproves of Samson's wild behavior, God still has a role for this undisciplined superman.

As Samson's life will make clear, his unbridled passions don't bring him happiness. Nevertheless, God uses this powerful man to begin to deliver Israel.

—BQ

Daily Contemplation

In what area has God given you special strength?

DAY 87

Samson and Delilah
Judges 16:1–31

The most famous of all the judges has made an appearance toward the end of the book, and the Bible devotes four chapters to the dramatic events of his life. If Gideon shows how a person with limited potential can be greatly used by God, Samson illustrates just the opposite: A person with enormous potential can squander it.

When Samson enters the picture, the Israelites are once again suffering under foreign domination. An angel announces his birth, making clear that God has great things in store for Samson and wants him specially set apart.

Indeed, Samson is blessed with extraordinary supernatural gifts. When the Spirit of the Lord comes upon him, he can tackle a lion or singlehandedly rout an entire army. And yet, as the stories from his youth reveal, Samson wields that strength in ways more befitting a juvenile delinquent than a spiritual leader.

Like any rebellious teenager, he chooses for a wife the kind of woman sure to cause his parents—and God—the most grief. That marriage barely survives a week, and next Samson takes up with a Philistine prostitute. This chapter describes how he, stupidly, forfeits his great strength in a dalliance with a third woman, the seductive Delilah.

Samson's story is like a morality play. No one in the world could match his physical strength; just about anyone could match his moral strength. His moral lapses would seem almost incomprehensible were they not repeated by spiritual leaders in almost every generation.

In the end, Samson, the designated savior of his people, is led out to perform like a trained bear for his captors. It appears that the God of the Israelites has been soundly defeated by the pagans and their gods. But Samson, and God, have one last surprise for the Philistine oppressors (16:23–31).

—PY

―――――――― *Daily Contemplation* ――――――――

In what areas are you living up to your potential? In what areas are you falling short?

DAY 88

A Strong Need for God
Reflection

Strength. Independence. Self-sufficiency.

Sound familiar? These traits have become the rule rather than the exception in present-day Western culture. We have absorbed subconsciously a definition for strength that excludes any show of neediness. Strong people live life on their own. When they hit bumps in the road, they grit their teeth a little harder and keep to themselves until they get past the struggle and regain control. Mental and emotional strength are the name of the game, and image is where it's at—if you look strong, you're there.

But as we see in the life of Samson, appearance and reality are two decidedly different things. Samson had physical strength, undoubtedly. In his day, physical prowess was probably the most coveted kind of strength a man or woman could have. The ability to overpower both animals and people gave Samson supreme status. Yet his physical strength couldn't overcome his sexual appetite or his weakness for ungodly women. His strength didn't enable him to make good decisions or to find joy in living.

Samson needed not only the physical strength God provided; he needed God's daily guidance. He needed God's Spirit to supply the power to resist temptation, to desire God's best, to forego instant gratification in exchange for more fulfilling choices. More than he realized, Samson needed God to meet his weakness.

We resemble Samson in our need for God's strength. No matter how capable we are, we need God every day, living in us and acting through us. We need his strength and his hope, his love and his companionship. We need his salvation. We can't live without God.

When we try to live by the cool-and-collected strength of our culture, we might mask our need, but we don't meet it. Underneath we are, all of us, weak. Not far beneath the surface we all have an aching place that needs God. As we live each day, we can defy our prescribed roles and reach out in our need for one another. We can speak of our need for God. And we can cry out to God daily in that need for him. Nothing could be more powerful.

—BQ

Daily Contemplation

How aware are you of your need for others and for God? Express your need for God by repeating this prayer several times: "Lord, I need you."

DAY 89

Naomi and Ruth
Ruth 1:1–22

This tale about two scrappy women has nothing like the broad sweep of history found in Judges. Rather, Ruth narrows its focus to the story of one family trying to cope during chaotic, tumultuous times.

Things got so bad in Canaan, especially after a severe famine, that Naomi's Israelite family migrated into enemy territory just to survive. There, her two sons married local pagan women and settled down. Years later, after both those sons and her husband die, Naomi decides to return to the land of her birth. This book mainly tells of the stubborn loyalty of Naomi's daughter-in-law named Ruth.

Ruth and Naomi make unlikely friends. Ruth is young and strong; Naomi past middle age and brokenhearted. In addition, they come from completely different ethnic and religious backgrounds. Who would have put them together? But somewhere along the way Ruth has converted to the worship of the true God, and she insists on returning with Naomi to the land of the Israelites.

In a few brief chapters, the book of Ruth manages to capture a slice of agrarian life in ancient times. The male-dominated society poses problems for unattached women, and these two live in harsh, trying times. Ruth serves for a while as a migrant farmworker, surviving on the "gleanings" left in the fields by the harvesters.

You can read this small book in several ways: as a tiny, elegant portrait of life in ancient times, as a record of God's faithfulness to the needy, or as an inspiring story of undying friendship. Perhaps the most accurate way to read this story, however, is as a missionary story. God not only accepts Ruth, a member of the despised Moabites, into his family, but also uses her to produce Israel's greatest king. Ruth's great-grandson turns out to be David. To anyone who thought God's love was for Israelites only, Ruth's life makes a striking contradiction.

—PY

---- *Daily Contemplation* ----

When has a friend gone out on a limb for you?

Ruth Meets Boaz
Ruth 2:1–23

And Ruth the Moabite said to Naomi, "Let me go to the fields and pick up the leftover grain behind anyone in whose eyes I find favor." Naomi said to her, "Go ahead, my daughter." So she went out, entered a field and began to glean behind the harvesters. As it turned out, she was working in a field belonging to Boaz, who was from the clan of Elimelek. Just then Boaz arrived from Bethlehem and greeted the harvesters, "The LORD be with you!" "The LORD bless you!" they answered. Boaz asked the overseer of his harvesters, "Who does that young woman belong to?" The overseer replied, "She is the Moabite who came back from Moab with Naomi." (Ruth 2:2–6)

God has guided Ruth to the field belonging to Boaz (BOH-az) and has blessed her with grain and the favor of her relative. In return for Ruth's faithfulness to God and to her widowed mother-in-law, God provides for her needs. Boaz tells Ruth she may continue to glean in his field.

Harvesting of barley and wheat took place from April through July, and typically the gleaners would begin gathering after the harvesters left the area. But Ruth is allowed to stay in the fields with the workers and even drink from their water jars. Boaz promises Ruth protection from the male workers.

Here in Bethlehem, where centuries later the Savior will be born, God is weaving together a way to bring his plans about. He has guided two unlikely people, Naomi and Ruth, on a journey and brought them to a town where a child will be born. This child, like the Child to come, will reaffirm God's covenant promise of love and faithfulness to his people. And in Ruth's story, as in Jesus' story, God reminds us that the world's ways are not his ways. Though life has seemed bitter to Naomi, God will turn despairing circumstances into a time of newfound joy.

—BQ

Daily Contemplation

Whom have you met recently who has brought good to your life in an unexpected way?

DAY 91

Boaz Marries Ruth
Ruth 3:1–4:17

So Boaz took Ruth and she became his wife. When he made love to her, the LORD enabled her to conceive, and she gave birth to a son. The women said to Naomi: "Praise be to the LORD, who this day has not left you without a guardian-redeemer. May he become famous throughout Israel!" (Ruth 4:13–14)

The relationship of Ruth and Boaz grows closer in this passage. Naomi becomes a matchmaker, and Ruth doesn't shy from Naomi's bold plan. Boaz acts responsibly by letting Ruth stay with him in safety for the night and by recognizing the rights of her nearer kinsman. Honored by Ruth's willingness to marry an older man, Boaz is nevertheless ready to receive Ruth only if she becomes rightfully his.

Boaz completes the formalities necessary to take Ruth as his wife. Her nearer kinsman, who in that culture had first option, forfeits his right to Ruth and her land, probably because if she bore him a son, this son would be entitled to a share of the kinsman's current estate, causing dissension in the family. Boaz is prepared to buy the land and marry Ruth.

Though barren for ten years in Moab, Ruth conceives after marrying Boaz and gives birth to a son. Obed (OH-bed) will become the grandfather of King David and an ancestor of Jesus. Just as Boaz becomes the kinsman-redeemer for Naomi's family, Jesus Christ will become the Kinsman-Redeemer for the family of all humankind, redeeming us from death and providing hope for a future. In a small family circle in Bethlehem, God gives us a preview of how he will bring the bitterness of life on earth to an end through an unexpected but trustworthy Redeemer.

—BQ

Daily Contemplation

Can you think of someone whom God placed in your life to help you through a dark time and remind you of his promises?

DAY 92

The Looks of a Believer
Reflection

How well do you fit the image of a follower of God? Chances are, you don't feel like you really belong. Maybe it's your appearance. Or your background. Maybe it's your language or the people you do life with.

If you feel like an outsider, you're not alone. Many feel the way you do, and indeed believers as far back as Ruth, and further, share those feelings. Ruth was the daughter of non-Israelite parents. Barren and recently widowed, she then chose to leave her homeland of Moab to accompany her depressed mother-in-law to another city, where the two would try to forge a new life with some extended relatives. Ruth didn't really fit in.

In fact, the plot thickens. Ruth's family traces all the way back to Lot, Abraham's nephew. As you may recall, Lot chose the fertile land of the Jordan plain as his home, settling his family near the evil city of Sodom. Later, after God destroyed Sodom, Lot's daughters got him drunk and had sex with him. They gave birth to two sons, Moab (MOH-ab) and Ben-Ammi (ben-AM-ee), whose people later became the Moabites and the Ammonites, nations with a history of warring against Israel. And these Moabites were the people Ruth called her own.

But in marrying into Naomi's family, Ruth switched allegiance to the true God of the Hebrews. She renounced the god of the Moabites and stayed with the new family God had given her. In many ways Ruth became a loner. She belonged with Naomi yet was very different from her and from the others in Bethlehem as well. She could only hope for their kindness.

Ruth did fit in with God, however. She chose to believe in him, and to God nothing else mattered. Ruth lived out her faith by making difficult choices and following through with them. She had a humble heart, and although she undertook some uncommon methods for survival—gleaning behind workers in the fields, approaching an older man in the middle of the night—she remained faithful to God.

As a believer, you may not feel like you belong. But God sees things differently. He called Ruth his own, and others like her who didn't seem to fit. God doesn't care about outward traits, the looks of your life. He cares about the look of your heart.

—BQ

Daily Contemplation

In what ways do you feel different from other God-followers? Thank God that he has made you the way you are for a reason, to be used by him in a unique way.

DAY 93

The Birth of Samuel
1 Samuel 1:1–28

> Eli the priest was sitting on his chair by the doorpost of the LORD's house. In her deep anguish Hannah prayed to the LORD, weeping bitterly. . . . As she kept on praying to the LORD, Eli observed her mouth. Hannah was praying in her heart, and her lips were moving but her voice was not heard. Eli thought she was drunk and said to her, "How long are you going to stay drunk? Put away your wine." "Not so, my lord," Hannah replied, "I am a woman who is deeply troubled. . . . I was pouring out my soul to the LORD." Eli answered, "Go in peace, and may the God of Israel grant you what you have asked of him." . . . Early the next morning they arose and worshiped before the LORD and then went back to their home at Ramah. Elkanah made love to his wife Hannah, and the LORD remembered her. So in the course of time Hannah became pregnant and gave birth to a son. She named him Samuel, saying, "Because I asked the LORD for him." (1 Samuel 1:9–10, 12–15, 17, 19–20)

In a situation similar to that of Rachel and Leah, Hannah and Peninnah (peh-NIN-uh) become rivals for their husband's love, their competition centering around the fertility of their wombs. They live toward the end of the period of the judges, and theirs is a moral and spiritual climate grown progressively wayward and corrupt. Hannah so desires a child that she is willing to give him away in a life of service to God.

In response to Hannah's sincere prayer for a son, God raises up Samuel to be used as a leader of the Israelites. Samuel will serve as a judge, prophet, and priest. He will anoint Israel's first king and later will anoint King David.

—BQ

Daily Contemplation

Have you ever made a promise to God? Have you kept it?

DAY 94

The Lord Calls Samuel
1 Samuel 2:18–21; 3:1–21

By the time of the judges, most terms in the Israelites' covenant with God have already been fulfilled. Abraham's descendants, twelve tribes many thousands strong, have a land of their own. Yet something is clearly lacking: No one could begin to call the crazy quilt of tribal territories a unified "nation." In fact, throughout the judges' era, the Israelites have fought each other as often as they have fought their hostile neighbors.

As this book opens, the Philistines, a traditional enemy, are exploiting the Israelites' disunity, pushing ever deeper into their territory. The Philistines have superior weapons—chariots, in particular—and Israel has neither a central administration nor a regular army to mount an effective defense. A crisis of leadership is building, one that threatens the very existence of Israel. This military weakness leads to one of the darkest days of Jewish history, when the Philistines capture the sacred ark of the covenant. Some Israelites wonder whether God has abandoned them and thus forsaken the covenant.

"In those days the word of the LORD was rare; there were not many visions," begins 1 Samuel 3. But the chapter goes on to relate how God steps in directly, as he did with Abraham and Moses, calling out a leader for his people. "See, I am about to do something in Israel that will make the ears of everyone who hears about it tingle," God announces. He answers the desperate prayer of Samuel, who will grow into his role as one of Israel's greatest leaders.

Ultimately, Samuel will serve the Israelites in many capacities, as both judge and prophet. A priest by training, he will also lead the nation's worship. When the need arises, he even functions as a military general, spearheading a victorious recapture of disputed territories. Finally, under God's direction, Samuel will anoint Israel's first two kings. By performing these varied roles, Samuel leaves an important legacy: he manages to unite the tribes for the first time in a century. Under his leadership, Israel comes to the very brink of nationhood. God has not forgotten the covenant after all.

—PY

Daily Contemplation

Have you ever felt called by God for a certain task? How have you responded?

DAY 95

Israel Asks for a King
1 Samuel 8:1–22

> So all the elders of Israel gathered together and came to Samuel at Ramah. They said to him, "You are old, and your sons do not follow your ways; now appoint a king to lead us, such as all the other nations have." But when they said, "Give us a king to lead us," this displeased Samuel; so he prayed to the LORD. And the LORD told him: "Listen to all that the people are saying to you; it is not you they have rejected, but they have rejected me as their king." (1 Samuel 8:4–7)

Despite Samuel's military prowess, the Philistine threat doesn't entirely go away. As Samuel ages, Israel needs continuing vigorous leadership, but Samuel's sons hardly measure up to the task. What can be done? Looking around them, the tribes see that virtually every other country has a king. *Aha, that's the answer*, they conclude, and urge Samuel to appoint an Israelite king.

The idea of a king seems popular with everyone except Samuel and God, who sense in the request an underlying rejection of God's own leadership. Samuel warns the elders bluntly against the problems they might be inviting: tyranny, oppression, a military draft, high taxes, maybe even slavery. But the people beg for a king despite his warnings.

Does God oppose the very notion of a king? Probably not. Many years before, Moses predicted the Israelites would someday have a king (see Genesis 17:6; Deuteronomy 17:14–20), and God will eventually use the royal line to produce his own Son, Jesus, King of Kings. But the Bible makes one thing clear: God opposes the people's motives, as expressed by the elders: "Then we will be like all the other nations." God does not want them to be like all the other nations. He, no human king, is the true ruler of the Israelites.

—PY

Daily Contemplation

What do you feel in need of today? What motivates your sense of need?

DAY 96

Samuel Anoints Saul
1 Samuel 9:1–10:8

There was a Benjamite, a man of standing, whose name was Kish son of Abiel, the son of Zeror, the son of Bekorath, the son of Aphiah of Benjamin. Kish had a son named Saul, as handsome a young man as could be found anywhere in Israel, and he was a head taller than anyone else. . . . Now the day before Saul came, the LORD had revealed this to Samuel: "About this time tomorrow I will send you a man from the land of Benjamin. Anoint him ruler over my people Israel; he will deliver them from the hand of the Philistines. I have looked on my people, for their cry has reached me." When Samuel caught sight of Saul, the LORD said to him, "This is the man I spoke to you about; he will govern my people." . . . Then Samuel took a flask of olive oil and poured it on Saul's head and kissed him, saying, "Has not the LORD anointed you ruler over his inheritance?" (1 Samuel 9:1–2, 15–17; 10:1)

After warning the Israelites of the pain and sorrow that will come from having a human king lord over them, God finally agrees to give the people the ruler they want. Saul (SAWL) measures up to God's standard of a good king (Deuteronomy 17), at least outwardly. Initially he is humble, claiming to be unworthy of such an honor. Later, however, Saul will lose his humility, becoming arrogant and vindictive toward any who threaten him.

From Saul we'll learn something about leadership and power. All leaders who take on a position of authority face the danger of becoming prideful and unbending. When they succumb, as does Saul, they lose their effectiveness as well as the love and support of the people.

—BQ

―――――――――――――――― *Daily Contemplation* ――――――――――――――――

Where are you currently serving as a leader? Have you maintained a humble spirit?

DAY 97

Passionate Prayer
Reflection

Maybe you've heard the tongue-in-cheek admonition "Be careful what you pray for—you might get it."

This warning applies to the story of the Israelites' request for a king. The years of leadership by judges had plunged the nation into a period of immorality, and the people were tired of being manipulated by men who had only their own interests at heart. So they prayed for a king just like all the nations around them had. They got what they asked for. Soon Saul began following his own ways rather than God's.

How can we avoid the Israelites' blunder in offering our own prayers? We need to take caution in how we pray. Jesus gave us the essentials of praying in the Lord's Prayer, and they have nothing to do with speaking eloquently or religiously; they concern the attitude behind the words: "Our Father in heaven, hallowed be your name, your kingdom come, your will be done, on earth as it is in heaven" (Matthew 6:9–10).

"Hallowing" God's name means that we respect him, revere him. Praying for his kingdom to come puts our hearts next to God's heart, expressing that we want his big-picture plans to be fulfilled. Asking for his will to be done on earth as in heaven tells God we know that what he wants is more important and ultimately better for us than what we want. With these words, we're asking God to pray a better prayer for us than we know how to pray, and then to answer that prayer. We are opening our hands filled with needs and burning desires and placing these hands in God's.

If the people of Israel had approached God like this, God might have responded by saying, "Wait. I'll provide for your needs now in a different way. If you'll wait, I'll give you the best. Right now, a king will only complicate things."

In this way God has answered many a prayer for a relationship, a job, a home, a child, and scores of others. Like the Israelites, many believers anticipate God's response and shut their ears, insisting on their own way. God eventually grants the request, allowing also the difficulties that may accompany this choice. Other believers accept God's answer and wait, only to find that their desire has changed or that God's timing and choice is abundantly better than what their own had been.

Be careful what you pray for—you might get it. Make your prayer God's by offering your requests and then, with open hands, letting his prayer become your own.

—BQ

Daily Contemplation

What is the desire that burns within you today? Tell God that you want what is truly good for you, knowing that he knows so much better what you need.

DAY 98

The Lord Rejects Saul as King
1 Samuel 15:1–29

> Then the word of the LORD came to Samuel: "I regret that I have made Saul king, because he has turned away from me and has not carried out my instructions." Samuel was angry, and he cried out to the LORD all that night. . . . Then Saul said to Samuel, "I have sinned. I violated the LORD's command and your instructions." . . . But Samuel said to him, "I will not go back with you. You have rejected the word of the LORD, and the LORD has rejected you as king over Israel!" (1 Samuel 15:10–11, 24, 26)

This story reveals the first signs of Saul's disobedience to God. Saul wages war against the Amalekites, but he takes the liberty to bend God's instructions and allow for a little extra glory for himself and a few prime animals for his herds. He takes the Amalekite king alive as a visual aid for his people, broadcasting Saul's own power. When Samuel calls him out on these acts, Saul feigns innocence and claims that the animals are intended for sacrifice to the Lord. In this sequence of disobedience, Saul permanently loses God's approval. He will serve for fifteen more years as king, but in God's eyes he has already lost his position.

Although Saul entered into kingship with a humble spirit, in time he let the position go to his head, allowing pride and disobedience to replace humility. Later, fear will cause him to hold on to his place of power so tightly that he becomes irrational and destructive. Saul models the corrupting power that leadership can have over us when self-centered motives take hold. Like Saul, we may feel greedy at times, tempted to take for ourselves more than we should, or to maneuver for the limelight. Through God's grace we can refocus on his way—because, as this passage indicates, in God's eyes greed and pride are no small offense.

—BQ

Daily Contemplation

What is easier for you, obedience or sacrifice?

DAY 99

Samuel Anoints David
1 Samuel 16:1–23

The LORD said to Samuel, "How long will you mourn for Saul, since I have rejected him as king over Israel? Fill your horn with oil and be on your way; I am sending you to Jesse of Bethlehem. I have chosen one of his sons to be king." . . . Jesse had seven of his sons pass before Samuel, but Samuel said to him, "The LORD has not chosen these." So he asked Jesse, "Are these all the sons you have?" "There is still the youngest," Jesse answered. "He is tending the sheep." Samuel said, "Send for him; we will not sit down until he arrives." So he sent for him and had him brought in. . . . Then the LORD said, "Rise and anoint him; this is the one." So Samuel took the horn of oil and anointed him in the presence of his brothers, and from that day on the Spirit of the LORD came powerfully upon David. (1 Samuel 16:1, 10–13)

Israel's first king began his reign with enormous promise. Saul was a perfect physical specimen: handsome, strong, intelligent, a head taller than anyone else. Leadership qualities oozed out of him. But he failed, for one simple reason: He disobeyed God, refusing to acknowledge him as the true ruler. And without hesitation God ended that royal dynasty and looked elsewhere for a replacement.

The replacement king is utterly unlike the first king. No one imagined royalty potential in the shepherd boy David—not even his own father. But, as God says, "People look at the outward appearance, but the LORD looks at the heart" (1 Samuel 16:7). David has the kind of heart God can work with. Despite his humble beginnings, despite his many flaws, he will go on to become the greatest king in the history of the Israelites.

—PY

Daily Contemplation

Would the leadership qualities God values be an asset or a handicap to someone running for president of the United States?

DAY 100

A Shepherd's Song
Psalm 23:1–6

David is a well-rounded human being. Although he will have enough courage to take on the likes of Goliath, a nine-foot-tall Philistine, he certainly does not fit any "macho" warrior mold. In fact, David first gains King Saul's notice for his musical, not military, skills. Initially he is brought to the army camp because his harp playing soothes the frayed nerves of the troubled king.

Almost half of the 150 psalms in the Bible are credited to David, and it seems only appropriate to read a sampling in conjunction with his life history. This famous psalm reveals at once the secret of David's poetic abilities and the secret of his faith.

In his poetry David tends to start with the scene around him—rocks, caves, stars, battlefields, sheep—and work out from that physical world to express profound thoughts about God. Psalm 23, for instance, stems from his experience as a shepherd boy. Using metaphors that emerge from the tasks of sheepherding, David composes a few beautiful stanzas of worship poetry.

The psalm captures the essence of David's trust in God. Sheep have blind, absolute trust in a leader: If a lead sheep plunges off a cliff, an entire flock will follow. That kind of unshakable trust is what David seeks in his walk with God.

Yet no one can dismiss David as having a rosy, romantic view of life. The preceding Psalm 22 shows just how tough, gritty, and ruthlessly honest he could be: "My God, my God, why have you forsaken me?" Somehow David manages to make God the center of his life, regardless of circumstances—whether he feels specially comforted by God or cruelly abandoned. "Some trust in chariots and some in horses, but we trust in the name of the LORD our God," writes this soldier, who spends much of his time running from chariots and horses (Psalm 20:7).

The best way to read the Psalms is to make these ancient prayers your own by speaking them directly to God. Over the years, millions of people have found comfort and inspiration by "praying" the eloquent words of Psalm 23, written by the shepherd who would become king.

—PY

--- *Daily Contemplation* ---

Does your faith more resemble the childlike faith of Psalm 23 or the barely hanging-on faith of Psalm 22?

DAY 101

David and Goliath
1 Samuel 17:1–58

King David dominates much of the Old Testament and much of Jewish history. This exciting story from his boyhood, told in colorful eyewitness detail, is one of the most famous Bible stories, a beacon of hope for all outsized underdogs.

David will spend the better part of a decade trying to escape the wrath of King Saul, and Saul's enmity may trace back to this one scene. Saul, the leader of a large army, sits in his tent, terrorized by the taunts of the colossal Goliath. Meanwhile David, a mere boy too small for a suit of armor, strides out bravely to meet Goliath's challenge. Little wonder Saul comes to resent and fear the remarkable youth.

The scenario related here is not as far-fetched as it may seem. "Single combat" or "representative" warfare was an acceptable style of settling differences in ancient times. As Tom Wolfe explains it in *The Right Stuff*, "Originally it had a magical meaning . . . They believed that the gods determined the outcome of single combat; therefore, it was useless for the losing side to engage in a full-scale battle."[10]

During many lonely hours as a shepherd boy, David honed his slingshot skills to a state of perfection. But he takes no personal credit for the victory. "You come against me with sword and spear and javelin," he shouts to Goliath, "but I come against you in the name of the LORD Almighty, the God of the armies of Israel, whom you have defied." In the tradition of Joshua and Gideon, he places complete trust in God alone—a lesson that King Saul never learned.

Once Goliath falls, the rest of the Philistines quickly succumb. Soon the Israelites are dancing in the streets and singing this song: "Saul has slain his thousands, and David his tens of thousands" (1 Samuel 18:7). The nation is beginning to recognize in David the qualities that have marked him for potential kingship. Saul, however, will not relinquish his throne without a fight.

—PY

Daily Contemplation

Are you facing any great fear or danger about which God is telling you that you can rely utterly on him?

DAY 102

Outdoor Lessons
Psalm 19:1-14

David lived much of his life outdoors. It's not surprising, then, that a great love, even reverence, for the natural world shows through in many of his psalms.

The psalms present a world that fits together as a whole. At night wild animals hunt; at daybreak humans go out to work. As rain falls, nourishing crops for people and grass for cattle, it also waters the forest where wild animals live. Yet David doesn't just marvel over the complexity and beauty of nature; behind everything he sees the hand of God. The world works because an intimate, personal God watches over it. Every breath of life depends on his will. So do the weather, the winds and clouds, the very stability of the earth.

Psalm 19 combines two of David's favorite themes: God's care for the earth and his care for the chosen people of Israel. He begins with the natural world, marveling at the mantle of stars that covers the whole earth. Yet David and the Israelites, unlike their neighbors, do not worship the sun and stars as gods but rather see them as the workmanship of a great God who oversees all creation.

In the middle of the psalm, David turns his attention from nature to the "law of the Lord." To reflect that change, the poem in Hebrew uses a different, more personal name for God. The first six verses refer to God with a general name that anyone, of any religion, might use, much like our English word **God**. But from verse seven onward, God is called **Yahweh**, the personal name revealed to Moses from the burning bush. The heavens declare the glory of God, but God's law reveals even more—his personal voice to his chosen people.

David writes some of the psalms as a fugitive, while fleeing the wrath of King Saul. Even though God has promised him the throne of Israel, David must run for his life. He will have many nights of fear and many doubts, but he still believes that the God who has demonstrated his faithfulness to the natural world, and to the nation David will one day govern, will show that same faithfulness in fulfilling promises to David himself.

—PY

Daily Contemplation

Does nature reveal the glory of God to you? Does God's law—his guidelines for living—reveal to you his trustworthiness, wisdom, and rightness?

DAY 103

Fighting Giants
Reflection

Who are the giants in my life? I ponder as I (Brenda) read in fascination the story of David and Goliath. This is a delicious tale. A brave boy approaches a gargantuan ogre and without an ounce of fear announces God's victory in advance. I love David's bold attitude, his absolute belief that God will conquer.

Not just my love of a good story captivates me as I read; what thrills me more is this vision of conquered giants.

In David's day one boy faced one giant as all the others looked on. Today countless giants haunt the lives of many around us: addictions, feelings of personal inadequacy or unworthiness, fear of failure, brokenness from failed relationships, guilt over past mistakes, shame, feelings of isolation, depression, anxiety, fear of disease or death. The list goes on. In places deep inside, giants lurk, and often we are too frightened or ashamed to bring our battles into the open. Victory seems altogether unlikely.

When I sense these fears, I return to David's story. Unlike the Disney animations that set good against evil within romping, imaginative plots, this story took place in the life of a historical king of Israel. God really did overcome. His good conquered a giant bent on evil and destruction. If God did this for David, certainly he can do it for you and me.

As I consider my inner giants, I recall Ephesians 6:12: "Our struggle is not against flesh and blood, but against the rulers, against the authorities, against the powers of this dark world and against the spiritual forces of evil in the heavenly realms." God knows well the giants that stalk our lives, forces that aim to rob us of life and vitality, thus defeating God's presence in us. But as with David, these forces don't stand a chance against God. David used a stone. Paul tells us in Ephesians to use truth, righteousness, knowledge of the Bible, faith, salvation, and prayer in our fight. We can be as confident as David was that God will conquer.

—BQ

Daily Contemplation

What kind of armor have you been using as you battle the giant that plagues you? Do you trust God to make the story of David your story? Ask him to increase your confidence in what he will do and show you how to fight the battle.

DAY 104

Saul Tries to Kill David
1 Samuel 18:1–11; 19:1–24

When the men were returning home after David had killed the Philistine, the women came out from all the towns of Israel to meet King Saul with singing and dancing, with joyful songs and with timbrels and lyres. As they danced, they sang:
"Saul has slain his thousands,
and David his tens of thousands."

Saul was very angry; this refrain displeased him greatly. "They have credited David with tens of thousands," he thought, "but me with only thousands. What more can he get but the kingdom?" And from that time on Saul kept a close eye on David. The next day an evil spirit from God came forcefully on Saul. He was prophesying in his house, while David was playing the lyre, as he usually did. Saul had a spear in his hand and he hurled it, saying to himself, "I'll pin David to the wall." But David eluded him twice. (1 Samuel 18:6–11)

Saul's jealousy toward David emerges in these chapters. Though God has removed his presence from Saul's life and rulership, Saul still clings to the throne. The people, however, are giving David more acclaim than Saul. Even Jonathan and Michal (MI-kuhl), Saul's children, love David. Although no one is trying to dislodge Saul, he senses his position as king slowly slipping from his grasp. Jealousy and fear overwhelm him.

After several failed attempts by Saul's men to kill David, Saul sets out to do it himself. In an ironic, almost comic scene, he is overcome by the Spirit of God and falls into an ecstatic, trancelike state that immobilizes him (1 Samuel 19:19–24). It should be obvious that no harm Saul intends David will succeed, and little that David does will ultimately fail to succeed. God continues to fulfill his purposes for the man he has chosen to found the messianic dynasty of kings.

—BQ

Daily Contemplation

Can you remember a time when you felt overpowering jealousy toward someone?

DAY 105

David and Jonathan
1 Samuel 20:1–42

You can sense the force of David's personality by observing his effect on people around him. This chapter tells of an undying friendship from his early days, before the radical break with King Saul. The king's son Jonathan values friendship with David so much that he forfeits his chance at succession to the throne.

Saul reveals his true, murderous intent to Jonathan in a dramatic scene at the dinner table. Jonathan warns David, and thus begins the terrible struggle between the competing kings. Saul, the king rejected by God, lives on in luxury while David, secretly anointed as his replacement, lives in the wilderness, scrabbling to survive. Saul has a professional army; David a guerrilla band made up of family members and an assortment of outlaws.

The events of the next few years will play out the inner character of the two men. Saul knows God's will about the rightful king of Israel but will spend his life resisting it. In contrast, David will show amazing patience, waiting for the prophecy to come true. Twice when Saul accidentally falls into his hands, David refuses to kill him.

In the remainder of 1 Samuel, a long, Shakespearean-style drama unfolds. King Saul, an ancient Macbeth, has lost his grip and is clearly deteriorating. His son has sided with David; his daughter, married to David, has shifted her loyalties as well. Saul, insane with rage, turns up the heat. Can David hold on long enough to outlast him?

At times, David despairs. "One of these days I will be destroyed by the hand of Saul," he thinks (1 Samuel 27:1). His position is desperate. David has one precious asset only: God's promise that he will be king. Although his faith in that promise is tested to the extreme, David learns to wait for God's timing. In the end, like the hero of a Shakespearean tragedy, Saul takes his own life. Meanwhile, David inherits the throne of Israel.

—PY

Daily Contemplation

Do you have a close friendship like David and Jonathan had?

DAY 106

Ups and Downs
Psalm 27:1–14

The psalms open a window into the inner life of King David. That window discloses some surprises, however. David is surely no saint, and seldom does he show the peace and serenity normally associated with "spiritual" people. In fact, he often cries out against God, blaming him when things go wrong and begging for relief.

The psalms are not pious devotionals. They are filled with accounts of enemies who scheme and gossip and plot violence. For the psalmists, faith in God involves a constant struggle against powerful forces that often seem more real than God. The writers frequently ask, "Where are you, God? Why don't you help me?" They often feel abandoned, misused, betrayed.

As an example, consider Psalm 27, which shifts in mood with every stanza. The first stanza opens with a bold declaration of confidence in God from an author who seems downright fearless. The second stanza hints at the author's true condition: Tired of running, he yearns for the day when he can rest safely in God's dwelling and rise above all his enemies. By the third stanza, all confidence has melted and the psalmist is pleading for help. The psalm ends in a calmer tone, with a word of practical advice David often had opportunity to put into practice: "Wait for the LORD."

Yet out of such trials a strong, toughened faith in God emerges. In the years when David is an outlaw hiding from King Saul, his hideouts include a "rock" in the desert and a "stronghold." As an experienced fighter, David knows the value of such defenses. But when he writes about these days—as in this psalm—he calls God his rock and his fortress. He readily credits God as the true source of his protection.

Danger will not fade away even after David becomes king. He will face unceasing hostility from enemies, as well as numerous internal rebellions and coup attempts. But David has learned a pattern of helpless dependence in the wilderness that he will practice throughout his life.

—PY

―――――――― *Daily Contemplation* ――――――――

Is your emotional life fairly even or full of peaks and valleys? What about your spiritual life?

DAY 107

David Spares Saul's Life
1 Samuel 24:1–22

> Then David went out of the cave and called out to Saul, "My lord the king!" When Saul looked behind him, David bowed down and prostrated himself with his face to the ground. He said to Saul, "Why do you listen when men say, 'David is bent on harming you'? This day you have seen with your own eyes how the LORD delivered you into my hands in the cave. Some urged me to kill you, but I spared you; I said, 'I will not lay my hand on my lord, because he is the LORD's anointed.' See, my father, look at this piece of your robe in my hand! I cut off the corner of your robe but did not kill you. . . . I have not wronged you, but you are hunting me down to take my life." (1 Samuel 24:8–11)

No more than twenty years old, David is forced to flee to the Wilderness of Judah and take refuge in caves in order to escape the wrath of King Saul. For ten years he will live a sort of Robin Hood existence before Saul finally dies in battle.

This passage shows one instance of David's loyalty to God while on the run. Saul is pursuing David, intent on finding and killing him. Suddenly, in a dramatic twist, David gains the chance to quickly and easily end Saul's life. But David has such a sense of reverence for the one God anointed that he can't even entertain the thought of killing this bloodthirsty man. He is committed to letting God bring justice.

The Bible records another similar incident, in which David again has the chance to take Saul's life and chooses to let him live (1 Samuel 26). In the end God will deliver the justice David has trusted him to provide.

—BQ

Daily Contemplation

What difficulty are you facing today (apart from abuse or domestic violence, in which case you should leave and seek help immediately) that could tempt you to use your own methods rather than God's in seeking an escape?

DAY 108

David, Nabal, and Abigail
1 Samuel 25:1-42

A certain man in Maon, who had property there at Carmel, was very wealthy. He had a thousand goats and three thousand sheep, which he was shearing in Carmel. His name was Nabal and his wife's name was Abigail. She was an intelligent and beautiful woman, but her husband was surly and mean in his dealings. . . . Nabal answered David's servants, "Who is this David? Who is this son of Jesse? . . . Why should I take my bread and water, and the meat I have slaughtered for my shearers, and give it to men coming from who knows where?" David's men turned around and went back. When they arrived, they reported every word. David said to his men, "Each of you strap on your sword!" . . . When Abigail saw David, she quickly got off her donkey and bowed down before David with her face to the ground. She fell at his feet and said: "Pardon your servant, my lord, and let me speak to you; hear what your servant has to say. . . . And let this gift, which your servant has brought to my lord, be given to the men who follow you." (1 Samuel 25:2–3, 10–13, 23–24, 27)

David's frustration reaches a peak in this passage, in which foolish Nabal (NAY-buhl) refuses to help David and his men in return for their prior kindness. David may well have taken Nabal's punishment into his own hands this time, but a remarkably resourceful woman named Abigail restrains him. Abigail offers another portrait of a strong woman with a deep reverence for God. Like Rahab and Ruth before her, Abigail chooses loyalty to God and God's people. She acts quickly, decisively, and wisely to prevent David from taking vengeance that belongs to God. God uses Abigail to mercifully spare David from his own violent inclination. Then Abigail marries David and continues to support him in her strength and wisdom.

—BQ

Daily Contemplation

Who has God put in your life to support you and give you wise counsel?

DAY 109

Taking Risks, Trusting God
Reflection

Life is a risky business. We face situational risks that stem from finances, jobs, schooling, or homes. We may also face physical risks from sports, violence, travel in cars or planes, poor eating habits, smoking, or drug use. And we encounter relational risks, especially with the people in our lives to whom we are closest—family, spouse, children, friends, coworkers.

David certainly knew a life of risk. His decision to spare Saul's life involved a risk that Saul could again turn on David, hunting him down in a matter of hours or days. Jonathan, too, may easily have betrayed David out of loyalty to his father and desire for the throne. The stranger Abigail could have been deceptively seeking to save the life of her husband, setting David up for destruction. But David boldly trusted God's protection and trusted those whom God put in his life to help him. He refused to become a skeptic or a cynic.

We may have many reasons to distrust the people and situations in our lives. Sometimes our distrust protects us from making wrong decisions or relying on people who are unsafe. Yet sometimes it is not wise caution but rather improper fear that holds us back from the ways God seeks to bless us. How can we know the difference? Like David, we must turn to God again and again, asking for the wisdom to respond properly.

David prays, "Teach me your way, LORD; lead me in a straight path" (Psalm 27:11). We can trust God for wisdom and protection. As we do so, we leave our lives open for his blessing through those people and circumstances he chooses.

—BQ

Daily Contemplation

Where is the bulk of your distrust focused today? Do you sense God asking you to let go of your distrust and let him protect you instead? Take a moment to ask God for his wisdom and protection.

King David Brings the Ark to Jerusalem
2 Samuel 6:1-23

An unavoidable question dangles over the Bible's account of David's life. How could anyone so obviously flawed—he did, as we shall see, commit adultery and murder—be called "a man after God's own heart"? The central event in this chapter may point to an answer.

David consistently acknowledges that God, not a human king, is the true ruler of Israel, and so in one of his first official acts he sends for the sacred ark of the Lord that was captured by the Philistines half a century before. He plans to install it in Jerusalem, the new capital city he is building, as a symbol of God's reign.

It takes a few false starts to get the ark to Jerusalem. Without looking up the regulations given to Moses, the Israelites try transporting the ark on an ox cart, as the Philistines parade their gods, rather than on the shoulders of the Levites, as God has commanded. Somebody dies, David gets mad, and the ark sits in a private home for three months.

Nevertheless, when the ark finally does move to Jerusalem, to the accompaniment of a brass band and the shouts of a huge crowd, King David completely loses control. Wild with joy, he cartwheels in the streets like an Olympic gymnast who has just won the gold medal and is out strutting his stuff.

The scene of a dignified king doing backflips in a scanty robe breaks every rule ever devised by a politician's image-builders. David's wife, for one, is scandalized. But David sets her straight: He is dancing before God, no one else. And, king or no, he doesn't care what anyone thinks as long as that one-Person audience can sense his jubilation.

In short, David is a man of **_passion_**, and he feels more passionately about the God of Israel than about anything else in the world. The message gets through to the entire nation. As Frederick Buechner has written, "He had feet of clay like the rest of us if not more so—self-serving and deceitful, lustful and vain—but on the basis of that dance alone, you can see why it was David more than anybody else that Israel lost her heart to and why, when Jesus of Nazareth came riding into Jerusalem on his flea-bitten mule a thousand years later, it was as the Son of David that they hailed him."[11]

—PY

Daily Contemplation

Have you ever lost control in worship? How would you respond to someone who did?

DAY 111

God's Promise to David
1 Chronicles 17:1–27

After bringing the ark of God to Jerusalem, David begins to dream of building a splendid home for it, a temple devoted to the God of the Israelites. In a day when pagan temples ranked among the wonders of the world, he thinks it only fitting to lavish the wealth of his kingdom on a "house" for the true God. But God makes clear that David is not the one to build such a temple. Elsewhere (1 Chronicles 22:8), the Bible states the reason: As a warrior, David will shed much blood during his time on the throne, and God wants his house built by a man of peace. That task will fall on David's son.

Although God vetoes the plan to build a temple, he grants David far more. Harking back to his covenant with the Israelites, he promises—in a tender play on words—to build a "house" out of David's descendants that will last forever. Whatever his reservations about the Israelites' demand for a king, God has fully adopted the king as his representative within the nation. In a typically humble response, David erupts in a prayer of astonished thanksgiving.

This promise, given in an intimate exchange between God and David, sows the seed for what will become a longtime hope of the Jews: a royal "Messiah," or Anointed One. Saul's dynasty ends just as it began; David's will continue through a long line of kings and culminate in God's own Son, to be born into David's lineage in Bethlehem, the City of David. Has God's promise been fulfilled? This provides a hint: the fact that even in modern times people still pore over the lives of David and other kings of tiny Israel—though far grander, more impressive kings have faded from history—and recognize one descendant as the true Messiah. (The books of Samuel, Kings, and Chronicles often overlap, telling the same history from different perspectives. This chapter from 1 Chronicles repeats almost word-for-word the seventh chapter of 2 Samuel.)

—PY

Daily Contemplation

What have you wanted to do for God?

DAY 112

The Goodness of God
Psalm 103:1–22

David never gets over a sense of ***astonishment*** at all God has done for him. As he grows older and reviews his life, he realizes that, despite the hardships, God has always delivered him "from the pit." God has kept his promises. In gratitude, David writes many psalms praising God for his past faithfulness. The king serves, in effect, as a national reservoir of memory for his people, helping the whole nation remember God's benefits.

When the Israelites praise God, their thoughts center on God's actions in freeing them from slavery and leading them into a land of their own. Their psalms are like history recaps, designed to summon up the past, especially the hallmark days of deliverance under Moses. The faithful study those days in the Torah (the five books of Moses) and write songs to commemorate them.

The memories aren't all positive, and the Israelites' songs can be brutally frank about the ancestors' rebellions, complaints, and lack of gratitude. Yet the nation has one great, happy reason to rejoice: God has kept his promise to love them. To psalm writers like David, the events of Israel's history are unmistakable signs of God's grace. They have done nothing to deserve God's love, and yet he has showered love on them.

This psalm could be titled "The Goodness of God." It reviews the dark times of illness and oppression, of sin and rebellion, and then it points with amazement to the remarkable ways in which God transformed all those dark times. God understands and will not overwhelm human weakness: "He knows how we are formed, he remembers that we are dust." More, despite our failings, he has in store for us an unfathomable eternity of love.

David has one loud message to celebrate: We do not get what we deserve. We get far more. The psalm ends in a burst of praise, starting with the grand sweep of the universe and spiraling back to the setting of the very first verse—David praising God in his inmost being.

—PY

Daily Contemplation

When you review your past, do you tend to focus on the victories or the failures?

DAY 113

David and Bathsheba
2 Samuel 11:1–27

It is the simplest story in the world, this tale of David and Bathsheba (bath-SHEE-bah): man sees woman, man sleeps with woman, woman gets pregnant. Nothing unusual there. Every year the tabloids broadcast modern variations on the same theme. Substitute a politician—or a TV evangelist—for the king, and a beauty queen for Bathsheba. What else is new?

The scandal doesn't especially shock David's Israelite subjects. Like most people, they are resigned to the fact that the people on top, who make the rules, often don't bother to live by them. Lots of leaders in history have followed this course, taking the spoils they want, the money they want, the privileges they want. The Romans had a phrase for such behavior, **rex lex**—the king is law—rather than **lex rex**—the law is king.

Bathsheba's pregnancy complicates the picture somewhat. Today, a leader in David's situation might destroy the evidence with an abortion. David has his own cover-up plan. It starts as a clever attempt to deceive, making Bathsheba's husband appear as the likely father. Uriah's (yoor-I-uh) scruples, however, put King David to shame, or should. What follows is a classic case of "one crime leads to another."

In the end, David, the man after God's own heart, breaks the sixth, seventh, ninth, and tenth commandments. For his loyalty, David's soldier Uriah gets the reward of murder, and many other Israelites fall with him. This story shows David at his most Machiavellian: cold as iron, ruthless in use of his power. Even so, not a word of protest is filed. What the king wants the king gets, no questions asked. Such is life.

After a mourning period, Bathsheba moves into the palace and David marries her. By now many people must have surmised what had happened—the servants know, at any rate—but the Bible doesn't report that any of them protest. The story of David's infidelity might have ended here, and probably would have, except for one portentous sentence at the close of this chapter. It says merely, "The thing David had done displeased the Lord."

—PY

Daily Contemplation

Have you, like David, ever been caught in the act of a sin and tried to deceive your way out?

DAY 114

Sin and God's Love Through the Eyes of an Unbeliever
Reflection

These days, in Western culture, right and wrong vary depending on whom you ask. "Individual relativism . . . says the almighty Me defines reality, [and] cultural relativism . . . says the mightiest We defines reality,"[12] explains theologian and author Thaddeus Williams.

God followers, though, accept the Bible as the overarching standard of right and wrong, the final authority. God's words are set down in the Bible, which stands as the only true and reliable guidebook for living this life and preparing for eternity.

David knew God's law well, as given through Moses. During most of his life this shepherd-at-heart followed God's law, aware that God's rules are the boundaries that keep us, God's "sheep," within the pastures that are the richest and most fulfilling. Yet David shut his eyes to God's law on the evening he spied Bathsheba on a nearby roof. His unchecked passion propelled him into making a big mistake, and we'll see that he suffered much heartache as a result. Sin, wildly fun for a while, always brings pain in the end.

Like David, we each make mistakes. Some of them we make in ignorance before becoming believers; others we make while knowing well the wrong we are doing. Often our mistakes bring difficult consequences. But as we look at how tenderly God cares for us, we can echo David's words in Psalm 103:10: "He does not treat us as our sins deserve or repay us according to our iniquities." The price we pay for sin does not even approach the price we owe, all because of the payment Jesus made in our place.

Only with this understanding can we reach out to those in our culture who lack a center of authority. When unbelievers come to know God's deep love for them, they can begin to understand the love he's shown through the guidelines in his Word, the Bible. "There is beauty, truth, love, and justice that we don't invent, but discover,"[13] says Thaddeus Williams. We can share with others that what Jesus did out of love for us, he also did for them. They too can see the Bible as a long story of God's immeasurable love.

—BQ

Daily Contemplation

When has God spared you from your own mistakes? How has he surprised you with blessing beyond your dreams? Ask God to help you tell others about his love for you in spite of your mistakes.

DAY 115

Nathan Rebukes David
2 Samuel 12:1–25

Across the globe today, people who live under the thumb of tyrants ask the question, "Who holds the ruler accountable?" From the beginning God established Israel as his kingdom, with its ruler as his representative and not the final authority. After David's great sin, God sends the prophet Nathan to confront the king.

It was Nathan who conveyed to the king God's lavish promise to establish David's "house" (1 Chronicles 17). This time he comes with a heartrending tale of poverty, greed, and injustice. He presents the case to David, the highest judge in Israel, for a verdict. David knows exactly how to decide such a case: The man deserves to die! When he says so, Nathan delivers his own devastating verdict: "You are the man!"

In this dramatic scene David's greatness shows itself. He could have had Nathan killed. Or he could have laughed and thrown him out of the palace. Instead, David says to Nathan, "I have sinned against the LORD," immediately admitting guilt and acknowledging God as the true ruler.

To appreciate David's confession, you only have to think of the response of leaders "caught in the act" in more recent times: Richard Nixon grudgingly admitting, "Mistakes were made"; tobacco company executives making barefaced lies about their products' congressional hearings; Bill Clinton initially denying well-substantiated charges of womanizing. But King David sees at once the heart of the issue. He has sinned not just against Uriah and his country but against the Lord.

David is a great king partly because he does not act with the normal pride of a great king. Confronted with the truth, he repents. Forgiveness comes in an instant, but the consequences of David's actions will plague the kingdom for a generation. For one thing, he has lost moral authority within his own family. Over the next few years, one of David's sons will rape his half-sister, and another will kill his brother and launch a coup against David himself. King David has left a legacy of abuse of power, and not all his successors will be as quick to repent.

—PY

Daily Contemplation

How do you instinctively react when someone confronts you about wrongdoing?

DAY 116

True Confession
Psalm 51:1–17

This poem of remembrance may well be the most impressive outcome of David's sordid affair with Bathsheba. It is one thing for a king to confess a moral lapse in private to a prophet. It is quite another for him to compose a detailed account of that confession to be sung throughout the land!

All nations have heroes, but Israel may be alone in making epic literature about its greatest hero's failings. This eloquent psalm, possibly used in worship services as a guide for confession, shows that Israel ultimately remembered David more for his devotion to God than for his political achievements.

Step by step, the psalm takes the reader (or singer) through the stages of repentance. It describes the constant mental replays—"Oh, if only I had a chance to do it over"—the gnawing guilt, the shame, and finally the hope for a new beginning that springs from true repentance.

David lives under Old Testament law, which prescribes a harsh punishment for his crimes: death by stoning. But in a remarkable way this psalm transcends the rigid formulas of law and reveals the true nature of sin as a broken ***relationship*** with God. "Against you, you only, have I sinned," David cries out. He sees that no ritual sacrifices or religious ceremonies will cause his guilt to vanish; the sacrifices God wants are "a broken spirit, a broken and contrite heart." Those things David has in abundance.

In the midst of his prayer, David looks for possible good that might come out of his tragedy and sees a glimmer of light. He prays for God to use his experience as a moral lesson for others. Perhaps, by reading his story of sin, they might avoid the same pitfalls, or by reading his confession they might gain hope in forgiveness. David's prayer is fully answered and becomes his greatest legacy as king. The best king of Israel has fallen the farthest. But neither he, nor anyone, can fall beyond the reach of God's love and forgiveness.

—PY

Daily Contemplation

Would you lose respect for a leader if he or she admitted failures this openly?

DAY 117

David's Spiritual Secret
Psalm 139:1–24

In the end David—lusty, vengeful King David—gains a reputation as a friend of God. For a time in Israel, Yahweh is known as "the God of David"; the two are that closely identified. What is David's secret? This majestic psalm hints at an answer.

Mainly, Psalm 139 reveals the ***intimacy*** that exists between David and his God. Although his exploits—killing wild animals bare-handed, felling Goliath, surviving Saul's onslaughts, routing the Philistines—make him a hero in his nation's eyes, David always finds a way to make God the one on center stage. Throughout his life David believes, truly believes, that the spiritual world is every bit as real as his physical world of swords and spears and caves and thrones.

The psalms form a record of David's conscious effort to subject his own daily life to the reality of that spiritual world beyond him. Whatever the phrase "practicing the presence of God" means, David experiences it. He intentionally involves God in every detail of his life.

David firmly believes he ***matters*** to God. After one narrow escape he writes, "[God] rescued me because he delighted in me" (Psalm 18:19). Another time he argues, "What is gained if I am silenced, if I go down to the pit? Will the dust praise you?" (Psalm 30:9). And Psalm 139 beautifully expresses David's sense of wonder at God's love and concern.

Reading David's psalms, with all their emotional peaks and valleys, it may even seem that he writes them as a form of spiritual therapy, a way of talking himself into faith when his spirit and emotions are wavering. Now, centuries later, we can use these very same prayers as steps of faith, a path to lead us from an obsession with ourselves to the actual presence of God.

—PY

Daily Contemplation

How do you practice the presence of God in your life? Read Psalm 139 again and make it your prayer to God.

DAY 118

Practicing His Presence
Reflection

God is always with us. He's always focused on us, always thinking about us, always aware of what we're doing, thinking, and feeling. Not for a second does he turn his attention from us. And all his attention flows from a burning, passionate love that never grows cold, never tires.

If we in turn make God the center of our attention, we can be in a continual love relationship with God that will give us perspective on everything in life and fill the deepest needs of our souls. David understood God's constant presence and in return was often present to God. His understanding of God's nearness helped him to walk more closely with God.

Another man has helped believers understand this concept more fully. Brother Lawrence lived in a French Carmelite monastery during the seventeenth century, working in the kitchen of the monastery until he died at age eighty. His work held no special significance by this earth's standards, but Brother Lawrence transformed his work in a way that has left an impact on many who have come after him. During his years serving in the kitchen, Brother Lawrence grew in what he called "practicing the presence of God."

> I beheld him in my heart as my Father and as my God. I worshiped him as often as I could, keeping my mind in his holy presence and recalling it back to God as often as I found it had wandered from him . . . I make it my business only to persevere in his holy presence wherein I keep myself by a simple attention and a general fond regard to God, which I refer to as an ***actual presence*** of God. Or, to put it another way, an habitual, silent, and secret conversation of the soul with God . . . In short, by often repeating these acts they become ***habitual***, and the presence of God becomes something that comes naturally to us.[14]

David and Brother Lawrence were earthly people with human weaknesses and wandering hearts, yet through discipline and a real love for God, they discovered that it is possible to form a habit of being consciously present to God.

The apostle Paul, writing to church friends, asked them to "pray continually, give thanks in all circumstances; for this is God's will for you in Christ Jesus" (1 Thessalonians 5:17–18). Paul knew that the inner practice of sitting with God, sensing him and whispering to him, sometimes with words and sometimes just with the language of our hearts, not only is possible but is God's will for us.

—BQ

--- *Daily Contemplation* ---

How often during the day are you aware of God's presence? How often do you pray? Ask God to help turn your mind to him often, in both times of quiet and times of activity.

DAY 119

Solomon Asks for Wisdom
1 Kings 1:28-30; 3:1-28

The first half of 1 Kings describes a man who gets life handed to him on a silver platter. The favored son of King David and Queen Bathsheba, young Solomon grows up in the royal palace. God lavishes special gifts on Solomon. In an incredible dream sequence, young Solomon actually gets the opportunity every child secretly longs for. God offers him any wish—long life, riches, anything at all—and when Solomon chooses wisdom, God adds bonus gifts of wealth, honor, and peace. Early on, the precocious prince astounds others with his talent for songwriting and natural history.

A mere teenager when he takes over the throne of Israel, Solomon soon becomes the richest, most impressive ruler of his time. In Jerusalem during his reign, silver is as common as stones (1 Kings 10:27). And a fleet of trading ships brings exotica for the king's private collections—apes and baboons from Africa, ivory and gold by the ton. He is called the wisest man in the world, and kings and queens travel hundreds of miles to meet him. They leave dazzled by the genius of Israel's king and by the prosperity of his nation.

Israel reaches its Golden Age under King Solomon, a shining moment of tranquility in its long, tormented history. Almost all the Promised Land lies in Solomon's domain, and the nation is at peace. Literature and culture flourish. Of the common people, the Bible reports simply that "they ate, they drank and they were happy" (1 Kings 4:20).

However, even in the happy days, danger signs appear. King Solomon makes a shrewd political alliance with the Pharaoh of Egypt. Already he is looking to military strength, rather than to God, for security. In addition, Solomon has a passion for foreign-born women. Over time, he marries princesses from Moab, Ammon, Edom, Sidon, and other nations—seven hundred wives in all, and three hundred concubines! Eventually, to please his wives, Solomon will take a final, terrible step of building altars to all their gods.

—PY

Daily Contemplation

What gifts have you wanted in life? How have you used the gifts that God has given you?

DAY 120

The Ark Brought to the Temple
1 Kings 6:1–38; 8:1–66

Of Solomon's many accomplishments, one looms large above the rest. He spares no expense in building a place for God to dwell, and Solomon's temple, fashioned by two hundred thousand workmen, soon ranks as one of the wonders of the world. From a distance, it shines like a snowcapped mountain. Inside, all its walls and even its floors are plated with pure gold.

In many ways the scene in this chapter represents the high-water mark of the entire Old Testament, the fulfillment of God's covenant with Israel. Solomon calls the nation together to dedicate the temple to God, and as thousands of people look on in a huge public ceremony, the glory of the Lord comes down to fill the temple. Even the priests are driven back by the mighty force of God's presence.

God is making Solomon's temple the center of his activity on earth, and the crowd spontaneously decides to stay another two weeks to celebrate. Kneeling on a bronze platform, Solomon prays aloud, "I have indeed built a magnificent temple for you, a place for you to dwell forever" (1 Kings 8:13). Then he catches himself in astonishment. "But will God really dwell on earth? The heavens, even the highest heaven, cannot contain you. How much less this temple I have built!" (8:27).

God has done it! His promises to Abraham and Moses have finally come true. In one of the most magnificent prayers ever prayed, Solomon reviews the history of the covenant and asks God to seal that agreement with his presence in the temple. God responds: "I have heard the prayer and plea you have made before me; I have consecrated this temple . . . . My eyes and my heart will always be there" (9:3).

The Israelites now have land, a nation with secure boundaries, and a gleaming symbol of God's presence among them. All this comes to pass in a land rich with silver and gold. On the famous day of the temple dedication, everyone sees the fire and the cloud of his presence. No one can doubt God's faithfulness.

—PY

Daily Contemplation

What promise of God are you waiting on? What signs of God's faithfulness do you see?

DAY 121

More than a Building
Psalm 84:1–12

It is almost impossible to exaggerate the significance of the temple for Jews throughout history. They took pride in its beautiful architecture (as people today might honor the Notre Dame cathedral), but the temple was far more than a grand symbol. Israel's entire national religious life centered around this building, the house of God.

Faithful Jews turned and faced the temple daily in prayer. Each year they made pilgrimages there to celebrate three great festivals honoring God's covenant with them. The Israelites even came to believe that the temple magically protected them against foreign invasion. As long as the temple stood, some said, no foreign armies could enter Jerusalem—a belief the prophet Jeremiah roundly condemned.

This psalm captures some of the intense feelings about the temple. It is written by one of the "Sons of Korah," a priestly choir established by King David to provide music for worship. As the writer travels to the temple on pilgrimage, his joy and anticipation make the desert surroundings seem almost like an oasis. Perhaps using a little humor, he claims to envy the sparrows and swallows that build nests inside the walls of the temple and thus get to live there permanently. He sings, "Better is one day in your courts than a thousand elsewhere."

The object of the psalmist's enthusiasm, the glorious temple built by Solomon, stood for about 380 years, occasionally falling into disrepair. Destroyed by the Babylonians, it was partially rebuilt under the leadership of Ezra (EZ-ruh) and Nehemiah and then reconstructed by King Herod in Jesus' time. Jesus, who also made pilgrimages to the temple, walked on "Solomon's Porch," and the early church met on the temple grounds.

Herod's temple eventually fell to the Romans, and years later the Muslims built a mosque on the site. But the temple has never lost its sacred significance for the Jews, and even today some in Israel propose rebuilding the temple.

In the days since Jesus' resurrection, his followers now form a different kind of temple. God now dwells in our bodies rather than in a physical construct.

—PY

Daily Contemplation

Is worshiping God dull or exciting for you? Why? Read Psalm 84 again as a prayer to God for the continued living presence of his Spirit in you.

DAY 122

The Queen of Sheba Visits Solomon
1 Kings 10:1–13

> When the queen of Sheba heard about the fame of Solomon and his relationship to the LORD, she came to test Solomon with hard questions. . . . When the queen of Sheba saw all the wisdom of Solomon and the palace he had built, the food on his table, the seating of his officials, the attending servants in their robes, his cupbearers, and the burnt offerings he made at the temple of the LORD, she was overwhelmed. (1 Kings 10:1, 4–5)

This passage gives a glimpse of just one of the world rulers who came to see Solomon's magnificent kingdom firsthand and to observe his wisdom. The queen of Sheba (SHEE-buh) does not go away disappointed. Rather, what she sees overwhelms her. Solomon's reign of wisdom and wealth exceeds anything she could expect. It seems obvious even to this queen, likely a pagan ruler and wealthy in her own right, that the Lord of Solomon loves him and has chosen to bless Israel through Solomon's leadership.

Sheba was located south of Israel and Arabia in the country now called Yemen, which borders the Indian Ocean to the south. The queen's words to Solomon indicate that God has revealed to her, one outside the chosen nation of Israel, that God has an "eternal love for Israel" (1 Kings 10:9).

Jesus will later compare the queen of Sheba with the people of his time. "The Queen of the South will rise at the judgment with the people of this generation and condemn them, for she came from the ends of the earth to listen to Solomon's wisdom; and now something greater than Solomon is here," Jesus said (Luke 11:31). So impressed was the queen with Solomon's riches and wisdom that she traveled a great distance and brought him costly gifts. How much more should all those in Jesus' day have yearned to follow Jesus, who offered true riches and perfect wisdom.

—BQ

Daily Contemplation

How much effort are you expending in seeking Jesus?

DAY 123

Solomon's Splendor, Solomon's Wives
1 Kings 10:23–11:13

> King Solomon was greater in riches and wisdom than all the other kings of the earth. . . . King Solomon, however, loved many foreign women . . . . As Solomon grew old, his wives turned his heart after other gods, and his heart was not fully devoted to the LORD his God, as the heart of David his father had been. (1 Kings 10:23; 11:1, 4)

Part of God's law to the Israelites reads, "The king, moreover, must not acquire great numbers of horses for himself or make the people return to Egypt to get more of them, for the LORD has told you, 'You are not to go back that way again.' He must not take many wives, or his heart will be led astray. He must not accumulate large amounts of silver and gold" (Deuteronomy 17:16–17).

Clearly, God has warned Israel against the very patterns Solomon falls into. He imports horses from Egypt. He takes seven hundred wives and nearly half as many mistresses. And he accumulates more silver and gold than any other king on earth. He also amasses rich clothing, spices, mules, and apes and baboons, which may have been fashionable pets for royalty at the time (1 Kings 10:22).

God has specifically warned that many horses, an abundance of wives, and great wealth will harm Israel rather than help her. When Israel purchases horses to assist in battle, the nation's confidence will turn to its own power rather than to God for victory. When the nation grows wealthy, it will lose its sense of need for God. When the king surrounds himself with foreign wives, many of whom remain loyal to false gods, his heart will turn toward their loyalties.

In all these forms of disobedience, Solomon and Israel grieve God more deeply than David ever did. Israel has chosen not to love God with all her heart (Deuteronomy 6:5).

—BQ

--- *Daily Contemplation* ---

How might our nation resemble Israel during Solomon's reign?

DAY 124

Losing Sight of God
Reflection

With his accumulation of horses, women, and riches, Solomon put himself in a position where he could conquer anyone, enjoy exotic women at a moment's notice, and delight in the acclaim of all who valued wealth. In the eyes of his world Solomon had it all.

Yet while he was focused on his wealth and enjoying his popularity, Solomon was gradually drifting "back that way again." God had warned the Israelites in the desert, after freeing them from Egypt and leading them toward the Promised Land, not to return to their former ways. He had liberated them from the false promises of Egypt, leading them instead to a place where they could, through his power and blessing, enjoy true pleasure in life. In the Promised Land they would experience a full life with God as he continued to build their nation and care for them.

It didn't take long for the Israelites' hearts to start going "back that way again." The very son of David, who had heard from God himself and possessed more wisdom than anyone ever, could not see that in straying back toward security, seduction, and wealth, he was betraying the One who had given him life. He was forfeiting the deeper pleasures God offered in favor of cheap counterfeits. The world deceived even Solomon. In the end, as 1 Kings 11:5 states, he found himself worshiping Ashtoreth, a goddess of sex and fertility, and Molech, a god whose worship involved child sacrifice, a practice that God had strictly forbidden (Leviticus 18:21).

It's easy to lose sight of God. It's tempting to grow comfortable in this world, to enjoy God's gifts and then begin to believe that in them, rather than in God, lie our security and delight. Just as God warned Israel not to return to the ways of Egypt, he reminds us that he has freed us from the lies of this world.

We may never be as wise as Solomon, but we can understand the truth he missed. Only God can save us and bring us lasting joy. Earthly strength will not save, sex cannot satisfy, and possessions cannot hold a candle to God's approval and blessing. Why go back that way again?

—BQ

Daily Contemplation

What are the things that most pull your heart from God? Ask God to help you turn to him above all else. God answered Solomon's earnest prayer for wisdom; he will answer your prayer just as faithfully.

DAY 125

Uncommon Song
Song of Songs 2:1–17

Without doubt more songs have been written about romantic love than any other subject. And, to many people's surprise, the Bible itself contains an explicit love song—complete with erotic lyrics.

Solomon, with all his wives and mistresses, was a devoted student of romance. Ultimately, he fell victim to a love obsession that caused him much grief. But the Song of Songs (also known as the Song of Solomon) celebrates a high form of beautiful love. It shows no embarrassment about lovers enjoying each other's bodies and openly expressing that enjoyment.

Not everyone has felt comfortable with the frankness of this book. In medieval Spain, some church authorities led a campaign to remove all copies of Song of Songs from the Bible and burn them in public bonfires. Priests and teachers who refused were removed from their jobs and even imprisoned.

Over the centuries, many others have tried to read the song as though it had nothing to do with physical lovers, seeing it instead as an allegory of love between God and his people. But nowadays most scholars believe that the poem was intended to be taken at face value, as a celebration of love between two newlyweds.

These lovers look without shame on one another and tell each other what they feel. They revel in the sensuous: the beauty of nature, the scent of perfumes and spices. They are explicit and erotic. Yet Song of Songs creates a very different atmosphere than most modern love songs. It hearkens back to the original love in the Garden of Eden, when man and woman were naked and unashamed. Reading it, you sense no shame or guilt; you feel that God himself smiles upon their love.

—PY

Daily Contemplation

What did you learn about romantic love from your parents or teachers when you were growing up?

DAY 126

The Wedding
Song of Songs 3:6–4:16

Come with me from Lebanon, my bride,
    come with me from Lebanon.
Descend from the crest of Amana,
    from the top of Senir, the summit of Hermon,
from the lions' dens
    and the mountain haunts of leopards.
You have stolen my heart, my sister, my bride;
    you have stolen my heart
with one glance of your eyes,
    with one jewel of your necklace.
How delightful is your love, my sister, my bride!
    How much more pleasing is your love than wine,
and the fragrance of your perfume
    more than any spice!
Your lips drop sweetness as the honeycomb, my bride;
    milk and honey are under your tongue.
The fragrance of your garments
    is like the fragrance of Lebanon. (Song of Songs 4:8–11)

Solomon's Song of Songs progresses in stages, from the courtship of two lovers, to their wedding night—today's passage—and then on to mature marriage.

The custom in ancient Israel, still practiced in the Middle East today, is for the groom to lead a procession to his bride's home for the wedding ceremony. After the ceremony, the couple consummate their marriage with a beautiful wedding night together, each lavishing love on the other. Solomon's praise for his bride's physical beauty echoes the praise of every loving groom for his new spouse.

Later, in chapter 5, the beloved will praise the beauty she finds in her lover. As today's passage ends, the bride invites her new husband to come and enjoy her fully. She gives herself to him, like a tree offering its ripened fruit.

—BQ

Daily Contemplation

Did you grow up believing sex to be a beautiful and fulfilling part of marriage, or were you taught differently?

DAY 127

Maturing Marriage
Song of Songs 8:1–14

This last chapter of the Song of Songs portrays the lovers enjoying a maturing marriage that has sustained trials yet still possesses loving, passionate intimacy. The culture of Solomon's day frowned upon public displays of affection between husband and wife. Here in the first verses, the beloved expresses her desire to display casual affection for her husband, as a sister would be allowed to do for a brother. In a playful manner, the wife speaks of herself as a sister, a mother, and earlier as a friend (Song of Songs 5:16) to her lover. Clearly, this couple shares a multifaceted relationship in which each meets various needs of the other.

As the couple emerges from the desert in 8:5, we see a picture of two who have overcome trials in their marriage. Earlier they dealt with the insecurity of the beloved (1:5), "foxes" (2:15) representing obstacles or temptations that threaten their relationship, and indifference on the part of the beloved toward her husband (5:2–7). In the image of coming up out of the desert, the song suggests that the couple has worked to overcome the disharmony that became a part of marital life when sin entered the world (Genesis 3:16).

The song goes on to express the great power that love holds over a person. The beloved tells of her desire to be her husband's most valued possession. Once love takes hold, its power can bring a heightened energy for life, or it can bring destruction. If its passion is not kindled and preserved, jealousy will burn with a destructive force. Ultimately, love is a priceless gift from God that must be treasured and protected.

In the final two verses of the song, the lovers recall their days of courtship, expressing a love for each other still strong and intimate while also playful and passionate. The husband and wife have lived out a committed relationship with one another that in all its phases reflects God's intentions for marriage.

—BQ

Daily Contemplation

Do you know a couple who embody the marriage described in Song of Songs?

DAY 128

Loving God's Way
Reflection

How did Solomon get the privilege of writing a song on marital love for the Bible—he of the **seven hundred** wives and **three hundred** mistresses? Did God overlook his polygamy and adultery?

Some scholars believe that Solomon wrote Song of Songs after his marriage to his first wife. If so, it fits his pattern. Solomon could not control his appetites. When he found something good—horses, buildings, gold—he hoarded it like a greedy child.

Or maybe Solomon wrote when old and tired of his harem of women. Looking back on his life—as in Ecclesiastes—perhaps he saw the errors in his ways and recalled a time when his marriage reflected God's plan for a man and a woman.

Whatever the reason, it's clear that God gave us the song to teach about love. Throughout, the Song of Songs presents romantic love as a powerful, living force within us. Think of a blazing fire, a thirst that cannot be quenched, a boulder that can't be washed away. Love is consuming and unchangeable. Sound like God's love for us?

God intended love to have this power. It can unite us and fuel the energies needed to care for one another in all the peaks and valleys of life. Solomon alluded to this: "Above all else, guard your heart, for everything you do flows from it" (Proverbs 4:23).

Solomon's song celebrates the life-giving power of love, with sex as the ultimate expression of this love. Sex becomes the fulfillment of a loving relationship that through marital union will only keep growing. As the final gift of two people to one another, sex joins lives together for the duration of their time on earth.

The Bible never downplays the force of sex. This act taps into our emotions and wills, influencing all we do and even who we are. Although it may feel right outside the boundaries God set, we can trust his guidance and limits, as he is our wise creator.

God illustrates in Song of Songs that when we are following God's way, every part of a romantic, loving relationship is a gift from him. He also warns repeatedly, "Do not arouse or awaken love until it so desires" (Song of Songs 2:7). Because love is a wonderful gift, many desire it. But love cannot be bought or forced.

As we reflect on God's gift of love, we can celebrate his passionate, pursuing love of us. The romantic love we experience here on earth is merely a taste of the love God has for us and will reveal fully in eternity. "Now I know in part; then I shall know fully, even as I am fully known" (1 Corinthians 13:12).

—BQ

Daily Contemplation

Are you in a romantic relationship now? Are you seeking one? Are you questioning God's will for a relationship? Ask God for wisdom in the choices you make about love.

DAY 129

Life Advice
Proverbs 4:1–27

The happy days of Solomon's reign do not last. In a pointed editorial aside, the author of 1 Kings notes that after building the temple, Solomon spends twice as much time and energy on the construction of his own palace (7:1). He proves unable to control his extravagant appetite in any area: wealth, power, romance, political intrigue. He seems obsessed with a desire to outdo anyone who has ever lived, and gradually his devotion to God slips away. First Kings gives this summation of Solomon's days: "So Solomon did evil in the eyes of the LORD; he did not follow the LORD completely, as David his father had done" (11:6).

Yet, although Solomon ultimately fails to please God, he does use his enormous talent for much good. In the arts, he creates many fine works, among them several books of biblical literature. Inspired by God's supernatural gift of wisdom, he composes 1,005 songs and 3,000 proverbs—many of which are collected in the book of Proverbs.

This representative chapter captures the tone of the book of Proverbs: A wise old man, surrounded by eager young admirers, coyly unveils to them the secrets of his life. (A modern parallel: Millions of Americans will buy the latest how-to book by a famous sports figure or business executive—*Maybe it will help me achieve that same kind of success*, they think.)

Before revealing his secrets, however, the author of Proverbs wants to get one thing straight. The wisdom he is teaching cannot be reduced to a series of "Don't do this; do that" rules. There is no formula for "one-minute wisdom"; true wisdom demands a lifelong quest. The rewards of such a life, however, will repay any sacrifice, "though it cost all you have."

As the author contrasts "the path of the righteous" with "the way of the wicked," one cannot help wondering how Solomon might have fared if he had consistently followed his own advice. Now that his time is passing, he can only hope to convey that hard-bitten wisdom to future generations.

—PY

Daily Contemplation

Where did you look for wisdom before you became a believer or during times when you weren't following God?

DAY 130

How to Read Proverbs
Proverbs 10:1–23

Solomon had the ability to express his great wisdom in a very down-to-earth way. As a result, the book of Proverbs reads like a collection of folksy, commonsense advice. The practical guidance, intended to help you make your way in the world, skips from topic to topic. It comments on large issues as well as small ones: blabbermouthing, wearing out your welcome with neighbors, being unbearably cheerful too early in the morning.

Anybody can find exceptions to the generalities in Proverbs. For instance, Proverbs 10:4 says, "Lazy hands make a man poor, but diligent hands bring wealth" (TLV). Yet farmers who work diligently may go hungry during a drought, and lazy dreamers sometimes hit the lottery jackpot. Proverbs simply tells how life works most of the time; it gives the rule, not the exceptions. Normally, people who are godly, moral, hardworking, and wise will succeed in life. Fools and scoffers, though they appear successful, will pay a long-term price for their lifestyles.

The advice in Proverbs usually takes the form of brief, pungent "one-liners," so the book requires a different kind of reading than others in the Bible. It's hard to read several chapters in a row. Some people have made a practice of reading one chapter of Proverbs each day. With thirty-one chapters, the book can be read through once each month. The proverbs are meant to be taken in small doses, savored, digested, and gradually absorbed.

Many proverbs are written in a style called "parallelism," a word that describes the tendency of Hebrew poetry to repeat a thought in a slightly different way. In one such form, "synonymous parallelism," the second half of the proverb underscores and embellishes the message of the first half (10:10). In another form, "antithetical parallelism," a thought is followed by its opposite. In both kinds of parallelism, the trick is to compare each phrase with its pair in the other half of the proverb. For instance, in 10:4 "diligent hands" pairs with its opposite, "lazy hands," and "bring wealth" is the opposite of "make a man poor." Sometimes these comparisons bare subtle shades of meaning.

—PY

Daily Contemplation

Which of the proverbs in this chapter apply most directly to you?

DAY 131

Wisdom for Living
Proverbs 3:1–35

> Trust in the LORD with all your heart
>   and lean not on your own understanding;
> in all your ways submit to him,
>   and he will make your paths straight . . .
> Blessed are those who find wisdom,
>   those who gain understanding,
> for she is more profitable than silver
>   and yields better returns than gold.
> She is more precious than rubies;
>   nothing you desire can compare with her. (Proverbs 3:5–6, 13–15)

Who is the wisest person you know? Probably you'll come up with an elderly person, full of life experience, who has a wry twist of humor and a colorful way of putting things. Solomon must have been like that, and he passed down his observations about life in elegant, witty nuggets of insight.

Solomon did not sit around all day spouting proverbs in topical sequence. Most likely, those that survive in this book were assembled late in his life in no strict order. Thus reading Proverbs may at first remind you of reading the dictionary: You'll encounter short, self-contained items in a long list with little or no connection between them.

Even though the one-liners in Proverbs move quickly (and apparently randomly) from one subject to another, there is an overall objective behind the disorder. If you spend enough time in Proverbs, you will gain a subtle and practical understanding of life. Familiar themes keep showing up: the use and abuse of the tongue, wealth and poverty, keeping and losing one's temper, laziness, and hard work.

Yet for all its wisdom, Proverbs may well be the most misused book in the Bible. People often quote the proverbs as if they were absolute promises from God or rigid rules for living, when in fact few of them should be read that way. It's best to study the whole book to get its overall point of view on a subject. Or, you can spend a few minutes skimming through several chapters in search of key words such as *tongue*, *wealth*, or *lazy*.

—PY

Daily Contemplation

Have you ever asked God to grow you in wisdom? Take time now to pray for this growth.

DAY 132

A Time for Everything
Ecclesiastes 3:1–22

People surprised to find a book like Song of Songs in the Bible may be knocked flat by the book of Ecclesiastes. "Meaningless! Meaningless! Everything is meaningless!" cries the author of this bleak capitulation of despair (1:2).

Although Ecclesiastes mentions no author by name, it contains broad hints that King Solomon was, if not its author, at least its inspiration. It tells the story of the richest, wisest, most famous man in the world, who follows every pleasure impulse as far as it can lead him. This man, "the Teacher," finally collapses in regret and despair; he has squandered his life.

This early chapter gives a capsule summary of the book, beginning with an elegant poem about time and proceeding from there into musings about life typical of the Teacher's search for meaning. The author concludes that God has laid a "burden" on humanity that keeps us from finding ultimate satisfaction on earth. After a lifetime spent in the pursuit of pleasure, the Teacher asks, "Is that all there is?" Even the rare moments of peace and satisfaction he found were easily spoiled by the onrushing threat of death. According to the Teacher, life doesn't make sense outside of God and will, in fact, never fully make sense because we are not God.

But God has also "set eternity in the human heart" (3:11) We feel longings for something more: pleasures that will last forever, love that won't go sour, fulfillment and not boredom from our work.

The Teacher thus dangles between two states, feeling a steady drag toward despair but also a tug toward something higher. Much like a personal journal, the book of Ecclesiastes records a wise person's search for balance. The tension does not resolve in this chapter, and some readers wonder if it resolves at all. But Ecclesiastes ends with one final word of advice, the summation of all the Teacher's wisdom: "Fear God and keep his commandments, for this is the duty of all mankind" (12:13).

—PY

Daily Contemplation

The Teacher is painfully honest about his doubts and his despair. What portions of this chapter do you especially identify with?

DAY 133

Keys to Becoming Wise
Reflection

Solomon had no corner on wisdom. He may have been the wisest person to live, but he wasn't the only one with wisdom. His father, David, wrote about wisdom before Solomon was born. David in fact gives us the two most important cornerstones for acquiring wisdom: "You taught me wisdom in that secret place" (Psalm 51:6) and "The statutes of the Lord are trustworthy, making wise the simple" (Psalm 19:7). Wisdom comes straight from God to those in relationship with him, and following God's guidelines for living is the first step in moving from unwise to wise. Another psalmist echoes David's words: "The fear of the Lord is the beginning of wisdom" (Psalm 111:10).

Solomon writes more extensively about wisdom in Proverbs. He affirms that yes, "the Lord gives wisdom" (Proverbs 2:6). It was through his own request to God that he had received his wisdom. Then he gives several attitudes and actions that are key in gaining wisdom. The first involves humility. "With humility comes wisdom," he says (Proverbs 11:2). People who are quick to promote themselves aren't wise and won't become wise. When we're concerned with elevating ourselves in the eyes of others, we aim to determine our own destiny rather than letting God determine it, and this desire can never walk hand-in-hand with wisdom.

Solomon also writes about accepting advice and correction: "Wisdom is found in those who take advice" (Proverbs 13:10); "A rod and a reprimand impart wisdom" (Proverbs 29:15). When we're willing and able to accept wisdom from others, through both advice and criticism, we'll gain it more quickly than in trying to find it on our own.

People in our lives play a big role in making us wise or unwise. The choices we make in friends and in how we allot our time reflect how concerned we are with gaining wisdom. "Walk with the wise and become wise," Solomon says in Proverbs 13:20. The people with whom we surround ourselves help shape who we become. For example, those who know Jesus intimately will carry us into greater wisdom through him.

The way we interact with people in our lives provides another key to wisdom. The words we use and the things we say usher us deeper into wisdom or further from it. Impulsive rants usually result in regret. But when we choose our words carefully, knowing the impact they can have on other people and ourselves, we're displaying a heart that desires wisdom. "The hearts of the wise make their mouths prudent," Solomon says in Proverbs 16:23.

Where we place our energy and commitment represents the final key to wisdom. "The one who is wise saves lives," Solomon says in Proverbs 11:30. This is the final evidence of one who wants the things Jesus wants, who desires the same outlook on life he has. We can choose to focus our lives on ourselves and our interests or instead focus on God and his interests, which involve other people. If we focus on God, we will make time for those who need to know him. For a person growing in wisdom, this becomes a passion that is never quenched.

According to David and Solomon, wisdom is available to all who seek it in the right way. It's never too late. "Get wisdom," for it is "more precious than rubies" (Proverbs 4:7; 8:11). Who wouldn't want it? Only the unwise.

—BQ

Daily Contemplation

Where are you in possessing Solomon's keys to wisdom? Do you need to ask God for wisdom or for a commitment to his guidelines? Do you need to work on being humble, accepting advice or criticism, finding wise friends, or controlling your words? How much do you care about drawing other people to Jesus? Ask God to help you move further toward wisdom.

DAY 134

Israel Rebels Against Rehoboam
1 Kings 12:1–24

> The king answered the people harshly. . . . "My father made your yoke heavy; I will make it even heavier. My father scourged you with whips; I will scourge you with scorpions." So the king did not listen to the people, for this turn of events was from the LORD, to fulfill the word the LORD had spoken to Jeroboam . . . . When all the Israelites heard that Jeroboam had returned, they sent and called him to the assembly and made him king over all Israel. Only the tribe of Judah remained loyal to the house of David. (1 Kings 12:13–15, 20)

Under the leadership of David and Solomon, the nation of Israel finally becomes strong and prosperous. But even in their success, the twelve tribes display ongoing antagonism. Jealousy over land allotments and competing claims of superiority threaten to split them apart. And in the end Solomon's weaknesses seriously erode the kingdom. His lavish public projects lay a heavy tax burden on the citizens of Israel and force him to conscript some of them as virtual slaves. His moral failures undermine the spiritual unity of the nation, and the brief, shining vision of a covenant nation gradually fades away. After Solomon's death, Israel splits in two in 931 BC and slides toward ruin.

In a story reminiscent of Saul and David's early days, God makes known through a prophet his intentions to remove part of the kingdom of Israel from the hands of Rehoboam (REE-huh-BOH-uhm), Solomon's son and rightful heir to the throne, and give it to Jeroboam (JAIR-uh-BOH-uhm), a palace official. Like David, Jeroboam must go on the run after receiving the prophecy, because Solomon tries to kill him (1 Kings 11:26–40). When Solomon dies, the prophecy comes true. Rehoboam's greed for power turns all but the southern tribes of Judah and Benjamin against him. Jeroboam is crowned king of Israel, the northern kingdom, and Rehoboam rules over the southern kingdom of Judah.

—BQ

Daily Contemplation

Are you more focused on outward success, as was Rehoboam, or on the growth of your inner life with God?

PART 3

The Northern Kingdom—Israel

DAY 135

The Widow at Zarephath
1 Kings 17:1–24

The once-unified nation of Israel has split into the northern and southern kingdoms of Israel and Judah. The remaining part of the Old Testament can prove especially confusing: The two nations will have thirty-nine rulers between them, and a couple dozen prophets besides. To avoid getting hopelessly lost, keep these basic facts in mind: **Israel** is the breakaway northern kingdom, with a capital city of Samaria. All its rulers will prove unfaithful to God. **Judah** is the southern kingdom, with its capital of Jerusalem. In general, its rulers, descendants of David, will remain more faithful to God and his covenant, and consequently Judah survives 136 years longer.

Although the Bible discusses all thirty-nine rulers by name, after Solomon the stories of the kings speed up into a forgettable blur. God turns instead to his prophets.

Elijah, the wildest and woolliest prophet of all, first makes an appearance in this chapter. He illustrates better than anyone else the decisive change: Where King Solomon had worn jewelry and fine clothes and lived luxuriously in a gilded palace, Elijah wears a diaper-like covering of black camel's hair, sleeps in the wilderness, and has to beg—or pray—for handouts. He comes on the scene when Israel (the northern kingdom) is thriving politically but floundering spiritually. Queen Jezebel has just launched a murderous campaign to eliminate all true prophets of God and replace them with a thousand handpicked pagan priests.

This chapter shows glimpses of Elijah during his fugitive days. Although he is a moody prophet, subject to bouts of depression and self-doubt, he clearly has God on his side. The tender story of his healing a widow's son shows that God has not forgotten the "little people." Indeed, Jesus will later use this story as an example of God providing for a distraught Gentile woman outside the boundaries of Israel (Luke 4:24–26). The salvation of Israel will depend on how well they listen to prophets like Elijah.

—PY

Daily Contemplation

How has God reminded you this week that he cares about what matters to you?

DAY 136

Elijah on Mount Carmel
1 Kings 18:15–40

In ancient Africa, tribes would sometimes fight their battles single-combat style. Great armies would line up across from each other, waving their weapons menacingly and hurling insults back and forth. When tribal hatred reached a kind of critical mass, two warriors—only two—would step forward to fight on behalf of all the rest. Whoever drew blood first would prove the gods were on his side, and his opponent's army would surrender. Something like single-combat warfare takes place at a moment of deep crisis in Israel. As usual, the prophet Elijah occupies center stage.

Elijah journeys across Israel to a rugged mountain to confront his pagan enemies. Few scenes in history can match the one that transpires on windswept Mount Carmel (KAR-muhl). On one side stands a resplendent array of 850 prophets of Baal and Asherah (uh-SHEER-uh); on the other stands a lone, bedraggled desert prophet of God. Elijah lets the pagan prophets have the first turn. As they dance around an altar beseeching their gods, he sits back, enjoys the show, and taunts them to frenzy. "Maybe your god is traveling, or sleeping," he yells, and the priests slash themselves with swords until the blood runs.

Elijah may be outnumbered, but he proves a worthy adversary. When his time comes, he works the crowd like a master magician. He stacks the odds against a miracle by dousing the site with twelve large jars of water—the most precious commodity in Israel after a three-year drought. Just when it seems Elijah is perpetrating a huge national joke, the miracle happens: Fire falls from heaven. The heat melts even the stones and soil, and flames lick water from the trenches as if it were fuel. The crowd drops to the ground in fear and awe.

Elijah's very name means "The Lord is my God," and, in the final analysis, the showdown on Mount Carmel is no contest at all. Elijah goes on to orchestrate one of the greatest outbreaks of miracles in biblical history. It is as if God is sounding a loud, unmistakable final warning to the northern kingdom—a warning they fail to heed.

—PY

Daily Contemplation

In Old Testament times God was known to reveal himself in occasional spectacular public displays. Even if his power in your life hasn't been as showy, can you think of one instance in which it was clear to you that God was moving against all odds?

DAY 137

The Lord Appears to Elijah
1 Kings 19:1–18

> After the earthquake came a fire, but the LORD was not in the fire. And after the fire came a gentle whisper. When Elijah heard it, he pulled his cloak over his face and went out and stood at the mouth of the cave. (1 Kings 19:12–13)

Despite God's clear display of power on Mount Carmel, the prophet Elijah becomes terrified when King Ahab's (AY-hab) wife Jezebel vows to kill him. God has just rained down fire from heaven, resulting in the slaughter of hundreds of Baal prophets, but Elijah is emotionally drained. When the threat against him gets personal, it looms larger than the obvious truth of God's greater power. Although Elijah has been faithful in carrying out God's work, even this great man falters in his faith. Letting fear take hold, on impulse he runs for his life.

Nevertheless, God acts tenderly toward Elijah, even sending an angel to care for his needs. "Get up and eat, for the journey is too much for you" (1 Kings 19:7), an angel gently nourishes the exhausted prophet. In a journey that should have taken only fourteen days on foot, Elijah travels for forty, with God sustaining him along the way.

When he arrives at Mount Horeb—the mountain where God revealed himself to Moses and formed a covenant with Israel—Elijah confesses that he feels all alone in his loyalty to God. He has seen other prophets of God killed and feels sure he will be next. His vision is still one-sided. The great victories God wrought through Elijah have become buried under feelings of fear and failure.

This time God speaks not through a startling event but through a quiet whisper. Elijah has seen God's spectacular displays; now he needs to hear God's gentle voice. God will use Elijah in new ways—ways that will be easier on the prophet and will continue to reassure him of his calling as God's beloved servant.

—BQ

Daily Contemplation

When have you needed God to pick you up and care for you?

DAY 138

Elijah Taken Up to Heaven
2 Kings 2:1–18

As they were walking along and talking together, suddenly a chariot of fire and horses of fire appeared and separated the two of them, and Elijah went up to heaven in a whirlwind. Elisha saw this and cried out, "My father! My father! The chariots and horsemen of Israel!" And Elisha saw him no more. Then he took hold of his garment and tore it in two. Elisha then picked up Elijah's cloak that had fallen from him and went back and stood on the bank of the Jordan. He took the cloak that had fallen from Elijah and struck the water with it. "Where now is the LORD, the God of Elijah?" he asked. When he struck the water, it divided to the right and to the left, and he crossed over. The company of the prophets from Jericho, who were watching, said, "The spirit of Elijah is resting on Elisha." And they went to meet him and bowed to the ground before him. (2 Kings 2:11–15)

God had given two prophets, Elijah and Elisha, to one another as teacher and student, but also as partners for mutual support. The time, however, has come for Elijah to leave the earth and for Elisha to carry on his ministry. Only once before has God taken someone to heaven apart from death. Enoch was the first (Genesis 5:24). Now in a show of honor for a prophet who has served God well through a period of Israel's idolatry, God sends escorts to carry Elijah into his presence.

Elisha, a devoted spiritual son, takes up Elijah's deserted cloak and assumes the mantle of God-given authority that has passed to him. Having seen Elijah's departure, he now receives the double portion of his spirit as promised.

—BQ

Daily Contemplation

Whom has God placed in your life as a support and spiritual partner?

DAY 139

Hearing God's Voice
Reflection

At times Elijah acted without any apparent indication that he heard God's voice. He simply seemed to know what God wanted him to do. He told the widow her flour would not run out. He called on God to send fire from heaven and consume the altar. Both were clearly God's will. At other times God spoke distinctly and directly to Elijah. He heard God's audible voice question him in a cave, and later God merely whispered to him. Elijah heard God speak in many ways. Was he specially gifted, or can anyone who walks with God expect to hear him clearly?

In ***The Christian's Secret of a Happy Life***, Hannah Whitall Smith teaches that beyond a doubt we can still hear God's voice. Smith explains that God speaks through the Scriptures, providential circumstances, the convictions of our higher judgment, and the inward impressions of the Holy Spirit on our minds. "His voice will always be in harmony with itself, no matter how many different ways he may speak," she explains. "The voices may be many, the message can be but one. If God tells me in one voice to do or to leave undone anything, He cannot possibly tell me the opposite in another voice. If there is a contradiction in the voices, the speakers cannot be the same."[15]

The Bible gives us guidance on what we will encounter in life. As we become familiar with the Bible, we can make decisions that fall in line with God's voice found there. Smith gives one caution: "It is essential, however, in this connection to remember that the Bible is a book of principles, and not a book of disjointed aphorisms. Isolated texts may often be made to sanction things to which the principles of Scripture are totally opposed."[16]

Sometimes we will feel a need for more specific direction than what the Bible can provide. Then we must look also at how our circumstances are working to lead us one way or another, at our common sense "enlightened by the Spirit of God," and at any strong sense the Holy Spirit seems to be impressing upon us. "If any one of these tests fail, it is not safe to proceed, but you must wait in quiet trust until the Lord shows you the point of harmony, which He surely will, sooner or later, if it is His voice that is speaking."[17]

Smith reminds us that sometimes we will hear voices other than God's. These could come from the strong opinions of others around us, from our own moodiness or emotional state, or from spiritual enemies who would like to mislead us. We don't need to fear these voices, but we should be careful about letting them guide us. It's important to take time to discern whether we indeed hear God's voice.

We can trust God to make his voice clear if we are willing to hear it and be patient in waiting until God makes us sure.

> Take all your present perplexities, then, to the Lord. Tell Him you only want to know and obey His voice, and ask Him to make it plain to you. Promise Him that you will obey, whatever it may be. Believe implicitly that He is guiding you, according to His word. In all doubtful things, wait for clear light. Look and listen for His voice continually; and the moment you are sure of it, then, but not until then, yield an immediate obedience. Trust Him to make you forget the impression if it is not His will; and if it continues, and is in harmony with all His other voices, do not be afraid to obey.[18]

—BQ

Daily Contemplation

In which areas of your life do you need to hear God's voice? Ask God to help you hear him clearly and then to obey him completely.

DAY 140

The Widow's Oil; A Son Restored
2 Kings 4:1–36

> When Elisha reached the house, there was the boy lying dead on his couch. He went in, shut the door on the two of them and prayed to the LORD. Then he got on the bed and lay on the boy, mouth to mouth, eyes to eyes, hands to hands. As he stretched himself out on him, the boy's body grew warm. Elisha turned away and walked back and forth in the room and then got on the bed and stretched out on him once more. The boy sneezed seven times and opened his eyes. (2 Kings 4:32–35)

Today's stories demonstrate God's love for those who remain faithful to him in Israel. Although much of the nation has turned to Baal worship, some continue following God and honoring his prophets. God clearly cares for women, who were considered inferior in most Near Eastern societies of the time. God holds no gender bias in his concern for those who honor him.

In these stories both women demonstrate a strong faith in God's power to help them. The first, a widow, is doubly in need. Not only does she lack a husband to provide for her; she is the widow of a prophet and has been left with little. God provides in a way neither she nor anyone around her would have guessed.

The second woman, a Shunammite, professes her faith in God at a moment of crisis. She feels deceived and disappointed at receiving a son only to lose him again, yet she knows that God is greater than her disappointment. Even in her grief she acts on her belief. Most likely, the Shunammite woman's story of her son's birth and his return to life spread throughout Israel. Once more God shows his sovereignty over the popular Baal, hailed as a god of fertility.

—BQ

Daily Contemplation

When has God met your need in a way you didn't expect?

DAY 141

Naaman Healed of Leprosy
2 Kings 5:1-27

While Elijah was a loner, a fugitive, and a prophet who preached a stern message of judgment, his protégé Elisha lives among the common people and stresses hope and God's grace.

Elisha has a colorful life: He leads a school of prophets, serves as a military spy, advises kings, and even anoints revolutionaries. Easily recognizable with his bald head and wooden walking staff, he becomes a famous figure in Israel, especially as reports of his miracles spread. Elisha asked for a double portion of Elijah's spirit, and the Bible pointedly records about twice as many miracles performed by Elisha. Many of these miracles prefigure the miracles Jesus himself will later perform; they show God caring for the needs of poor and outcast people.

In this chapter Elisha is seen offering assistance to Naaman (NAY-uh-muhn), a high-ranking enemy general. Naaman's pilgrimage shows how far Elisha's fame has spread. A pagan king agrees to seek help from God's prophet in order to get a general's health restored.

Elisha's brusque treatment of generals and kings contrasts sharply with the tenderness he shows toward the poor and oppressed. The bizarre procedure he prescribes, along with his refusal to take payment, offends Naaman. Elisha, however, is making it clear that healing comes not through magical powers or a shaman's secret technique but through God—and God requires obedience and humility even of five-star generals with piles of gold.

Jesus will refer to this story at the beginning of his ministry (Luke 4:27). He makes the same point as Elisha: Don't try to "box in" God. He is to be obeyed, on his own terms, not manipulated.

—PY

Daily Contemplation

One of my colleagues has described the Christian life as "living by God's surprises." Has God ever surprised you?

DAY 142

Elisha and the Chariots of Fire
2 Kings 6:8–23

When the servant of the man of God got up and went out early the next morning, an army with horses and chariots had surrounded the city. "Oh no, my lord! What shall we do?" the servant asked. "Don't be afraid," the prophet answered. "Those who are with us are more than those who are with them." And Elisha prayed, "Open his eyes, LORD, so that he may see." Then the LORD opened the servant's eyes, and he looked and saw the hills full of horses and chariots of fire all around Elisha. As the enemy came down toward him, Elisha prayed to the LORD, "Strike this army with blindness." So he struck them with blindness, as Elisha had asked. (2 Kings 6:15–18)

Through Elisha, God has miraculously reversed a widow's financial situation, brought life to a childless woman and a dead boy, and healed a man from leprosy. In this passage, we see that God's miraculous care for his people can also extend to the battlefield.

At key times God has intervened in wartime to make his power known to the nations surrounding Israel. During Elisha's era, Israel was often raided by its neighbor Aram (AlR-uhm). This passage shows how God used his power in novel ways to defuse one tense military standoff.

Biblical prophets have an enhanced vision that lets them see things other people don't. In this account, Elisha is exercising his "seer" gifts as a secret weapon, to scout out the enemy's next moves. And when his servant sounds an alarm about their plight—surrounded by an army with horses and chariots—Elisha simply "opens the servant's eyes" to see God's invisible army of horses and chariots of fire.

In most cases we do not have access to see spiritual reality so directly, but this time Elisha's servant catches a momentary glimpse of that spiritual reality. In a stroke of delicious irony, the story contrasts Elisha's enhanced vision with a state of temporary blindness imposed on Aram's forces. Then, in a lovely display of peacemaking, Elisha treats the captives to a feast and sends them home. God has once again kept watch over his people and spared many lives.

—BQ

―――――――――― *Daily Contemplation* ――――――――――

What battle have you faced in the past and found that God came through in a powerful way?

DAY 143

Greater Is God in Us
Reflection

Jim Cymbala, longtime pastor of the Brooklyn Tabernacle in New York City, tells of his cry to God in the early days of the church. He had just begun as substitute pastor to this small, inner-city congregation. Services drew about twenty people, most of whom were poor and some vagrant. He recalls the church's plight when it lacked funds to pay the mortgage.

That Monday, my day off, I remember praying, "Lord, you have to help me. I don't know much—but I do know that we have to pay this mortgage."

I went to church on Tuesday. *Well, maybe someone will send some money out of the blue*, I told myself, *like what happened so often with George Mueller and his orphanage back in England—he just prayed and a letter or a visitor would arrive to meet his need.*

The mail came that day—and there was nothing but bills and fliers.

Now I was trapped. I went upstairs, sat at my little desk, put my head down, and began to cry. "God," I sobbed, "what can I do? We can't even pay the mortgage." . . .

I called out to the Lord for a full hour or so. Eventually, I dried my tears—and a new thought came. *Wait a minute! Besides the mail slot in the front door, the church also has a post office box. I'll go across the street and see what's there. Surely God will answer my prayer!*

With renewed confidence, I walked across the street, crossed the post office lobby, and twirled the knob on the little box. I peered inside . . .

Nothing.

As I stepped back into the sunshine, trucks roared down Atlantic Avenue. If one had flattened me just then, I wouldn't have felt any lower. Was God abandoning us? Was I doing something that displeased him? I trudged wearily back across the street to the little building.

As I unlocked the door, I was met with another surprise. There on the foyer floor was something that hadn't been there just three minutes earlier: a simple white envelope. No address, no stamp—nothing. Just a white envelope.

With trembling hands I opened it to find . . . ***two $50 bills***.

I began shouting all by myself in the empty church. "God, you came through! You came through!" We had $160 in the bank, and with this $100 we could make the mortgage payment. My soul let out a deep "Hallelujah!" What a lesson for a disheartened young pastor.

To this day I don't know where that money came from. I only know it was a sign to me that God was near—and faithful.[19]

This miracle was only the beginning for Cymbala. He took on the full-time pastorate of the Brooklyn Tabernacle and in twenty-five years watched God build the church to a congregation of six thousand each Sunday. Money couldn't hold God back. The seemingly hopeless situation of the homeless, drug addicts, and prostitutes didn't thwart God's Spirit. Steadily he drew these needy people to himself and to each other to establish a place of healing in New York City.

"Those who are with us are more than those who are with them" (2 Kings 6:16). The tempter loves to get us in situations in which hope seems lost. But, like Elisha, we have God's horses and chariots encircling us in the times we cry out in despair. Next time the cry of Elisha's servant passes your lips—"Oh, Lord, what will I do?"—take a look, in your mind's eye, at the battalion standing ready for you. God's strength is more real than the despair you are feeling.

—BQ

Daily Contemplation

What battle do you face? Ask God for help in seeing the forces of heaven that are standing guard ready to fight for you.

DAY 144

Rend Your Heart
Joel 2:1–32

Scenes from the lives of Elijah and Elisha—fire on Mount Carmel, the widow's oil, Naaman's healing, the chariots of fire—are among the most familiar of Old Testament stories. But the prophets who follow them perform few miracles, relying less on spectacular displays of power and more on the power of the Word.

The prophet Joel provides a brief introduction to the style of the writing prophets. No one knows for sure when he delivered his messages—they could have come anywhere within a four-century span. No one is even sure whether he lived in Israel in the north or Judah in the south. But in gripping prose he warns his people of a terrible disaster to come. This chapter captures as well as any the essential message of all the prophets.

A day of judgment. Nearly every prophet begins with words meant to inspire fear and dread. Some warn of invading armies, and some of natural disasters. For example, Joel paints vivid pictures of an army of locusts. The locusts could symbolically represent human armies but may also be taken literally. People who have lived through a locust invasion never forget the experience.

A call to repentance. The prophets raise alarm with good reason, for they see such disasters as a consequence of their nation's unfaithfulness to God. They urgently call on their people to turn from their evil ways. Joel 2:13 could stand as a single, eloquent summary of the heart of the prophets' message.

A future of hope. Every biblical prophet, no matter how dour, gets around to a word of hope. Taken together, prophets paint a picture of a future when God will make right everything wrong with the earth, a time when the world as it is will finally match the world as God wants it.

Joel 2 gives a fine capsule summary of this threefold message.

—PY

Daily Contemplation

Did you ever rend your heart before God? Do you think this is something a person does once or regularly?

DAY 145

Jonah Flees from the Lord
Jonah 1:1–2:10

> The word of the LORD came to Jonah son of Amittai: "Go to the great city of Ninevah and preach against it, because its wickedness has come up before me." (Jonah 1:1–2)

In one of the most illustrative stories of the Old Testament, a reluctant prophet runs from God's call and receives a most mysterious comeuppance. God tells Jonah to go to the great city of Nineveh (NIN-uh-vuh) in neighboring Assyria and preach to the people about their wickedness.

Such a task may sound unpleasant, but Jonah has deeper reasons for refusing to go. He discerns that God is not simply full of anger and vindictiveness toward people outside of God's chosen nation but has a heart big enough to love these wicked people if they will simply repent. Sensing God's compassion, Jonah reacts with the heart of a jealous son. No matter that God has offered him and his people eternity; Jonah can't stand the thought of allowing others into that future.

Jonah has barely begun to run when God puts a stop to the game. Jonah faces death at sea, then spends three days in the depths, and finally walks the earth once again—an experience that foreshadows Jesus' own story.

Some have suggested that Jonah's travail is too fantastic to be true, but others have noted that a Mediterranean sperm whale can swallow a man whole, and that its laryngeal pouch could hold enough air for a person to survive a few days. Regardless of natural explanations, the Bible presents the story of Jonah as a miraculous event displaying God's compassion both on his servant in Israel and on people outside of Israel.

Ezekiel declares that God takes "no pleasure in the death of the wicked, but [desires] rather that they turn from their ways and live" (Ezekiel 33:11). To those in Israel who joyfully claimed God's blessings for themselves but were quick to wish God's wrath upon their enemies, God gives a sobering revelation. Here in Jonah we see further proof of God's love for Gentiles—a love he will openly proclaim after his Son's final sacrifice.

—BQ

Daily Contemplation

Do you tend to reflect more of Jonah's jealousy or God's compassion for sinful people who need God?

DAY 146

Jonah Goes to Nineveh
Jonah 3:1–4:11

Jonah's journey to Nineveh, complete with an ocean storm and a detour in the belly of a whale, often becomes the focus of the account of Jonah. As a result, readers miss the central point, the reason for Jonah's misadventures in the first place. He is rebelling against God's mercy. Jonah offers a true-life study of how hard it is to follow the biblical command "love your enemies." While many people admire that command, few find it easy to put into practice.

Jonah has an understandable reason as to why he balked at God's orders to preach in Nineveh, for that city in his day was the capital of an empire renowned for its cruelty. Assyrian soldiers had no qualms about "scorched earth" military tactics; typically, after destroying an enemy's fields and cities they would slaughter the conquered peoples or hammer iron hooks through their noses or lower lips and lead them away as slaves. Jonah wants no part in giving such bullies a chance to repent. Amazingly, though, God loves Nineveh and wants to save the city, not destroy it. He knows the people are ripe for change.

The book of Jonah powerfully expresses God's yearning to forgive, and these two brief chapters fill in the lesser-known details of Jonah's mission. To the prophet's disgust, a simple announcement of doom sparks a spiritual revival in pagan Nineveh. And Jonah, sulking under a shriveled vine, admits he has suspected God's soft heart all along. He could not trust God—could not, that is, trust him to be harsh and unrelenting toward Nineveh. As one of Robert Frost's characters summed up the message of Jonah, "You can't trust God to be unmerciful."[20]

The book also reveals God's ultimate purpose for his chosen people: He wants them, like Jonah, to reach out to other people and demonstrate his love and forgiveness. Nineveh's wholehearted response puts the Israelites to shame, for not once have they responded to a prophet as these Assyrians have.

—PY

Daily Contemplation

Have you ever consciously tried to love the "enemies" in your life?

DAY 147

Working with God
Reflection

Following God involves hard work. His love and blessings may be easy to receive, but when obedience to God requires us to do something contrary to our human nature, a conflict sets in that tests our commitment. God desires his holiness to take root in us, and he can use precisely these trials of the will to make us more like himself.

As with Jonah, our greatest trials come when we feel threatened or hurt by others yet sense God's heart willing us to love anyway with a power that overcomes our fear and dislike. God sets the pattern: Despite countless reasons to dislike us, his heart of love overcomes his dislike and he opens his arms to us. Can we allow that supernatural love to spill into our hearts and then flow into the lives of those we dislike?

Corrie ten Boom tells of the ultimate test of her willingness to let God love through her a person she had every reason to hate. She was speaking about God's forgiveness to a crowd at a church in Munich, Germany, in 1947. Only a few years earlier, Corrie and her sister, Betsie, had been imprisoned in the Ravensbrück concentration camp for concealing Jews in their home during the Nazi occupation of Holland. Corrie had watched her sister die a slow, painful death in the camp.

Now, as Corrie stood watching people file out of the church, solemn after her challenging message, Corrie found herself being tested to the core. She spotted in the crowd a man wearing a nondescript hat and overcoat. In a flash she recalled the same face framed in a skull-and-crossbones cap and blue uniform—the garb of a Nazi guard. Suddenly she was back in the huge room at Ravensbrück, filing naked with her sister and the other prisoners past this same set of eyes. Although he didn't seem to recognize her, she had no doubt about his identity.

The man congratulated her on the message and expressed his relief at knowing his sins were, in her words, at the bottom of the sea. Corrie fumbled with her purse rather than taking his hand. This was the first time she had been confronted face-to-face with one of her captors. The man went on to explain that he had been a guard at Ravensbrück, the camp she had spoken of in her talk. And then he revealed that he had become a believer in Christ since the war. He'd accepted God's forgiveness, but could he have Corrie's forgiveness, he wondered? Again he extended his hand.

She froze, thoughts of Betsie's agonizing death running through her mind. How could she with the shake of a hand simply erase what had happened? She had to do it. Along with the images of Betsie came the words of Jesus, "For if you forgive other people when they sin against you, your heavenly Father will also forgive you. But if you do not forgive others their sins, your Father will not forgive your sins" (Matthew 6:14–15). Corrie knew that not only does God require forgiveness; it is the only way to rebuild life after tragedy. Those who nursed bitterness toward the Nazis were trapped in their hatred and consumed by it. She also knew that forgiveness is an affair of the will rather than the heart. We may not feel like forgiving, but we can make a decision to forgive and trust God to supply the feelings in time.

She lifted her hand and prayed for help. As she did, a warmth traveled down her arm and filled her whole body. Blinking back the tears, Corrie offered heartfelt words of forgiveness, sensing God's love gripping her more intensely than ever before. His love not only supplied what she lacked; it filled her in a greater way than she could have imagined.[21]

—BQ

Daily Contemplation

Who has been most difficult for you to forgive and love? How would you feel if this person reached out a hand and asked for your forgiveness? Do you want to forgive even if he or she doesn't request it? Ask God for help in forgiving and loving despite your feelings (and in the realization that love does not always require us to be in relationship with a person).

DAY 148

Israel Has Not Returned to God
Amos 4:1–13

Biblical prophets represent a wide spectrum of social backgrounds and personality types, but modern-day cartoonists tend to perpetuate a single stereotyped image. And the fact is, Amos fits the stereotype. He is the kind to stand on street corners with a signboard and rail against the whole miserable world.

Ironically, Amos appears on the scene when Israel, the northern kingdom, is booming. They have beaten back all their traditional enemies and even invaded neighboring Judah, seizing land and prisoners. For a change, the government is stable: King Jeroboam II presides over a half century of prosperity and strength. People are too busy enjoying the good life to listen to the rantings of a prophet, and for precisely that reason Amos speaks in italics and exclamation points.

Unlike Jonah, Amos is not a professional prophet. He is a man of the land, a shepherd and a tender of sycamore trees. A migrant to Israel from the south, he speaks with a rural accent and is probably the butt of many jokes by city sophisticates.

Amos the peasant cannot get over what he finds in the northern cities. The luxurious lifestyles shock him: gorgeous couches, beds of carved ivory, summer homes, top-grade meat, fine wine. To Amos it seems obvious that this extravagance is built on a foundation of injustice: oppression of the poor, slavery, dishonest business practices, court bribes, privilege bought with money.

Lulled into security by their powerful, victorious army, the Israelites think they are safe for generations. But, as Amos warns, Israel cannot forever push God into a small corner of their lives, to be brought out like a magic charm whenever they need him.

"Israel, prepare to meet your God!" Amos shouts from the street corners, but those words have about as much impact in his day as they do in ours. Nevertheless, the prophet's warnings prove true: In a remarkably short time, Israel will fall apart. A mere thirty years after Jeroboam II's reign, the northern kingdom of Israel ceases to exist.

Amos is not a comfortable book to read—its message hits too close to our own time, when nations judge success by the size of gross national product and military forces. For that reason alone, it deserves a close look.

—PY

Daily Contemplation

What parallels do you see between Amos's time and our own?

DAY 149

Hosea's Wife and Children
Hosea 1:1–3:5

God sent prophets to Israel and Judah to meet the need of the moment. When people were cocky, self-indulgent, and spiritually deaf, a screamer like Amos appeared on the scene. But suffering people called for another tone. Just a few years after Amos, as Israel was breaking apart and sliding toward chaos, a word from God came to Hosea (hoh-ZAY-uh). To a shattered nation, Hosea brings a hope-filled message of grace and forgiveness.

Most books of the prophets focus on the audience and all the things they've done wrong. Hosea, in contrast, shines the spotlight on God. What is it like to be God? How must he feel when his chosen people reject him and go panting after false gods? As if words alone are too weak to convey his passion, God asks the brave prophet Hosea to act out a living parable. He marries a loose woman named Gomer, who, true to form, soon runs away and commits adultery. Only by living out that drama could Hosea understand, and then express, something of how Israel's rebuke feels to God.

After all that Gomer has done, God instructs Hosea simply to invite her back and forgive her. The pattern hopelessly repeats itself. Gomer bears two children—but is Hosea really their father? According to the Mosaic law, he should turn his adulterous wife out on the street or have her tried in court. What Hosea does, and God does, is unheard of.

Hosea is one of the most emotional books in the Bible, an outpouring of suffering love from God's heart. Read aloud, this chapter sounds like a fight between a husband and wife overheard through thin walls. The book of Hosea, in fact, represents the first time God's covenant with Israel has been described in terms of marriage. It shows that God longs for his people with the tenderness and hunger that a lover feels toward his bride.

In the covenant, Israel agreed to love and obey God no matter what, "till death do us part." But as they prosper in the new land, that flame of love dies. The old covenant is fractured. As Hosea tells it, the death of their love breaks God's heart. God can only promise another chance, with a new covenant at a future time when "you will call me 'my husband'; you will no longer call me 'my master'" (Hosea 2:16).

—PY

Daily Contemplation

Hosea describes various stages in Israel's relationship to God: courtship, engagement, newly married, unfaithfulness, separation. What stage are you in with God?

DAY 150

God's Love for Israel
Hosea 11:1-11

Many people carry around the image of God as an impersonal force, something akin to the law of gravity. Hosea portrays almost the opposite: a God of passion and fury and tears and love. A God mourning over Israel's rejection of him.

God uses Hosea's unhappy story to illustrate his own whipsaw emotions. That first blush of love when he found Israel, he says, was like finding grapes in the desert. But as Israel breaks his trust again and again, he has to endure the awful shame of a wounded lover. God's words carry a tone surprisingly like self-pity: "I am like a moth to Ephraim (EE-free-uhm), like rot to the people of Judah" (Hosea 5:12).

The powerful image of a jilted lover explains why, in a chapter like Hosea 11, God's emotions seem to vacillate so. He is preparing to obliterate Israel—wait, now he is weeping, holding out open arms—no, he is sternly pronouncing judgment again. Those shifting moods seem hopelessly irrational, except to anyone who has been jilted by a lover.

Is there a more powerful human feeling than that of betrayal? Ask a high school girl whose boyfriend has just dumped her for someone more exciting. Or tune your radio to a country-western station and listen to the lyrics of infidelity. Or check out the murders reported in the daily newspaper, an amazing number of which trace back to a fight with an estranged lover. Hosea and God demonstrate in living color exactly what it is like to love someone desperately and get nothing in return. Not even God, with all his power, can force a human being to love him.

Virtually every chapter of Hosea talks about the "prostitution" or "adultery" of God's people. God the lover will not share his bride with anyone else. Yet, amazingly, even when she turns her back on him, he sticks with her. He is willing to suffer, in hope that someday she will change. Hosea proves that God longs not to punish but to love.

—PY

Daily Contemplation

What is your strongest memory of feeling betrayed?

DAY 151

Israel Exiled Because of Sin
2 Kings 17:1–41

An impressive lineup of prophets all tried their hand at convincing the northern kingdom, Israel, to change its ways. But neither the miracles of Elijah and Elisha nor the shouts of Amos nor the impassioned pleas of Hosea had much effect. When times of trouble came, the nation turned toward the gods of their neighbors and frantically signed up military allies; they never turned wholeheartedly to God.

The day of judgment so harrowingly foretold by the prophets is here recorded in the flat, matter-of-fact language of history. The end for the northern kingdom of Israel comes when Israel's kings, against all the prophets' advice, seek to purchase political protection, first from Assyria and then from Egypt. After discovering the double cross, Assyria sends an army against Israel.

In early wars Assyrian conquerors exterminated their enemies, but in later years they adopted the technique of deporting their victims and replacing them with foreigners from other conquered territories. The radical disruption of their societies tended to keep conquered peoples from regrouping and rising up as a new threat. In keeping with that policy, Assyria deports 27,290 captives from the land of Israel, dispersing the "ten lost tribes of Israel."

These émigrés the Assyrians replace with foreigners who form a new identity as "Samaritans," a group that will exist in New Testament times and in fact can still be found in modern Israel. Samaritan settlers combine their native religions with some reverence for the true God.

After this chapter, the Bible's attention turns south toward Judah, the collective name for the two surviving tribes of Israelites. Why does the Assyrian tragedy happen? Second Kings diagnoses idolatry as the chief cause of Israel's moral collapse. Unfortunately, the practice has already gained a foothold in the southern kingdom as well.

—PY

―――――― *Daily Contemplation* ――――――

What kind of idolatry might believers today fall into? The worship of possessions? People? Ideas? Image? Pleasure? Comfort? Family?

DAY 152

God's Love Story
Reflection

Everything beautiful and right—even embarrassingly so—about Solomon's Song of Songs is despoiled in the book of Hosea and in Israel's continuing story in 2 Kings. Song of Songs was a celebration of blossoming love between a newly married man and woman. Hosea is a lament over married love gone sour and crushed by repeated unfaithfulness.

If ever we wonder whether God could understand the thrill of new love, we need only read the Song of Songs. God preserved this song for the Bible to let us know that not only does he understand, but he also rejoices in new and enduring love between a man and a woman. This love is part of his plan, and he delights in it as deeply as we do.

If we wonder whether God could know the depths of pain we feel when betrayed or rejected, we have only to read Hosea. This oft-forgotten book of the Old Testament can provide words of empathy and solidarity to believers shaken by another's unfaithfulness. Not only does God understand such pain, but he actually endured it, and still does.

If God has the capacity to love far beyond our limited ability, he also has the capacity to hurt from betrayal more deeply than we could ever hurt. We cannot grasp all God has given to his people, a gift that includes, ultimately, the sacrifice of his Son, and to have that gift rejected again and again causes him indescribable pain. God knows the cries that escape from the wordless places within us—our cries are faint echoes of his own.

Each time we suffer in a relationship that should be filled with love and life, God embraces us and reminds us that he understands our pain intimately, personally. In this pain we move closer to him with a new appreciation of his faithful love.

—BQ

Daily Contemplation

Whose rejection or betrayal is hurting you? Ask God for the help you need in coping with your feelings. As you pray, thank God for this promise to you: "Great is our Lord and mighty in power; his understanding has no limit" (Psalm 147:5).

PART 4

The Southern Kingdom—Judah

DAY 153

Jehoshaphat Defeats Moab and Ammon
2 Chronicles 20:1–30

So far our readings have sampled the two-hundred-year history of Israel, which began sliding away from God from the very first days after its birth as a nation. Yet the Bible devotes far more space to the kings and prophets of the southern kingdom. Of the nineteen men and one woman who rule Judah, at least a handful demonstrate a quality of spiritual leadership unmatched in the northern kingdom. Judah proves more faithful in living up to the covenant with God, and chiefly for that reason it outlasts Israel by nearly a century and a half.

This chapter tells of the extraordinary king named Jehoshaphat, one of Judah's early rulers. No ruler of Judah had a wholly peaceful reign, and as a result much of the action in 2 Chronicles takes place on a battlefield, like this story. Here is the book's philosophy of war in a nutshell: *If you trust in your own military might or that of powerful neighbors, you will lose. Instead, humble yourself and rely totally on God—regardless of the odds against you.*

As the kings of Judah demonstrate with monotonous regularity, it requires uncommon courage to rely on God alone at a moment of great peril. Even the best of them dip into the royal treasury to purchase help from neighboring allies. But King Jehoshaphat provides a textbook example of the proper response. When invading armies threaten, he calls the entire nation together in a giant prayer meeting. On the day of battle, he sends a choir in front of his army to sing praises to God.

Although Jehoshaphat's tactics may seem more suitable for a church service than a battlefield, they actually work. The enemy forces all turn against each other, and Judah's army marches home victorious.

This bright moment of national faith shines out from a very mottled historical record. By his public prayer and personal example, King Jehoshaphat shows what can happen when a leader places complete trust in God.

—PY

Daily Contemplation

Do you know of a leader who has this kind of trust in God?

DAY 154

The Lord's Case Against Israel
Micah 6:1–16

Not every king of Judah has Jehoshaphat's faith and courage. As the years grind on, the same decadence that has characterized the northern kingdom of Israel spreads like an epidemic through Judah. Other parts of the Bible detail Judah's faults: One notorious king, Ahaz (AY-haz), sets up foreign altars, offers his own children in human sacrifice, and shutters the Lord's temple. Along with the religious corruption comes every other kind of sin: dishonesty, greed, bribery, injustice.

Around the same time that Amos is blasting Israel in the north, God calls another country preacher, Micah (MI-kuh), to deliver similar words of warning to Judah. Micah, a prophet who gets emotionally caught up in his message, lives in tumultuous times. At one point, Judah loses a hundred and twenty thousand soldiers in a single day (2 Chronicles 28:6). The nation watches in fear as Assyria, the chief power of the day, brutally smashes the northern kingdom. What will keep Judah from a similar fate? That very prospect of judgment is what makes Micah "howl like a jackal and moan like an owl" (1:8).

Chapter 6 of the book of Micah opens with an impassioned plea from God. "My people, what have I done to you?" God asks. He reviews the history of his chosen people, reminding them of his great works on their behalf. In his rhetorical response, Micah makes clear that God desires true, heartfelt changes, not just a veneer of religion: "What does the LORD require of you? To act justly and to love mercy and to walk humbly with your God" (6:8).

Micah concludes darkly that his people, afflicted with the same sickness as their relatives to the north, will meet the same end. Even so, Micah sees light ahead. Amid graphic predictions of destruction, Micah gives clear predictions of the Messiah, the future leader from the tiny town of Bethlehem who will offer new hope to the earth (5:2).

—PY

Daily Contemplation

How would you feel about adopting these words from Micah as a life motto: "To act justly and to love mercy and to walk humbly with your God"? Would anything have to change in your life?

DAY 155

Hezekiah Celebrates Passover
2 Chronicles 30:1–27

Toward the end of Micah's career, just as the situation in Judah is deteriorating, another great king takes the throne. In fact, 2 Chronicles spends more time on Hezekiah (HEZ-uh-KI-uh) than on anyone else. The very first year of his reign, he leads a program to restore the temple, which has fallen into disrepair from lack of use. Hezekiah turns the tables on Judah's priests: He stands in the temple square and delivers a rousing sermon to ***them***.

When Hezekiah decides to sponsor a huge religious festival, he encounters scorn and ridicule. But a king's proclamation carries certain weight, and the nation finally does come together in a remarkable scene of happiness and unity. Hezekiah even sends "missionary" couriers to the devastated lands to the north, and some survivors of the Assyrian scourge make their way to Jerusalem.

This chapter closely resembles 1 Kings 8 and its story of Solomon's dedication of the temple. Hezekiah intends to renew the covenant with God in hopes of forestalling God's judgment. The details of the festival celebration show just how badly Judah has neglected the covenant: There are too few priests to purify all the worshipers, and Hezekiah has to bend the rules in order to proceed.

It is no accident that Hezekiah organizes his festival around the Passover. That day marks the birth of a nation, when God freed his people from slavery in Egypt (see Exodus 12). In a real sense, the Passover sealed the covenant, and Hezekiah is determined to remind the nation of its heritage.

Despite the initial skepticism, the people of Judah get caught up in the celebration and, as in Solomon's day, spontaneously decide to stay another seven days. "There was great joy in Jerusalem," the Bible reports, "for since the days of Solomon son of David king of Israel there had been nothing like this in Jerusalem" (2 Chronicles 30:26).

—PY

Daily Contemplation

What spiritual event have you attended that has had a great impact on you? Did you get the feeling God was honored at this event?

DAY 156

Isaiah's Commission
Isaiah 6:1–13

This chapter flashes back to a scene that took place two decades before Hezekiah became king. The prophet Isaiah, a giant of Jewish history, received a direct, dramatic call from God, as recounted in this chapter.

As Isaiah begins his work, Judah seems strong and wealthy. Yet Isaiah sees signs of grave danger—the very same signs that have alarmed his contemporary, the prophet Micah. Men go around drunk. Women care more about their clothes than about their neighbors' hunger. People give lip service to God and keep up the outward appearance of religion but little more.

External dangers loom even larger: On all sides, monster empires are burgeoning. The nation of Judah, says Isaiah, stands at a crossroads. It can either regain its footing or begin a dangerous slide downward.

Two kings, Jotham (JAH-thuhm) and Ahaz, pay Isaiah little heed. Nevertheless, in a remarkable turnaround the new king Hezekiah appoints Isaiah as one of his most trusted advisors. In any moment of crisis, he calls upon the prophet.

Not every prophet blasts the establishment from street corners. Isaiah spends his days in the corridors of power, offering political advice and helping set the course of his nation. Although he sometimes stands alone against a crowd of contrary advisors, he never tempers his message. Isaiah outlasts four kings, but he finally offends one beyond repair. Tradition records that the last of these rulers, King Manasseh, has Isaiah killed by fastening him between two planks of wood and sawing his body in half.

It seems likely that much of Hezekiah's zeal for reform traces back to the influence of the prophet Isaiah. The divine call recorded in this chapter shows where Isaiah got the courage and commitment that made him such an important force in Judah's history.

—PY

---- *Daily Contemplation* ----

Have you ever felt compelled to volunteer for a difficult task for God?

DAY 157

Praise to the Lord
Isaiah 25:1–26:21

In addition to his role as advisor to kings, Isaiah was a writer of enormous talent. No other biblical author can match his rich vocabulary and use of imagery, and the New Testament quotes him more than all the other prophets combined. Many of his majestic phrases have become a familiar part of the English vocabulary.

Using his great ability, Isaiah tries to awaken Judah from its spiritual slump. Like most of the prophets, he preaches a two-part message of ***judgment*** that will surely come unless people radically change their ways, and ***hope*** in a future when God will restore not only the Israelites but the whole world.

During the period when Judah is fat, self-indulgent, and reveling in luxury, Isaiah warns of a reckoning day. But later, when Jerusalem is surrounded by foreign troops, Isaiah offers stirring words of hope. World-class tyrants don't intimidate Isaiah; he knows that God can toss them aside like twigs.

Isaiah summons up latent human longings for a better world. He has no doubt that God will one day transform this pockmarked planet into a new earth that has no tears, no pain, and no death. In the future world as pictured by Isaiah, wild animals will lie beside each other in peace. Weapons will be melted into farm tools.

At any given point in history, God may appear powerless or blithely unconcerned about the violence and evil that plague this planet. The people of Jerusalem certainly question his lack of concern in the face of the Assyrian invasion. Isaiah gives them a local message of hope: Entrust your future to God alone. And he expands that message to encompass the entire world.

Isaiah 24 through 27 gives a preview of the end of all history. First will come a difficult time, when God purifies the stained earth. Like a woman in childbirth, the earth will undergo pain and struggle. What follows next, however, will be a future life so wonderful, we can scarcely imagine it.

—PY

Daily Contemplation

What gives you hope about the future?

Ready to Be Used by God
Reflection

God has created you with a unique personality, a one-of-a-kind perspective, custom talents, and particular circumstances, all with the purpose of using you for something that only you can step forward and accomplish. Because you are uniquely equipped, your service to God will fulfill the deepest part of you. As the author Frederick Buechner puts it, "The place God calls you to is the place where your deep gladness and the world's deep hunger meet."[22]

Isaiah, for instance, stood specially poised for his work in several ways. Living in Jerusalem, he had regular, privileged contact with Judah's kings. He was married to a prophetess and had two sons. Isaiah lived at a time when powerful neighbors threatened both Israel and Judah, and God was withdrawing his help because of the people's repeated unfaithfulness. God used Isaiah to bring bold prophetic warnings to his nation as well as eloquent visions of future blessing.

As he delivered his prophecies, Isaiah skillfully painted pictures with words that would endure for centuries and be quoted by Jesus and many New Testament writers. Isaiah's faithfulness to his unique calling rendered an important service both for God and for us.

Before he could serve, however, Isaiah needed a right understanding of himself and God. In his vision recounted in Isaiah 6, Isaiah had the opportunity to see God in all his majesty. This sight struck Isaiah with the reality of his own sin and his unworthiness to stand before a holy God. Then God touched Isaiah's lips with a hot coal in a symbolic gesture, purifying and preparing him for service.

"Whom shall I send? And who will go for us?" God asked, priming Isaiah for the answer only he could offer. God was asking Isaiah to tell the people they desperately needed God's forgiveness and leadership, despite their blindness to their need.

"Here am I. Send me!" Isaiah replied. He was ready to let God take everything he had, and use everything he was, for God's own purposes.

Each of us has a calling different from Isaiah's, but the process God will use as he prepares us will be the same. God will give us a greater understanding of his almighty power and glory. He will help us see our great need for his cleansing and guidance. He will purify us and ask if we are willing to be used. Then we can respond with heartfelt availability, "Here am I. Send me!"

Nothing will bring greater satisfaction than joining God in the work for which he has made us. Author Richard Foster affirms, "Service that flows out of our inward person is life, and joy and peace."[23]

—BQ

--- *Daily Contemplation* ---

How well do you know yourself? Have you sensed how God wants to use you? Ask God for a revelation of his greatness and your sinfulness, and tell him of your desire to be made ready to serve him.

DAY 159

Sennacherib Threatens Jerusalem
2 Chronicles 32:1–31

It is the greatest crisis that Hezekiah and Isaiah would ever face. The very survival of Judah is in peril. Assyria, ever thirsty for more conquests, has just rolled into Judah, leveling forty-six walled cities and taking 200,150 captives. The Assyrian king demands huge sums of money from Hezekiah, whom he mockingly describes in his annals as "a bird in a cage." Hezekiah may as well be in a cage, for siege armies completely surround his city.

Cowering behind his city's walls, Hezekiah once more turns to Isaiah for advice. Should he surrender? Negotiate? Outside, the Assyrians are directing a barrage of propaganda at Jerusalem's demoralized citizens. They scoff at Israelite hopes for a miracle from God. No gods have helped any other nation withstand the Assyrian juggernaut.

Isaiah, however, refuses to panic. Against all odds, he calmly advises prayer and reliance on the power of God. ***Have faith,*** he says. ***Don't surrender and don't fear. Assyria will return home, wounded.***

Jerusalem looks like a doomed city during the siege by Assyria. But two things happen to fulfill Isaiah's prophecy. First, a great plague strikes the Assyrians (Isaiah 37), a plague also recorded by the historian Herodotus. Later, the murder of Assyria's leader brings internal chaos to that empire and cancels out the Assyrian threat.

The miraculous deliverance saves Judah, but only temporarily. In his latter days, Hezekiah foolishly flaunts his country's wealth before envoys from Babylon, a rising power in the east. The citizens of Judah grow proud as well; they become convinced that Jerusalem, God's city, is indestructible—a belief that will be proved tragically false.

—PY

Daily Contemplation

Why might God sometimes seem close to you and sometimes seem more distant? What does he care most about when he looks at your heart?

DAY 160

The Lord's Anger Against Nineveh
Nahum 1:1–15

Nahum (NAY-hum) has one distinct advantage over most biblical prophets: He is addressing an enemy. Prophets like Micah and Isaiah sometimes collapsed in grief as they thought about the judgments that would befall their own people. But Nahum lowers the boom on Assyria, a nation that has just obliterated the northern kingdom of Israel and, except for God's miraculous intervention in Hezekiah's day, would have done the same to Nahum's homeland of Judah.

Assyria is an easy enemy to hate—something along the lines of Hitler's Germany. Its soldiers decimate cities, lead captives away with hooks in their noses, and plow salt into fertile ground. In fact, Assyria's very obnoxiousness lies at the heart of what Nahum has to say.

A question nags at the citizens of Judah, who have experienced the full force of Assyria's "endless cruelty." Assyria has trampled a huge path of destruction from the region of modern-day Turkey down the Persian Gulf all the way to Egypt. Judah, in contrast, is a tiny vassal state barely clinging to existence. Why would God hold Judah accountable but allow Assyria to go unpunished?

Nahum brashly predicts that even mighty Assyria will meet its end. Its people repented once, in Jonah's day, but have reverted to old patterns that will bring on God's judgment. Undoubtedly, the people of Judah applaud Nahum's prophecies—but who can believe them? Assyria, the most powerful empire in the world for two centuries, will not simply disappear.

Nahum delivers these prophecies sometime around 700 BC. In 612 BC Nineveh, the last Assyrian stronghold, falls to the Babylonians and Persians. Over time a carpet of grass will cover the pile of rubble marking what had been the greatest city of its time. Years later, both Alexander the Great and Napoleon will camp nearby, with no clue that a city had ever been there.

Like all the biblical prophets, Nahum sees beyond the intimidating forces of history. He knows that behind the rise and fall of empires an even greater force is at work, determining the ultimate outcome. Though God's justice may seem slow, nothing can finally escape it.

—PY

Daily Contemplation

What modern-day injustices do you most want to see punished?

DAY 161

The Future of Jerusalem
Zephaniah 3:1–20

Through the influence of prophets such as Micah and Isaiah, King Hezekiah helped set the land of Judah back on course. However, Hezekiah's death vacated the throne for Manasseh (muh-NAS-uh), who proved to be one of Judah's all-time worst monarchs. In his fifty-year reign—the longest of any king of Israel or Judah—Manasseh reversed all the good that Hezekiah had accomplished.

An unabashed tyrant, Manasseh filled the streets of Jerusalem with blood. He made child sacrifice common practice, built astrology altars in God's temple, and encouraged male prostitution as part of religious ritual. By the time he died, very few reminders of the covenant with God remained in Judah. Public shrines abounded, and storefronts in Jerusalem advertised household gods, mediums, and spiritists. God's chosen people were out-paganizing the pagans.

The next king, Manasseh's son Amon (UH-muhn), started out in his father's footsteps, but this time his own officials rose up in revolt and assassinated him after two years. The nation of Judah, cut loose from its moorings, begins drifting toward total anarchy. And Josiah, the pint-sized prince newly crowned by Amon's supporters, hardly gives much reason for optimism.

In the early days of Josiah's reign, the prophet Zephaniah (ZEF-uh-NI-uh) speaks out against the decadence spreading throughout Judah. Other prophets have come from peasant stock; Zephaniah proudly traces his ancestry back to King Hezekiah. Yet, unlike others of high social standing, he doesn't try to defend the upper classes. Rather, he accuses them of chief responsibility for the decay in Judah. The officials, the priests, the rulers, the judges, even the prophets—these are the targets of Zephaniah's rage.

The leaders of Judah are pointing the entire nation on a course of self-destruction. Unless they reverse directions, Jerusalem will face the same fate as many of its fallen neighbors.

—PY

Daily Contemplation

When you have plenty of money and life seems easy, do you tend to move closer to God or farther from him?

DAY 162

Josiah Renews the Covenant
2 Kings 22:1–23:3

The Bible does not record what specific effect Zephaniah's words had within Judah. But it does give a thrilling account of a turnaround that occurred during his days, a revival led by the king himself.

King Josiah inherits the throne at the age of eight in the midst of a crisis seemingly beyond all healing. Josiah, however, is no ordinary eight-year-old. Raised by a wicked king in a wicked time, he somehow emerges with a spiritual vision that has no equal. Against the odds, Josiah steers his nation back toward God.

Josiah devotes much time and energy to a favorite public works project: repairing the temple. And one busy day, as carpenters cut new joists and beams, and masons chisel new stones for the temple walls, and workmen haul off rubble from the idols Josiah has smashed—in the midst of that din and clutter, a priest makes an amazing discovery. He finds a scroll that looks like—***Could it be?***—the Book of the Covenant, the original record of the agreement between the Israelites and their God. (Most scholars believe the scroll contained part or all of the book of Deuteronomy.)

The neglect of such an important document, long buried and forgotten, shows the extent of Judah's slide away from God. And Josiah's response shows the depth of his commitment. Hearing those sacred words for the first time, he tears his robes in shame and repentance. After a prophetess confirms the scroll's authenticity, Josiah pledges himself and his nation to the terms of the long-lost covenant.

This chapter tells the story of the dramatic discovery, and the next tells of Josiah's fervent campaign to call his nation back to God. His actions will change the landscape of Judah and stave off certain destruction. All this comes about because a young king takes seriously the words of God.

—PY

Daily Contemplation

When have you experienced an awakening similar to King Josiah's?

DAY 163

What Does It Take to Be Faithful?
Reflection

The story of Josiah offers great inspiration. Descended from a father and grandfather who modeled corrupt, God-hating leadership, Josiah nevertheless broke the mold and reversed his nation's slide. As no other king had done, Josiah turned to God "with all his heart and with all his soul and with all his strength" (2 Kings 23:25). Yet as time wore on Josiah made a mistake that cost him his life and put Judah in the hands of a puppet ruler who answered to Egypt. Though Josiah was committed to obeying God, at some point he faltered, with tragic consequences.

Why do Israel and Judah fail so consistently? Why does even Josiah go astray eventually? Are all believers doomed to start out well and fizzle at the finish?

In Israel and Judah's case, the leaders lacked long-term obedience. They worshiped God one year and abandoned him the next. They got in trouble and turned to him, then got delivered and reverted to their own ways. Like a car out of alignment, they kept veering off the road and into the path of the world around them.

We face the same challenge. We too find it difficult to stick with something over the long haul, to grow stronger in commitment rather than weaker. We are not accustomed to pursuing "a long obedience in the same direction," explains author, professor, and former pastor Eugene Peterson. "We assume that if something can be done at all, it can be done quickly and efficiently. Our attention spans have been conditioned by thirty-second commercials. Our sense of reality has been flattened by thirty-page abridgments . . . Everyone is in a hurry . . . They are impatient for results. They have adopted the lifestyle of a tourist and only want the high points."[24]

This pattern sets believers up for a fall. We can't form a relationship with God once and be done. We can't achieve spiritual maturity in a few weeks or months. We must go ever deeper in knowing God and experiencing his work in us. When we're committed to a life of ongoing growth and obedience, we safeguard ourselves against the mistakes of the Israelites.

Peterson writes, "In going against the stream of the world's ways there are two biblical designations for people of faith that are extremely useful: **disciple** and **pilgrim. Disciple (mathetes)** says we are people who spend our lives apprenticed to our master, Jesus Christ. We are in a growing, learning relationship always . . . **Pilgrim (parepidemos)** tells us we are people who spend our lives going someplace, going to God, and whose path for getting there is the way, Jesus Christ."[25]

As disciples, we walk daily with Jesus and learn from him. And the more we learn, the more we see how much we don't know. The relationship continually opens new worlds and, as we stay with it, our love for him will grow deeper and deeper. As pilgrims, we will encounter a multitude of experiences and emotions. Through it all, Jesus is the goal of our journey; he is also our companion, traveling with us and guiding us through each landscape.

We can be faithful if we commit to a long obedience in the direction of Jesus Christ.

—BQ

―――――――――― *Daily Contemplation* ――――――――――

Do you tend to persevere, staying determined and focused, or do you tire easily of one pursuit and move on to another? How is this tendency affecting your pursuit of God? Ask God to help you be faithful to the end.

DAY 164

Israel Forsakes God
Jeremiah 2:1–37

Zephaniah was not the only prophet active during King Josiah's days. Just as Josiah is reaching adulthood, the doleful voice of Jeremiah begins to be heard in the streets of Jerusalem. Later, Jeremiah's messages will be collected into a book that is the Bible's longest and easily its most passionate. Jeremiah is subject to violent swings of mood, and his book reflects that same emotional temperament. The English word ***jeremiad***, which means "a prolonged complaint," conveys something of the prophet's tone.

This chapter, full of strong images and rhetorical blasts, typifies Jeremiah's style. Using sexual imagery, he presents Judah's crisis as a kind of lover's quarrel between God and Judah. She is like a prostitute who lies down under every spreading tree; like a rutting she-camel; like a donkey in heat driven wild with desire.

But what is the object of Judah's desire? Incredibly, she is trading the glory of God for worthless idols of wood and stone. God, the wounded lover, cannot comprehend his people's actions, and neither can Jeremiah.

Jeremiah has two main complaints against Judah: She prostitutes herself through idol worship and also through alliances with foreign nations. When a military threat looms, Judah turns to empires like Assyria, Egypt, or Babylon for help, not to God.

Josiah, one of Judah's all-time best kings, conducts a mostly successful campaign to rid the nation of idols. But not even Josiah can resist the temptation of foreign entanglements. Against Jeremiah's counsel, he leads an ill-advised march against Egyptian armies. Josiah dies in that battle, and his death shocks the nation. A grieving Jeremiah writes laments in honor of the great king.

Judah will never recover from Josiah's fatal mistake. Egypt installs a puppet king over Judah, and from then on no one has the ability to rally Judah's religious or political strength. Jeremiah lives through the reigns of four weakling kings, and the messages collected in this book heap scorn upon them.

—PY

Daily Contemplation

To whom do you show the most consistent loyalty? Are you loyal to God?

DAY 165

Death, Famine, Sword
Jeremiah 15:1–21

For most of his life Jeremiah must deliver a gloomy message, and no one feels the weight of that burden more than he. "Since my people are crushed, I am crushed; I mourn, and horror grips me. . . . Oh, that my head were a spring of water and my eyes a fountain of tears!" (8:21; 9:1). That spirit comes through so strongly in his writings that Jeremiah has become known as "the Weeping Prophet."

More than the future of Judah distresses Jeremiah; he also fears for his personal safety. From the very beginning he protested his assignment as a prophet. "I do not know how to speak; I am too young," he told God (1:6). When God proceeds to make tough demands, Jeremiah responds in typical fashion: by whining, complaining, feeling sorry for himself, and even lashing out against God's cruelty. The book includes a remarkable series of conversations—more like arguments—in which Jeremiah tells God exactly how he feels.

This chapter includes one such conversation with God. Quotation marks surround God's speeches: He begins by pronouncing judgment on the nation of Judah. But at verse 10 Jeremiah butts in with his agenda. What will people think of a prophet delivering a message like that? His name is a national swear word already. He'd be better off unborn. To him, God seems unreliable, like a brook that dries up, a spring that fails.

Despite Jeremiah's fits and protests, God never gives up on him. He promises to make the weepy prophet "a fortified wall of bronze," able to stand against the whole land. Likewise, Jeremiah, for all his diatribes, never gives up on God. The word of God is inside him and he can't stop talking about it. "But if I say, 'I will not mention his word or speak anymore in his name,' his word is in my heart like a fire, a fire shut up in my bones. I am weary of holding it in; indeed, I cannot" (20:9).

—PY

Daily Contemplation

What complaints would you bring to God? Do you, like Jeremiah, ever feel unappreciated by God?

DAY 166

Restoration of Israel
Jeremiah 31:1–40

Born into a priestly family, Jeremiah learned at an early age the story of the covenant between God and his chosen people. Yet he also knew the more recent history of the ten Israelite tribes being dispersed by the Assyrians. Suddenly he is ordered to prophesy that the two surviving tribes in Judah will undergo a similar trial—a message no one wants to hear. In Jeremiah's own lifetime, Babylonian armies will desecrate the holy city of Jerusalem and take captive many more Israelites.

Has God abandoned the covenant? Has he cast aside his chosen people? In this chapter, Jeremiah receives a dream sequence that hints at an answer. He sees that a "remnant" will survive the Babylonian invasion. God has not permanently rejected his people but is allowing them to undergo temporary punishment for the sake of purging. Moreover, God promises that the future of the Israelites will be far grander than anything in the past.

Bible interpreters disagree on the full meaning of these promises. Some things are clear. For example, God promises a "new covenant" to replace and improve on the old, broken one. Hebrews 8 quotes a key passage from this chapter in Jeremiah and applies the prophecy to Jesus, who made possible the new covenant of grace.

But what of the predictions that seem to apply geographically to the land? Some of the exiled Israelites, led by Ezra and Nehemiah, will eventually return from captivity in Babylon, but that sparse resettlement of a devastated land hardly calls to mind the glorious new society described here. Jewish theologians disagree on the meaning: Some point to the modern-day state of Israel as a direct fulfillment of this prophecy, while others strongly disagree. And some Christian theologians believe that these promises, under the new covenant, apply to the church in a more general sense and not to the Jewish race and its settlement of the land.

Jeremiah does not get a detailed blueprint of future history, but he does get a resounding confirmation of how God feels about his people.

—PY

Daily Contemplation

What promises does God keep renewing in your life?

DAY 167

Jeremiah Thrown into a Cistern
Jeremiah 38:1–28

Jeremiah has good reason for being a weeping, balky prophet. Four kings succeeded Josiah, but each of them served as a surrogate for a larger empire, and each of them gave the prophet Jeremiah a hard time. One king scheduled a private reading of Jeremiah's prophecies in his winter apartment. As each scroll was read, the king casually hacked it to pieces with a knife and tossed it into the fireplace (36:23). On other occasions the prophet was beaten and put in stocks, or locked in a dungeon or, as this chapter relates, thrown in a well. The best state Jeremiah could hope for was house arrest or confinement in the king's courtyard.

The mistreatment, however, only serves to harden Jeremiah's resolve. He curses his tormentors even as they release him from the stocks. Evidently, he reserves his fears and doubts for God's ears alone.

The events in this chapter take place in Jerusalem in the midst of a terrible two-year siege by the Babylonians. The city's starving residents, barely clinging to survival, have resorted to cannibalism. City officials are frantically trying to improve morale and whip up courage. Little wonder they object to Jeremiah's dour advice: "We're going to lose anyway—might as well defect over the walls or open the gates and let the Babylonians in."

The following chapter (Jeremiah 39) tells of Jeremiah's prophecies coming true. Babylon's army does breach the walls and then captures and tortures the weak king Zedekiah. The conquerors treat Jeremiah with respect, however, having heard of his counsel to surrender.

Not long after the fall of Jerusalem, a gang of Israelites rebel against their captors and run to Egypt, with the angry prophet in tow. They think they have reached safety. But in his last recorded words, Jeremiah, a browbeaten seventy-year-old, announces that those runaways will meet a tragic end. They ignore him—just like everyone else in Jeremiah's hapless career.

—PY

Daily Contemplation

When have you felt as if everyone were out to get you? Can you identify with Jeremiah's feelings?

DAY 168

Serving from a Sensitive Spirit
Reflection

The prophet Jeremiah had a tough life. Although God used him in a significant way to speak words of both punishment and hope to the people of Judah, much of the time Jeremiah struggled with his role. In a time of crisis, the nation's leaders didn't like his doomsday message. If the message itself was hard to deliver, Jeremiah found that their opposition made his life even more difficult. Regarding him as a traitor, they beat him and threw him in a dungeon.

Jeremiah's temperament, sensitive and moody, did not help. He's called the "Weeping Prophet" for good reason. Anyone would weep in Jeremiah's circumstances, watching his people and holy city fall into the hands of another nation. But not only did he weep; Jeremiah also complained to God and loudly bemoaned his lot in life. Against the people, Jeremiah retaliated with curses.

What can we learn from this prophet, who was so clearly loved and chosen by God for important work yet struggled so intensely? God told Jeremiah, "Before I formed you in the womb I knew you, before you were born I set you apart; I appointed you as a prophet to the nations" (1:5). Despite his frequent outbursts, Jeremiah loved God, too, and he embraced the truth of the message he delivered. "When your words came, I ate them; they were my joy and my heart's delight" (15:16).

We see in Jeremiah's life that following God faithfully and doing his work won't always be easy. We may suffer, experience unfair treatment, and feel unpopular. Jesus said that if he himself got such treatment, his followers should expect the same (John 15:20). When we feel discouraged, as Jeremiah did, we can bare our souls to God. We can reveal our questions and even voice our complaints. God can handle our true feelings. Maybe God chose Jeremiah, and chooses people today who have sensitive spirits, precisely because he needs those with soft hearts to complete the special assignments he is giving.

Yet as we mature in our walk with God, we can hope and pray to reach a place of deepened trust and fulfillment in the place he has put us. Struggles are never easy, and physical pain never pleasant. Yet as God hears our cries and shares our pain, he can also bring us to a place of oneness with him, where we can rise above the hard times and sense God's presence as more real than even our physical surroundings. This ability comes only through God and through time spent training ourselves, as disciples in the presence of God, to trust and rely on him rather than our outward circumstances.

Jeremiah reveals that God cherishes his children who are temperamental and emotional. He walks closely with them and continues to give his hand of guidance and protection. We also learn from Jeremiah that God's promises are fulfilled in the end. He will care for us and remain faithful throughout our lifetime. We can trust him, and with God's help that trust can affect how we react to our circumstances. We have a choice—to let our emotions control us or to let God embrace and transcend those emotions, giving us his own mind and heart.

—BQ

Daily Contemplation

How do you react to suffering? Ask God to help you mature in your relationship with Jesus. "Consider it pure joy, my brothers, whenever you face trials of many kinds, because you know that the testing of your faith produces perseverance. Let perseverance finish its work so that you may be mature and complete, not lacking anything" (James 1:2–4).

DAY 169

Habakkuk's Complaint
Habakkuk 1:1–17

Everyone has a built-in sense of justice. If a careless driver runs down a small child and nonchalantly drives on, other drivers will follow in hot pursuit. **He can't get away with that!** We may disagree on specific rules of fairness, but we all follow some inner code.

Frankly, much of the time life seems unfair. What child "deserves" to grow up in the slums of Calcutta, Rio de Janeiro, or the East Bronx? Why should people like Adolf Hitler, Joseph Stalin, and Saddam Hussein get away with tyrannizing millions of people? Why are some kind, gentle people struck down in the prime of life while other, meaner people live into cantankerous old age?

We all ask different versions of such questions. And the prophet named Habakkuk (huh-BAK-kuhk) asked them of God directly—and got a no-holds-barred reply. Habakkuk does not mince words. He demands that God explain why he isn't responding to the injustice, violence, and evil that the prophet can see around him.

God answers with the same message he has told Jeremiah, that he will send the Babylonians to punish Judah. But such words hardly reassure Habakkuk, for the Babylonians are ruthless, savage people. Can this be justice—using an even more evil nation to punish Judah?

The book of Habakkuk does not solve the problem of evil. But Habakkuk's conversations with God convince him of one certainty: God has not lost control. As a God of justice, he cannot let evil win. First, he will deal with the Babylonians on their own terms. Then, later, he will intervene with great force, shaking the very foundations of the earth until no sign of injustice remains.

"The earth will be filled with the knowledge of the glory of the Lord, as the waters cover the sea," God promises Habakkuk (2:14). A glimpse of that awe-inspiring glory changes the prophet's attitude from outrage to joy. In the course of his "debate" with God, Habakkuk learns new lessons about faith, which are eloquently expressed in the last chapter. God's answers so satisfy Habakkuk that his book, which begins with a complaint, ends with one of the most beautiful songs in the Bible.

—PY

Daily Contemplation

Can you think of an instance in your life in which, after some doubtful times, you eventually saw God deliver justice?

DAY 170

His Compassion Never Fails
Lamentations 3:1-40

This chapter begins with the words "I am the man who has seen affliction," and that doleful sentence captures the tone of this entire book. Judah's king is now shackled and blinded, and his sons, the princes, have been slaughtered. Jerusalem—the capital city, the holy city—is no more. The poet writes this book in a state of dazed grief. He wanders the empty streets, piled high with corpses, and tries to make sense of a tragedy that defies all comprehension.

Beyond the human tragedy, a different kind of distress gnaws at the author. Babylonian soldiers have entered the temple—pagans in the Most Holy Place!—looted it, then burned it to the ground. The dream of the covenant died on that day. Historians record that as the Babylonians entered the temple, they swept the empty air with their spears, seeking the unseen God of Israel. But they found nothing. God had given up and fled the premises. Modern Jews still mourn the event: Each year on the anniversary of the day the temple was destroyed, Orthodox Jews read the book of Lamentations aloud.

The tone of this anonymous book may sound familiar, for the prophet Jeremiah is the likely author. An old man now, with shriveled skin and broken bones, he has been hunted, jailed, tortured, thrown in a pit, and left for dead. Yet nothing can match the grief he feels as he stares not at his own wounds but at the gaping wounds of Jerusalem.

God is an enemy, the prophet concludes, in an outburst familiar to any reader of Jeremiah. He lets his venom spill out. And yet, in the middle of this dark chapter, the author remembers what he once learned about God in the brighter, happier times. He recalls the goodness of God, the love, the compassion. In the midst of this bleak book come words that a writer would later craft into a hymn: "Great Is Thy Faithfulness." At the moment of terrible tragedy, those qualities of God may seem very far away—but where else can we turn? As Lamentations shows, without God's hope, there is no hope.

—PY

Daily Contemplation

In your darkest times, do your thoughts turn to God? What helps you find relief?

DAY 171

Your Deeds Will Return
Obadiah 1–21

As Psalm 137:7 proclaims: "Remember, LORD, what the Edomites did on the day Jerusalem fell. 'Tear it down,' they cried, 'tear it down to its foundations!'" Survivors of the sacking of Jerusalem would never forget the reactions of their neighbors the Edomites, who had watched the carnage with open glee. The Edomites cheered on the conquering Babylonian army, looted the fleeing refugees, and helped plunder Jerusalem. Psalm 137, one of the saddest passages in the Bible, voices the Israelites' acrid bitterness over this offense.

As if to rub salt in Judah's wounds, the Edomites were actually distant relatives. Their nation traces back to the feud between twin brothers Jacob and Esau. While Jacob fathered the Israelites, Esau, having traded away his birthright for a meal, moved to desolate mountain country and founded the nation of Edom (EE-duhm). The twins' descendants continued the quarrel for hundreds of years, and now the Edomites are gloating over the Israelites' calamity. True sons of Esau, they think primarily of the immediate gain available to them from plunder.

The Edomites' attitude contrasts sharply with the sorrow expressed in the book of Lamentations. And Obadiah, the shortest book in the Old Testament, makes clear that the Edomites will pay for their callousness and cruelty: "As you have done, it will be done to you." Those who have betrayed Judah will be repaid with treachery from their own allies.

Obadiah predicts opposite futures for Israel and Edom. According to the prophet, downtrodden Israel will rise again, but Edom will disappear from the face of the earth. History will bear out the latter prediction in 70 AD, when Roman legions destroy the last remnant of the Edomites during a siege of Jerusalem.

—PY

Daily Contemplation

Edom was basing its security on its strategic location "on the heights" and "in the clefts of the rocks." On what do you base your security?

DAY 172

To Love or Leave Unbelievers?
Reflection

How are God's people supposed to live when they're surrounded by unbelievers? It finally happened to Judah. Like Israel, Judah lost its land and its freedom as an independent nation of God. Tens of thousands were deported to Babylon and forced to make new lives in a foreign society. Now, worshiping the true God—suddenly a more attractive pursuit—became more difficult. Surrounded by the worship of false gods and by worldly religions, the Jews had to learn to live *in* the world without being *of* the world.

Richard Mouw, former president of Fuller Seminary, writes,

> When the children of Israel were taken off to Babylon as captives, they faced some serious questions about civility. For a long time they had been living in their own land, with familiar rulers and institutions. They had experienced the unity of a people who were committed (officially at least!) to obeying the will of God in all aspects of their lives.
>
> But they were aliens in a strange environment, surrounded by a pervasively pagan culture. Psalm 137 records their poignant plea: "How could we sing the Lord's song in a foreign land?" (v. 4). God answered their query through the prophet Jeremiah. You are to settle into the land for the long haul, the prophet told the people: construct homes to live in, raise crops, get married and have children; "multiply there, and do not decrease" (Jer. 29:4–6). And then a very important "policy statement" is added: "But seek the welfare of the city where I have sent you into exile, and pray to the Lord on its behalf, for in its welfare you will find your welfare" (v. 7).[26]

God was telling the people not to deplore their new neighbors but to care for them, to engage with them, to seek their good. God hates the worship of false gods and despises religions that serve the self rather than God, but he doesn't hate the people themselves. Repeatedly God reminds us through the prophets that he hates wickedness but does not hate the wicked. He desires that all people come to him and be saved. The Bible itself is a long message of God's love and forgiveness for those who don't deserve him.

Like the people of Judah, we live alongside many who don't follow God. Just as he stresses the importance of holding firmly to our beliefs without compromising, God also stresses the need for us to love others with the love he has shown us.

Mouw explains,

> God is telling the Israelites—and us—that neither indifference nor hostility is a proper way of treating our pagan neighbors. We must seek their welfare. Indeed, it is in pursuing the well-being of others that we realize our own well-being. When Christians fail to measure up to the standards of kindness and gentleness, we are not the people God meant us to be.[27]

Before Jesus died, in prayer he voiced God's greatest desire: "As you sent me into the world, I have sent them into the world. . . . May [they] be brought to complete unity. Then the world will know that you sent me and have loved them even as you have loved me" (John 17:18, 23). God delights not in punishing sin but in bringing sinners to himself. He has chosen to use us to live out that message.

—BQ

Daily Contemplation

What is your attitude toward those who don't follow Jesus? Do you struggle more in speaking to them about your beliefs or in treating them with love and kindness? Pray that the apostle Peter's words would become real in your life: "Always be prepared to give an answer to everyone who asks you to give the reason for the hope that you have. But do this with gentleness and respect" (1 Peter 3:15).

PART 5

Starting Over—
In Exile and
Returning
from Exile

DAY 173

The Living Creatures and the Glory of the Lord
Ezekiel 1:1–28

About the same time that Jeremiah, Habakkuk, and Obadiah are prophesying in Judah, a man named Ezekiel (ee-ZEE-kee-uhl) receives a dramatic call to minister to their unfortunate countrymen in exile. The Babylonian army has been plundering Judah for twenty years before Jerusalem's fall, and Ezekiel is among the first wave of captives taken to Babylon nearly five hundred miles away. There he lives with the Israelites in a refugee settlement beside a river.

Like refugees everywhere, those in Babylon long for nothing more than a chance to return to their homeland. They receive comfort from letters written by the prophet Jeremiah, but cringe at reports of rebellion by Judah's kings, lest any rebellion arouse the wrath of Babylon. They wonder anxiously whether their beleaguered nation can survive and whether they'll ever see home again.

Uprooted, dispirited people such as these need a strong, authoritative voice, and in Ezekiel they get exactly that. As a young man in training for the priesthood, he found his career plans interrupted by the foreign deportations. **What good is a priest in Babylon when the temple is in Jerusalem?** he must have wondered. God summons Ezekiel to a new role, as prophet to the Jews in exile.

Ezekiel begins with a description so unearthly that some have suggested the prophet saw a UFO. Indeed, there are similarities: glowing lights, quick movements, inhuman figures. But there are also differences in this account of a "close encounter." This majestic being was not mysteriously rushing off to disappear. He wanted to be known by everyone. And he had chosen the prophet Ezekiel as the one privileged to make him known.

Confronted with such splendor, Ezekiel falls on his face. But the Spirit of God raises him to his feet and gives him an assignment. After this vision, Ezekiel will never again wonder about a question that often bothers the other refugees: Has God abandoned them? Ezekiel's encounter of the closest kind convinces him permanently that God still cares about his people—even the exiles in Babylon.

—PY

Daily Contemplation

Have you ever felt abandoned by God? What helped?

DAY 174

Ezekiel's Call
Ezekiel 2:1–3:27

Orthodox Jewish rabbis forbid anyone under the age of thirty to read the first three chapters of Ezekiel. No young person, they reason, is ready for such a direct encounter with the glory of the Lord. Indeed, Ezekiel himself barely survives the experience. He falls on his face repeatedly and is knocked speechless for seven days.

Such exalted revelations are part of God's training regimen to toughen up the prophet for a demanding task. With Isaiah sawn in two and Jeremiah thrown in a well, the prophets of Judah have plenty of reason for concern. What might befall Ezekiel as he takes the word of God to an ornery people in the heart of enemy territory? Thus, in the beginning God gives Ezekiel an experience he will never forget or doubt, no matter what difficulties he may confront.

God warns Ezekiel that few Israelites, if any, will listen to his message. He will have to become as stubborn and unyielding as the audience he addresses. As a result, Ezekiel lives a lonely life. People think of him as a dreamy storyteller and scoff at his pessimistic predictions of Jerusalem's fall. Still, despite the negative tone of his prophecies, Ezekiel never once loses hope. He can see past the tragedies of the present day to a future time when God will restore his people and his temple.

Ezekiel's faith cannot be shaken, because he has received a vision of the glory of the Lord. Due to his priestly training, he undoubtedly recognizes the light, the fire, and the glow—Israelites have seen those images in the pillar of fire in the wilderness, and in the cloud that descended into Solomon's temple. Now the nation is in shambles, its chief citizens in exile. But even here, in Babylon, the glory of the Lord appears to Ezekiel. This experience alone gives him the courage he will need to fight off the enemies that surround him.

—PY

Daily Contemplation

What obstacles do you face when you try to talk to people about God?

DAY 175

Siege of Jerusalem Symbolized
Ezekiel 4:1–17

When someone asked Flannery O'Connor why she populated her novels with such exaggerated, eccentric characters, she replied, "To the hard of hearing you shout, and for the almost-blind you draw large and startling figures."[28] The same answer may help explain the oddities of Ezekiel. He too faces a stubborn, dense audience with little tolerance for his message. And God instructs him to use some bizarre methods to get that message across.

The book records twelve public "object lessons" acted out by the prophet. For example, one year he lies on his side every day, bound by ropes and facing a clay model of Jerusalem. Strange? When a car is headed toward the edge of a cliff, you may scream and gesture so wildly that people think you insane. So it is with Ezekiel, who will do anything to force people to pay attention.

The first part of Ezekiel mainly focuses on the political situation back in the homeland of Judah. False prophets are assuring the exiles that God would never allow his temple or holy city to be destroyed. Ezekiel blasts these phony optimists and broadcasts God's plan of judgment in strong words and public protests. He takes no great delight in the doomsday message. Twice, seeing the future, he falls facedown, crying out in horror (9:8; 11:13). In this chapter, when God tells him to cook food on human excrement as a symbolic act, he is too appalled to agree.

Ezekiel delivers an undiluted message from God, presented in a way that the Israelites cannot ignore. The prophet's exaggerated style says much about the One who gives him orders. God will not let go of his people until he has done all in his power to turn them around. No device is too undignified, no carnival ploy too corny, as long as he has the slightest hope of breaking through. "As surely as I live, declares the Sovereign LORD, I take no pleasure in the death of the wicked, but rather that they turn from their ways and live. Turn! Turn from your evil ways! Why will you die, people of Israel?" (33:11).

—PY

Daily Contemplation

How does God get your attention?

DAY 176

The Valley of Dry Bones
Ezekiel 37:1–28

> So I prophesied as he commanded me, and breath entered them; they came to life and stood up on their feet—a vast army. (Ezekiel 37:10)

Why would Jerusalem be destroyed? Why would all Judah's enemies come to a violent end? So that they would "know that I am the Lord." This phrase gets repeated more than sixty times in the book of Ezekiel. In a sudden change of tone, God uses that same phrase to explain why he will bring about a time of future happiness.

After all the gloom, Ezekiel at last gets to pronounce words of great joy and hope. In the early days, he alone prophesied doom, and no one listened. Next, for a period of seven years he maintained a virtual silence. But now he opens his mouth again, and bright words of hope issue forth.

Ezekiel enjoys a sudden surge in popularity among the exiles, since only he has predicted current events accurately. As people flock to hear his words, he scolds them for their unchanged hearts, then confirms the rumor of good news to come.

No part of Ezekiel captures that message of hope more effectively than this startling vision of the valley of dry bones. Like a graveyard of scattered, bleached bones coming gloriously to life, the deadest of the dead will live.

Ezekiel's congregation of exiles in Babylon is still trying to absorb the staggering news that the temple has been razed, with God apparently having departed. But Ezekiel assures them God has not given up; the split kingdoms of Judah and Israel will join together again at last. God is coming back to his home, to live with his people.

The book ends with a shining vision of a new Jerusalem arising from the ruins of the old. Scholars disagree on whether Ezekiel's words apply literally or symbolically to the nation of Israel. But it is clear that the good news will affect the whole world. The triumphant name of that new city says it all: "And the name of the city from that time on will be: THE LORD IS THERE" (Ezekiel 48:35).

—PY

Daily Contemplation

Where are you spiritually? With the dry bones? Barely stirring? Alive and well?

DAY 177

God's Bizarre Ways of Showing Love
Reflection

The story of Ezekiel gives us one of the most startling pictures of God in all the Bible. We see a God who is willing to go to any lengths to reach people he loves.

Using outrageous symbolism, God warns the people about the upcoming destruction of Jerusalem. Ezekiel must draw Jerusalem under siege and then lie on his side for a year while eating food cooked on cow dung. He must shave his head and burn the hair, strike some with a sword, scatter some to the wind, and tuck some in his cloak. He must clap and stamp while prophesying the consequences of Israel's wicked behavior. He must wail, preaching doom and destruction. He must pack his belongings and crawl out of his house through a hole in the wall. He must tremble with the people while eating and drinking. Then when Ezekiel's wife dies, he must not mourn. All to illustrate God's distress over their sin, and the consequences.

God will later change the message to one of hope, promising a new temple. He plans to forgive and cleanse the people, putting a new heart within them and establishing eternal peace.

In Ezekiel, God speaks with intensity, using the bizarre behavior of a prophet who comes off looking psychotic. If God tempers his passion, the people won't get the message they will soon be desperate to hear.

Today God is still willing to go to any length to help us know him. Brent Curtis and John Eldredge write about God as a wild pursuer engaging us in a sacred romance with himself. "How is God wooing us through flat tires . . . and rained-out picnics? What is he after as we face cancer, sexual struggles, and abandonment?"[29]

"Our Story is written by God who is more than author, he is the romantic lead in our personal dramas," they conclude. "He created us for himself and now he is moving heaven and earth to restore us to his side. His wooing seems wild because he seeks to free our heart from the attachments and addictions we've chosen."[30]

God acts as a lover who seeks in every situation to reunite with his beloved. God is so wild about us that he uses whatever strategy will intimately fit us and draw us to himself. "We lose heart when we lose the eternal Romance," Curtis and Eldredge write, "which reminds us that God sought to bring us into his sacred circle from all eternity, and . . . despite our rejection of him, he pursues us still."[31]

—BQ

Daily Contemplation

Can you see times in your life when God was romancing you, even in unconventional ways? Thank God now for loving you so passionately. Or, ask God for the eyes to recognize his pursuit.

DAY 178

Daniel's Training in Babylon
Daniel 1:1–21

Whereas Ezekiel spent his days preaching (and acting out) sermons to the Jewish exiles, Daniel was recruited for a job in the king's palace.

In fact, Daniel's life in the palace more closely resembles that of the ancient character Joseph, who also rose to a position of prominence in a foreign government. As this chapter underscores, Daniel achieves success without bending his own principles of integrity. Somehow he manages to thrive in an environment marked by ambition and intrigue, while still holding to his high-minded Jewish ideals.

The Babylonians do their best to purge the young Jews of their heritage. They force on them new, pagan names and ply them with wine and food that has been offered to idols. Even the study course for diplomats-in-training is distasteful to a Jew: It covers sorcery, magic, and a pagan, polytheistic religion. Daniel and his three friends overcome these obstacles and excel enough to attract the attention of the king, who can't help noticing that the four are more impressive than anyone else in the kingdom.

Taken together, the biblical prophets offer not one but many models of how a person can serve both God and the state. On the one extreme stand men like Amos and Elijah, who, as outsiders, railed against the evils of society. Others, such as Jeremiah and Nathan, gave occasional counsel to kings but kept a safe distance. The prophets Isaiah and Samuel, however, worked for the king as official advisors. And in this book the prophet Daniel shows that a person can stay pure even while functioning within a tyrannical regime.

For at least sixty-six years Daniel serves pagan kings with great diligence and resourcefulness. Yet he never once compromises his faith, even when threatened with death. The Bible offers no better model of how to live among people who do not share or respect your beliefs.

—PY

Daily Contemplation

When have you taken a difficult or unpopular stand as a matter of integrity?

DAY 179

Nebuchadnezzar's Dream
Daniel 2:1–23

Nebuchadnezzar [Neb-uh-kuhd-NEZ-urh] had dreams; his mind was troubled and he could not sleep. So the king summoned the magicians, enchanters, sorcerers and astrologers . . . He said to them, "I have had a dream that troubles me and I want to know what it means." Then the astrologers answered the king, . . . "Tell your servants the dream, and we will interpret it." The king replied to the astrologers, "This is what I have firmly decided: If you do not tell me what my dream was and interpret it, I will have you cut into pieces." . . . When Arioch, the commander of the king's guard, had gone out to put to death the wise men of Babylon, Daniel spoke to him . . . "Why did the king issue such a harsh decree?" Arioch then explained the matter to Daniel. At this, Daniel went in to the king and asked for time, so that he might interpret the dream for him. (Daniel 2:1–5, 14–16)

Whether to remind his own people of his power or to proclaim it to the Gentiles, God frequently allows a crisis in the lives of his most faithful followers and lets them resolve it by relying on him. Here God positions Daniel and his friends in close proximity to the king and then gives them the opportunity to do what none of the wisest in Babylon can do.

Even the astrologers admit that only the gods could meet the king's absurd demands. They are almost right. Only the one true God can know a person's dream. And although the pagan gods don't live among men, God does. Four men who are slated to die will give the proof. Once again God will proclaim to his chosen people and the Babylonians that he reigns. For all their mystique and showmanship, sorcerers, magicians, and astrologers can only offer empty promises when arrayed against the God of heaven.

—BQ

---— *Daily Contemplation* ---—

When have you recently been reminded of God's power through his actions in another person's life?

DAY 180

Daniel Interprets the Dream
Daniel 2:24–49

The king asked Daniel (also called Belteshazzar), "Are you able to tell me what I saw in my dream and interpret it?" Daniel replied, "No wise man, enchanter, magician or diviner can explain to the king the mystery he has asked about, but there is a God in heaven who reveals mysteries. He has shown King Nebuchadnezzar what will happen in days to come." . . . Then King Nebuchadnezzar fell prostrate before Daniel and paid him honor and ordered that an offering and incense be presented to him. The king said to Daniel, "Surely your God is the God of gods and the Lord of kings and a revealer of mysteries, for you were able to reveal this mystery." (Daniel 2:26–28, 46–47)

God not only shows his power through Daniel's interpretation of the king's dream; he also reveals the future of the Near East and of God's own eternal kingdom. The statue in Nebuchadnezzar's dream depicts the successive kingdoms that will rule over the land of Israel and the Jewish people. The gold head represents the Neo-Babylonian Empire; the silver chest and arms the Medo-Persian Empire; the bronze belly and thighs the Greek Empire; and the iron legs and feet the Roman Empire. The metals symbolize the decreasing power and grandeur of the empires and also their increasing toughness, with each empire lasting longer than the preceding one.

The four kingdoms will be destroyed not by another earthly power but by the God of heaven, who will establish a different kind of kingdom. Like the rock that strikes the statue and causes it to crumble, this kingdom will crush all others and replace them with an eternal kingdom.

—BQ

Daily Contemplation

What "kingdom" of today are you eager for Jesus to overthrow? The influence of a political or social group? The repressive government of a particular nation? A destructive cultural trend?

DAY 181

The Image of Gold and the Blazing Furnace
Daniel 3:1–29

Stories from Daniel have become famous, and in fact any of the first six chapters would make a script for a thriller. In this account, Daniel's three friends face a tyrant's decree that brings their dual loyalties into irreconcilable conflict. Fully aware of the king's threats against them, the three decide they cannot serve both the kingdom of God and the kingdom of Babylon. There can be no compromise.

Idolatry is in fact Judah's stubborn sin that has brought on the Babylonian punishment in the first place. The Jews can never expect God's blessing if they choose to bow down to Nebuchadnezzar and his gold image. The uncompromising response of Daniel's friends shows that the Babylonian captivity is having a purifying effect on a whole generation of Jewish exiles.

The book of Daniel makes for exciting reading because, at this most precarious time in Israelite history, God lets loose with a burst of miraculous activity: supernatural dreams, handwriting on the wall, rescues from a fiery furnace and a lions' den. Not since Elisha's day have the Israelites seen such signs and wonders.

The story of the fiery furnace has a happy ending, far beyond anything the three courageous Jews might have hoped for. Not only do they survive; the event ensures that Nebuchadnezzar will treat the Jewish religion with tolerance throughout his reign.

The Israelites are still thinking of God in terms of their own small community, but God has never intended for his blessings to stop with the Jews. When he first revealed the covenant to Abraham, he promised that Abraham's offspring would bless the whole earth (Genesis 12:3). Ironically, at a time of deep humiliation, while living as unwilling captives in Babylon, the Jews begin to convince others that their God deserves honor. The proclamations by Nebuchadnezzar and later Darius (Daniel 6:26–27) honor God more than anything a king of Judah has done in years.

—PY

Daily Contemplation

What do you learn about faith from the reply of Daniel's friends (Daniel 3:16–18)?

DAY 182

The Writing on the Wall
Daniel 5:1–30

A miracle may make someone sit up and take notice, but it does not guarantee long-term change. Despite Nebuchadnezzar's newfound enthusiasm for the God of the Hebrews, in time he apparently forgets all about his religious zeal.

The king's son Belshazzar (bel-SHAZ-uhr), who grew up in the midst of the flurry of miracles, has an even shorter memory. Chapter 5 introduces the new king at a state orgy as he boozes it up with a thousand nobles and assorted women. The revelers are carousing in a kind of "hurricane party" to show their disdain over reports of enemy armies advancing on the capital. The party even includes a pseudo-religious element: They worship idols and use sacred relics stolen from the temple in Jerusalem to hold their wine.

Belshazzar's raucous party provides the setting for a scene straight out of a horror film: A human hand, eerily disconnected from any body, writes a message on the wall. The king trembles and turns pale, terrified until the queen remembers the supernatural gifts of an old Jewish prophet. Daniel hasn't changed a bit over the years. He respectfully declines the king's bribes but interprets the dream anyway, after delivering an impromptu sermon.

That night, Daniel gets another high-ranking appointment in the government of a tyrant. But the job doesn't last long. The same night, Babylon falls victim to a sneak attack, and Darius the Mede takes over the kingdom.

A phrase has come down from this story—"The handwriting on the wall"—to signify a final warning just before the end. The prophets of Israel and Judah tried to interpret God's "handwriting" for their countrymen, with little success, and God used Babylon to punish them. Now Babylon, having disregarded the warnings of a spiritual giant like Daniel, is itself ripe for punishment. They have ignored handwriting on the wall long enough.

—PY

Daily Contemplation

Has God ever used "handwriting on the wall" in your life?

DAY 183

Daniel in the Den of Lions
Daniel 6:1–26

"My God sent his angel, and he shut the mouths of the lions." (Daniel 6:22)

After six decades of service, Daniel finally confronts a situation like the one that landed his three friends in a blazing furnace: an unresolvable conflict between the law of God and the law of the land. During these years Daniel has lost much of his Jewish heritage and has even taken on a Babylonian name. Yet, although he can't worship God in the way he wishes, at the temple in Jerusalem, his devotion to God never wavers. In defiance of the king's new law, the old prophet keeps orienting himself toward Jerusalem three times a day in prayer.

The story of Daniel in the lions' den has special meaning for both Jews and Christians because, sadly, history has repeated itself so often. The Roman Empire, Stalin's Russia, Hitler's Germany, Chairman Mao's China—they've all taken their turn at restricting worship, yet the church has survived, and even thrived, during times of intense persecution. Not everyone who undergoes religious persecution receives miraculous deliverance like Daniel's, but the martyrs, too, give witness to the watching world that true faith cannot be stamped out, regardless of the penalty.

While a miracle spares Daniel's life, an even greater miracle occurs in those around him. Stirred by Daniel's faith, the Persian ruler issues a proclamation that everyone in his kingdom must fear and reverence "the God of Daniel." Soon, the same empire that has passed laws against Jewish worship will escort the Jewish exiles back to their homeland and allow them to rebuild the temple.

The harsh times in Babylon have their effect on the Jewish community as well. Led by the examples of people such as Daniel and his friends, they begin a new practice of meeting together to study the law and to pray. And they will return to their homeland purged of the sin that has brought them so much anguish: Jews never again will be known to practice idolatry. The refining fire has done its work.

—PY

Daily Contemplation

Has God used a "refining fire" to teach you or cleanse you from sin?

DAY 184

An Excellent Example
Reflection

If you want a biblical character to emulate, Daniel is one excellent choice, mainly because of his strength of character. The Bible tells of many weak people who made mistakes and were still used by God. Daniel was one of the rare people who, as far as we know, made no great mistakes. According to all the Bible tells us, his commitment to God remained strong and steady, and he lived out that commitment for everyone to see.

"It's too late," you may sigh. "I've already made big mistakes, and I'll likely never become a Daniel." No matter what your past holds, you can pursue excellence of the kind Daniel exhibited. Ted Engstrom, former president of World Vision and author of the book *The Pursuit of Excellence*, writes, "Striving for excellence in our work, whatever it is, is not only our Christian duty, but a basic form of Christian witness. And our nonverbal communication speaks so loudly that people often cannot hear a single word we say."[32]

Our actions speak loudly about our caliber. Who we are reflects to others something of what it means to be a believer. In the way we live our lives, we, often unknowingly, tell unbelievers something about following God.

Take a look at Daniel's actions. In the beginning of the book we see Daniel declining the expensive food and wine offered him. Because this food has first been sacrificed to idols, Daniel's principles won't allow him to enjoy such a repast. He politely asks the guard to give him and his men a chance to eat only vegetables and water, trusting that God will keep them healthy.

Then, before interpreting a dream for the king, Daniel first acknowledges that he possesses no more wisdom than others. He is able to interpret the dream simply because God has chosen to reveal its meaning through him. Daniel has no concern for promoting himself. He cares rather about the duty at hand.

Later, when another king comes to power and asks Daniel to read some strange writing on a wall, Daniel turns down the gifts and rewards offered yet agrees to interpret the writing anyway. Again he knows God has given him a job to do, and taking rewards from an ungodly king would compromise Daniel's own devotion to God.

Under yet another king, Daniel "so distinguished himself among the administrators and the satraps by his exceptional qualities that the king planned to set him over the whole kingdom" (6:3). They could find nothing wrong with Daniel, "because he was trustworthy and neither corrupt nor negligent" (6:4). Once more Daniel's integrity shines through in his actions. The jealous people around him soon conclude they can only pin something on him if it sets up a conflict with God's law.

Finally, when Daniel survives a night on the verge of death, he doesn't complain about the king throwing him into the lions' den but instead honors the king and focuses on God. "May the king live forever! My God sent his angel, and he shut the mouths of the lions" (6:21–22).

Daniel may have been born into a noble family, but he wasn't born into excellence. That, he earned for himself. John Gardner, in his book **Excellence**, explains, "Some people have greatness thrust upon them. Very few have excellence thrust upon them . . . They achieve it. They do not achieve it unwittingly by 'doing what comes naturally' and they don't stumble into it in the course of amusing themselves. All excellence involves discipline and tenacity of purpose."[33]

Daniel did show discipline. He knew his purpose and held to it over the long haul. Daniel was committed to doing things God's way, and he never lost sight of that commitment.

—BQ

Daily Contemplation

How much do you think about excellence in day-to-day life? How concerned are you with doing your best and acting consistently? Ask God to help you develop, or continue developing in you, a fortitude that helps you maintain the virtue you have through Jesus.

DAY 185

Rebuilding the Altar
Ezra 3:1–4:5

For more than half a century Jewish exiles, among them Daniel and Ezekiel, were held captive in Babylon. Some, like Daniel, prospered in the foreign land, but no true Israelite ever felt totally at peace there. Always, a longing gnawed inside, a longing for home and for the temple of God. As one poet in exile wrote, "If I forget you, Jerusalem, may my right hand forget its skill. May my tongue cling to the roof of my mouth if I do not remember you, if I do not consider Jerusalem my highest joy" (Psalm 137:5–6).

Daniel's new boss, in keeping with the Persian policy of religious tolerance, granted permission for the first wave of Jewish exiles to return to Jerusalem, and the book of Ezra tells their story. The sight that greets the returning exiles in Jerusalem dismays them: The city is a ghost town, burned and pillaged by the conquering Babylonians. The temple of God is a mound of rubble.

The settlers go to work at once, making temple reconstruction their highest priority. They have hope: The Persians have even given back the pilfered silver and gold temple articles. When the Jews finally lay the foundation, the sound of their shouting can be heard from far away. The temple, after all, is the place where they will meet God and, as such, symbolizes a new start with him.

Yet the shouts of joy mingle with loud cries of weeping as well. The older returnees, those who remember Solomon's temple in all its splendor, weep at the comparison. They have lost political independence and need permission from a foreign government just to rebuild the temple. The Jews have regained only a tiny portion of their former territory. They are very far from the glory days of David and Solomon.

The book of Ezra thus introduces a new period in the Israelites' history—a period in which they become more like a "church" than a nation. Their leaders focus energy not on fighting enemy armies but on fighting sin and spiritual compromise. They fear repeating the mistakes that sent them into exile.

—PY

Daily Contemplation

In your spiritual life, what are you fighting? Sin? Spiritual compromise? Repeat of past mistakes? Lack of trust in God?

DAY 186

A Call to Build the House of the Lord
Haggai 1:1–2:9

The burst of energy described in Ezra does not last long. Opposition soon arises among the tribes bordering Israel, who do not look kindly on the resurgence of a traditional enemy. The temple project especially alarms them in view of all the stories they have heard about the miraculous power of Israel's God. And surely, they reason, a rebuilt temple will only inflame the Israelites' religious zeal. Even Israel's protector, Persia, begins to waver on its promises to the Jews.

In the face of this stiff opposition, the Jews lose enthusiasm and redirect their energy toward other projects. Just a few years after the exiles' return, work on the temple grinds to a halt. The Jews begin to concentrate instead on building their own homes and regaining their former prosperity. They have forgotten the original motive for returning to Jerusalem.

About twenty years after the first migration, a prophet named Haggai (HAG-i) appears in Jerusalem to confront the growing apathy and confusion. He does not rage like Jeremiah or act out public object lessons like Ezekiel. He simply urges these pioneers to give careful thought to their situation. "Is it a time for you yourselves to be living in your paneled houses, while this house [the temple] remains a ruin?" he asks in Haggai 1:4.

Haggai puts things simply and logically. The settlers have worked hard, but what has it earned them? Their crops are unsuccessful. Their money disappears as soon as they earn it. Haggai's diagnosis of the problem: wrong priorities. The Israelites need to put God first, and for starters that means rebuilding his temple. God's reputation is at stake. If the temple symbolizes God's presence, how can he be properly honored when his house lies in ruins?

A statement made by Jesus years later summarizes Haggai's message well: "Do not worry, saying, 'What shall we eat?' or 'What shall we drink?' or 'What shall we wear?' . . . But seek first his [God's] kingdom and his righteousness, and all these things will be given to you as well" (Matthew 6:31, 33). Amazingly, Haggai strikes an immediate chord of response in his audience. Prophets before him, such as Amos, Isaiah, or Jeremiah, spoke for decades without seeing such a heartfelt reaction.

—PY

Daily Contemplation

What tends to distract you from spiritual priorities today?

DAY 187

The Lord Promises to Bless Jerusalem
Zechariah 8:1–23

Another younger prophet named Zechariah (ZEK-uh-RI-uh) joins Haggai in his campaign to lift the spirits of the settlers in Jerusalem (Ezra 5:1 lists both these prophets by name). The two have a similar message but a different approach. Whereas Haggai asks the Jews to look around at their current conditions and then make some needed changes, Zechariah calls them to look beyond the present and envision a new Jerusalem, a "Faithful City."

At the time, the pioneers are focusing on immediate goals: the next planting of crops, basic shelter for their families, repopulating the deserted city. Zechariah lifts their sights toward a far more glorious future, when Jerusalem will be a light to the world and people from many nations will stream to the city "because we have heard that God is with you." The prophet gives his prescription for reaching such a state: The new society must be built on justice, honesty, integrity, and peace.

It will take years to rebuild the city of Jerusalem, and centuries for Israel to regain some form of political independence. The Jews who are laboring so hard must ask themselves often, "Is this all God has in mind for us?" Zechariah replies with a resounding "No!" He insists that the small refugee community in fact holds the key to the world's future: Their new beginning will lead the way to a Messiah who will bring hope to the whole earth.

Following Haggai's lead, Zechariah seizes upon the need to rebuild the temple as a vital first step. These prophets see that as long as the temple lies in ruins, Israel's distinctive character as a people of God is suspect. Together, the two men have a remarkable effect on their countrymen. They urge the Jews to build again, and within four years the temple is completed, giving the nation a central reminder of its original covenant with God.

—PY

Daily Contemplation

When was the last time you asked, "Is this all God has in mind for me?"

DAY 188

Artaxerxes Sends Nehemiah to Jerusalem
Nehemiah 1:1–2:20

Sixty-five years have passed. The Jews have a temple in Jerusalem, yes, but little else. The holy city is sparsely occupied; most Jews have settled in the outlying villages and towns rather than inside its walls. Indeed, with all the intermarriage and mixing with foreigners, the entire community seems on the verge of losing its unique identity. The Jews' cultural and religious heritage is slipping away.

What can stop the downhill slide? One man, a Jewish exile who has stayed behind in Babylon, has an idea. Like Daniel before him, Nehemiah (NEE-uh-MI-uh) has risen in the ranks of a foreign government (Persia) and is prospering. Nevertheless, his heart is with his countrymen back in Jerusalem, and when he hears the dismaying reports from that city, he feels compelled to act. He obtains the king's permission to lead an expedition to Jerusalem with the goal of rebuilding the city's wall.

In an age when nomadic warriors pose a constant danger, a wall offers a city its only security. It was for lack of a wall that the Jews scattered among their neighbors and are now facing permanent assimilation into other cultures. By constructing a wall, Nehemiah can help make Jerusalem into a sacred city again and protect its residents by controlling who comes and goes.

Nehemiah stands in a long line of remarkable Israelite leaders such as Moses, Samuel, David, Hezekiah, and Josiah. Strictly speaking, he is not a prophet, although he is surely a man of God. He does not act without prayer, and he does not pray without acting. Although he has enormous skills in management and leadership, he does not seek after earthly status—if he did, he would have never left Persia.

Nehemiah improvises as he goes, meeting each new challenge with a combination of business savvy, courage, and dependence on God. He mobilizes work crews, fights off opposition, reforms the court system, purifies religious practices, and, when necessary, rallies the troops with stirring speeches. And he does all this while "on leave" from his responsibilities as a statesman in the Persian court.

—PY

Daily Contemplation

Do you see any secrets of success in this record of Nehemiah's actions?

DAY 189

Ezra Reads the Law
Nehemiah 7:33–8:18

Nehemiah, an impressive leader, is downright indomitable when paired with Ezra. The two make a perfect combination. Nehemiah, emboldened by good political connections, inspires others with his hands-on management style and his fearless optimism. Ezra leads more by moral force than by personality. He can trace his priestly lineage all the way back to Moses' brother Aaron, and he seems singularly determined to restore integrity to that office.

Upon his arrival in Jerusalem some years before, Ezra was shocked by the Jews' spiritual apathy. Rather than mounting a soapbox and scolding them for their failures, he tore his hair and beard, threw himself on the ground, and began a fast of repentance (see Ezra 9). His remarkable display of contrition so startled the Jewish settlers that they all agreed to repent and change their ways. Ezra had that kind of moral influence over people.

The action in this chapter takes place after Nehemiah has completed the arduous task of repairing the wall. Safe at last from their enemies, the Jews gather in hopes of regaining some sense of national identity. As spiritual leader, Ezra addresses the huge crowd. He stands on a newly built platform and begins to read from an ancient document, the scroll that contains the Israelites' original covenant with God.

As Ezra reads, a sound of weeping begins to rise, spreading throughout the multitude. The Bible does not explain the reason for the tears. Are the people feeling guilt over their long history of breaking that covenant? Or nostalgia over the favored days when Israel had full independence?

Whatever the reason, this is no time for grieving. Nehemiah and Ezra send out orders to prepare for a huge feast and celebration. God wants joy, not mourning. His chosen people are being rebuilt, just as surely as the stone walls of Jerusalem have been rebuilt.

The central image of this chapter—a lone figure atop a wooden platform reading from a scroll—comes to symbolize the Jewish people. They are becoming "people of the Book." The Jews have not regained the territory and splendor their nation once enjoyed under David and Solomon. The temple they have painstakingly constructed will eventually fall to looters, just like the one it replaced. But the returnees will never forget the lesson of Ezra. He becomes the prototype for a new leader of the Jews: a scribe, a student of Scripture.

—PY

Daily Contemplation

How important is the Bible in your life?

DAY 190

Building God into Our Lives
Reflection

Who and what have you built into your life? Whether consciously or not, we all build space into our lives for what we most value. A glance at your calendar over the last months will reveal what holds the highest priority. How often does God appear in the pages of your calendar? How much of a priority does the reading and study of his Word represent? Do appointments with God get scheduled as often as business lunches and visits to the hair salon?

For many years the people of Israel and Judah increasingly let other people and pursuits take priority over their worship of God and attention to his Word. In time they almost completely lost their knowledge of the law. God didn't force himself on them; rather, he let them walk away and stay away for a long time. Only by experiencing life without God would they remember what they were missing.

Through Ezra, Haggai, Zechariah, and Nehemiah, the Jewish people understood again their deep-seated need to walk closely with God and live by his Word. They celebrated with great joy upon hearing the law again for the first time, "because they now understood the words that had been made known to them" (Nehemiah 8:12). Hearing God again helped them find sense in living as well as guidance for the present and hope for the future. The people understood, as David had, that "your word is a lamp for my feet, a light on my path" (Psalm 119:105).

In rebuilding the temple and Jerusalem, the Jewish people declared they were once more building God into their lives. They needed him and needed to live near his holiness and close to his teaching. Apart from him they would have no real joy.

Today it's not a sacred building or city or priest that defines God's presence in our lives. Now God's Spirit dwells inside us. Each believer has become a living, breathing temple of God. We need to work at staying in touch with God, however. We must be intentional about building a prominent place for God in our lives.

God's Word serves as our foundation. Never will we outgrow our need for studying the Bible. Never can we know it well enough. Stone by stone, reading and learning, we build God an enduring home in our hearts.

—BQ

Daily Contemplation

What have you done to intentionally build God into your life?

DAY 191

Queen Vashti Deposed
Esther 1:1–22

At that time King Xerxes [ZERK-seez] reigned from his royal throne in the citadel of Susa, and in the third year of his reign he gave a banquet for all his nobles and officials. . . . On the seventh day, when King Xerxes was in high spirits from wine, he commanded the seven eunuchs who served him . . . to bring before him Queen Vashti [VASH-ti], wearing her royal crown, in order to display her beauty to the people and nobles, for she was lovely to look at. But when the attendants delivered the king's command, Queen Vashti refused to come. Then the king became furious and burned with anger. (Esther 1:2–3, 10–12)

Not every Jewish exile took the opportunity to return to their homeland. Some had put down roots during the half century of Babylonian captivity, and when the more tolerant Persian regime took charge, many of them decided to stay. (Communities of Jews in present-day Iraq and Syria trace their ancestry to this group of exiles.) This adventure story concerns two such Jews who stay behind, a beautiful woman named Esther and her cousin Mordecai (MOHR-duh-ki).

Before the Israelites were seized by Babylon, Isaiah and Jeremiah prophesied about their future, urging the remnant to leave Babylon after seventy years' captivity. They encouraged the Israelites of the future to return to the land where God would fulfill his covenant promises.

Although Esther and Mordecai do not leave, they play a crucial role in preserving the Jews who remain behind. God reminds his people through the book of Esther that he will keep his promises, whether they live in Jerusalem, surrounded by powerful nations, or in the midst of the Babylonian Empire.

—BQ

Daily Contemplation

What situation in your life causes you to need God's reassurance that he will care for you and preserve you?

DAY 192

Esther Made Queen
Esther 2:1–23

Then the king's personal attendants proposed, "Let a search be made for beautiful young virgins for the king. . . . Then let the young woman who pleases the king be queen instead of Vashti." This advice appealed to the king, and he followed it. Now there was in the citadel of Susa a Jew of the tribe of Benjamin, named Mordecai . . . Mordecai had a cousin named Hadassah . . . . This young woman, who was also known as Esther, had a lovely figure and was beautiful. Mordecai had taken her as his own daughter when her father and mother died. When the king's order and edict had been proclaimed, many young women were brought to the citadel of Susa . . . . Esther also was taken to the king's palace . . ." Now the king was attracted to Esther more than to any of the other women . . . . So he set a royal crown on her head and made her queen instead of Vashti. (Esther 2:2, 4–5, 7–8, 17)

Esther's story begins with intrigue as she enters the running for Queen Vashti's replacement. Esther handles her position in the royal palace very differently than Daniel did, however. Whereas Daniel refused to eat food from the king's table because it would be considered unclean by Jewish law, Esther accepts the special food she is given, and then eventually marries an unbeliever—both actions forbidden in God's law.

We don't know how much of the law Esther and Mordecai knew, nor do we know why they chose not to return to Jerusalem. But rather than condoning Esther's actions, God uses the book of Esther to remind his people that he can protect and use them whatever their situation. His grace shines through, illuminating once more his great love for his people.

—BQ

Daily Contemplation

How have you seen God's grace in your life despite a past mistake?

DAY 193

Haman's Plot and Moredecai's Plan
Esther 3:1–4:17

The Jews in Persia face a grave crisis. Their success has attracted so much jealousy that a powerful man is leading a conspiracy to kill every Jew in the land. Tragically, the underlying "plot" of Esther is an old and familiar one to Jews, for throughout history—Roman campaigns, medieval Jew hunts, Russian pogroms, Hitler's "final solution"—no other group has faced such a constant threat of extermination.

Although the book of Esther never once mentions the word **God**, the story highlights the many "coincidences" that work together on the Jews' behalf. By the "accident" of her beauty and the "accident" of the former queen's dismissal, Esther has risen from obscurity to become queen of the Persian Empire. She alone, of all the Jews, has access to the king. As her cousin Mordecai puts it, "Who knows but that you have come to your royal position for such a time as this?" (Esther 4:14).

Yet in Esther's day a queen does not easily stand up to her husband—especially a husband like Xerxes, who has already summarily dismissed one queen for insubordination. By intervening for the sake of her race, Esther might be putting her own life in jeopardy.

The book of Esther recounts a thrilling chapter in the story of God's love for the Jews. While no other group has been so persecuted, no other group has shown the Jews' ability to overcome adversity. How? Esther reveals God's exquisite timing combined with the courage of individuals who "happen" to be in the right place at the right time.

—PY

--- *Daily Contemplation* ---

Someone has called coincidences "God's way of working anonymously." Do you tend to give God credit for the coincidences in your life?

DAY 194

Esther's Request to the King
Esther 5:1–6:14

That night the king could not sleep; so he ordered the book of the chronicles, the record of his reign, to be brought in and read to him. It was found recorded there that Mordecai had exposed Bigthana and Teresh, two of the king's officers who guarded the doorway, who had conspired to assassinate King Xerxes. . . . "Go at once," the king commanded Haman. "Get the robe and the horse and do just as you have suggested for Mordecai the Jew, who sits at the king's gate. Do not neglect anything you have recommended." So Haman got the robe and the horse. He robed Mordecai, and led him on horseback through the city streets, proclaiming before him, "This is what is done for the man the king delights to honor!" (Esther 6:1–2, 10–11)

In one of the most epic stories of the Bible, God reverses the flow of history and brings justice and honor to his people. Every sign points to the destruction of Jews, including Mordecai and Esther. The evil are favored and the good are overlooked. But grim as the circumstances appear, God has not lost control. Through what seems crazy happenstance, God elevates Mordecai and humiliates Haman.

The story is too good to be true—the stuff of fairy tales. But God, the author of history, proves himself capable of "finding a way when there is no way." After everything the Jewish people have experienced in recent decades of exile and rebuilding, Esther's story brings a strong reminder that nothing is impossible with God. Indeed God, a miracle worker, delights in weaving his miracles into the everyday happenings of life. Esther reminds us that we can never be sure when God will move to turn a situation around through some sort of baffling and curious coincidence.

—BQ

Daily Contemplation

When was the last time you suspected God might have something to do with a positive development in your life?

DAY 195

Haman Impaled
Esther 7:1–8:17

Esther again pleaded with the king, falling at his feet and weeping. She begged him to put an end to the evil plan of Haman the Agagite, which he had devised against the Jews . . . . "If it pleases the king," she said, "and if he regards me with favor and thinks it the right thing to do, and if he is pleased with me, let an order be written overruling the dispatches that Haman son of Hammedatha, the Agagite, devised and wrote to destroy the Jews in all the king's provinces. For how can I bear to see disaster fall on my people? How can I bear to see the destruction of my family?" King Xerxes replied to Queen Esther and to Mordecai the Jew, "Because Haman attacked the Jews, I have given his estate to Esther, and they have impaled him on the pole he set up. Now write another decree in the king's name in behalf of the Jews as seems best to you, and seal it with the king's signet ring." (Esther 8:3, 5–8)

God finishes Esther's story in a royal fashion. The king grants all her requests, taking Mordecai into the palace and sparing the Jews from mandated destruction. To cap off the story, many Gentiles become Jews, turning to the God who has awed them and evoked their respect. Not only does God save his own people, he draws others to himself as well. The book of Esther shows God's care for justice and mercy both.

In yet another unforgettable Old Testament scene, God expresses his deep love for people who, though imperfect, show courage in carrying out his plan. In their faithfulness they find his unending forgiveness and care.

—BQ

Daily Contemplation

What was it about God that first caught your attention?

DAY 196

God's Strategic Ways
Reflection

When was the last time you were in the right place at the right time? People tell stories about getting jobs, meeting spouses, winning prizes, and finding bargains, all because they were in the right place at the right time. Often these seemingly accidental strokes of fortune are explained with, "It was meant to be." If the job is offered, it was meant to be. If the relationship flourishes, it was meant to be. On the converse, if the job falls through or the relationship sours, it wasn't meant to be.

What lies behind these words? Are we speaking in a roundabout way of God's hand in our lives? Or are we attributing our successes and failures to the more general and impersonal hand of fate?

Esther had several such fortunate experiences. First selected as a contestant to become queen, she then won the king's favor. She was living in the palace at the time a plot to kill the Jews developed. She gained the trust of the king by informing him of an assassination plot, and then prepared a banquet to present her bold request. Esther often found herself in the right place at the right time to save her people, and she responded courageously. Her circumstances were more than "meant to be." They were arranged by a sovereign God who had a plan for Esther's life and for the lives of his people.

We serve the same God as did the Jews of Esther's day. God tells us, "I the LORD do not change" (Malachi 3:6). His ways of moving in our lives may look different from what we see in the Old Testament, but God has not changed, nor have his purposes. Just as he had a plan for his people then, he has a plan for those who belong to him now. We can trust that whenever we find ourselves in the right place at the right time, God's hand is present.

"Every good and perfect gift is from above, coming down from the Father of the heavenly lights, who does not change like shifting shadows" (James 1:17). We can thank God for each stroke of good fortune, each providential gift. Sometimes they are simple blessings. Other times they are his strategic ways of fulfilling the bigger purposes he has for us.

—BQ

Daily Contemplation

Do you wonder about the way your life has unfolded? Do you have questions about failures or missed opportunities? Ask God to help you better see your life through his eyes, and place yourself in his care, trusting that his good purpose for you will be achieved.

DAY 197

Airing Complaints
Malachi 2:17–3:18

Malachi (MAL-uh-ki) is the last Old Testament voice, and his book serves as a good prelude to the next four hundred years of biblical silence. From the Jews' point of view, those four centuries could be termed "the era of lowered expectations." They have returned to the land, but that land remains a backwater province under the domination of several imperial armies. The grand future of triumph and world peace described by the prophets seems a distant pipe dream. Even the restored temple causes stabs of nostalgic pain: It hardly rivals Solomon's majestic building, and no one has seen God's glory descend on this new temple as it did in Solomon's day.

A general malaise sets in among the Jews, a low-grade disappointment with God that shows in their complaints and also in their actions. They are not notorious sinners like the people before the exile, who practiced child sacrifice and brought idols into the temple. They go through the motions of religion but have lost intimate contact with their God.

The prophet Malachi writes in the form of a dialogue, with the "children" of Israel bringing their grievances to God, the Father. One gripe bothers them more than any: Following God has not brought the anticipated reward. "It is futile to serve God," they complain. "What do we gain by carrying out his requirements and going about like mourners before the LORD Almighty?"

In reply, Malachi calls his people to rise above their selfishness and to trust the God of the covenant; he has not abandoned his treasured possession. "Test me in this," says God, "and see if I will not throw open the floodgates of heaven and pour out so much blessing that there will not be room enough to store it" (3:10).

At least some of Malachi's message will take hold. During the next four centuries, reform movements like the Pharisees become increasingly devoted to keeping the law. Unfortunately, many of them will cling fiercely to that law even when Jesus, the "messenger of the covenant" predicted by Malachi, brings a new emphasis on forgiveness and grace.

—PY

Daily Contemplation

When was the last time you questioned God's love and fairness? Did God prove himself to you?

PART 6

Cries of Pain

DAY 198

Job Is Tested
Job 1:1–2:10

One book of the Bible is virtually ageless. It relates the story of Job (JOHB), a rich "patriarch" who might have lived in Abraham's time but whose story was likely reduced to this poetic form hundreds of years later during Israel's literary Golden Age. Regardless, the book raises questions so urgent and universal that it speaks to every era.

In the period between the Old and New Testaments, the book of Job became a favorite of the Jews. His story centers on a question that has haunted the Jews from the earliest days, when they were first chosen as God's covenant people. To put it bluntly, they expected better treatment. Job has the courage to voice the question aloud—***Is God unfair?***—and no one has asked that question more eloquently or profoundly.

The book seems meant to explore the outer limits of unfairness. Job, the most upright, outstanding man in all the earth, must endure the worst calamities. He suffers unbearable punishment—but for what? What has he done wrong?

The book reads like a detective story in which the readers know more than the central characters. The very first two chapters answer Job's main concern: He has done nothing to deserve such suffering. We, the readers, know that, but nobody tells Job and his friends. As the prologue reveals, Job is involved in a cosmic test, a contest proposed in heaven but staged on earth.

People in Malachi's day asked, "What do we gain by following God?" and that question gets at the heart of Job's test. Satan claims that people love God only because of his good gifts. According to Satan, no one would ever follow God apart from some selfish gain. ***Of course*** Job is blameless and upright; he is also rich and healthy. Remove those good things from Job's life, Satan challenges, and Job's faith will melt away along with his riches and health.

God's reputation is on the line in this book, resting suspensefully on the response of a shattered man. Will Job continue to trust God's goodness, even as his world crumples around him? Will he believe in a God of justice, even when life seems grotesquely unfair?

—PY

Daily Contemplation

What situation has caused you to question why bad things happen to good people?

DAY 199

The Lord Speaks
Job 38:1–41

It seems a travesty to skip thirty-five chapters and rush to the conclusion, for those middle chapters of Job express the human dilemma as well as it has ever been expressed. Like all grieving persons, Job drifts on emotional currents, alternately whining, exploding, cajoling, and collapsing into self-pity. Sometimes he agrees with his friends, who blame Job himself for his suffering, and sometimes he violently disagrees with them. Occasionally, in the midst of deepest despair, he comes up with a statement of brilliant hope.

Nearly every argument on the problem of pain appears somewhere in the book of Job, but the disputation never seems to help Job much. He's experiencing a crisis of relationship more than a crisis of intellectual doubt. **Can he trust God?** Job wants one thing above all else: an appearance by the one Person who can explain his miserable fate. He wants to meet God himself, face-to-face.

Eventually, as this chapter relates, Job gets his wish. God shows up in person. He times his entrance with perfect irony, just as Job's friend Elihu (el-LI-hoo) is expounding on why Job has no right to expect a visit from God.

No one—not Job or any of his friends—is prepared for what God has to say. Job has saved up a long list of questions, but it is God, not Job, who asks the questions. "Brace yourself like a man," he begins, "I will question you, and you shall answer me." Brushing aside thirty-five chapters' worth of debates on the problem of pain, God plunges instead into a majestic poem on the wonders of the natural world. He guides Job through the gallery of creation, pointing out with pride such favorites as mountain goats, wild donkeys, ostriches, and eagles (Job 39).

Above all, God's speech defines the vast difference between a God of all creation and one puny man like Job. "Do you have an arm like God's?" he asks at one point (40:9). God reels off natural phenomena—the solar system, constellations, thunderstorms, wild animals—that Job cannot begin to explain. God's point is obvious: *If you can't comprehend the visible world you live in, how dare you expect to comprehend a world you cannot even see!*

—PY

Daily Contemplation

Does God's reply to Job surprise you? In Job's place, what kind of answer would you have wanted from God?

DAY 200

Job Is Restored
Job 42:1-17

What God says is not nearly so important as the mere fact that he shows up. God's presence spectacularly answers Job's biggest question: Is anybody out there? "Surely I spoke of things I did not understand," Job confesses, "things too wonderful for me to know." Catching sight of the big picture at last, Job repents in dust and ashes.

God has some words of correction for Job. No one, not Job and especially not his friends, has the evidence needed to make judgments about how he runs the world. But mainly God praises Job, calling him "my servant." (Ezekiel 14:14 mentions Job in God's list of the finest human examples of righteousness.)

Satan wagered with God that Job would "surely curse you to your face" (1:11). He lost. Despite all that happens, Job does not curse God. He clings to his belief in a just God even though everything in his experience seems to contradict it. Significantly, Job speaks his contrite words *before* any of his losses have been restored, while still sitting in a pile of ashes, naked, covered with sores. He has learned to believe even in the dark, with no hope of reward.

The book of Job ends with some surprising twists. Job's friends, who spouted all the right pieties and cliches, have to plead for forgiveness. Job, who raged and cried out, receives twice as much as he ever had before: fourteen thousand sheep, six thousand camels, one thousand donkeys, and ten new children.

The book of Job will give much comfort to Jews during the harsh period between the Old and New Testaments. It demonstrates the important lesson that not all suffering comes as punishment; a person's trials may in fact be used to win a great spiritual victory. And the happy ending of Job also echoes the promises of the prophets, awakening hopes for a future time of peace and restoration.

Christians, looking back, see yet another message in Job, who stands as an early prototype of the Messiah. Job, the best man of his day, suffered terribly; Jesus, a perfect man, would suffer even more.

—PY

Daily Contemplation

Have you experienced any Job-like trials in your life? What were the results?

DAY 201

Loving God Freely
Reflection

On the surface, the book of Job centers on the problem of suffering. Underneath, a different issue is at stake: the doctrine of human freedom. Job had to endure undeserved suffering in order to demonstrate that God is ultimately interested in freely given love.

The contest posed between Satan and God was no trivial exercise. Satan's accusation that Job loved God only because God had "put a hedge around him" (Job 1:10) stands as an attack on God's character. It implies that God is not worthy of love in himself; faithful people like Job follow him only because they are "bribed" to do so. Job's response when all the props of faith were removed would prove or disprove Satan's challenge.

To understand this issue of human freedom, it may help to imagine a world in which everyone truly does get what he or she deserves. That imaginary world has a certain appeal. It would be just and consistent, and everyone would clearly know what God expected. Fairness would reign. There is, however, one huge problem with such a tidy world: It's not at all what God wants to accomplish on earth. He wants from us love, freely given love, and we dare not underestimate the premium God places on that love. Freely given love is so important to God that he allows our planet to be a cancer of evil in his universe—for a time.

Throughout the Bible, an analogy that illustrates the relationship between God and his people keeps surfacing. God, the husband, is pictured as wooing the bride to himself. He wants her love. If the world were constructed so that every sin earned a punishment and every good deed a reward, the parallel would not hold. The closest analogue to that relationship would be a kept woman, who is pampered and bribed and locked away in a room so that the lover can be sure of her faithfulness. God does not "keep" his people. He loves us, gives himself to us, and eagerly awaits our free response.

God wants us to choose to love him freely, even when that choice involves pain, because we are committed to *him*, not to our own good feelings and rewards. He wants us to cleave to him, as Job did, even when we have every reason to deny him hotly. Job clung to God's justice when he was the best example in history of God's apparent injustice. He did not seek the Giver because of his gifts; when all gifts were removed, he still sought the Giver.[34]

—PY

Daily Contemplation

Talk with God about your attitude toward suffering. Let him know you want your love for him to be bigger than anger or dismay over your circumstances.

DAY 202

Comfort for God's People
Isaiah 40:1–31

The book of Job concerns the sufferings of one man. The prophets of Israel and Judah speak to the sufferings of an entire race. Most of the Jews at the end of the Old Testament are scattered across the Middle East, dispersed by Assyrian and Babylonian armies. The minority who have returned to Jerusalem live under the total domination of a foreign government in Persia. The same questions Job asked while scratching himself with shards of pottery the Jews ask now about their people. Has God abandoned them? Will they have a future?

The Jews' hope for the future centers in a Messiah, who has been promised by almost all the prophets. After Malachi, as the years drag on, the Jews scour the scrolls of these prophets, seeking clues into their destiny. Of all the prophets, Isaiah gives perhaps the clearest picture of what the Jews can expect. His earlier messages blast his nation's sin and unfaithfulness. But beginning with chapter 40, Isaiah shifts into a new key. Gone are the bleak predictions of judgment. Instead, a message of hope and joy and light breaks in. "Speak tenderly to Jerusalem, and proclaim to her that her hard service has been completed" (40:2).

According to Isaiah, what happened to Judah was not God's defeat. God has in mind a new thing, a plan far more wonderful than anything seen before. The book of Isaiah explains why the future holds hope—not just for the Jews but for the whole world. A mysterious figure called "the servant" will, through his suffering, provide a means of rescue. Later, in a faraway time, God will usher in peace for all, in a new heaven and new earth.

Chapter 40 introduces a new tone in Isaiah with the sweeping declaration that God reigns over all. In many ways, these soaring words restate in a global sense God's personal message to Job. "Surely the nations are like a drop in a bucket; . . . He sits enthroned above the circle of the earth, and its people are like grasshoppers." God makes himself known as the master of nature, of history—indeed, of the entire universe.

—PY

Daily Contemplation

What do Isaiah's words "Those who hope in the LORD will renew their strength" (40:31) mean to you today?

DAY 203

The Suffering Servant
Isaiah 52:1–15

Isaiah's four songs about a "suffering servant" are among the richest, and most closely studied, passages in the Old Testament. The first part of this chapter stirs anticipation for a glorious time when God will restore Jerusalem and prove to all "Your God reigns!" It looks as if Israel will gain revenge on their enemies at last.

But the author explains how God will redeem Jerusalem by introducing the mysterious figure of the suffering servant, whose appearance was "disfigured beyond that of any human being." Who is this suffering servant? And how will such a wounded person bring about a great victory?

Jewish scholars puzzled over these passages for centuries. What exactly did the prophet mean? Some of the servant songs refer to the nation of Israel as a whole, but passages like this one portray the servant as a specific individual, a great leader who suffers terribly. Although Isaiah holds him up as the deliverer of all humankind, he more resembles a tragic figure than a hero.

Some Jewish scholars speculated the prophet was describing himself or perhaps a colleague, such as Jeremiah. Still others focused their hopes on a Messiah to come. In general, however, the idea of the suffering servant never really caught on among the Jewish nation. They longed for a victorious Messiah, not a suffering one.

The image of the suffering servant went underground, as it were, lying dormant for centuries. Then, in a dramatic scene early in his ministry, Jesus quoted from one of Isaiah's servant passages. After reading aloud in the synagogue, Jesus "rolled up the scroll, gave it back to the attendant, and sat down. The eyes of everyone in the synagogue were fastened on him. He began by saying to them, 'Today this scripture is fulfilled in your hearing'" (Luke 4:20–21).

A link snapped into place for some, but not all, of Jesus' listeners. The Messiah had come at last—not as a conquering general but as a carpenter's son from Nazareth.

—PY

Daily Contemplation

What kind of Savior were you looking for when you found Jesus?

DAY 204

The Glory of the Servant
Isaiah 53:1–12

> We all, like sheep, have gone astray,
>   each of us has turned to our own way;
> and the LORD has laid on him
>   the iniquity of us all. (Isaiah 53:6)

New Testament writers leave no doubt as to the identity of the suffering servant: At least ten times they apply Isaiah's four songs directly to Jesus (for example, Matthew 8:17, Luke 22:37, 1 Peter 2:22–24). In one instance, Philip corrects an Ethiopian official who wonders if the suffering servant refers to an ancient prophet (Acts 8:26–35).

Isaiah 53 reads almost like an eyewitness account of Jesus' last days on earth. The physical description is shocking. The servant "had no beauty or majesty to attract us to him"; he was "like one from whom people hide their faces." As this chapter foretells, Jesus did not open his mouth to answer accusers at his trial. He left no descendants. He was cut off in the prime of life and, thanks to a gracious friend, was buried in a rich man's tomb. But that was not the end. After three days he saw "the light of life."

According to Isaiah, the servant died for a very specific purpose: "He was pierced for our transgressions." He took on pain for the sake of others, for *our* sakes. His wounds, an apparent defeat, made possible a great victory. His death sealed a future triumph when all that is wrong on earth will be set right. Significantly, the book of Isaiah does not end with the suffering servant image but goes on to describe life in a new heaven and new earth. But the time of travail was a necessary first step, for the servant absorbed in himself the punishment that was due for all the evils of the world.

Isaiah 53 forms an underlying foundation for much New Testament theology. In addition, these detailed prophecies, recorded many centuries before Jesus' birth, offer convincing proof that God is revealing his plan for the ages through the ancient prophets. He has not permanently severed his covenant with the Jews. Rather, out of Jewish roots—King David's own stock—he will bring forth a new king, a king like no other, to reclaim all the earth.

—PY

Daily Contemplation

Who in your life needs to hear about the Messiah, Jesus, prophesied here in Isaiah?

DAY 205

Invitation to the Thirsty
Isaiah 55:1–13

Isaiah has seen a glimpse of the future, and that glimpse convinces him that good news lies ahead. No invading armies, no terrible calamities can interfere with God's final purpose for the earth.

"For a brief moment I abandoned you, but with deep compassion I will bring you back," God says to Israel (Isaiah 54:7). Isaiah foretells a time when the ruined holy city, now rebuilt, will achieve an unprecedented level of greatness. Yet the promise in these chapters goes far beyond what has ever been realized in Jerusalem. It merges into a vision of a future state where sin and sorrow no longer exist and we live in final peace with God.

This last part of Isaiah, addressed to a people facing deep despair, opens the door for the Jews to become a gift to all people. According to Isaiah, word about God will go out to nations nearby and faraway, and to distant islands that have never heard of him (66:18–21). This prophecy finds fulfillment in Jesus, who recruits disciples to carry his message worldwide. Through his life and death, the suffering servant indeed proclaims the gospel to the entire world.

In this and other soaring chapters, Isaiah describes the future with such eloquence that New Testament books like Revelation cannot improve on the language; they merely quote Isaiah. Whatever longings we feel on earth—for peace, for an end to suffering, for an unspoiled planet—will someday be fulfilled. Isaiah assures us that one day our very best dreams, all of them, will come true.

We may not understand the process the world must go through to arrive at that future time: "'For my thoughts are not your thoughts, neither are your ways my ways,' declares the LORD." But, as this chapter makes clear, God's covenant with his people is everlasting. Nothing can cancel it.

As the decades, even centuries, pass, empires—Babylonian, Persian, Egyptian, Greek, Roman—rise and fall, their armies chasing each other across the hills and plains. Each new empire subjugates the Jews with ease. Sometimes the entire race verges on extinction. Four centuries separate the last words of the prophets in the Old Testament and the first words of Matthew in the New Testament—"The four hundred silent years," they are called. Does God care? Is he even alive? In desperation the common people wait for a Messiah; they have no other hope.

—PY

Daily Contemplation

What would you most like to see changed in the world? Does Isaiah speak to that change?

DAY 206

Jesus, Our Highest Choice, Our Greatest Promise
Reflection

What are your deepest hopes, your most-cherished dreams? Isaiah has given us, as well as the beleaguered Jewish people, a vision of hope for the future. Sickness and sorrow, oppression and injustice are not the final outcome for those who walk with God. Isaiah proclaims strength for the weary, joy and peace for believers, and God's power one day revealed to everyone in every nation. Ours is a future replete with goodness and promise.

Isaiah intends not only to clue us in to this future but also to impact our lives in the present. For this reason, he pleads with believers to make choices in light of our future. We know only a shadow of the redeemed world that awaits us, and we live with the mistaken values of a fallen human race. Many of the goals and aspirations of the people of our world are mere counterfeits of the lasting reality God has set in place. In Isaiah's words, we spend money on what is not bread, and labor on what does not satisfy.

Author and futures consultant Tom Sine writes, "We have bought into an image of the better future that equates happiness with acquisition. We have really come to believe that the more we accumulate in our garages, ring up on our charge cards, and invest in the newest novelties, the happier we will be."[35] Especially for those in the Western world, this pattern of acquisition has become the norm. There is a real danger that the pursuit of possessions can distract our souls. We await a glorious future, yet as we are drawn into the world's pursuits, we lose all sight of what brings authentic joy.

We find—and observe in others—that the world's quest never fully satisfies. In fact, often in direct proportion, those who are most successful at the quest are the most dissatisfied. Sine notes the words of British missionary and author Lesslie Newbigin: "Technology continues to forge ahead with more and more brilliant achievements; but the novels, the drama and the general literature of the West are full of nihilism and despair."[36]

"Listen, listen to me," Isaiah pleads. "Eat what is good, and you will delight in the richest of fare" (Isaiah 55:2). Only Jesus can offer food that will fill us and satisfy us. Believers have learned this secret, and God has given us power to make the secret known to all who need the Bread of Life.

"Our vocation is not the preservation and advancement of the present order, but cooperation with God in the inbreaking of a radical new one," Sine writes. "Never has it been more urgent for people of faith and people of concern to question the visions and values to which we have given our lives and to begin to dream new dreams while there is yet time."[37]

—BQ

--- *Daily Contemplation* ---

What are your dreams? How do you spend your money and your labor? Talk with God about your pursuits and ask him to help you dream his dreams. Ask him to make Isaiah's vision for the present and the future more of an abiding vision in your life.

PART 7

A Surprising Messiah

DAY 207

The Births of John the Baptist and Jesus Foretold
Luke 1:5–52

Does any human emotion run as deep as hope? Fairy tales, for example, pass down from generation to generation a belief in the impossibly happy ending, an irrepressible sense that in the end the forces of evil will lose the struggle and the brave and good will somehow triumph.

For Jews at the dawn of the first millennium, all hope seems like a fairy tale. As Middle Eastern empires rise and fall, the Jewish people can never break free from the domination of greater powers. No prophet has spoken to them in four hundred years. At the end of the Old Testament, God is in hiding. He has long threatened to hide his face, and as he does so, a dark shadow falls across the planet.

During the four centuries of God's silence, the Jews wait and wonder. God seems passive, unconcerned, and deaf to their prayers. Only one hope remains, the ancient promise of a Messiah. On that promise the Jews stake everything. And then something momentous happens. The birth of a baby is announced—a birth unlike any that have come before.

You can catch the excitement just by reading the reactions of people in this chapter. The way Luke tells it, events surrounding Jesus' birth resemble a joy-filled musical. Characters crowd into the scene: a white-haired great uncle, an astonished virgin, and later a tottery old prophetess (Luke 2). They all smile broadly and, as likely as not, burst into song. Once Mary overcomes the shock from seeing an angel, she lets loose with a beautiful hymn. Even an unborn cousin kicks for joy inside his mother's womb.

Luke takes care to make direct connections to Old Testament promises of a Messiah; the angel Gabriel even calls John the Baptist an "Elijah" sent to prepare the way for the Lord. Clearly, something is brewing on planet Earth. Among dreary, defeated villagers in a remote corner of the Roman Empire, something climactically good is breaking out.

—PY

Daily Contemplation

If an angel appeared to you, would you likely respond like Zechariah, in disbelief, or like Mary, in humble assent?

DAY 208

An Angel Appears to Joseph
Matthew 1:1–25

"Joseph son of David, do not be afraid to take Mary home as your wife, because what is conceived in her is from the Holy Spirit. She will give birth to a son, and you are to give him the name Jesus, because he will save his people from their sins." (Matthew 1:20–21)

Matthew, the author of this gospel, was a Jewish tax collector who became one of Jesus' twelve disciples. In the first passage of this gospel Matthew offers a genealogy of Jesus, a feature that certainly would have interested any Jewish readers, who would be especially concerned about the ancestry of Jesus. The prophesied Messiah would come from the line of David, and unless the Jews see this to be true, they will not believe in Jesus as that Messiah.

Glance back at the genealogy and you'll see many familiar names: Abraham, Isaac, Jacob, Judah, Boaz, Rahab, Ruth, David, and Solomon. Through the line of his legal father, Joseph, Jesus does indeed trace back to David and to Abraham. Notice the women listed in the genealogy. The only ones who appear are those who were, in some sense, outsiders and unlikely members of a Messianic lineage. Tamar (TAY-mar) and Rahab had scandalous reputations. Ruth was a foreigner, and Bathsheba, Uriah's wife, committed adultery with David. Together with the men who are mentioned, these imperfect people experienced God's grace and became important links in the line of the Messiah.

Jesus' closest relatives, Mary and Joseph, each need great faith to play their part in Jesus' birth. Matthew focuses in this chapter on Joseph. Seven hundred years earlier God had prophesied through Isaiah that "the virgin will conceive and give birth to a son, and will call him Immanuel" (Isaiah 7:14). Now the prophecy is being realized, and Joseph has been chosen to fill the role of father. In faith, Joseph cuts short the expected one-year betrothal period and brings Mary into his home. He takes her home as his wife and cares for her during her pregnancy. No doubt the couple became the object of village gossip—just the beginning of a lifetime of misunderstanding awaiting their son Jesus.

—BQ

Daily Contemplation

Have you ever had to endure reproach from others when you knew you were in the right?

DAY 209

The Birth of John the Baptist
Luke 1:57–80

> When it was time for Elizabeth to have her baby, she gave birth to a son. . . . On the eighth day they came to circumcise the child, and they were going to name him after his father Zechariah, but his mother spoke up and said, "No! He is to be called John." . . . And the child grew and became strong in spirit; and he lived in the wilderness until he appeared publicly to Israel. (Luke 1:57, 59–60, 80)

As did Matthew in the first chapter of his Gospel, Luke also demonstrates that everything surrounding the coming of Jesus falls in line with the Old Testament prophecies of the Messiah. Luke adds details about the birth of Jesus' cousin John, who would become known as John the Baptist.

The prophet Malachi announced that God would send "my messenger, who will prepare the way before me" (Malachi 3:1). He likened this messenger to Elijah, saying, "See, I will send the prophet Elijah to you before that great and dreadful day of the LORD comes" (Malachi 4:5). Earlier in this chapter of Luke, an angel appears to Zechariah, John's father, and in announcing John's coming birth declares that John will "go on before the Lord" and minister "in the spirit and power of Elijah" (Luke 1:17).

Prophecy finds fulfillment in the life of John. Just as Elijah brought a message of judgment and redemption, so John will be a powerful forerunner announcing the coming of the awaited Messiah, the ultimate Judge and Redeemer. Just as Elijah prepared for his ministry in a desolate area, so John lives in the desert until his ministry begins. He does not fit the image of a typical Jewish holy man, donning rich robes and frequenting the temple. His style is only fitting, for he precedes a Savior who does not match the expectations of a waiting Jewish world. John will succeed in getting the attention of many people, and Jesus will fulfill the promises that many are familiar with but too few understand.

—BQ

Daily Contemplation

How do you respond when God does something unconventional in your life?

DAY 210

The Birth of Jesus
Luke 2:1–40

Nearly every time an angel appears in the Bible, the first words he says are "Don't be afraid!" Little wonder. When the supernatural makes contact with planet Earth, it usually leaves the human observers flat on their faces in catatonic fear. But Luke tells of God making an appearance on earth in a form that does not frighten. In Jesus, born in a barn and laid in a feeding trough, God achieves a mode of approach that we need not fear. What could be less scary than a newborn baby?

Imagine becoming a baby again: giving up language and muscle coordination and the ability to eat solid food and control your bladder. That gives just a hint of the "emptying" that God goes through.

According to the Bible, Jesus is both God and man. As God, he can work miracles, forgive sins, conquer death, and predict the future. Jesus does all that, provoking awe in the people around him. But for Jews accustomed to images of God as a bright cloud or pillar of fire, Jesus also causes much confusion. How could a baby in Bethlehem, a carpenter's son, a man from Nazareth, be the Messiah from God? Jesus' skin gets in the way.

Puzzled skeptics will stalk Jesus throughout his ministry. But this chapter shows that God confirms Jesus' identity from his earliest days. A group of shepherds in a field have no doubt—they hear the message of good news straight from a choir of angels. And an old prophet and prophetess recognize him also. Even the skeptical teachers in the temple are amazed.

Why does God empty himself and take on human form? The Bible gives many reasons, some densely theological and some quite practical. The upcoming scene of Jesus as an adolescent lecturing rabbis in the temple gives one clue. For the first time, ordinary people can hold a conversation, even a debate, with God in visible form. Jesus can talk to anyone—his parents, a rabbi, a poor widow—without first having to announce, "Don't be afraid!" In Jesus, God comes close.

—PY

Daily Contemplation

If Jesus were to come to hang out with you in person today, what would you want to talk to him about?

DAY 211

The Word Became Flesh
John 1:1–18

> The Word became flesh and made his dwelling among us. We have seen his glory, the glory of the one and only Son, who came from the Father, full of grace and truth. (John 1:14)

From the first words of his Gospel, John is writing about one person: Jesus. He doesn't begin with a narrative, as Matthew and Luke have done. Rather, he chooses to open his account by reaching back to the beginning of time to reveal the eternity of Jesus in his relationship to God the Father.

The passage is beautiful and filled with important theology, although in some places it may seem difficult to understand. For example, John's initial reference to Christ as "the Word" (Greek: *logos*) can be confusing. Greeks used this term *logos* in several ways. It may refer to the words spoken with the mouth, or the unspoken words of the reasoning mind. In addition, when speaking of the universe, the Greeks used *logos* to describe the rational principle that governs all things. Greek-speaking Jews, on the other hand, used *logos* in reference to God and God speaking creation into existence. Therefore John's description of Jesus as the Word is appropriate for both Jews and Greeks. Jesus, John declares, is the source of all reason, the only one with true understanding, creative power, and the capacity to rule. Jesus is the final word.

John asserts plainly that Jesus was with God in the beginning and he is God. This Messiah Jesus was not, as many claim, just a good man or a messenger from God present at the creation of the world; he is God's own Son who is also living today.

Jesus as a distinct being yet one with God seems contradictory. But that is the mystery of the Trinity: one God in three persons, Father, Son, and Holy Spirit. As part of this triune Godhead, Jesus fills the role of uniting us with God. Our eternal future depends neither on our biological family nor on the arbitrary decisions of our parents, but simply on our belief in his name. Jesus offers us the love of God in all its fullness.

—BQ

Daily Contemplation

What questions do you have about Jesus? Pray now that God would help you understand Jesus, and the Trinity, in "Spirit and in truth" (John 4:24).

DAY 212

Jesus, Our Picture of God
Reflection

What is it about Jesus that makes Christianity unique among all other religions? What sets Jesus apart from other religious leaders in world history?

John gives us the answer in the first chapter of his Gospel. He calls Jesus "the Word" and declares that Jesus both was with God and was God. Then John explains that Jesus, the Word, "became flesh and made his dwelling among us . . . full of grace and truth" (1:14). As he walked the earth in the flesh of a man, Jesus embodied the fullness of God. In his words and actions, Jesus in human form revealed God in a way God had never revealed himself before. Not only did Jesus exhibit in flesh the *truth* found only in God; he displayed the grace that defines God and sets him apart from any other purported deity from any time or place.

The book *What's So Amazing About Grace?* tells a story about British author and scholar C. S. Lewis.

> During a British conference on comparative religions, experts from around the world debated what, if any, belief was unique to the Christian faith. They began eliminating possibilities. Incarnation? Other religions had different versions of gods appearing in human forms. Resurrection? Again, other religions had accounts of return from death. The debate went on for some time until C. S. Lewis wandered into the room. "What's the rumpus about?" he asked, and heard in reply that his colleagues were discussing Christianity's unique contribution among world religions. Lewis responded, "Oh, that's easy. It's grace."
>
> After some discussion, the conferees had to agree. The notion of God's love coming to us free of charge, no strings attached, seems to go against every instinct of humanity. The Buddhist eight-fold path, the Hindu doctrine of karma, the Jewish covenant, and Muslim code of law—each of these offers a way to earn approval. Only Christianity dares to make God's love unconditional.[38]

Before Jesus came, God repeatedly exhibited his grace to the Israelite people by forgiving them for disobeying and turning their backs on him. God even showed grace toward Gentiles—people like Rahab, Ruth, and the Persians of Esther's day who turned to him. But his standard had not changed: Adherence to the law was still necessary for people to qualify to live for eternity in the presence of a holy God.

Early in the Old Testament, however, God was already foretelling a way for people to come to him apart from the law. No one in the Old Testament kept the law perfectly as God required, so only faith would ultimately qualify a person for heaven. Salvation was possible only because of the yet-to-be-completed sacrifice of Christ, the perfect God who took on the world's sin. Jesus was God's way of paying sin's debt once and for all, and his death on the cross gives us the greatest picture of God's grace and his love for us.

God has every reason to abandon us because of our failures at loving him well. Instead, through Jesus, he welcomes us and forever answers our pleas for mercy. Jesus is our picture of a holy, loving God who draws believers near once and forever.

—BQ

Daily Contemplation

How well do you know Jesus? How much has your understanding of Jesus transformed the way you see God? Talk to Jesus about your desire to get to know him better. Ask him to help you see God more clearly in the days ahead as we look at Jesus' life in the Gospels.

DAY 213

The Visit of the Magi, Travels to Egypt and Nazareth
Matthew 2:1–23

Not just a few select Jews recognize Jesus as the Messiah early on. Even some non-Jewish astronomers travel a great distance to worship the newborn King of the Jews. Tradition tells us three Magi made the trip, although no one is certain how many actually came. Whatever their number, they came prepared with special gifts. Theirs was no casual journey.

Some have speculated that the gifts the Magi brought were symbolic, not merely expensive offerings. Perhaps these precious gifts reflected the character of the child's life, with the gold representing his deity or purity, the incense his fragrant, priestly life, and the myrrh his sacrifice and death (myrrh was used for embalming). Jesus was King, Priest, and Prophet.

After receiving the acclaim of foreign visitors, Jesus' parents learn of the first threat to his life. Herod the Great, on the throne at the time of Jesus' birth, has a reputation for cruelty not only toward Jews but even toward his own family. During his lifetime he puts to death, among others, a few of his wives and several of his own children. Herod's son Archelaus (ahr-kuh-LAY-uhs) takes over one region after Herod's death and follows in his father's footsteps of tyranny and murder. (Eventually he will go insane, possibly a result of close family intermarriages.)

A few years after Jesus' birth, Joseph avoids the dangers of Archelaus and returns with his family to Nazareth, a town in Galilee ruled by another, more capable son of Herod. Joseph and Mary had left Nazareth to register for the census in Bethlehem. Now they again make the town of Nazareth their home, despite its unlikely setting for an up-and-coming Messiah.

As the military post of the north for Roman soldiers, Nazareth has earned the Jews' disdain. Jewish residents of Nazareth are thought to be sympathizers with the enemy, Rome. This reputation will help color Jesus' reputation. A later disciple, Nathanael, will first react to Jesus in reference to his Nazarene status. "Can anything good come from there?" (John 1:46). As a Nazarene, Jesus fulfills Old Testament prophecy speaking of his lowliness and the contempt many Israelites will feel toward him.

—BQ

Daily Contemplation

Can you identify in any way with the rejection Jesus felt because of the place he called home?

DAY 214

The Boy Jesus at the Temple; John the Baptist Prepares the Way
Luke 2:41–52; Matthew 3:1–12

At twelve Jesus already understands his purpose on earth, focusing even at this young age on revealing the intent of his Father. Lingering at the temple in Jerusalem despite his parents' departure may appear insensitive. As Jesus sees it, though, he is merely concentrating on pleasing his Father in heaven and completing the mission he has been sent to accomplish.

His cousin John the Baptist knows exactly why Jesus has been sent. As John prepares people for Jesus' ministry, he encounters two religious groups who will question Jesus throughout his public life. The Pharisees (FAIR-uh-sees) are a legalistic group who keep themselves separate from other Jews in a belief that they, more than any others, succeed in keeping the written law of Moses and the unwritten tradition of the Jewish elders. The Pharisees pride themselves on their knowledge of the law and Scriptures. Yet, as both John and Jesus point out, they are often hypocritical in their adherence to the law, accusing others yet rationalizing their own sin. The Sadducees (SAD-yoo-sees) concern themselves with the world and the political realm. They deny belief in such matters as angels, spirits, and the resurrection of the dead.

John addresses the mistaken assumption among many of the Pharisees and Sadducees that as children of Abraham they will automatically enter the kingdom of God. John cries a different message: "Repent, for the kingdom of heaven has come near." Only through repentance can a person be saved and transformed. Lineage won't do it, and no amount of knowledge, status, or good behavior will suffice. God requires a repentant heart and a new mind for his ways.

Many will reject Jesus for these reasons. They would rather cling to belief in their own goodness or hold to a previously conceived personal understanding of God. Jesus will have no patience with their stubbornness, continuing to offer them a place in his kingdom only if they will accept the message he has come to embody.

—BQ

Daily Contemplation

Has it been hard for you to accept that Jesus is more concerned about your repentant heart than about your knowledge or your good deeds?

DAY 215

Jesus Is Baptized, Tempted, and Begins His Work
Mark 1:9–45

Although the four Gospels all cover basically the same ground, each one looks at Jesus' life from a unique angle. Matthew and Luke both begin with a genealogy, taking pains to verify Jesus' Old Testament connections. Mark, however, plunges right in to report on Jesus' ministry, covering his baptism and temptation, the calling of his disciples, and a series of miracles in the first chapter alone.

Mark reads like a newspaper account, jam-packed with action and with little space for parables, speeches, or editorial comments. Thus the book gives an ideal "bird's-eye view" of Jesus' life. Its style—simple sentences without complicated transitions or long speeches—makes understanding easier.

After John the Baptist fans enthusiasm for Jesus—so much enthusiasm, in fact, that John lands in jail—Jesus openly announces his ministry. He has some surprises in store for the eager audience. For one thing, Jesus goes not to Jerusalem, the natural center of activity for any aspiring leader, but to small towns in the hill country of Galilee.

In other ways, too, Jesus does not fit the expected image of a prophet. His cousin John personifies the severe ascetic image: He lives in a desert, eats insects, and preaches a harsh message of judgment. But Jesus lives in the midst of people, dines in their homes, and brings a message of "the good news of God."

When Jesus begins healing people, his reputation swells overnight. Mark shows stadium-sized crowds pressing around Jesus so tightly that he has to plan escape routes. News of his miraculous powers spreads even when he tries to hush it up. Wherever Jesus goes, the crowds follow, buzzing about his remarkable life. "Is he the Holy One of God?" "Is he mad?" "Isn't this the carpenter's boy?" The word is out.

—PY

Daily Contemplation

Considering what you have read about Jesus so far, what characteristic about him surprises you most?

DAY 216

The Temptation of Jesus
Matthew 4:1–11

> Then Jesus was led by the Spirit into the wilderness to be tempted by the devil.... Jesus answered, "It is written: 'Man shall not live on bread alone, but on every word that comes from the mouth of God.'" (Matthew 4:1, 4)

The story of Jesus' temptation brings to mind two Old Testament stories. Whereas Jesus is tempted for forty days in the desert, the Israelites wandered forty years in the desert. Moses described God's purpose in the Israelites' wanderings: "To humble and test you in order to know what was in your heart, whether or not you would keep his commands" (Deuteronomy 8:2). Although the Israelites failed their test, Jesus shows himself to be a true Israelite. He endures, staying faithful to God and his purposes.

Jesus' temptation also reflects an earlier scene—Eve's encounter with the serpent in the Garden of Eden. Although God tested the children of Israel to try their loyalty to him, it was Satan who tempted Eve to do evil. More than simply a negative force or influence, Satan acted as a living being with both Eve and Jesus, using the same tactics he uses with us today. He makes an appeal to the physical appetite, to questions about God's care, and to the longing for a shortcut path to power and prestige.

Jesus believes the Scriptures he quotes in resisting Satan. He knows that only God can satisfy our hunger, that God is trustworthy, and that only God should be worshiped. In resisting Satan's ploys, Jesus shows he is qualified to be the Savior of all who receive him. He understands what we experience, and he can help us when we are tempted.

—BQ

Daily Contemplation

What has been your most recent temptation? Does it resemble any of Jesus' three temptations?

Jesus' Pattern of Restraint
Reflection

As I (Philip) look back on the three temptations, I see that Satan proposed an enticing improvement. He tempted Jesus toward the good parts of being human without the bad: to savor the taste of bread without being subject to the fixed rules of hunger and of agriculture, to confront risk with no real danger, to enjoy fame and power without the prospect of painful rejection—in short, to wear a crown but not a cross. The temptations that Jesus resisted, many of us, his followers, still long for.

The temptation in the desert reveals a profound difference between God's power and Satan's power. Satan has the power to coerce, to dazzle, to force obedience, to destroy. Humans have learned much from that power, and governments draw deeply from its reservoir. With a bullwhip or a billy club or an AK-47, human beings can force other humans to do just about anything they want. Satan's power is external and coercive.

God's power, in contrast, is internal and noncoercive. "You would not enslave man by a miracle, and craved faith given freely, not based on miracle," said the Inquisitor to Jesus in Dostoevsky's novel *The Brothers Karamazov*. Such power may seem at times like weakness. In its commitment to transform gently from the inside out and in its relentless dependence on human choice, God's power may resemble a kind of abdication. As every parent and every lover knows, love can be rendered powerless if the beloved chooses to spurn it.

Sometimes, I concede, I wish that God used a heavier touch. My faith suffers from too much freedom, too many temptations to disbelieve. At times I want God to overwhelm me, to overcome my doubts with certainty, to give final proofs of his existence and his concern.

I want God to take a more active role in my personal history too. I want quick and spectacular answers to my prayers, healing for my diseases, protection and safety for my loved ones. I want a God without ambiguity, one to whom I can point for the sake of my doubting friends.

When I think these thoughts, I recognize in myself a thin, hollow echo of the challenge that Satan hurled at Jesus two thousand years ago. God resists those temptations now just as Jesus resisted them on earth, settling instead for a slower, gentler way.

As I survey the rest of Jesus' life, I see that the pattern of restraint established in the desert persisted throughout his life. I never sense Jesus twisting a person's arm. Rather, he stated the consequences of a choice, then threw the decision back to the other party. He answered a wealthy man's question with uncompromising words and then let him walk away. Mark pointedly adds this comment: "Jesus looked at him and loved him" (Mark 10:21). Jesus had a realistic view of how the world would respond to him: "Because of the increase of wickedness, the love of most will grow cold" (Matthew 24:12).

When I examine myself, I find that I, too, am vulnerable to temptation. I lack the willpower to resist shortcut solutions to human needs. I lack the patience to allow God to work in a slow, "gentlemanly" way. I want to seize control myself, to compel others to help accomplish the causes I believe in. I am willing to trade away certain freedoms for the guarantee of safety and protection. I am willing to trade away even more for the chance to realize my ambitions.

When I feel those temptations rising within me, I return to the story of Jesus and Satan in the desert. Jesus' resistance against Satan's temptations preserved for me the very freedom I exercise when I face my own temptations. I pray for the same trust and patience that Jesus showed. And I rejoice that, as Hebrews said, "We do not have a high priest who is unable to empathize with our weaknesses, but we have one who has been tempted in every way, just as we are—yet he did not sin. . . . Because he himself suffered when he was tempted, he is able to help those who are being tempted" (Hebrews 4:15; 2:18).[39]

—PY

Daily Contemplation

What kinds of temptations seem to nag you most frequently? Can you look back and see Jesus' pattern of restraint in your life? Thank Jesus for drawing you to him gently, without coercion. Ask for his Spirit to increasingly pervade you as you fight the temptation to wear a crown but not a cross.

DAY 218

Jesus Changes Water to Wine
John 2:1-11

John tells the story of Jesus' first miracle, and the following story makes it clear that, as with all his miracles, Jesus performed more than magic. His miracles joined the natural world with God's supernatural power and brought results that even today are impacting our world.

Dr. Richard Eby tells about his father, an employee with General Electric in the early 1900s, and some modern-day repercussions of Jesus' first miracle. In 1908 the president of GE believed that the future of America would depend on vast voltages of electrical energy. At the time, proper insulators, or bushings, had not yet been developed, and without them grand-scale electricity was impossible. Eugene Eby, a young engineer, was given the job of solving the problem.

Many months of research and trial and error produced no answers. Eby and his staff were unable to identify a type of porcelain insulator that could withstand the surge of electricity produced by lightning storms that daily would hit electrical substations and cross-country tension lines. Every bushing they developed was quickly destroyed, even with the zap of a man-made bolt of lightning.

One Saturday morning at breakfast, Eby felt suddenly hopeful. He and his staff of engineers, mechanics, test operators, chemists, and porcelain specialists had been ready to give up. Exhausted, they were no closer to finding a solution. But the night before, Eby told his family, he'd told God in prayer that he would have to provide an answer or else let the problem of electricity remain unsolved.

When he'd woken in the morning, Eby had opened his Bible and let it fall to the story of Jesus' first miracle. Reading this familiar passage again, he began to think like an engineer. Jesus used six large pots and his power to change the water to wine. The pots held twenty to thirty gallons each; such pottery would have to be very strong. Furthermore, in the chemical change of water to alcohol, millions of volts would be needed to rearrange the molecules, as if bombs were exploding in the pots as the miracle occurred. Yet the pots withstood all the pressure.

Eby had no clear answers, he told his family, but the next day he would give his staff a month's vacation and await further insight.

A month later no answers had come. A wire arrived from President Hoover in the White House, addressing the topic of the Boulder Dam, later to be renamed the Hoover Dam. Its construction well underway, it promised to be the world's greatest dam. But it would prove useless as a power source apart from adequate bushings. The problem was urgent and needed a quick resolution.

Eby made a phone call to his Schenectady office, where a Mr. Cermak headed the porcelain research. Cermak had just returned from a trip to Europe and Egypt, and in the course of small talk mentioned that while in Egypt he learned of a tomb that had just been opened, housing the remains of King Tut. Touring the tomb, Cermak said, he had pocketed a small "souvenir" while the guard's back was turned. Business talk followed, with discussion of the president's orders, but no solutions became apparent.

That night Eby couldn't shake a feeling that some connection was waiting to be made. In the dark hours of the morning he knew he needed to phone Cermak immediately. Sure enough, the souvenir Cermak took was a piece of pottery, probably from some kind of pitcher, roughly three thousand years old, dating further back than Jesus' time on earth. Cermak agreed to test its composition right away. Two weeks later in the lightning lab, Eby, with his son standing by, tested a newly formed bushing made from the same material as the Tut pottery. An electric volt that shook the building didn't budge the bushing. President Hoover was notified. The dam would work. It would become the largest power plant, and the world would have its answer to grand-scale electricity.[40]

—BQ

---- *Daily Contemplation* ----

When has God used an experience from your past to affect your future unexpectedly yet profoundly?

DAY 219

Jesus Teaches Nicodemus
John 3:1–21

> "Very truly I tell you, no one can see the kingdom of God unless they are born again." (John 3:3)

A simultaneous reading of John 3 and Mark 2 (scheduled for day 224) reveals a chief difference between Mark's and John's Gospels. Mark gives the panoramic view: action, crowds, short scenes spliced together to create an overall impact. John tightens the camera angle, closing in on a few individual faces—a woman at a well, a blind man, a member of the Jewish ruling council—to compose a more intimate, in-depth portrait.

A simple word or phrase with a profound meaning—that is the style of Jesus' teaching as presented in John. No biblical author uses simpler, more commonplace words: *water, world, light, life, birth, love, truth.* Yet John uses them with such depth and skill that hundreds of authors since have tried to plumb their meaning.

Consider, for instance, this conversation with Nicodemus (NIK-uh-DEE-muhs). He comes to Jesus at night, in order to avoid detection. He risks his reputation and safety even by meeting with Jesus, whom his fellow Pharisees will eventually seek to kill. But Nicodemus has questions, burning questions, the most important questions anyone could ask. *Who are you, Jesus? Have you really come from God?* Jesus responds with the image of a second birth, using words that have become some of the most familiar in the Bible.

Evidently, some of Jesus' words to Nicodemus sink in. Later he will stand up for Jesus at the Jewish ruling council and, after the crucifixion, help prepare Jesus' body for burial.

John follows this conversation with a report from John the Baptist. People are questioning him, too, about the new teacher across the river who is drawing all the crowds. In words that echo Jesus' own, John the Baptist confirms that Jesus holds the keys to eternal life. He is indeed the one John has come to herald: "He must become greater; I must become less" (John 3:30).

—PY

Daily Contemplation

What has been your understanding of the term "born again"? Does this passage change how you think of the term? Does it apply to you?

DAY 220

Jesus Talks with a Samaritan Woman
John 4:1–42

> Jesus answered, "Everyone who drinks this water will be thirsty again, but whoever drinks the water I give them will never thirst. Indeed, the water I give them will become in them a spring of water welling up to eternal life." The woman said to him, "Sir, give me this water so that I won't get thirsty and have to keep coming here to draw water." (John 4:13–15)

In ways not so obvious today, Jesus' actions in this story border on outrageous. The Jews of Jesus' day, you see, have nothing but contempt for Samaritans, a mixed-race minority. When Assyria conquered the northern kingdom of Israel in 722 BC, overrunning its capital, Samaria, most Israelites were deported and replaced with other conquered peoples. These new settlers intermarried with the remaining Israelites and adopted some of their religious practices, combining them with worship of their own gods. For this reason, the Jews came to despise the "impostor" Samaritans.

Because of their hatred, the Jews of Jesus' day shunned contact with Samaritans. Deliberately avoiding the shortest route from Judea to Galilee through Samaria, the Jews would often cross over the Jordan River to the east side and travel north or south through Perea in order to bypass Samaria. Not Jesus. He chooses to travel directly through Samaria, and en route he upsets yet another Jewish tradition. In talking with the Samaritan woman, Jesus also defies a prejudice that frowns on conversation between men and women.

Jesus reveals his identity as Messiah, and this Samaritan woman becomes the first to hear him speak of himself so clearly. In Jewish territories Jesus must use care in revealing himself, so as not to incite political friction too soon. But here in Samaria political danger remains low. In speaking so openly to the woman and others in town, Jesus again expresses his great love for people outside the Jewish community. The result? An unlikely revival breaks out among the despised Samaritans.

—BQ

Daily Contemplation

What kind of thirst can Jesus quench in your life?

DAY 221

Jesus Rejected at Nazareth
Luke 4:14–30

Jesus returned to Galilee in the power of the Spirit, and news about him spread through the whole countryside. He was teaching in their synagogues.... He went to Nazareth, where he had been brought up, and on the Sabbath day he went into the synagogue, as was his custom. He stood up to read, and the scroll of the prophet Isaiah was handed to him. Unrolling it, he found the place where it is written:

> "The Spirit of the Lord is on me,
>   because he has anointed me
>   to proclaim good news to the poor.
> He has sent me to proclaim freedom for the prisoners
>   and recovery of sight for the blind,
> to set the oppressed free,
>   to proclaim the year of the Lord's favor."

Then he rolled up the scroll, gave it back to the attendant and sat down. The eyes of everyone in the synagogue were fastened on him. He began by saying to them, "Today this scripture is fulfilled in your hearing." (Luke 4:14–20)

Jesus' homecoming nearly sparks a riot when he reveals who he is and whom he came to help. Jesus has returned to Galilee, visiting his hometown of Nazareth. In this dramatic scene he identifies himself as the Messiah whom Isaiah has prophesied to all nations. His wisdom and authority impress them, and all goes well until he turns the emphasis to God's love for all people, not just the Jews. Whether from racism, pride, or historical enmity, his hometown audience is not ready for that message. Jesus brings up stories from Israel's past to prove his point, but that only inflames the crowd. This, his inaugural sermon, ends with the congregation's attempt to kill him. His message of God's amazing grace is too radical for his own hometown—and for many others in Israel as well.

—BQ

Daily Contemplation

What is helping you to see Jesus with new eyes?

DAY 222

Jesus Came for All People
Reflection

It's hard to peg Jesus' taste in friends. Already it seems clear that he came to reach out to a varied group of people. In one instance he met with the most Jewish of Jews: Nicodemus, a teacher, a Pharisee, and a member of the Sanhedrin (san-HEE-druhn), the Jewish ruling council comprising only seventy members. Jesus also cared for a Samaritan woman and many in her town. He healed outcasts such as a man with an evil spirit and several with leprosy. He called common fishermen and a tax collector—the latter a profession considered dishonest by the Jews—to join his closest circle.

Jesus came to let all people know of the love of God reaching fulfillment through his presence on earth. He came to tell us that our lives are precious to God, valuable into eternity. Jesus is looking not for a particular appearance or life story but for a heart that recognizes its need for him. Belief in Jesus and salvation through him are what matter.

When we give our lives to him, Jesus' love for all people will become a part of our own hearts. Mother Teresa, founder of the Missionaries of Charity, spoke often about extending Jesus' love to everyone, beginning with those immediately surrounding us:

> When you know how much God is in love with you then you can only live your life radiating that love. I always say that love starts at home: family first, and then your own town or city. It is easy to love people who are far away but it is not always so easy to love those who live with us or right next to us. I do not agree with the big way of doing things—love needs to start with an individual. To get to love a person, you must contact that person, become close. Everyone needs love. All must know that they're wanted and that they are important to God.[41]

Often it seems we decide whom we want to love and then keep ourselves mentally and emotionally detached from others, especially if they strike us as unattractive or unable to give back. But that isn't Jesus' way. He came not just for the rich but for the poor, not just for the Jews but for everyone else, not just for the healthy but for the sick, not just for the "together" but for the outcasts. And he came for people most undeserving—the egotistical, the self-righteous, the cheaters, the obnoxious, the ones who know all the answers.

When Jesus comes again, he will know his followers by the way they have cared for others. "Truly I tell you, whatever you did for one of the least of these brothers and sisters of mine, you did for me" (Matthew 25:40). Mother Teresa reflects that "the least of these" includes:

> the hungry and the lonely, not only for food but for the Word of God; the thirsty and the ignorant, not only for water but also for knowledge, peace, truth, justice, and love; the naked and the unloved, not only for clothes but also for human dignity; the unwanted, the unborn child; the racially discriminated against; the homeless and abandoned, not only for a shelter made of bricks, but for a heart that understands, that covers, that loves; the sick, the dying destitutes, and the captives, not only in body but also in mind and spirit: all those who have lost all hope and faith in life, the alcoholics and drug addicts and all those who have lost God . . . and who have lost all hope in the power of the Spirit.[42]

—BQ

Daily Contemplation

Who are the people most difficult for you to love? Be honest! Who are you afraid to love? Ask God to help you begin to love these people with Jesus' love.

DAY 223

The Calling of the First Disciples
Luke 5:1–11

> One day as Jesus was standing by the Lake of Gennesaret... He saw at the water's edge two boats, left there by the fishermen, who were washing their nets.... Then Jesus said to Simon... "From now on you will fish for people." So they pulled their boats up on shore, left everything and followed him. (Luke 5:1–2, 10–11)

Jesus now begins to assemble an official following. Other Gospel passages record Jesus in contact with Simon Peter and other disciples prior to this call on the shores of Gennesaret (geh-NES-uh-ret), indicating that these men have been loosely following Jesus. As he moves into the full swing of his ministry, Jesus demonstrates his authority once more and calls them to leave their fishnets and follow him.

Jesus isn't asking these men simply to tag along after him and marvel at his teaching and miracles. He is calling them to join in relationship with him, be filled with his Spirit, and carry on his ministry. They become the first believers to be mentored by God in the person of Christ. Privileged to know Jesus more intimately than anyone else during his time on earth, they will go on to lead the early church after Jesus' death. Some will write parts of the New Testament as letters to these new Christian outposts.

Jesus calls believers today to follow him as well. Although he isn't here in body, he remains present to us through the Bible and through his living Spirit. Still today he asks us to drop our nets into deep water and trust for his provision. As he meets our needs, Jesus calls us to put down the things that preoccupy us and turn our attention to him. He will use us, as he used the twelve disciples, to catch up men and women in his message of hope and new life.

—BQ

Daily Contemplation

How is Jesus calling you now to be his disciple?

DAY 224

Jesus Meets Opposition
Mark 2:1–28

When a new leader starts making waves, opposition surely follows. While on earth, Jesus makes an extravagant claim: He claims to be the Messiah, sent from God. And opposition to him springs up soon after the wild surge of popularity in Galilee. This chapter tells of three different criticisms that people will make against Jesus throughout his life.

He blasphemes. The teachers of the law are scandalized by Jesus' forgiving of sins. "Who can forgive sins but God alone?" they mutter. Jesus readily agrees that only God can forgive sins—that is his point, exactly.

Throughout his life, Jesus faces the strongest opposition from the most pious followers of Old Testament law; they can never accept that the awesome, distant God of Israel could take up residence inside a human body. Eventually, they have Jesus executed for making that claim. People who accept Jesus as a "good man and enlightened teacher" today often overlook the scenes where Jesus blatantly identifies himself with God. When the Pharisees react violently to Jesus in his day, it is because they have heard him correctly—they simply refuse to believe him.

He keeps disreputable company. Jesus shows a distinct preference for the most unseemly sort of people. He offends politicians and religious leaders by calling them names. Even after becoming famous, he dines with an outcast tax collector and his lowlife friends. On hearing the gossip about this strange behavior, Jesus says simply, "It is not the healthy who need a doctor, but the sick. I have not come to call the righteous, but sinners."

He goes against tradition. To the Pharisees, it seems Jesus' disciples are playing fast and loose with the holy Sabbath. Jesus' response: It's time for a new cloth; the old one has been patched together long enough. Before long, he will introduce the "new covenant." God has some major changes in store for the human race, and the narrow, confining covenant with the Israelites simply can't hold all those changes.

—PY

Daily Contemplation

What attracts you most to Jesus: that he is frank about who he is, that he spends time with outcasts, or that he goes against tradition in revealing God? What troubles you most?

DAY 225

Jesus Teaches and Heals
Mark 3:1–35

The Gospels record some three dozen miracles performed by Jesus, and he states plainly why he does them: "Believe me when I say that I am in the Father and the Father is in me; or at least believe on the evidence of the works themselves" (John 14:11). They serve as convincing proofs that he is the Messiah, the Son of God.

Large crowds flock from far away as word of Jesus' power spreads. Some people come for healing, others just to witness the extraordinary phenomena. Who but a messenger from God could perform such works? Yet Jesus himself has an odd ambivalence toward miracles. He never does "tricks" on demand, like a magician. "A wicked and adulterous generation looks for a sign," he says to those who seek a display of magic (Matthew 16:4).

Jesus seems not to trust miracles to produce the kind of faith he is interested in. Mark reports that on seven separate occasions he warns a person just healed, "Tell no one!" He is suspicious of the popular acclaim that his miracles stir up, for he has a hard message of obedience and sacrifice, and miracles tend to attract gawkers and sensation seekers.

Mainly, Jesus uses his powers in compassionate response to human needs. Every time someone asks directly, he heals. When his disciples grow frightened on a stormy lake, he walks to them across the water or calms the wind. When his audience gets hungry he feeds them, and when wedding guests grow thirsty he makes wine.

Much like people today, Jesus' contemporaries look for ways to explain away his powers, even when faced with irrefutable evidence. Here, the Pharisees seek to credit the miracles to Satan's power. On another occasion they arrange a formal tribunal, complete with judges and witnesses, to examine a man Jesus has healed. The man's parents confirm his story ("One thing I do know. I was blind but now I see!"), but still the doubters hurl insults and throw him out of court (John 9).

In short, the crowd's mixed responses bear out Jesus' suspicions about the limited value of miracles. They rarely create faith but rather affirm it in true seekers.

—PY

Daily Contemplation

If you were to ask Jesus for one miracle today, what would it be? Do you have a hard time believing that Jesus has as much compassion for your need as he had for the people he encountered when he was on earth? Pray now about your need.

DAY 226

Jesus Tells Parables, Calms the Storm
Mark 4:1–41

The story about the sower of seed summarizes well the mixed results Jesus himself gets while on earth. We who live two thousand years later, with such events as Christmas and Easter marked plainly on our calendars, may easily miss the sheer incredulity that greets Jesus in the flesh.

Neighbors have watched him play in the streets with their own children; Jesus is simply too familiar for them to believe he was sent from God. "Isn't this the carpenter?" they ask. "Isn't this Mary's son and the brother of James, Joseph, Judas and Simon? . . . What's this wisdom that has been given him? What are these remarkable miracles he is performing?" (Mark 6:3, 2).

Not even Jesus' family can easily reconcile the wondrous and the ordinary. Mark casually mentions that one time Jesus' mother and brothers arrive to take charge of him because they have concluded, "He is out of his mind" (3:21). Nor can common people make up their minds about Jesus. They judge him "raving mad" (John 10:20) one moment, then forcibly try to crown him king the next.

The scribes and Pharisees, who pore over the Prophets, should have the clearest notion of what the Messiah will look like. But no group causes Jesus more trouble. They criticize his theology, his lifestyle, and his choice of friends. When he performs miracles, they attribute his ability to evil powers.

When a storm nearly capsizes the boat transporting Jesus, he yells into the wind, "Quiet! Be still!" The disciples shrink back in terror. What kind of person can shout down the weather, as if correcting an unruly child? That scene helps convince them Jesus is unlike anyone else on earth. Yet it suggests a reason for their confusion about him. Jesus had, after all, fallen asleep in the boat from sheer fatigue, a symptom of his human frailty.

The early church will argue for three centuries about exactly what happened when God became man, but their creeds will do little to dispel the sense of mystery. In a way, Jesus is just like everyone else—he has a race, an occupation, a family background, a body shape. In a way, he is something entirely new in the history of the universe. In between those two statements lies the mystery that never completely goes away.

—PY

Daily Contemplation

In Jesus' story of the sower and the soil, which soil best represents your response to the gospel?

DAY 227

Jesus Heals and Restores Life
Mark 5:1–43

At one point some of the controversy about Jesus even affects John the Baptist, the prophet who more than anyone has raised the people's hopes about a Messiah. It is he who has baptized Jesus and pronounced him the Son of God. But two years later, as he languishes on death row, John the Baptist himself begins to wonder. He sends Jesus a direct question: "Are you the one who is to come, or should we expect someone else?" (Luke 7:20).

This is Jesus' reply: "Go back and report to John what you have seen and heard: The blind receive sight, the lame walk, those who have leprosy are cleansed, the deaf hear, the dead are raised, and the good news is proclaimed to the poor. Blessed is anyone who does not stumble on account of me" (Luke 7:22–23). Clearly, Jesus sees his miracles of healing as important proofs of who he is.

The healings do something else as well: They overturn common notions about how God views sick people. During Jesus' lifetime, the Pharisees taught a very strict principle (along the lines of Job's friends' beliefs) that all suffering comes from sin. They judged a deranged or demon-possessed person as permanently cursed by God. They saw God's hand of punishment in natural disasters, birth defects, and such long-term conditions as blindness and paralysis. Leprosy victims were viewed as unclean and were excluded from worship in the temple.

But Jesus contradicts such teaching. This chapter shows him curing a demon-possessed man, touching and healing an "unclean" woman, and resurrecting a child. On other occasions, he directly refutes this doctrine about sin and suffering. He denies that a man's blindness comes from his own or his parents' sin, and he dismisses the common opinion that tragedies happen to those who deserve them (see John 9 and Luke 13).

Jesus does not heal everyone on earth or even in Palestine. But his treatment of the sick and needy shows they are especially loved, not cursed, by God. The healings also provide a "sign" of what will happen in the future, when all diseases, and even death, will be destroyed.

—PY

Daily Contemplation

Did you ever believe that an illness or time of suffering came to you as a punishment?

DAY 228

Jesus Desires to Touch and Heal
Reflection

Jesus had a big heart. The Gospels are filled with stories of his touch on those who suffered from blindness, leprosy, paralysis, bleeding, evil spirits, deafness, and other unspecified illnesses. He healed to confirm to the people his claim that he was God incarnate. But just as importantly, he healed because he had compassion on the ones who suffered.

This profile of the tender, sympathetic Jesus may sometimes seem in conflict with his more difficult teaching and his often-harsh words to those who feigned real love for God. But to people of his day, Jesus' actions spoke volumes. His love was more real than any other characteristic he displayed.

If Jesus was truly the tenderhearted God we see in the Gospels, surely his heart has not changed. Does he desire to touch and heal today as he did then? Author Catherine Marshall asked this question as she lay confined to bed with tuberculosis for more than two years. As she studied the Bible closely, she began to understand the truth about the Jesus of two thousand years ago and the Jesus of today.

> One of my initial, joyous discoveries about Jesus' will is that having Himself created these awesomely constructed bodies of ours, *of course* He wants us to be well. All over the gospels is Jesus' positive zest for healing the diseased or the handicapped or the blind. In fact, he drew vicious criticism from the religious authorities because He could not wait even 24 hours to heal certain sufferers, thus unabashedly proceeding to break the Jewish Sabbath law, since in Jewish law, healing was "work."
>
> And Scripture makes it plain that Jesus is "the same yesterday, today, and forever," projecting into the future ages the same power He had while on earth in the flesh, and specifically passing on that power to future disciples who accept His full Lordship . . .
>
> Since this very different message from Scripture was living water for my thirsty spirit and needy body, I received it with overwhelming eagerness.[43]

Marshall struggled for many more months after this discovery before finally experiencing clear lungs and a return to health. This foundational truth of Jesus' deep compassion sustained her as she searched the Bible and her own heart for the things God would reveal to her during her illness. She later wrote, "Jesus came to earth to show us the Father's will. He who created the incredible human body still heals today, but not as a divine magician. We need to seek His way, His timing, and the lessons He wants us to learn along the way."[44]

Marshall would later learn, through the death of her young husband, the respected pastor Peter Marshall, that Jesus doesn't always bring physical healing. Yet even then his compassion endures. "Most important of all, He had shown me through more than two years of illness that I would always need Him every day for the rest of my life and more, throughout eternity . . . Christ is still the greatest Physician to the spirit."[45]

—BQ

---- *Daily Contemplation* ----

Are you in need of healing from Jesus right now? Let Jesus reach out and touch you, lovingly assuring you of how much he cares about your need. Let the truth of his deep love for you fill your mind and body. Ask for healing in his time and his way as he continues to teach you about himself.

DAY 229

The Sermon on the Mount
Matthew 5:1–48

If Jesus had avoided one emotionally charged word, *kingdom*, everything might have been different. Whenever he said it, images would dance in the minds of his audience: bright banners, glittering armies, the gold and ivory of Solomon's day, the nation of Israel restored to glory. Jesus often used this word that quickened the pulse of Israel, starting with his very first message: "Repent, for the kingdom of heaven has come near" (Matthew 4:17).

By boldly comparing himself to Solomon, Israel's most powerful king (12:42), Jesus taps into the reservoir of his nation's deepest longings. More, he claims that the promises of the prophets are coming true in him. What is about to happen, he says, is a new thing and will far surpass anything from the past: "For I tell you that many prophets and kings wanted to see what you see but did not see it, and to hear what you hear but did not hear it" (Luke 10:24).

The expectations raised by such statements lead to confusion and, finally, angry rejection. Disappointment displaces the initial excitement over Jesus' miracles when he fails to restore the long-awaited kingdom. For, as it turns out, the word *kingdom* means one thing to the crowd and quite another to Jesus.

Winds of change are blowing through Israel as Jesus speaks. Armed and well-organized, guerrilla fighters called Zealots are spoiling for a fight against oppressive Rome. But the signal for revolt never comes. To their dismay, it gradually becomes clear that Jesus is not talking about a political or military kingdom.

Jesus indicates that we live in a visible world of families and people and cities and nations, "the kingdom of this world." But he calls for people to commit their lives to an *invisible* kingdom, the "kingdom of heaven," more important and more valuable than anything in the visible world.

Success in the kingdom of heaven involves a great reversal of values, as seen in this major address, the Sermon on the Mount. "Blessed are the poor in spirit," Jesus says, and also those who mourn, and the meek, and those who hunger and thirst, and the persecuted, "for theirs is the kingdom of heaven." Status in this world is no guarantee of status in the kingdom of heaven and may even signal the opposite.

—PY

Daily Contemplation

Are you more focused on achieving success in the kingdom of this world or in the kingdom of heaven?

DAY 230

The Sermon on the Mount, Part 2
Matthew 6:1–34

Matthew 6, a continuation of the Sermon on the Mount, contains the Lord's Prayer, perhaps the most famous prayer of all. Jesus gives it as a model of prayer, and it captures well the message of the kingdom: "Your kingdom come, your will be done, on earth as it is in heaven." Jesus seeks to bring the two worlds together, and the Sermon on the Mount explains how.

At first glance, some of the advice may seem downright foolish: Give to everyone who asks, love your enemies, turn the other cheek, grant interest-free loans, don't worry about clothes or food. Can such idealism ever work in the "real," or visible, world? That is Jesus' point precisely: Break your obsession with safety, security, thriftiness, and self-righteousness. Depend instead on the Father, letting him take care of the personal injustices that come your way, trusting him to look after your daily needs. In a nutshell, the message of the kingdom is this: Live for God, not for other people.

The message applies to rewards as well. Most of us look to friends and colleagues for our rewards: a slap on the back, a raise and promotion, applause, a lavish compliment. But according to Jesus, by far the more important rewards await us after death. Therefore, the most significant human acts of all may be carried out in secret, seen by no one but God.

As Jesus explains it, we are accumulating a kind of savings account, "storing up treasures" in heaven rather than on earth—treasures so great that they will pay back any amount of suffering in this life. The Old Testament has dropped a few scant hints about an afterlife, but Jesus speaks plainly about a place where "the righteous will shine like the sun in the kingdom of their Father" (Matthew 13:43).

In their quest for a kingdom, the Jews of Jesus' day were looking for signs of God's approval in this life, primarily through prosperity and political power. Beginning with this speech, Jesus changes the focus to the life to come. He discounts success in this visible world. Invest in the future life, he cautions—after all, rust, a thief, or a lowly insect can destroy all else that we accumulate.

—PY

Daily Contemplation

Of the people you know, who best puts the principles of the Sermon on the Mount into practice?

DAY 231

The Sermon on the Mount, Part 3
Matthew 7:1–29

> "Therefore everyone who hears these words of mine and puts them into practice is like a wise man who built his house on the rock . . . it did not fall, because it had its foundation on the rock." (Matthew 7:24–25)

Drawing on familiar images to illustrate his teaching, Jesus completes his Sermon on the Mount in this passage. At the end lies an illustration that reveals the purpose of the entire sermon. Jesus' followers, those who hear the sermon in person and those who have read it since, will build a life foundation either on the promises of this world or on the promises of God. They will rely on the ways of the world or on the ways of Christ.

The Pharisees, who make up a large portion of Jesus' hillside audience, are banking on a self-produced righteousness to usher them to heaven. Pleasure seekers also stay to hear Jesus out. Living for the moment, they are trusting in earthly things to build a good life. Others in the audience, however, are truly searching for the way to follow God. They will choose the small gate and narrow road Jesus describes. He speaks to these people throughout his sermon. Rather than simply following the "letter of the law," they will seek to follow the spirit of the law, as he explains.

Authentic God seekers will pay much more attention to their own faults than to others'. Although they will be concerned enough to correct others, they will make sure their own lives are in order first. They will talk to God as to their true Father, confident that he delights in hearing their needs. And they will follow fellow pilgrims who show the fruit of God's Spirit in their lives.

Mere words or signs will never take the place of a personal relationship with Jesus. On Jesus, the Rock, the people of God will build a long-standing house, a shelter for the storms of this life and a home forever in the presence of the King.

—BQ

Daily Contemplation

What can you see in yourself that resembles a Pharisee, a pleasure seeker, and a God seeker?

DAY 232

Seeing Through God's Eyes
Reflection

The Sermon on the Mount haunted my adolescence. I (Philip) would read a book like Charles Sheldon's *In His Steps*, solemnly vow to act "as Jesus would act," and turn to Matthew 5–7 for guidance. What to make of such advice? Should I offer myself to be pummeled by the motorcycle-riding ruffians in school? Tear out my tongue after speaking a harsh word to my brother?

Now that I am an adult, the crisis of the Sermon on the Mount still has not gone away. Though I have tried at times to dismiss it as rhetorical excess, the more I study Jesus, the more I realize that the statements contained here lie at the heart of his message. If I fail to understand his teaching, I fail to understand him.

To begin, are the Beatitudes true? Gradually I have come to recognize them as important truths. To me, they apply on at least three levels.

Delayed justice. The Beatitudes are not merely Jesus' hollow words of consolation to the unfortunates. For convicts in the Soviet Gulag, enslaved people in antebellum America, and ancient Christians in Roman cages awaiting their turn with the wild beasts, the promise of reward has been a source of hope. It keeps you alive. It allows you to believe in a just God after all.

The great reversal. I have also come to believe that the Beatitudes describe the present as well as the future. They neatly contrast how to succeed in the kingdom of heaven with how to succeed in the kingdom of this world. The Beatitudes express quite plainly that God views the world through a different set of lenses.

Psychological reality. The Beatitudes reveal that what brings us success in the kingdom of heaven also benefits us most in this life here and now. I would rather spend time among the servants of this world than among the stars. The servants clearly emerge as the favored ones, the graced ones. They possess qualities of depth and richness and even joy that I have not found elsewhere. Somehow, as Jesus promises, in the process of losing their lives, they find them.

The Beatitudes represent only the first step toward understanding the Sermon on the Mount. Long after I came to recognize the enduring truth of the Beatitudes, I still brooded over the uncompromising harshness of the rest of Jesus' sermon. "Be perfect, therefore, as your heavenly Father is perfect," Jesus said (Matthew 5:48), his statement tucked almost casually between commands to love enemies and give away money. Be perfect like God? Whatever did he mean?

Ultimately I found a key to understanding the Sermon on the Mount in an unlikely place: the writings of two nineteenth-century Russian novelists, Tolstoy and Dostoevsky.

From Tolstoy I learned a deep respect for God's inflexible, absolute ideal. Tolstoy strove to follow the Sermon on the Mount literally. Sometimes he accomplished great good. His philosophy of nonviolence, lifted directly from the Sermon on the Mount, had an impact that long outlived him in ideological descendants like Gandhi and Martin Luther King, Jr. Yet his intensity soon caused his family to feel like victims of his quest for holiness.

Tolstoy failed to practice what he preached; and he never found peace. Despite his failures, though, Tolstoy's relentless pursuit of pure faith has made an indelible impression on me. Having grown up with many whom, in my arrogance of youth, I considered frauds, Tolstoy as an author accomplished for me the most difficult of tasks: to make goodness as believable and appealing as evil.

Fyodor Dostoevsky was the opposite of Tolstoy in every way, but he got one thing right: His novels communicate grace and forgiveness with a Tolstoyan force. He spent ten years in exile poring over the New Testament and emerged with unshakable Christian convictions. In prison he came to believe that only through being loved is a human being capable of love. He went on to write about grace in his novels.

These two authors helped me come to terms with a central paradox of the Christian life. From Tolstoy I learned the need to look inside to the kingdom of God that is within me. I saw how miserably I had failed to meet the lofty ideals of the gospel. From Dostoevsky I learned the full extent of grace. Not only is the kingdom of God within me; Christ himself dwells there. There is only one way for us to resolve the tension between the gospel's high ideals and the grim reality of ourselves: to accept that we will never measure up, but that we do not have to. We are judged by the righteousness of the Christ who lives within, not by our own.

Why did Jesus give us the Sermon on the Mount? Not to burden us but to tell us what God is like. He gave us God's ideal to teach us that we should never stop striving yet also to show us that none of us will ever reach that ideal.[46]

—PY

Daily Contemplation

In what ways do you struggle in living out God's ideals? Ask forgiveness for the ways in which you fail, and thank God for always holding out grace. Ask Jesus to make his life more and more evident in you.

DAY 233

Rest for the Weary; Jesus' Teaching on Prayer
Matthew 11:25–30; Luke 11:1–13

"Come to me, all you who are weary and burdened, and I will give you rest. Take my yoke upon you and learn from me, for I am gentle and humble in heart, and you will find rest for your souls. For my yoke is easy and my burden is light." (Matthew 11:28–30)

"Which of you fathers, if your son asks for a fish, will give him a snake instead? Or if he asks for an egg, will give him a scorpion? If you then, though you are evil, know how to give good gifts to your children, how much more will your Father in heaven give the Holy Spirit to those who ask him!" (Luke 11:11–13)

Jesus brings a message of love and of the better life his love will provide, presenting it to people who face struggles daily and who are weary of the cares of life. He offers what can be found nowhere else: rest for the soul.

Following Jesus isn't meant to be a burden, he reveals with compassion. By coming to him, we can finally find relief from the concerns that weigh on us. He responds to us in gentleness with a humble heart. Jesus, God's own Son, shows kindness toward those who draw near to him.

In a passage reminiscent of the Sermon on the Mount, Jesus again teaches his followers how to pray, using simple statements and requests. Prayer need not be impressive and eloquent. Rather, Jesus teaches that it consists in approaching God with a reverent attitude, placing our will alongside his, and asking humbly for God to meet our daily needs, forgive our sins, and keep us from situations where evil might overwhelm us.

Yes, Jesus is perfect and holy—transcendent qualities. He is also humble and compassionate. What we learn of the Son, we also learn of the Father. We can talk with God about our needs, as children speaking to a loving parent.

—BQ

Daily Contemplation

When you pray to God, which emotion do you usually feel the most? Fear or awkwardness? A sense of distance, comfort, relief, or love?

DAY 234

Parable of the Weeds, Mustard Seed, and Others
Matthew 13:24–58

Writers have long marveled at Jesus' skill in communicating profound truth through parables—short, simple, everyday stories with a moral.

The parables serve Jesus' purposes perfectly. When he first tells the stories in this chapter, he is floating offshore in a boat, shouting to the large crowds that have gathered. Because the stories concern their daily lives—farming, baking bread, hunting buried treasure, fishing—he is able to hold their attention. And yet the parables simultaneously allow Jesus to train his disciples "privately"; later on, he can take the disciples aside and explain the deeper meaning.

As Jesus tells his disciples, parables also help to winnow the audience. Spectators seeking entertainment can go home with a few stories to mull over, but more serious inquirers will need to come back for further interpretation. Parables also help preserve his message. Years later, as people reflect on what Jesus taught, his parables will come to mind in vivid detail.

Matthew 13 collects several of Jesus' stories about the "kingdom of heaven." Although Jesus never concisely defines the term, he gives many clues about the nature of his kingdom. Unlike, say, Greece or China or Spain, it has no geographical boundaries and can't be charted on a map. Kingdom followers live right among their enemies, not separated from them by a moat or a wall. Jesus predicts that the kingdom will show remarkable growth even in an evil environment bent on its destruction.

In summary, the kingdom of heaven consists of the rule of God in the world. It comprises people of all races and from all nations who loyally follow God's will on earth. The disciples, accustomed to more traditional images of power and leadership, can't quite grasp Jesus' concept of the kingdom. They keep asking him to explain his parables even as they jockey vainly for status. Not until he dies and then comes back do they comprehend his mission on earth.

—PY

Daily Contemplation

When do you most feel like wheat among weeds, a follower of Jesus living among forces that seek to smother the gospel?

DAY 235

Two Kinds of Power: Jesus' and Herod's
Mark 6:14–56

This chapter brings together scenes that illustrate very different kinds of power in the two kingdoms. Herod Antipas, ruler of Galilee, personifies one type. Rich and ruthless, he has legions of Roman soldiers to carry out his every command. He leaves impressive monuments all over the region. Mark tells how Herod Antipas uses power: He steals his brother's wife, locks up John the Baptist, and then has the prophet beheaded as a party trick. Killing John isn't Herod's preference, but he feels the need to honor a careless vow in order to protect his image.

Jesus, too, is a leader—a king, in fact—but one who breaks stereotypes. Though possessing undeniable power, he uses that power compassionately, to feed the hungry and heal the sick. At the beginning of his ministry, Jesus declined a tempting offer of glory and territory, and after that he seems to give no thought to cultivating an image of power or importance. He spends his time telling stories, not raising an army. He seeks to please God, not to satisfy people's false expectations.

Herod Antipas has built a lavish palace in Jesus' home province of Galilee, but Jesus carefully avoids that fashionable area. As Herod wines and dines prominent guests in the resort town of Tiberias, Jesus roams the countryside with his ragtag followers. He too serves a banquet, of sorts, to five thousand unexpected guests. His simple message of love, forgiveness, and healing has its own kind of power. Mark tells of crowds chasing Jesus around a lake, running to fetch their sick friends, pressing in close to touch the Teacher.

Jesus contemptuously dismisses Herod Antipas as "that fox" (Luke 13:32). But as talk about Jesus spreads, Herod longs for a chance to meet him. Eventually he'll get his chance at Jesus' trial (Luke 23:7–15). Eager to see a miracle, Herod Antipas uses charm, ridicule, and military force to try to coax some response from Jesus. He fails—Jesus never succumbs to that kind of power.

—PY

Daily Contemplation

To which kind of power are most people attracted? To which kind are you attracted?

DAY 236

Parables: Shrewd Manager; The Rich Man and Lazarus
Luke 16:1–31

A story is told about Rabbi Joseph Schneerson, a Hasidic leader during the early days of Russian communism. The rabbi spent much time in jail, persecuted for his faith. One morning in 1927, as he prayed in a Leningrad synagogue, secret police rushed in and arrested him. They took him to a police station and worked him over, demanding that he give up his religious activities. He refused. The interrogator brandished a gun in his face and said, "This little toy has made many a man change his mind." Rabbi Schneerson answered, "That little toy can intimidate only the kind of man who has many gods and but one world. Because I have only one God and two worlds, I am not impressed by your little toy."[47]

The theme of "two worlds," or two kingdoms, emerges often in Jesus' teaching, and two stories in this chapter draw a sharp distinction between the two worlds. "What people value highly is detestable in God's sight," Jesus says, commenting on the first story, a parable about a shrewd manager. The second story, of the rich man and Lazarus (LAZ-uh-ruhs), elaborates on that difference in values between the two worlds. The rich man prospers in this world yet neglects to make any provision for eternal life and thus suffers the consequences. Meanwhile a half-starved beggar, who by any standard would be judged a failure in this life, receives an eternal reward.

Jesus tells such stories to a Jewish audience with a tradition of wealthy patriarchs, strong kings, and victorious heroes. But Jesus keeps emphasizing his stunning reversal of values. People who have little value in the eyes of this world (the poor, the persecuted—people like Lazarus) may in fact have great stature in God's kingdom. Consistently Jesus presents the visible world as a place to invest for the future, to store up treasure for the life to come.

In a question that brings the two worlds starkly together, Jesus asks, "What good will it be for someone to gain the whole world, yet forfeit their soul?" (Matthew 16:26).

—PY

Daily Contemplation

How would you rate yourself using the standards of success and failure in this world? What if you used Jesus' standards?

DAY 237

Jesus Teaches on Money
Luke 12:13–48

Jesus has more to say on money than almost any other topic. Yet two thousand years later Christians have trouble agreeing on exactly what he *does* say. One reason is that he rarely gives "practical" advice. He avoids comment on specific economic systems and, as in this chapter, refuses to get involved in personal disputes about finances. Jesus sees money primarily as a *spiritual* force.

For years I (Philip) attended a church in Chicago positioned halfway between the richest and poorest zip codes in the city. Understandably, our pastor often spoke about the power of money. In one sermon, he presented money issues in the form of three questions:

1. How did you get it? (Through any injustice, cheating, exploitation?)
2. What are you doing with it? (Taking advantage of others?)
3. What is it doing to you?

Although Jesus speaks to all three of these issues, he concentrates on the last one. As he explains it, money operates much like idolatry. It can dominate a person's life, diverting attention away from God. Jesus challenges people to break free of money's power—even if it means giving it all away.

This chapter offers a good summary of Jesus' attitude toward money. He does not condemn all possessions ("your Father knows that you need [food, drink, and clothes]"). But he strongly warns against putting faith in money to secure the future. As his story of the rich man shows, money will fail to solve life's biggest problems.

Jesus urges his listeners to seek treasure in the kingdom of God, for such treasure can benefit them in this life and the next one too. "Do not worry," he says. Rather, trust God to provide your basic needs. To emphasize his point, he brings up the example of King Solomon, the richest man in the Old Testament. To most nationalistic Jews, Solomon is a hero, but Jesus sees him in a different light: Solomon's wealth has long since vanished—and even in his prime he was no more impressive than a common wildflower.

—PY

Daily Contemplation

How do you fit together Jesus' teaching and our culture's emphasis on financial security for the future?

DAY 238

God's Loving Nature
Reflection

As the sayings go, "The clothes make the man," and "Dress for success." These are among the prescriptions given for making it in the world. Jesus offered another plan. "Do not worry about your life, what you will eat; or about your body, what you will wear. For life is more than food, and the body more than clothes," he said (Luke 12:22–23), to illustrate that nothing we can do for ourselves compares with what God can do for us. Our worries are unfounded if only we will see how God cares for the details of our lives.

Take nature, for instance. According to Jesus, no garment of clothing could match the splendor of a wildflower. Nothing made with human hands can match the beauty God lavishes on the natural world. Nature itself is a message from God, his proclamation of love and care for all he created.

A man named John Muir agreed. Living a century ago, Muir spent most of his life so enamored with nature's beauty that he virtually made his home in the wild, roaming both summer and winter through Canada, the South, and the western United States. Journals preserve the sentiments of this man who in his lifetime helped preserve Yosemite, the Grand Canyon, and other wilderness areas. Muir's writings speak often of, among other loves, his enchantment with wildflowers: "The radiant, honeyful corollas, touching and overlapping, and rising above one another glowed in the living light like a sunset sky—one sheet of purple and gold, with the bright Sacramento [River] pouring through the midst of it from the north."[48]

The study of botany deepened Muir's awe for God's creation. "Like everybody else I was always fond of flowers, attracted by their external beauty and purity. Now my eyes were opened to their inner beauty, all alike revealing glorious traces of the thoughts of God, and leading on and on into the infinite cosmos."[49]

While his skills as an inventor could have made him rich, Muir chose instead to enjoy the land's wealth, spending countless hours and days traveling afoot and observing. "I have not yet in all my wanderings found a single person so free as myself," he mused. "When in the woods I sit at times for hours watching birds or squirrels or looking down into the faces of flowers without suffering any feeling of haste."[50]

A black-and-white photograph of Muir captures him seated on a rock outcropping gazing into the reflections falling across a mountain lake. The picture mirrors God's intense love for a creation that day after day, moment by moment, receives care and attention, God's uninterrupted gaze. "How much more valuable you are than birds!"

Jesus cries; "How much more will he clothe you!" (Luke 12:24, 28). If God's Spirit roams the world with such devotion and delight, caring more than anything else for the people of his creation, should we doubt he will meet our needs? Should we fear not "making it"?

—BQ

--- *Daily Contemplation* ---

What are your worries today? Imagine God gazing on your life with affection and deep love, seeing also the ripples of anxiety disturbing your spirit. Ask him to calm your fears. Ask for his help in trusting, letting go of worry and instead receiving the care he lavishes on you.

DAY 239

Jesus Teaches, Heals, and Welcomes the Children
Luke 18:1–43

A series of vignettes in this chapter reinforces the message about money and about two worlds. In Luke's typical style, the stories feature underdogs: a mistreated widow, a despised tax collector, little children, a blind beggar (Luke 18:35–43). A rich man makes an appearance, but, like the rich man in the story of Lazarus, only as a negative example.

Even Jesus' closest disciples have trouble swallowing his teaching that money represents a grave danger. Yet Jesus sternly warns that wealth can keep people from the kingdom of God by tempting them to depend on themselves rather than on God. The story of the Pharisee and the tax collector expands that message. Not only wealth but *any* form of pride or self-dependence tends to lead away from God.

An effort to become "holy," for example, may accomplish just the opposite if it produces spiritual pride and a feeling of superiority. Human beings have an incurable tendency to feed their own egos, to take credit, to compete. The way to God, said Jesus, is just the opposite: Trust God like a little child, admit wrong, let go.

Jesus reveals the key to true success in the very first story in this collection, a parable to illustrate why we "should always pray and not give up." The persistent widow endures much frustration and apparent injustice before the judge finally grants her request. Similarly, Jesus implies, we may go through desert periods when it looks as if God is ignoring our heartfelt requests. But in the end God himself will settle accounts. And all those whose faith holds firm, even in the hard times, will see justice.

—PY

Daily Contemplation

In what area of your life do you tend to feed your ego and compete? How have you seen this tendency lead you away from God?

DAY 240

Healing at the Pool; Life Through the Son
John 5:1–47

Some time later, Jesus went up to Jerusalem for one of the Jewish festivals. Now there is in Jerusalem near the Sheep Gate a pool, which in Aramaic is called Bethesda . . . Here a great number of disabled people used to lie . . . One who was there had been an invalid for thirty-eight years. When Jesus saw him lying there and learned that he had been in this condition for a long time, he asked him, "Do you want to get well?" "Sir," the invalid replied, "I have no one to help me into the pool when the water is stirred." . . . Then Jesus said to him, "Get up! Pick up your mat and walk." At once the man was cured; he picked up his mat and walked. (John 5:1–9)

According to the tradition of Jesus' day, disabled people who lay near the Pool of Bethesda would be healed if they made it quickly into the pool when an angel came and stirred the waters. This superstition was not from God, who would never create such a contest for those suffering illness. Yet despite the misguided beliefs of these people, Jesus feels compassion for one of them and chooses to heal him.

After restoring the disabled man's health, Jesus lets him know that there are more serious problems than physical suffering. He should use the opportunity to change his life.

Facing opposition once more to his work of healing on the Sabbath, Jesus explains to his detractors who he is and how God has made himself known before their eyes. He opens the door for any who will listen and soften their hearts to the truth he preaches. Those who hear and believe will have eternal life, he explains. They will pass, like invalids suddenly healed, from death to life.

—BQ

Daily Contemplation

What did it—or will it—take to make you hear and believe in Jesus as your Savior?

DAY 241

Parable of the Workers in the Vineyard
Matthew 20:1–16

"The owner of the vineyard said to his foreman, 'Call the workers and pay them their wages,' . . . The workers who were hired about five in the afternoon came and each received a denarius. So when those came who were hired first, they expected to receive more. But each one of them also received a denarius. . . . They began to grumble against the landowner. 'These who were hired last worked only one hour,' they said . . . But he answered one of them, 'I am not being unfair to you, friend. Didn't you agree to work for a denarius? Take your pay and go. . . . Don't I have the right to do what I want with my own money?' . . . So the last will be first, and the first will be last." (Matthew 20:8–16)

In this parable Jesus teaches about an issue close to all our hearts: fairness. By nature we expect reward proportionate to what we have earned. We'll accept more, of course, but if given less we will usually protest. Although life can throw curves that defy this sense of justice, we expect that when dealing with rational beings—especially God—fairness should prevail.

God has his own definition of what is fair, Jesus teaches. His generosity may take us by surprise. God is sovereign, so nothing can happen beyond his control and will. Above all, God is good; his ways are perfect and always right, so we can trust his choices.

Echoes of Jonah ring through the parable. Jesus reminds us that God's heart is bigger than ours, and he lavishes grace on the undeserving. Ultimately, of course, God's magnanimous generosity extends to *all* of us. How, then, can we complain?

—BQ

Daily Contemplation

When was the last time you questioned God about an unfairness you experienced?

DAY 242

Parable of the Ten Virgins and the Parable of the Talents
Matthew 25:1–30

"Then all the virgins woke up and trimmed their lamps. The foolish ones said to the wise, 'Give us some of your oil; our lamps are going out.' 'No,' they replied, 'there may not be enough for both us and you. Instead, go to those who sell oil and buy some for yourselves.' But while they were on their way to buy the oil, the bridegroom arrived. The virgins who were ready went in with him to the wedding banquet. And the door was shut. Later the others also came. 'Lord, Lord,' they said, 'open the door for us!' But he replied, 'Truly I tell you, I don't know you.' Therefore keep watch, because you do not know the day or the hour." (Matthew 25:7–13)

"Well done, good and faithful servant! You have been faithful with a few things; I will put you in charge of many things. Come and share your master's happiness!" (Matthew 25:23)

A parable of a simple wedding carries with it a serious message. Some Bible scholars believe that the parable of the ten virgins speaks specifically about the Jewish people during the time of trials just before Jesus' second coming. They will know of Christ's imminent return, but only some will choose to enter relationship with him while there is still time.

Whether this parable speaks to the Jews or to all people, it stands as a sober reminder that we should live with future consequences in view. Some like to believe they have ample time to get their spiritual lives in order, but they risk being caught off guard. As a result, like the foolish virgins, they will remain in darkness when Jesus comes for those who have the Light.

In a similar vein, the parable of the talents teaches believers that God holds us responsible for the work he has given us to do until Jesus' return. The kingdom of God is real, Jesus stresses, and we should live in view of eternity.

—BQ

Daily Contemplation

What is the work of preparation or "kingdom building" that you feel God may want of you?

DAY 243

Obedience Is the Thing
Reflection

Jesus' parables are simply stories. He told them to common people as well as to the religious elite, and yet Jesus declared that many of these people would be "ever hearing but never understanding" (Matthew 13:14). What about these simple stories made them confusing then, and still today can leave us wondering about Jesus' intent?

It seems that Jesus was referring primarily to people who had already rejected his kingdom message when he spoke of never understanding. For those who would accept Jesus as God's promised Savior, and would seek to follow him, the stories usually carried a single main message. We, too, can learn from his parables without trying too hard.

Author and pastor Eugene Peterson writes about the importance of our participation in the story as we read, and more, of our obedience.

> We enter the world of the text, the world in which God is subject, in order to become participants in the text. We have our part to play in this text, a part that is given to us by the Holy Spirit. As we play our part we become participants.
>
> We are given this book so that we can imaginatively and believingly enter the world of the text and follow Jesus. John Calvin in his treatment of Holy Scripture is commonly cited in this regard: "all right knowledge of God is born of obedience."
>
> If we have not entered this text as participants, we aren't going to understand what is going on. This text cannot be understood by watching from the bleachers—even from expensive box seats. We are in on it.[51]

Peterson tells of his experience as a runner and how he eagerly read magazines on the sport, until he had an injury and needed many weeks of healing. He soon realized that his interest in the magazines had completely halted since he'd stopped running. Yet,

> The moment I began running again I started reading again. . . . I was reading about running not primarily to find out something, not to learn something, but for companionship and validation and confirmation of the experience of running. . . . The parallel with reading Scripture seems to me almost exact: if I am not participating in the reality—the God reality, the creation/salvation/holiness reality—revealed in

the Bible, not involved in the obedience Calvin wrote of, I am probably not going to be much interested in reading about it—at least not for long.

Obedience is the thing, living in active response to the living God. The most important question we ask of this text is not, "What does this mean?" but "What can I obey?" A simple act of obedience will open up our lives to this text far more quickly than any number of Bible studies and dictionaries and concordances.

Not that the study is not important. A Jewish rabbi I once studied with would often say, "For us Jews studying the Bible is more important than obeying it, because if you don't understand it rightly you will obey it wrongly and your obedience will be disobedience." This is also true.[52]

Peterson continues with a story of Anthony, a truck driver in his congregation who had left school in the eighth grade, never read a book, and then became a Christian as an adult. Anthony read through the Bible three times in his first year. His wife was also interested but had a lot of questions. She had trouble with the parables. They invited Peterson to their mobile home, papered with Elvis Presley posters, and Eugene tried to explain how to makes sense of the stories. When Mary still wasn't understanding, Anthony interrupted, 'Mary, you got to live 'em, then you'll understand 'em; you can't figger 'em out from the outside, you got to git inside 'em—or let them git inside you.'"[53]

—BQ

Daily Contemplation

Which of Jesus' parables or teachings is God asking you to "get inside, or let it get inside of you"? How can you start obeying what Jesus is teaching?

DAY 244

The Sheep and the Goats
Matthew 25:31–46

"When the Son of Man comes in his glory, and all the angels with him, he will sit on his glorious throne. All the nations will be gathered before him, and he will separate the people one from another as a shepherd separates the sheep from the goats. He will put the sheep on his right and the goats on his left. Then the King will say to those on his right, 'Come, you who are blessed by my Father; take your inheritance, the kingdom prepared for you since the creation of the world. For I was hungry and you gave me something to eat, I was thirsty and you gave me something to drink, I was a stranger and you invited me in.'" (Matthew 25:31–35)

Using another simple parable, Jesus explains the coming day of judgment, when he will separate those who have genuinely loved him from those who have not. Jesus uses the parable to make clear the direct correlation between loving him and loving others in need. Love for Jesus is not simply an inward feeling that issues from us to his Spirit. If it is true love, it will manifest itself in caring for people toward whom Christ feels compassion. That same love he showed for every kind of person while here on earth will become a living love that flows from him through us and touches others.

Jesus does not imply that a list of good deeds will save us in the end. The Bible is clear—we are saved by grace through our faith in him. But here he tells us that the proof of our love is how we care for others. Our faith saves us, and our faith also compels us to help people in need. Each one we help, Jesus explains, carries a part of himself. In loving them, we are directly loving him.

—BQ

Daily Contemplation

Whom have you helped lately who was hungry, thirsty, lonely, unclothed, sick, or in prison?

DAY 245

Parable of the Great Banquet; Cost of Being a Disciple
Luke 14:15–35

> "Go out quickly into the streets and alleys of the town and bring in the poor, the crippled, the blind and the lame. . . . Go out to the roads and country lanes and compel them to come in, so that my house will be full."
>
> (LUKE 14:21, 23)

> Large crowds were traveling with Jesus, and turning to them he said: "If anyone comes to me and does not hate father and mother, wife and children, brothers and sisters—yes, even their own life—such a person cannot be my disciple. And whoever does not carry their cross and follow me cannot be my disciple."
>
> (LUKE 14:25–27)

Jesus told several parables about the coming day when God will judge believers and unbelievers. Some people in his parables were unprepared for his second coming, some didn't invest in God's kingdom while here on earth, and some didn't exhibit a genuine love for him by caring for others.

In this parable, Jesus tells of people who at first accepted an invitation to God's kingdom, then let other priorities crowd God out of their lives. Once again Jesus teaches that not all will enter his kingdom. Those who take for granted what he offers will eventually lose the chance to dine with him in eternity—at a banquet far more satisfying than anything the earth offers.

Faith will cost believers something here on earth, Jesus cautions. Much of his teaching has focused on God's love and faithfulness. Following Christ leads to fulfillment and peace that we can find nowhere else. Yet following him may also, for a time, bring difficulty, heartache, and sacrifice.

For instance, Jesus takes priority even over our families. Although he teaches us to love and honor family, he asks us to love him more. If we have to choose one over the other, Jesus must come first. It's a commitment not to be taken lightly nor in ignorance and may involve rejection or persecution by others. Nonetheless, if we choose to follow him, the reward will far outweigh the suffering.

—BQ

Daily Contemplation

What cost have you had to pay for being a disciple of Jesus?

PART 8

Responses to Jesus

DAY 246

Parables of the Lost Sheep and the Lost Coin
Luke 15:1–10

> "Suppose a woman has ten silver coins and loses one. Doesn't she light a lamp, sweep the house and search carefully until she finds it? And when she finds it, she calls her friends and neighbors together and says, 'Rejoice with me; I have found my lost coin.' In the same way, I tell you, there is rejoicing in the presence of the angels of God over one sinner who repents." (Luke 15:8–10)

This passage relays two of three parables Jesus tells about God's love for the lost. Luke sets the scene in the first verse: "Now the tax collectors and sinners were all gathering around to hear Jesus." Meanwhile, the Pharisees and teachers of the law were muttering about the unsavory people attracted to Jesus' message. Once again, Jesus turns the tables on his self-righteous opponents. They may consider themselves the spiritual ones worthy of God's attention and approval, but they earn Jesus' rebuke because in his eyes they are as lost as those in the crowds he encounters on the hillsides.

Jesus repeated one message throughout his time on earth: No one is righteous. All are sinners in need of God's forgiveness and grace, and these two poignant stories show God's eagerness to bring the lost into his fold. God goes to any length to find those who are hopelessly lost, and the Shepherd and all heaven rejoice when a straying sheep is found. No doubt the listening Pharisees got the point, for Jesus contrasted the one renegade sheep with "the ninety-nine righteous persons who do not need to repent." The ninety-nine probably represent his religious opponents, who do not recognize their need. If they also genuinely turned to him, heaven's rejoicing would be great indeed.

Carrying a similar message, the parable of the lost coin illustrates how God values those who don't know him. The Pharisees might disapprove of Jesus' attention to tax collectors and sinners, but God approves. He sent his Son to earth for these very people and wants them to be found.

—BQ

Daily Contemplation

When did you lose something important and then find it again?

DAY 247

The Parable of the Lost Son (Prodigal)
Luke 15:11–32

Luke reports that "the chief priests, the teachers of the law and the leaders among the people were trying to kill [Jesus]. Yet they could not find any way to do it, because all the people hung on his words" (Luke 19:47–48). Using simple, homespun images, Jesus expresses profound truths in a way that holds his audience captive. His parables, or concise short stories, have won high praise even from literary experts who do not accept their message. Some of the most famous of these parables, including the three in Luke 15, appear only in Luke's Gospel.

Although trained as a physician, Luke demonstrates great skill as a writer. The introduction to his book mentions that he carefully investigated reports from eyewitnesses before writing the book that bears his name. Using the finest Greek found in the New Testament, he brings characters and scenes vividly to life.

Luke especially excels at conveying the plight of the poor and the outcast. Women, largely ignored by ancient historians, play a large role in his book (he introduces thirteen mentioned nowhere else), as do children. It may seem strange that a man belonging to the upper class would emerge as a champion of the underdog—evidently, Jesus' own compassion has affected Luke deeply.

The three stories in Luke 15 all stir up feelings for the underdog. A shepherd scours the hillside in a frantic search for a missing sheep. A woman turns her house upside down over a lost silver coin. And a runaway son thumbs his nose at a life of comfort and ends up half-starved in a pigpen. In a few brief sentences, the parables tug at feelings of loss and remorse that lie buried just beneath the surface in all of us. And yet all three parables end the same: Spectacular good news floods in to replace the sadness, and partying breaks out.

The word *gospel* itself comes from the Old English word *godspell*. It means, simply, "good news"—a message that Luke never loses sight of. Even for the saddest story, there can be a happy ending after all.

—PY

Daily Contemplation

In the story of the lost son, which of the two brothers do you more resemble?

DAY 248

Zacchaeus the Tax Collector
Luke 19:1–10

> Jesus entered Jericho and was passing through. A man was there by the name of Zacchaeus; he was a chief tax collector and was wealthy. . . . He ran ahead and climbed a sycamore-fig tree to see him . . . When Jesus reached the spot, he looked up and said to him, "Zacchaeus, come down immediately. I must stay at your house today." So he came down at once and welcomed him gladly . . . . Zacchaeus stood up and said to the Lord, "Look, Lord! Here and now I give half of my possessions to the poor, and if I have cheated anybody out of anything, I will pay back four times the amount." Jesus said to him, "Today salvation has come to this house, because this man, too, is a son of Abraham. For the Son of Man came to seek and to save the lost." (Luke 19:1–2, 4–6, 8–10)

Zacchaeus (za-KEE-uhs) is an underdog of sorts, although the people of his day resent rather than pity him. A rich exploiter of his neighbors as one who worked on behalf of the hated Roman occupiers, Zacchaeus would seem an unlikely target for Jesus' love and attention. More, Zacchaeus is a chief tax collector, probably in charge of a group of collectors and very wealthy. Members of his profession have a reputation for fleecing people and getting rich off the profits. In the eyes of the Jewish people, Zacchaeus, like Matthew, ranks at the bottom.

Yet Jesus sees past the surface to the heart of a man in need of salvation. Zacchaeus's response shows that not only does he qualify as a Jew by heritage, but he also has the faith of Abraham and a heart eager for the Messiah. Jesus looks past outward appearances to care for even the most hopeless unbeliever. His love reveals that every person, no matter how unlikely, has the potential of transformation.

—BQ

Daily Contemplation

Who in your life needs Jesus but seems most unlikely to ever receive him?

DAY 249

Jesus, the Bread of Life; Deserted by Many Disciples
John 6:24-71

"I am the bread of life. Whoever comes to me will never go hungry, and whoever believes in me will never be thirsty." (John 6:35)

All four gospels include an account of the feeding of the five thousand, but John adds the most detail, describing the effect of the miracle on the ordinary people who saw it. At first, dazzled by the miracle, they forcibly try to crown Jesus as king. When he, characteristically, slips away, the persistent crowd commandeers boats and sails across a lake in pursuit.

The next day when the crowds catch up with him, Jesus meets them with a blunt warning: "Very truly I tell you, you are looking for me, not because you saw the signs I performed but because you ate the loaves and had your fill. Do not work for food that spoils, but for food that endures to eternal life, which the Son of Man will give you."

That response shows why Jesus distrusts sensation-seeking crowds: They care far more for physical spectacle than for spiritual truth. And what happens next certainly bears out his suspicion. As he is interpreting the spiritual meaning of the miracle, all the enthusiasm of the previous day melts away. The crowd grows downright restless when he openly avows his true identity as the one sent from God. They cannot reconcile such exalted claims ("I have come down from heaven") with their knowledge that he is a local man, whose family they know.

Jesus uses the miracle they have seen firsthand as a way of introducing his topic of the bread of life (his words are later applied to the Lord's Supper, or the Eucharist). But in the end the people in the crowd—who have proof of Jesus' supernatural power digesting in their bellies—abandon him, unbelieving. Many of his disciples turn back, too, never to follow him again.

—PY

Daily Contemplation

Have you ever taken offense at Jesus? Why?

DAY 250

The Woman Caught in Adultery
John 8:2-11

"Let any one of you who is without sin be the first to throw a stone at her." (Luke 8:7)

This story, one of the most memorable in the Gospels, is not found in some of the earliest and most reliable manuscripts of John. Yet surely it gives us another reliable glimpse of Jesus' heart.

Once again Jesus shows compassion toward an underdog. His attention to women in his ministry is unusual in itself, especially for the Jewish culture of the day. Many of the Gospel stories tell of Jesus' friendship with women and his attention to their physical, emotional, and spiritual needs. Far ahead of his time, Jesus treats women as equally worthy.

In this story he cares for a woman who has committed sexual sin. According to the law, both she and her partner deserve death. But Romans do not allow Jews to carry out death sentences, so the Pharisees try to trap Jesus between Jewish and Roman regulations.

Jesus will not be duped by conniving, heartless legalists. He cuts to the core of the matter: sin. God gave his law to define sin and to punish it, and because she broke the law, the adulteress deserves punishment. Yet God's law encompasses more than sexual sin. No person is guiltless in the face of the law, and no one should know that fact better than these legal experts. Jesus puts them in their place, proclaiming that his Father's business is vastly different—more merciful—from the business they have taken upon themselves in the guise of acting in the Father's name.

Jesus came to convict of sin, yes, but also to offer forgiveness. The Pharisees, on the other hand, remain stuck in a self-made maze called law.

—BQ

Daily Contemplation

Do you tend to categorize sin, considering some sins less serious than others, and some worse?

DAY 251

Finding Jesus
Reflection

Inside all of us is a yearning that only God can meet. The North African bishop Saint Augustine once wrote, "Thou hast made us for Thyself, and the heart of man is restless until it finds its rest in Thee."⁵⁴ French mathematician, philosopher, and scientist Blaise Pascal wrote of an infinite abyss that "can be filled only with an infinite and immutable object; in other words by God himself."⁵⁵

Whether or not we are in tune with our need for God, he stands as the only one who can fill us. Jesus spoke of God's filling this way: "I am the bread of life. Whoever comes to me will never go hungry, and whoever believes in me will never be thirsty" (John 6:35). Jesus meets a need more basic than physical hunger—the need for bread that satisfies forever. Jesus can fill us now and also promise us eternal life.

Often we find ourselves most aware of our need for Jesus in times of struggle. With our senses sharpened by the raw edges of pain, life takes on fresh perspective. The incidentals fall away, and we see that God is a part of everything that really matters. If we don't have union with him, life holds no hope. We will continue to hunger and thirst.

The death of a loved one, or the prospect of our own death, dramatically brings us face-to-face with that God-shaped abyss inside. In a very different way, so does the mundane pursuit of everyday life. Without God to fill the days with more than routine, life becomes heavy, our souls restless. What is the point? What gives life meaning?

Any circumstance of life, in the end, gives occasion to a yearning for God. Why then do many still resist him, and others continue to search, looking everywhere but to God?

John 6 gives one insight. After hearing Jesus reveal himself as the bread of life, many of his disciples responded, "This is a hard teaching. Who can accept it?" (6:60). Today, many face similar roadblocks. Why follow a God who became man and died a humiliating death? Why follow a God who asks us to give up our lives for him? Why follow One we don't understand? In each case Jesus responds, "No one can come to me unless the Father has enabled them" (6:65). In a seeming dichotomy, we have the free will to choose Jesus, yet we need God's help in doing even that.

Those who have found the answer to the infinite abyss can thank God for enabling us to see and respond to his love. As we pray for those who have yet to accept the love of Jesus, we ask for God's help. They, too, need his enabling in order to respond.

—BQ

---- *Daily Contemplation* ----

What turned your heart to Jesus? Thank God for his enabling. Think of others who still need him, and ask God to help them in their search.

DAY 252

Jesus Goads Hypocrites; Heals Man and Young Girl
Mark 7:1–37

Although the crowds sometimes have difficulty swallowing Jesus' message, as long as he keeps healing people, they tag along. On the other hand, the religious, political, and intellectual establishments all strongly oppose Jesus but cannot manage to loosen his grip on the common people. The Pharisees, in particular, keep trying to trap him in a major blunder that might turn the people—or the government—against him.

In many ways, the Pharisees make for an odd set of enemies. They are, in fact, among the most religious people of Jesus' day. More than any other group, they strive to follow the letter of the Old Testament law. But Jesus can see right through the Pharisees' pious behavior. He blasts them for focusing on the "outside" while neglecting the far greater dangers within.

The Pharisees of Jesus' day are strict legalists who proudly embellish Jewish law with their own traditions. For example, they have determined that a person can ride a donkey without breaking the Sabbath rules, but not use a switch to speed up the animal. It is permissible to give to a beggar on the Sabbath only if the beggar sticks his hand inside the home, so the giver needn't reach outside. A woman cannot look in the mirror on the Sabbath—she might see a gray hair and be tempted to pull it out.

Jesus reacts with surprising harshness to such seemingly petty matters. By concentrating on all the rules, the Pharisees risk missing the whole point of the gospel. Such external, showy forms of legalism do not get anyone closer to God; just the opposite, they tend to make people proud and cliquish and self-righteous.

One way Jesus exposes the hypocrisy in the Pharisees' attitude is by publicly healing people on the sacred Sabbath. Fully aware that such acts will scandalize strict Pharisees, he goes ahead anyway, insisting that compassion for needy people must take precedence over any tradition.

—PY

Daily Contemplation

In what ways can you try to focus on your own heart and avoid being overly judgmental of the sins of others?

DAY 253

Jesus Teaches on Forgiveness; On Divorce
Matthew 18:21–19:12

Legalists, people who follow strict rules of conduct, at first glance may seem "righteous." But Jesus warns against the subtle dangers of legalism. Oddly, it tends to lower a person's view of God. If I manage to meet all the requirements of a strict rule book, I may begin to feel secure about my own goodness. I may think that I have earned God's approval through my own efforts.

People in the Gospels who question Jesus in person—both his enemies the Pharisees and his friends the disciples—seek a precise list of rules so that they can strive to meet those obligations and thus feel satisfied. To such people, Jesus shouts a loud "No!" We never outgrow our need for God; we never *complete* the Christian life. We survive spiritually only if we constantly depend on God.

In the first story in this passage, Peter tries almost ludicrously to reduce forgiveness to a mathematical formula. *Let's see, exactly how many times must I forgive someone? Six? Seven?* Jesus mocks the question and tells a profound story about God's forgiveness, so great and all-encompassing that it defies all mathematics.

Next, the Pharisees try to pin down a formula for divorce. Once again Jesus avoids the answer they want to hear and points instead to the principles that undergird all marriage.

These examples illustrate how Jesus usually responds to questions about specific problems. When a pious man asks which neighbors he should go about loving, Jesus tells of the Good Samaritan who shows love even to his enemies. Jesus doesn't tell a rich person to give away 18.5 percent of his belongings; he says to give them all away. He doesn't restrict adultery to the act of intercourse; he connects it to lust, adultery of the heart. Murder? In principle, that's no different from anger.

In short, Jesus always refuses to lower the sights. He lashes out at every form of legalism, every human attempt to accumulate a list of credits. The credit goes to God, not us. The chief danger facing legalists is that they risk missing the whole point of the gospel: that it is a gift freely given by God to people who don't deserve it.

—PY

Daily Contemplation

When have you had to forgive someone repeatedly?

DAY 254

The Good Shepherd; His Sheep; The Unbelievers
John 10:1–40

Every few years an author or movie director comes out with a new work raising questions about Jesus' identity. Often such portrayals show him wandering around the earth in a daze, trying to figure out why he came and what he is supposed to be doing. Nothing could be further from the account given us by John, Jesus' closest friend. According to John, Jesus was no "man who fell to earth" but God's Son, sent on a mission from the Father. "I know where I came from and where I am going," Jesus said (John 8:14).

Of the four Gospel writers, John dwells most prominently on Jesus' identity as the true Messiah, the Son of God. He states his purpose in writing very clearly: "These are written that you may believe that Jesus is the Messiah, the Son of God, and that by believing you may have life in his name" (20:31). His book includes incidents from no more than twenty days in Jesus' life, arranged so as to demonstrate who Jesus is. Significantly, most of these incidents come from Jesus' final days, when he is declaring his mission openly.

"I am the gate," Jesus says in this chapter; "I am the good shepherd." Jews who hear those words undoubtedly think back to Old Testament kings like David, who were known as the shepherds of Israel. When some challenge him bluntly, "If you are the Christ, tell us plainly," Jesus answers with equal bluntness, "I and the Father are one." The pious Jews understand him perfectly: They pick up stones to execute him for blasphemy.

Not even these hostile reactions surprise Jesus. He expects opposition, even execution. As he explains, a truly good shepherd, unlike a hired hand, "lays down his life for the sheep." He is the only person in history who chooses to be born, chooses to die, and chooses to come back again. This chapter explains why he makes those choices.

—PY

Daily Contemplation

What difference does it make to you that Jesus is God and not just a man?

Jesus Feeds, Teaches, and Heals
Mark 8:1–38

As this chapter opens, Jesus is exasperated with his disciples. They have seen him feed five thousand people, and then four thousand, and yet still they worry about their next meal. "Do you have eyes but fail to see, and ears but fail to hear?" Jesus asks them reproachfully. Still, for all their denseness the disciples have grasped something that eludes most others. The crowds see Jesus as a reincarnation of a prophet: Elijah, maybe, or John the Baptist. But in this scene Peter boldly pronounces Jesus as the "Christ," the very Messiah long predicted by the prophets.

It is difficult for us to comprehend the importance of that single word to first-century Jews. Ground down by centuries of foreign domination, they staked all their hopes on a Messiah who would lead their nation back to glory. Matthew records that Jesus, pleased by Peter's impulsive declaration, lavishes praise on him (16:17–19). Yet Peter's brightest moment is immediately followed by one of his dullest, for a few paragraphs later Jesus identifies Peter with Satan. What transpires between those two scenes marks an important turning point in the story of Jesus' life.

To Peter and the other disciples, "Messiah" stands for wealth and fame and political power, the very temptations of an earthly kingdom that Jesus has resisted from Satan. Jesus knows that the true Messiah will first have to endure scorn, humiliation, suffering, and even death. He is the suffering servant prophesied by Isaiah, destined for an executioner's cross and not a worldly position of honor.

Jesus accepts Peter's designation; he is indeed the true Messiah. But from that moment on, Jesus makes a strategic shift. He leaves Galilee and heads toward the capital of Jerusalem. Instead of addressing the crowds, he narrows his scope to the twelve disciples and works to prepare them for the suffering and death to come. Peter may have grasped Jesus' identity, but he has much to learn about his mission. He wants Jesus to avoid pain, not understanding that the pain of the cross will bring salvation to the whole world.

—PY

Daily Contemplation

If someone were to ask you who Jesus is, what would you say?

DAY 256

The Transfiguration; Jesus Heals and Teaches
Mark 9:1–41

Despite the increased attention, Jesus' closest disciples, the Twelve, do not distinguish themselves—to put it mildly. "Are you so dull?" Jesus asks them at one point (Mark 7:18), and later in Mark 9:19 he sighs in exasperation, "How long shall I put up with you?" This chapter alone shows the disciples bungling a work of healing, misunderstanding Jesus' hints about his coming death and resurrection, squabbling about status, and trying to shut down the work of another disciple. Obviously, there is much in Jesus' mission they fail to comprehend.

Three of the disciples observe a dramatic scene that should quell any lingering doubts. "The Transfiguration," reported in vivid detail by Matthew, Mark, and Luke, affords absolute proof of God's approval. Jesus' face shines like the sun and his clothes become dazzling, "whiter than anyone in the world could bleach them" (Mark 9:3). A cloud envelops the disciples and inside that cloud, to their astonishment, they find two long-dead giants of Jewish history: Moses and Elijah. It is too much to take in; when God speaks audibly in the cloud, the disciples fall down terrified. (Most scholars believe Mark got his details from Peter, one of the eyewitnesses. Peter describes the long-term impact of this experience in 2 Peter 1:16–18.)

Yet what impact does such a stupendous event have on the disciples? Does it permanently silence their questions and fill them with solid faith? A few weeks later, each one of the Twelve—including the three eyewitnesses of the Transfiguration—abandon Jesus in his hour of deepest need. Somehow the import of who Jesus is, God in flesh, never really sinks in until after he has left and then comes back.

Actually, the fact of the disciples' abrupt change makes compelling evidence for Jesus' resurrection. The cowering disciples portrayed in Mark hardly resemble the bold, confident figures in the book of Acts. Something incredible had to happen to turn this bunch of bumblers into heroes of the faith.

—PY

Daily Contemplation

This chapter includes both highs and lows in the disciples' experience. What would a graph of your spiritual journey look like?

DAY 257

Still Trying to Figure Jesus Out
Reflection

I'm often relieved, when I (Brenda) read the Gospels, that God chose to put me on earth now rather than back in Jesus' day. A part of me envies those who got to see, hear, and touch Jesus in person. This part of me surmises that life would be much easier if he were here before me in the flesh. But a bigger part of me suspects that would not be true. Would I find more clarity in making decisions after hearing Jesus voice his perspective? Would my life become easier after seeing and touching him?

I know my suspicious nature. Were I living back then, I'd probably fit right in with the crowds who followed Jesus, astonished by his miracles and touched by his love yet skeptical about his claim to be God. I hope that I would discern the truth of who Jesus was, but since so many in the crowds didn't, would I?

Worse, would I have responded to Jesus any better than the Pharisees did? I too can be self-righteous, convinced that I know the mind of God. As I read of Jesus chiding the Pharisees, I sometimes shudder, feeling his reproach hitting too close to home.

I can also identify with Jesus' disciples. Even in seeing my leader transfigured on the mountain and hearing God audibly commend him, I would likely be gripped with fear, as was Peter, and say something stupid. Or, despite my literary bent, I too might puzzle in ignorance over Jesus' obvious use of metaphor. "'Watch out for the yeast of the Pharisees'? Well of course, Jesus wants us to bring more bread next time."

Yes, I'm afraid that I would exasperate Jesus in the same way the majority of those who knew him did. Today I have the Bible spread before me. I can see his life from beginning to end and read prophecies about his coming as well as teaching by the apostles written after he was gone. I have access to countless books and teachers who can open to me the truths Jesus came to reveal. More, I have his Spirit living inside—Jesus in me revealing himself. I can't complain. I have everything I need to know Jesus as he is and love him with my life.

Despite all this knowledge, I'm still trying to figure Jesus out. I've walked with him for years, yet I've hardly scratched the surface in knowing this Savior I call my own. "My sheep know me," Jesus said. I know I couldn't live without him. I know he's changed me. And I know I need to keep learning to know him better.

—BQ

Daily Contemplation

Bring to Jesus your questions about who he is. Pray for Jesus to draw you more deeply into intimacy with him.

DAY 258

Jesus Sends Out Seventy-Two Disciples
Luke 10:1–24

"All things have been committed to me by my Father. No one knows who the Son is except the Father, and no one knows who the Father is except the Son and those to whom the Son chooses to reveal him." (Luke 10:22)

Jesus' time on earth is running out. Only a few weeks remain for him to prepare others to carry on his work, and he uses that time for a crash training course. The opening scene in this chapter shows a major advance in his plan of turning over his work to his followers. This time he commissions not twelve but seventy-two followers in a hazardous assignment.

A seismic change is rumbling. As Jesus describes the mission of the seventy-two, he does not disguise his alarm. "Go! I am sending you out like lambs among wolves," he says. Finally, in a voice that commands attention, he gives this mysterious charge: "Whoever listens to you listens to me; whoever rejects you rejects me."

Luke's next view of Jesus is almost unprecedented in the Gospels. Nowhere else will you find Jesus so happy, so bubbling with joy. The caution in his face has given way to exuberance. It really has worked, the dangerous mission into the hill country, and Jesus celebrates the enormous breakthrough with these seventy-two disciples.

In that triumphant response Jesus reveals the significance of the final phase of his mission. He has come to earth to establish a *church*, a group of people who will carry on his will after his departure. And as these seventy-two disciples plod the dusty roads of Judea, knocking on doors, explaining the Messiah, and healing the sick, Jesus watches Satan fall like lightning from heaven. Their actions win a cosmic victory. Jesus' own mission, his own life, is being lived out through seventy-two very ordinary human beings.

—PY

Daily Contemplation

When did you last sense Jesus' life being lived out through you?

DAY 259

The Parable of the Good Samaritan
Luke 10:25–37

"But a Samaritan, as he traveled, came where the man was; and when he saw him, he took pity on him. He went to him and bandaged his wounds, pouring on oil and wine. Then he put the man on his own donkey, brought him to an inn and took care of him. . . . Which of these three do you think was a neighbor to the man who fell into the hands of robbers?" The expert in the law replied, "The one who had mercy on him." Jesus told him, "Go and do likewise." (Luke 10:33–34, 36–37)

Jesus tells a story about another way in which his followers will live out his life. Jesus, like the Samaritan in the story, has come to care for hurting people who are neglected by the religious leaders, the very ones who should be their caregivers. Like the priest and Levite, many of these leaders are too busy to interrupt their important agendas and help someone in dire need. They are too busy working *for* God to care *like* God.

Jesus has another message, another approach. Love for God can't be an ethereal commitment of the head. Rather, it must impact the daily, moment-by-moment decisions a person makes. A heart that looks like Jesus' will fill with compassion upon seeing someone in need. A soul committed to him will resonate with his likeness. A mind surrendered to Jesus will decide like him regardless of feelings or convenience. And a person yielded to him will expend strength in loving God actively. Heart, soul, mind, and strength devoted to God will translate into practical, compassionate love for our neighbors.

—BQ

Daily Contemplation

When was the last time you went out of your way to help a neighbor in need?

DAY 260

At the Home of Mary and Martha
Luke 10:38–42

> But Martha was distracted by all the preparations that had to be made. She came to him and asked, "Lord, don't you care that my sister has left me to do the work by myself? Tell her to help me!" "Martha, Martha," the Lord answered, "you are worried and upset about many things, but few things are needed—or indeed only one. Mary has chosen what is better, and it will not be taken away from her." (Luke 10:40–42)

Jesus spends part of his final week on earth in Bethany, located less than two miles from Jerusalem. Here he visits with two good friends whose brother, Lazarus, Jesus will raise from the dead.

In this introduction to Mary and Martha, Luke gives a portrait of two distinct personality types. Though short, the vignette is packed with meaning. In fact, this scene often disturbs those believers who identify more readily with Martha than with Mary. Martha is responsible, concerned about meeting the needs of others and being a proper hostess—certainly respectable qualities. Mary can come across as somewhat lazy and uncaring toward her sister.

If God creates people with individual personalities for his use, why did Jesus commend Mary over Martha? Why does he fault Martha for seeking to be a competent hostess and commend Mary for sitting around doing nothing?

In this situation Mary has a deeper sense of priority. Under other circumstances she might be at fault for not helping her sister. But with Jesus as a guest, time with him takes precedence over all else.

Jesus teaches that ways of loving him won't always look the same. In every situation we should seek the Spirit's guidance on how best to serve him. That may mean sometimes following our natural bent, and other times doing the opposite!

—BQ

Daily Contemplation

Do you identify more with Mary or Martha?

DAY 261

Jesus Raises Lazarus from the Dead
John 11:1–44

"I am the resurrection and the life. The one who believes in me will live, even though they die; and whoever lives by believing in me will never die. Do you believe this?" (John 11:25)

Performing his most startling miracle yet, Jesus demonstrates that he is "the resurrection and the life." In doing so, Jesus seals his own death. After this miracle, the Jewish leaders won't risk letting him draw more crowds. Rome might become concerned and clamp down on the Jewish leaders to maintain control.

Ironically, though Jesus' greatest exhibition of God's power will endanger his own life, it will ultimately accomplish what God intends. God receives glory both now and in the coming week when, after the death of his Son, a far greater resurrection will take place.

The mourners, including Jesus' disciples, don't understand any of this yet. They have simply gathered in good Jewish custom to support and comfort their grieving friends. Many have heard Jesus and seen him do miraculous things, but this time it appears Jesus' help has come too late. Lazarus is long dead, and Jesus doesn't show up till well after the fact.

Imagine being at the tomb when Jesus comes, weeping, and asks to have the stone removed. "Now what?" the people must have thought. "The teacher has some wild ideas, but this time he's really making a spectacle of himself and of Mary and Martha too. Can't he mourn properly, like the rest of us?"

The words are hardly out of their mouths when they wonder if they're seeing a ghost. "How could it be? This is too much! Lazarus can't be alive—he's been dead for four days!"

"You're right," Jesus responds. "This *is* too much. God has much more in store than you could imagine. Now, if you believe, you'll see the glory of God as you've never seen it before."

—BQ

Daily Contemplation

Has Jesus ever astonished you by doing something you never would have expected?

DAY 262

Jesus Predicts His Death; Heals; Enters Jerusalem
Mark 10:32–11:11

This scene opens with yet another prediction of Jesus' death. Showing incredible insensitivity, two of the disciples immediately lapse into a petty dispute about status. They cannot grasp the message that Jesus patiently repeats for them: In his kingdom, the greatest is the one who *serves*.

Jesus uses curious techniques to gain recruits for his kingdom. His job descriptions include such words as *cross* and *slave*—rather like a Marine Corps recruiter displaying photos of war amputees and dead soldiers. Not even his closest friends can comprehend how the ugly image of an executioner's cross fits their dreams of a new kingdom. No matter how many times Jesus explains the way of the cross, it never seems to sink in.

As the group reaches Jerusalem, however, Jesus does permit one display of public adulation. Always before, he has shrunk away from the crowds who try to coronate him. But in the "Triumphal Entry" of Palm Sunday he lets people honor him as the conquering Messiah.

In some ways, the procession is a slapstick affair compared with the lavish processions of the Romans—Jesus rides on a donkey, after all, not a stallion or a gilded chariot. But the event, foretold by the prophets, has deep meaning for the Jews. Jesus is openly declaring himself as Messiah, and the Triumphal Entry sets all Jerusalem astir.

Jewish leaders who oppose Jesus raise an alarm, and even the Romans take note of a man claiming to be a king. The rest of the Gospel accounts, however, record how tragically short-lived Jesus' public acceptance proves to be. The crowds, like the disciples, are wholly unprepared for Jesus' style of kingdom. Its demands are too hard, its rewards too vague.

—PY

Daily Contemplation

How can you demonstrate servant leadership today?

DAY 263

Waiting on God
Reflection

Just when I (Brenda) think I know what God is up to in my life, he changes directions and does something I'm not expecting. Although it's disorienting at times, I know God has a bigger and more intricate plan for me than I'll ever foresee. Each change of direction reminds me that I'll always need an attitude of waiting.

Jesus' disciples had to learn this lesson too. Just a week before his crucifixion, Jesus told them for at least the second time that in Jerusalem he would be betrayed and killed, only to rise again. He was preparing them for difficult days soon to come. However, two of the disciples, James and John, rather than letting Jesus' words soak in and waiting for further guidance from him, impulsively tried to ensure for themselves the best place in heaven. Although they were two of Jesus' closest friends, they couldn't quiet their own ambitions enough to realize that God was doing something monumental and that they needed to take direction from him rather than proposing their own plan.

Writer Macrina Wiederkehr uses a fitting illustration from her childhood of helping her mother bake bread. The ritual taught her something important about waiting.

> While she mixed and kneaded the dough we talked of many things, but when she covered the dough and put it in a warm place to rise, it was time to be quiet and wait. For me, it became a sacred, mystery hour, a holy hour, an hour of watching and waiting for the miracle of rising.
>
> During that time of waiting she would always tell me not to frighten the dough. It seems that dough grew best in a silent, peaceful atmosphere. And so if friends came over to play at that time, I would always tell them: Don't scare the dough! They would look at me strangely and never quite seem to understand. But I understood.[56]

In the wisdom of Ecclesiastes, there is "a time to be silent and a time to speak" (3:7), and for the disciples this was a time for silence, a time to wait for the miracle of rising. In a brief while God's greatest act of love would come to pass, and shortly afterward his Spirit would make a home in these men. They didn't understand, but they would see more clearly if only they would continue to watch and wait for the sacred mystery to unfold.

Even God's followers in the Old Testament knew of their need to wait. Job said, "I will wait for my renewal to come" (14:14), and David wrote often about waiting, saying in one psalm, "Be still before the LORD and wait patiently for him" (Psalm 37:7). The apostles of Christ would sense this continued need for waiting. Paul cautioned Titus to say "'no' to ungodliness and worldly passions . . . while we wait for the blessed hope" of Jesus' second coming (Titus 2:12–13).

God's work is always in process. Always there will be a warm stovetop place in my life that calls me to be silent and wait on God, a place where his sacred mysteries continue to rise. I am wise to heed David's, and Macrina's mother's, caution: "Be still, and don't scare the dough!"

—BQ

Daily Contemplation

Where in your life is God asking you to wait on him?

DAY 264

Jesus Clears the Temple and Teaches
Mark 11:12–12:12

> On reaching Jerusalem, Jesus entered the temple courts and began driving out those who were buying and selling there. He overturned the tables of the money changers and the benches of those selling doves, and would not allow anyone to carry merchandise through the temple courts. And as he taught them, he said, "Is it not written: 'My house will be called a house of prayer for all nations'? But you have made it 'a den of robbers.'" (Mark 11:15–17)

The last week of Jesus' life shows a mounting sense of urgency, as seen in several dramatic confrontations at the temple. That sacred site, supposedly the center for worship of God, has taken on a commercial cast. Merchants, who sell sacrificial animals to pilgrims and foreigners at inflated prices, seem more interested in profit than in true worship. In the spirit of the Old Testament prophets, Jesus brands them "robbers" and forcibly drives them out.

Mark folds that scene into an account of a fig tree cursed by Jesus because of its lack of fruit. He is probably drawing a direct parallel to the religious establishment of the day: It too has "withered," and Jesus plans to take decisive action against it.

Jesus does nothing to temper his harsh message. On the contrary, he tells a parable of a vineyard that seems deliberately provocative. He presents himself as God's last resort, one final attempt to break through stubborn resistance. But he too will be killed, by the same people whose ancestors have mocked and killed the prophets.

Battle lines are drawn. On one side is Jesus, kept safe only by his widespread popularity. On the other are leaders of the religious and political establishments. Threatened by Jesus' radical message of repentance and reform, they determine to find a way to trap Jesus and turn the crowd against him.

—PY

Daily Contemplation

In what way can you identify with Jesus' feelings in these stories?

DAY 265

The Law; Greatest Commandment; Widow's Offering
Mark 12:13–44

Mark 12 records three different skirmishes between Jesus and the groups seeking to trap him.

The Pharisees, allied with a party following Herod Antipas, cynically praise Jesus and then spring on him a trick question: "Is it right to pay taxes to Caesar or not?" If Jesus says, "Pay the taxes," he will lose popular support among the independence-minded Jews, who despise Roman occupation forces. If he says, "Don't pay," he could be arrested for breaking the Roman law.

Next, a small but powerful religious group tries to stump Jesus with a theological question. The Sadducees, who do not believe in an afterlife, propose a complicated riddle about life after death.

Finally, Jesus' perennial enemies the Pharisees take their turn. Jewish rabbis of that day counted 613 commandments in the law, and various splinter groups would bicker over which ones were most important. Here a teacher of the law asks Jesus to select just one as the greatest commandment of all, knowing his choice will offend some of those groups.

Jesus avoids each of these verbal traps, succeeding so brilliantly that Mark concludes, "And from then on no one dared ask him any more questions" (Mark 12:34). In all these skirmishes, Jesus does not try to placate his adversaries. Instead, he uses the occasions of conflict to warn his disciples and the watching crowds against those adversaries, whose fury only increases.

After he has fended off the last critic, Jesus points to a poor widow who has just made a tiny but sacrificial offering for the temple treasury. Her faithfulness, says Jesus, is far more impressive than that of the greedy religious establishment, who "devour widows' houses and for a show make lengthy prayers."

—PY

Daily Contemplation

What can you learn from Jesus' style in handling his enemies?

DAY 266

Signs of the End of the Age
Mark 13:1–37

Move forward a few days, beyond the events of this chapter, as Jesus is prodded by Roman soldiers toward the place of execution. A group of women follows behind, hysterical with grief. Suddenly Jesus turns and silences them with these words, "Daughters of Jerusalem, do not weep for me; weep for yourselves and for your children. . . . For if people do these things when the tree is green, what will happen when it is dry?" (Luke 23:28, 31).

Even in Jesus' childhood, rumors about him provoked a king's bloody campaign of infanticide. And as this chapter spells out in grim detail, Jesus does not expect the war against God's kingdom to end with his own death. He predicts that evil will only intensify until at last, in one final spasm of rebellion, the earth will give way to God's final restoration.

The words of this chapter echo and quote from the Old Testament prophets, who often saw the future in dreadful apocalyptic visions. At the end of time, God will take off all the wraps. And when Jesus returns, he will appear in a new form: not as a helpless babe in a manger, not nailed to a crosspiece of wood, but as "the Son of Man coming in clouds with great power and glory" (Mark 13:26).

Some of Jesus' dire predictions find fulfillment in AD 70, when Roman soldiers would break through the walls of Jerusalem and demolish Herod's temple—the same temple Jesus' disciples are admiring when Jesus first speaks these words. Other predictions, clearly, have not yet been fulfilled. In this passage, Jesus gives direct clues to events that will precede his second coming. But he ends with a warning that no one can calculate the precise time of his return to earth.

It doesn't take long for doubters to appear on the scene. Just a few decades later scoffers are already mocking the notion of the second coming of Christ. "Where is this 'coming' he promised? Ever since our ancestors died, everything goes on as it has since the beginning of creation" (2 Peter 3:4). For all such scoffers, Jesus and the prophets have one ominous word of advice: Just wait. God will not remain silent forever. One day, earth and sky will flee from his presence.

—PY

Daily Contemplation

What response does Jesus want from those who hear these words?

DAY 267

Woman Anoints Jesus; The Last Supper
Mark 14:1–31

The Passover, an annual commemoration of the Israelites' deliverance from Egypt, marks one of the high points of the Jewish calendar. In Jesus' day, all males older than twelve would travel to Jerusalem for the holiday, filling the city with hundreds of thousands of pilgrims.

Jesus has entered that festive scene in a moment of triumph on Palm Sunday, but very soon a sense of doom steals in. He seems obsessed with death. When a woman splashes him with expensive perfume, he calls it a form of burial preparation.

Passover festivities in Jesus' day culminated in a solemn meal, where family and close friends would gather to remember the Exodus, the time of liberation. They'd taste morsels of food, sip wine, and read aloud the stories from the Old Testament. They would also select a lamb to take to the temple and offer as a sacrifice to God. Thus the holiday ended on a sad and bloody note.

Outside the room, Jesus' enemies are stalking, waiting for an occasion to seize him. Inside, the disciples swear loyalty to their leader, even as he insists that all of them will soon forsake him. It is at this somber meal that Jesus makes a profound declaration. "This is the blood of the new covenant," he says as he pours the wine. "Take it, this is my body," he says, breaking bread.

What the disciples do not fully understand is that a dream is dying—a dream of a mighty nation, God's covenant nation. Jesus is announcing a new covenant, sealed not with the blood of lambs but with his own blood. The new kingdom, the kingdom of God, will be led not by Jewish generals and kings but rather by the scared band of disciples gathered around the table—the very disciples who will soon betray him.

Today, virtually all Christian churches continue the practice of Communion (also known as the Eucharist, or the Lord's Supper) in some form. This solemn ceremony dates back to the original Passover meal when Jesus instituted the new covenant.

—PY

Daily Contemplation

What does the celebration of the Lord's Supper mean to you?

DAY 268

Loving Jesus Extravagantly
Reflection

When I (Brenda) hear the word *extravagance*, I think of beautiful possessions, rich foods, a lavish lifestyle. It's a word we use most often in connection with luxuries.

The Bible, though it does not use the word directly, suggests another use for extravagance: to describe ways of loving. The woman who anointed Jesus' feet with perfume, for instance, knew a lot about extravagant loving. John identifies her as Mary, the sister of Martha and Lazarus. Only days earlier Mary had sat at Jesus' feet, absorbed in his company while her sister complained of her laziness. Now Mary takes a valuable jar of perfume and pours it on Jesus' feet out of love for him. Again her actions are misunderstood and criticized. Some protest that she is careless and wasteful, foolishly emptying a valuable flask that could have been sold for the poor.

Jesus observes another woman in a "foolish" act of extravagant love: a widow who dropped all the money she had into the temple offering. Another man, in a parable Jesus told, interrupted his journey and "wasted" time and money to help a wounded traveler, one from a group who had oppressed his own people.

A glimpse of a wild, uninhibited King David provides a vivid picture of extravagant love. Leading a procession in bringing the ark of God back to Jerusalem, David danced "before the LORD with all his might" (2 Samuel 6:14), while wearing only a skimpy garment. David's wife Michal watched from a window, grimacing in anger. No king should act in such an undignified manner, she felt.

I think of these Bible characters and look at my own life. How extravagantly do I love Jesus? How willing am I to give my most costly possession away? How eager am I to spend stretches of time with God? How apt to offer money I really need? How likely to spend time on someone I don't know and don't particularly care about? How often do I shed my inhibitions to worship God in a physical, demonstrative, even ecstatic way?

Tough questions. Ones I'd rather not look at too honestly. Love for God is good and right, but extravagant love? It feels scary and risky; it threatens to take a lot from me and guarantees nothing in return. What is more challenging, I need to offer this love spontaneously. Rarely planned or manufactured, extravagant love simply lives out daily God's greatest commandment: to "love the Lord your God with all your heart and with all your soul and with all your mind and with all your strength" (Mark 12:30). Extravagant lovers in the Bible displayed an inner love that flowed naturally from them.

With that same love real in my life, I may not look like Mary, the widow, the Good Samaritan, or David. I'll love God extravagantly in ways that flow from the person God made me to be. I'll love God with all my might, no expenses spared, and I'll smile to myself when someday I'm labeled "foolish."

—BQ

Daily Contemplation

Does the thought of loving Jesus in an extravagant way scare you? Rather than focusing on what you can do to love Jesus, focus simply on loving him. Ask God to bring you deeper each day into a love relationship with him. Extravagant acts will flow from this life-giving bond.

PART 9

Jesus' Final Hours

DAY 269

Jesus Washes His Disciples' Feet
John 13:1–17

> When he had finished washing their feet, he put on his clothes and returned to his place. "Do you understand what I have done for you?" he asked them. "You call me 'Teacher' and 'Lord,' and rightly so, for that is what I am. Now that I, your Lord and Teacher, have washed your feet, you also should wash one another's feet." (John 13:12–14)

Once again Jesus teaches his disciples by doing something that dumbfounds them. Throughout his ministry Jesus has resisted the outward status that usually accompanies leadership. Although clearly a leader, he has refused to pull rank. On this night he demonstrates a humility that will only be exceeded when he goes to the cross.

People in ancient Judea often traveled dusty roads by foot, wearing sandals on bare feet, which made foot washing a daily necessity. Sometimes a servant or a woman would wash the feet of guests, or more typically the visitors did it themselves. Since people normally washed before meals, Jesus' act in the middle of a meal is especially surprising.

You can easily understand the disciples' chagrin at seeing Jesus remove some of his clothes mid-meal and begin to wash the grime of a day's travel from the feet of his friends. On the eve of his death, despite his many clues, they are still hoping for a Messiah to exalt. The posture of a foot-washing servant just doesn't fit their image of God's Son.

Jesus' demonstration of love and servanthood lives on as a reminder to believers that nothing we could do for another person is beneath what Jesus would do. No matter what we feel we deserve from others, we can't bend too low in caring for others. Service doesn't demean one's dignity; rather, as Jesus shows, it defines it.

—BQ

Daily Contemplation

Can you recall a recent time when it was difficult to serve someone else?

DAY 270

Jesus Offers Comfort, The Father, The Holy Spirit
John 14:1–31

The apostle John devotes one-third of his gospel to the last twenty-four hours of Jesus' life. John stretches out the Passover meal over five chapters (John 13–17), and nothing like these chapters exists elsewhere in the Bible. Their slow-motion, realistic detail provides an intimate memoir of Jesus' most anguished evening on earth.

Leonardo da Vinci immortalized the setting of the Last Supper in his famous mural painting, arranging the participants on one side of the table as if they were posing for the artist. John avoids physical details and focuses instead on the swirl of human emotions. He holds a light to the disciples' faces, and you can almost see the awareness flickering in their eyes. All that Jesus has told them over the past three years is settling in.

Never before has Jesus been so direct with them. It is his last chance to communicate to them the significance of his life and his death. He refrains from parables and painstakingly answers the disciples' redundant questions. The world is about to undergo a convulsive trauma, and the fearful men with him are his hope for that world.

"I am going away, and I am coming back to you," Jesus keeps repeating, until at last the disciples show signs of comprehension. God's Son has entered the world to reside in one body. He is now leaving earth to return to the Father. But someone else—the Spirit of truth, their Advocate—will come to take up residence in many bodies, in *their* bodies.

Jesus is planning to die, yes. He is leaving them. But in some mysterious way, he is not leaving. He will not stay dead. This night, Jesus gives them an intimacy with the Father such as they have never known, yet he promises an even greater intimacy to come. He seems fully aware that much of what they nod their heads at now will not sink in until later.

—PY

Daily Contemplation

Which of Jesus' words in this chapter mean the most to you today?

DAY 271

The True Vine; The World; The Holy Spirit
John 15:1–16:4

The sense of urgency grows inside the stuffy, crowded room. Jesus has just a few more hours to prepare his disciples for the tumult that lies ahead. More, these are his closest friends in all the world, and he is about to leave them.

In this passage, Jesus envisions what will happen to the little band after his departure. He foresees fierce opposition and hatred and beatings and executions. The disciples will face all these trials on his behalf and without his physical presence to protect them.

As he has done so often, Jesus reaches for an allegory, a parable from nature to drive home his point. Just outside Jerusalem, rows of vineyards cover the hills—probably, he and his disciples have walked through them on their way to the city—and Jesus summons up two images from those vineyards.

First, the image of lush, juicy grapes. Not long before, the disciples drank the product of those grapes as they listened to Jesus' deeply symbolic words about the blood of the covenant. In order to bear fruit, Jesus says, one thing is essential: They must remain in intimate connection with the vine. Jesus also reminds the Twelve that he has handpicked them for a specific mission: "to go and bear fruit—fruit that will last."

Then Jesus mentions one more image: a pile of dead sticks at the edge of the vineyard. Somehow, these branches have lost their connection with the vine, the source of nourishment. A farmer has snapped them off and thrown them in a heap for burning. They no longer have a useful function.

Most likely, Jesus' disciples do not fully understand his meaning that night. But the symbol, with its abrupt contrast between juicy grapes and withered branches, will stay with them. The spectacular history of the early church gives certain proof that they eventually heed his heartfelt words about "remaining" in him.

—PY

Daily Contemplation

In what ways do you work at remaining in Jesus?

DAY 272

The Spirit of Truth; Return of Joy
John 16:5–33

"I have told you these things, so that in me you may have peace. In this world you will have trouble. But take heart! I have overcome the world." (John 16:33)

After the allegory of the vine and branches, Jesus turns from word pictures and speaks directly about what will happen to the disciples. Never is he more "theological" with them. Some of it they understand, some of it they do not. John shows them whispering to each other, trying to figure out his meaning.

Perhaps the strangest words of all are these: "It is for your good that I am going away" (John 16:7). Good? How could it possibly be good for him to abandon them, thus dashing their hopes of a restored kingdom? Jesus tries to explain the advantages to come, when the Spirit will live inside them, but the disciples are too busy discussing what he means by "going away" to comprehend.

Jesus' analogy of childbirth gives a further clue. Although childbirth may involve great pain, the pain is productive. The effort of giving birth produces something—new life!—and results in joy. In the same way, the great sorrow he and the disciples are about to undergo will not be useless. His suffering will bring about the salvation of the world; their grief will turn to joy.

Jesus concludes his teaching this fateful evening with a ringing declaration: "Take heart! I have overcome the world." How hollow this statement will seem the next evening when his pale, abused body hangs on an executioner's cross, and the disciples slink away in the darkness. Their emotions, and faith, are to rise and plummet in one unforgettable day—just as Jesus has predicted in his analogy of childbirth.

—PY

Daily Contemplation

When have you experienced great pain that in the end brought joy?

DAY 273

Jesus Prays
John 17:1–26

When the disciples respond to Jesus' speech with the bold pronouncement "This makes us believe that you came from God" (John 16:30), it seems to settle something in Jesus' mind. Then he concludes the intimate get-together with this, his longest recorded prayer. In it, Jesus sums up his feelings and his plans for the tight circle of friends gathered around him.

Their previous missions, the preaching and healing ministries in the countryside, have been mere warm-up exercises. Now he is turning everything over to them. "I confer on you a kingdom, just as my Father conferred one on me," he once said (Luke 22:29). This prayer represents a kind of commissioning or graduation.

Using language full of mystery, Jesus informs the Twelve that he must leave the world but they must remain in it to proclaim him. They will now attract the hatred and hostility that have previously been directed against him. And yet, although they live "in the world," they are not quite "of the world." Something sets them apart from the world and binds them together with him in unity with God—a unity so close as to defy all explanation.

Jesus prays too for the other believers who will follow them, stretching in an unbroken chain throughout history. "I pray . . . that all of them may be one, Father, just as you are in me and I am in you. May they also be in us so that the world may believe that you have sent me." And then he leads the frightened little band to his appointment with death.

—PY

Daily Contemplation

Based on this prayer, how would you sum up Jesus' goals for the church? How well do Christians today fulfill those goals?

DAY 274

Abiding in Jesus
Reflection

In John 15:4 Jesus says, "Remain in me, as I also remain in you. No branch can bear fruit by itself; it must remain in the vine." When I'm reading the Bible on a regular basis, and especially when I'm reading about Jesus, I (Brenda) am more connected to him. I feel more in tune with who he is, what he cares about, how he lived, what he means in my life. I know a Christian leader who recommends reading something from the Gospels every day to fill our minds with the words and works of Jesus in daily doses. Now I can see the value.

Yet Bible reading is not the only way I come to know Christ. When Jesus left the earth, he gave his followers the Holy Spirit as the constant presence of himself. The Holy Spirit reveals Jesus to me as I walk with him; and more, if I'm willing, the Spirit makes me increasingly like Jesus. My mind and actions gradually become one with his.

Oswald Chambers, a teacher and missionary who lived in the early twentieth century, talks about this process known as *sanctification*. "Sanctification means being made one with Jesus so that the disposition that ruled Him will rule us."[57] The term has largely fallen out of use in the church today, but Jesus prayed about it in John 17: "Sanctify them by the truth; your word is truth. As you sent me into the world, I have sent them into the world. For them I sanctify myself, that they too may be truly sanctified" (17:17–19). He spoke about setting himself apart for the Father's work so that in turn his disciples could be set apart to do God's work through the Spirit living in them.

There is a big difference between living for Jesus and having Jesus live in us. Attempts to live for him often turn out more Pharisee-like, disciple-like, or crowd-like than Christ-like. Only Jesus can produce the life of himself in us. When he inhabits us and his life becomes ours, he acts in all the surprising fullness of himself.

Soaking in the Bible, especially the Gospels, is a way of remaining in Jesus, abiding in the vine so that I can bear his fruit in the world. I need that help. Daily I'm surrounded by much that encourages another way of living—an ultimately destructive way. Keeping the Bible, with its stories of Jesus' life, before me provides the link I need to keep drawing sustenance from his roots, growing through his Spirit into the branch that extends from himself.

—BQ

Daily Contemplation

Where are you in the process of sanctification? Ask Jesus to continue shaping you, nourishing you, and living through you as you abide in him.

DAY 275

Jesus in Gethsemane; Arrested; Faces Sanhedrin
Matthew 26:36–75

In a stroke of bitter irony, the intimate scene of the Last Supper butts up against the scene of betrayal in Gethsemane (geth-SEM-uh-nee). The ordeal begins with Jesus praying in a quiet, cool grove of olive trees, with three of his disciples waiting sleepily outside and a large armed mob making its way toward the garden to seize and torture him.

Jesus feels afraid and abandoned. Falling facedown on the ground, he prays for some way out. The future of the human race and of the entire universe comes down to this one weeping figure whose sweat falls to the ground in large drops, like blood.

The deep ironies of Jesus' life come crashing together this evening in the garden, when the one whom wise men crossed a continent to worship is sold like a slave for thirty pieces of silver. Jesus' disciples still have not come to terms with the kind of "kingdom" their leader wants to establish. Blustery Peter is prepared to install a kingdom the traditional way—by force. When he hacks off a servant's ear, however, Jesus stops the violence and performs his last miracle: Notably, he heals the servant. Still, Peter later denies knowing Jesus.

With a single prayer, Jesus reminds his friends, he could dispatch squadrons of angels. He has the power to defend himself, but he will not use it. When the disciples realize that they can expect no last-minute rescue operations from the invisible world, they all flee. Their last flicker of hope has been extinguished. If Jesus will not protect himself, how can he protect them?

Matthew's account of what transpires in Gethsemane and before the Sanhedrin shows that, in an odd inversion, the "victim" dominates all that takes place. Jesus—not Judas, not the mob, and not the high priest—acts like one truly in control. "Tell us if you are the Messiah, the Son of God," they demand. That single admission condemns Jesus to death, for the Sanhedrin have a different expectation of the Messiah. They want a conqueror to set them free by force. Jesus knows that only one thing—his death—will truly set them free. For that reason he has come to earth.

—PY

---- *Daily Contemplation* ----

How would you respond if your life were threatened because you were a follower of Christ?

DAY 276

Judas Hangs Himself; Jesus Before Pilate
Matthew 27:1–31

The Gospels record a pass-the-buck sequence in Jesus' encounter with "justice." Roman law has granted the Jews many freedoms, including the right to their own court system, the Sanhedrin. When Jesus identifies himself as the Messiah, the Sanhedrin convicts him of the religious charge of blasphemy, a capital offense. However, the Sanhedrin has no authority to carry out a death sentence; that requires the sanction of Roman justice. Thus Jesus' opponents send him to Pilate (PI-luht), the Roman governor of Judea.

Along the way, the accusers change the charge against Jesus from a religious one (which would not have impressed Pilate) to a political one. They portray Jesus as a dangerous revolutionary who has declared himself king of the Jews in defiance of Roman rule. Pilate has grave misgivings about the charge, and his wife's premonitions compound his sense of unease.

Luke's version of this moment records that Pilate at first declares Jesus innocent, despite pressure from the crowd. Then he seeks a way out of his dilemma by deferring the case to Herod Antipas, who has jurisdiction over Jesus' home region. Herod, disappointed by Jesus' silence and his refusal to perform miracles, soon sends him back to Pilate.

As Pilate tries three times to get the Jewish leaders to release their prisoner, the fury of the crowd against Jesus only swells. At last, facing a mob scene, the canny governor yields to their demands, but only after ostentatiously washing his hands of innocent blood.

Through all these legal proceedings, Jesus maintains an almost unbroken silence. He is acknowledged king at last—with a crown of thorns jammed onto his head and a royal robe draped across his bloodied back. Pilate seems to recognize, at some level, the enormity of the injustice he has participated in. He prepares a notice of Jesus' "crime" to be fastened to the cross, which reads, in three languages, "JESUS OF NAZARETH, THE KING OF THE JEWS." When the chief priests protest that it should read only that Jesus claimed to be king, Pilate answers, "What I have written, I have written" (John 19:19–22).

—PY

Daily Contemplation

When have you been punished undeservedly? How did you respond?

DAY 277

The Crucifixion, Death, and Burial of Jesus
Mark 15:21–47

Long before, at the very beginning of his ministry, Jesus resisted Satan's temptation toward an easier path of safety and physical comfort. Now, as the moment of truth draws near, that temptation must seem more alluring than ever.

On the cross, a criminal at Jesus' left taunts him: "Aren't you the Messiah? Save yourself and us!" (Luke 23:39). The crowd milling about the site takes up the cry: "Let him come down now from the cross, and we will believe in him. . . . Let God rescue him now if he wants him" (Matthew 27:42–43).

But there is no rescue, no miracle. There is only silence. The Father has turned his back, or so it seems, letting history take its course, letting everything evil in the world triumph over everything good. For Jesus to save others, quite simply, he cannot save himself.

Why does Jesus have to die? Theologians who ponder such things have debated various theories of "the Atonement" for centuries, with little agreement. Somehow it requires love, sacrificial love, to win what cannot be won by force.

One detail Mark includes may provide a clue. Jesus has just uttered the awful cry, "My God, my God, why have you forsaken me?" He, God's Son, identifies so closely with human beings—taking on their sin!—that God the Father has to turn away. The gulf is that great. But, just as Jesus breathes his last, "the curtain of the temple was torn in two from top to bottom."

That massive curtain served to seal off the Most Holy Place, where God's presence dwelt. No one except the high priest was allowed inside, and he could enter only once a year on a designated day. As the author of Hebrews will later note (Hebrews 10), the tearing of that curtain showed beyond a doubt exactly what was accomplished by Jesus' death on the cross. No more sacrifices would ever be required. Jesus has won for all of us—ordinary people, not just priests—immediate access to God's presence. By taking on the burden of human sin and bearing its punishment, Jesus has removed forever the barrier between God and us.

—PY

Daily Contemplation

When have you most wanted a miracle in your life and been disappointed? What did you learn from the experience?

DAY 278

The Resurrection
Matthew 27:62–28:15

"He is not here; he has risen, just as he said. Come and see the place where he lay." (Matthew 28:6)

When the greatest miracle of all history occurs, the only eyewitnesses are soldiers standing guard outside Jesus' tomb. When the earth shakes and an angel appears, bright as lightning, these guards tremble and become like dead men. Then, with an incurably human reflex, they flee to the authorities to report the disturbance.

Yet here is an astounding fact: Later that afternoon the soldiers, who have seen proof of the resurrection with their own eyes, change their story. The resurrection of the Son of God does not seem nearly as significant as, say, stacks of freshly minted silver.

A few women, grieving friends of Jesus, are next to learn of the miracle of miracles. Matthew reports that when an angel breaks the news of Jesus' resurrection, the women hurry away "afraid yet filled with joy." *Fear,* the reflexive human response to a supernatural encounter—when the women hear from a glowing angel news of an event beyond comprehension, of course they feel afraid. *Yet filled with joy*—the news they hear is the best news of all, news too good to be true, news so good it has to be true. Jesus is back! He has returned, as promised. The dreams of a Messiah come surging back as the women run fearfully and joyfully to tell the disciples.

Even as the women run, the soldiers are rehearsing an alibi, their part in an elaborate cover-up scheme. Like everything else in Jesus' life, his resurrection draws forth two contrasting responses. Those who believe are transformed, finding enough hope and courage to go out and change the world. But those who choose not to believe find ways to ignore evidence they have seen firsthand.

—PY

Daily Contemplation

Why do you believe in Jesus?

DAY 279

Jesus' Resurrection and Appearances
John 20:1-31

People who discount Jesus' resurrection tend to portray the disciples as gullible country bumpkins with a weakness for ghost stories, or as shrewd conspirators who hatch a resurrection plot in order to attract popular support for their movement. The Bible presents a radically different picture. It shows Jesus' followers themselves as the ones most skeptical of rumors about a risen Jesus.

Mary Magdalene is still bewildered and afraid even after an angel breaks the news plainly to her. When she encounters Jesus himself, she doesn't recognize him until he speaks her name.

Reports from the women of an empty tomb fail to convince the disciples, so Peter and a companion run to the graveyard to see for themselves. That same night all the disciples huddle in a locked room, afraid of the Jewish leaders, apparently still skeptical.

For his part, Jesus goes out of his way to allay the disciples' fears and suspicions. In broad daylight he visits and fishes with them. Once he asks a dubious Thomas to test his scarred skin by touch. Another time he eats a piece of broiled fish in their presence to prove he is not a ghost (Luke 24). This is no mirage, no hallucination; it is Jesus, their leader, no one else.

The appearances of the risen Christ recorded in the Bible, fewer than a dozen, follow a pattern. With one exception (found in 1 Corinthians 15:6), Jesus visits small groups of people closeted indoors or in a remote area. By the garden tomb, in a locked room, on the road to Emmaus (eh-MAY-us), beside the Sea of Galilee, atop the Mount of Olives—such private encounters bolster the faith of people who already believe in him. As far as we know, not a single unbeliever sees Jesus after his death.

What would happen if Jesus reappeared on Pilate's porch or before the Sanhedrin, this time with a withering blast against those who ordered his death? Surely such a public scene would cause a sensation. But would it kindle faith? Jesus has already answered that question in his story of Lazarus and the rich man: "If they do not listen to Moses and the Prophets, they will not be convinced even if someone rises from the dead" (Luke 16:31). Instead, Jesus chooses another way: to let the disciples themselves spread the word, as his witnesses.

—PY

Daily Contemplation

Would you have greeted the news of Jesus' resurrection like Mary? Like Peter? Like Thomas?

DAY 280

On the Road to Emmaus
Luke 24:13–49

In this scene at the end of Luke's Gospel, two followers are walking away from Jerusalem, downhearted and perplexed. Their dream of "the one who was going to redeem Israel" has died along with their leader on the cross. And yet they too have heard the crazy rumors of an empty tomb. What does it all mean?

A stranger appears beside the two forlorn disciples. According to him, the prophets have predicted all along that the Messiah would suffer these things. The stranger fascinates them, so much so that they beg him to stay longer. Then at mealtime, the last link snaps into place. It is Jesus—sitting at their table! Without a doubt, he is alive.

They are two ordinary people, not even counted among the twelve intimates of Jesus. But the encounter with the risen Christ changes them forever. "Were not our hearts burning within us while he talked with us on the road and opened the Scriptures to us?" they recall. They dash to meet the Twelve (now the eleven, with Judas's betrayal), only to learn that Peter too has seen Jesus. Suddenly, amid that chaotic scene of joy and confusion, Jesus himself appears. He explains once and for all that his death and resurrection were not unforeseen but rather lay at the heart of God's plan all along.

Jesus has one last promise to keep: He will depart earth and in his place leave the band of believers to carry out his mission. These people, common people with more than a touch of cowardice, have followed Jesus, listened to him, and watched him die. Yet seeing Jesus alive changes all that. They return to Jerusalem with great joy, and before long they are out telling the world the good news.

—PY

Daily Contemplation

How did the truth about Jesus' resurrection dawn on you?

Jesus and the Miraculous Catch of Fish; Jesus Reinstates Peter
John 21:1–25

Jesus performs a miracle similar to one he performed in his first days with the disciples: He fills their nets with a great catch of fish. He is the same Lord they came to know three years ago in that familiar setting. Now he has returned for a few weeks to finish his mission.

These final scenes will cement the disciples' understanding of Christ and his plan for them. They have struggled to understand his true mission, but soon, with the Holy Spirit's help, they will know why he came and what part they should play. Buoyed by that knowledge, they will then carry the message to the world.

Peter has grievously failed Jesus by denying him three times. Now Jesus offers him a chance at rehabilitation. Three times he asks whether Peter loves him, and that third time must have felt to Peter like an arrow to the heart. Jesus' tender care for Peter sends the message that God's grace extends to believers even when we fail God in a major way.

John chooses two different Greek words for *love*. Some scholars speculate that Jesus was indicating two kinds of love, the first referring to a love of one's whole being, including the will, and the second to a more spontaneous, emotional kind of love.

Whether or not John or Jesus intended this distinction, the Bible teaches that Jesus wants us to love him with a complete love. He wants us to choose to love him with our will, in the good times and bad, when we feel loving toward him and when we don't. At the same time, he desires love that is free-flowing with emotion—impulsive, affectionate love issuing from the heart. Just as with a lasting romantic love, our love for Jesus should be passionate yet also involve a decision of the mind and will.

Each time Peter replies, Jesus asks him to care for his sheep. In some of his final words on earth, Jesus reminds his disciples that loving him means taking care of the people he places in our lives. Jesus called himself "the Good Shepherd" and spent his time on earth caring for many who came across his path or whom he sought out. Now all believers will carry on that mission, temporarily keeping watch over God's flock until the Shepherd returns.

—BQ

Daily Contemplation

In what ways are you feeding and taking care of Jesus' sheep?

DAY 282

Remembering Jesus' Death and Victory
Reflection

This section of the Gospels contains some of my least as well as some of my most favorite scenes in the Bible. Although central to my faith, the passages about Jesus' torture and crucifixion make me recoil inwardly when I (Brenda) read them. I want to pass quickly through to get to his resurrection. Then my spirits soar, relieved again that God wins, overshadowing all the horrific suffering with his victory.

I once attended a seminar in which the speaker spent hours describing in detail the physical trauma Jesus underwent in his last hours before death. The physical agony Jesus experienced defies understanding. Weighing on him even more heavily was the staggering burden of sin that he carried. For him, holy God, the sin of one human being alone would have been a crushing weight to bear. But to carry the sin of all humankind exacted suffering beyond our comprehension.

Our hearts may rightly cringe at the story of Jesus' suffering, yet he hasn't asked us to turn away. Rather, he has guided us, "This is my body given for you; do this in remembrance of me" (Luke 22:19). We *celebrate* the Lord's Supper to remember Jesus' death. Many observe the season of Lent as another way of focusing on his sacrifice.

Without Jesus' death, there could be no resurrection, no final victory over evil in his life or in ours. An observance of Jesus' resurrection without a proper remembrance of his suffering would lead to a cheapening of the victory we celebrate at Easter. Jesus' resurrection is our greatest cause for celebration, yet the ending we relish and love to relive goes hand-in-hand with his death.

I have a fondness for happy endings, which makes the Gospels especially satisfying. God knows how to write—and live—a story. He knows that we yearn for the winners to win and the losers to lose in the end. He has both crafted and starred in a real-life drama that beats any Pulitzer Prize winner. Each time we engage fully, entering into Jesus' life, death, and resurrection, we take hold once more of the story that has become ours for now and eternity.

—BQ

Daily Contemplation

How do you respond to Jesus' suffering and death? Are you inclined to pass quickly through these passages? Do you do anything on a regular basis to remember his death? Thank Jesus for the pain he endured for you.

PART 10

The Word Spreads

DAY 283

The Great Commission; Jesus Taken Up into Heaven
Matthew 28:16–20; Acts 1:1–26

The disciples' obsession with Israel's restored kingdom does not fade even after Jesus dies and comes back to life. For forty days after the resurrection he appears and disappears seemingly at will. When he shows up, his followers listen eagerly to his explanations from Scripture of all that has happened. When he leaves, they plot the structure of the new kingdom that he will surely inaugurate. Think of it: Jerusalem free at last from Roman domination.

Jesus gives some mystifying orders, however. He tells his followers to return to Jerusalem and simply wait. Something more is needed. Do not leave the city, he says, until the Holy Spirit comes. At last, one of the disciples puts to Jesus the question they have all been debating together: "Lord, are you at this time going to restore the kingdom to Israel?"

No one is prepared for Jesus' reaction. He seems to brush the question aside, deflecting attention away from Israel toward neighboring countries, all the way to the ends of the earth. He mentions the Holy Spirit again, and then, to everyone's utter amazement, his body lifts off the ground, suspends there for a moment, then disappears into a cloud. And they never see him again.

Christians believe that all of history revolves around the life of Jesus the Christ. But the plain fact is that Jesus left earth after thirty-three years. Furthermore, he declared it a good thing: "You are filled with grief because I have said these things. But very truly I tell you, it is for your good that I am going away. Unless I go away, the Advocate will not come to you" (John 16:6–7).

The book of Acts, written by the same author as the Gospel of Luke, tells what happens after Jesus' departure when the Advocate comes at last. First, though, the disciples begin adjusting to new realities: They select a replacement for Judas, make plans to follow Jesus' final instructions, and return to Jerusalem to await the Holy Spirit.

—PY

Daily Contemplation

When have you realized that Jesus' plans in your life were different from what you had assumed them to be?

DAY 284

The Holy Spirit Comes at Pentecost
Acts 2:1–41

> Suddenly a sound like the blowing of a violent wind came from heaven and filled the whole house where they were sitting. They saw what seemed to be tongues of fire that separated and came to rest on each of them. (Acts 2:2–3)

On the Jewish feast day of Pentecost, the disciples get what they have been waiting for. The Holy Spirit, the presence of God himself, takes up residence inside ordinary bodies—their bodies. The disciples hit the streets with a bold new style that the world has never recovered from. Soon everyone in Jerusalem is talking about the Jesus followers. Clearly, something is afoot. To their amazement, pilgrims from all over the world hear the Galileans' message in their own native languages.

Peter, the disgraced apostle who denied Christ three times to save his own neck, brazenly takes on both Jewish and Roman authorities. Quoting from King David and the prophet Joel, he proclaims that his audience has just lived through the most important event in all of history. "God has raised this Jesus to life, and we are all witnesses of it," he says, and goes on to declare Jesus as the very Messiah, the fulfillment of the Jews' long-awaited dream. Three thousand people respond to Peter's powerful message on that first day. And thus the Christian church is born.

Beginning with this boisterous scene in Jerusalem, Luke weaves a historical adventure tale. The group of new believers, at first a mere annoyance to the Jews and the Romans, will not stop growing. Just as Jesus has predicted, the message spreads throughout Judea and Samaria and in less than one generation penetrates into Rome, the center of civilization. In an era when new religions are a dime a dozen, the Christian faith becomes a worldwide phenomenon. It all begins with this scene on the day of Pentecost.

—PY

Daily Contemplation

Have you ever been in a place where God moved in many people at one time? Did you sense the Holy Spirit's presence?

DAY 285

Peter Heals a Beggar
Acts 3:1–26

> One day Peter and John were going up to the temple at the time of prayer... Now a man who was lame from birth was being carried to the temple gate... When he saw Peter and John about to enter, he asked them for money.... Then Peter said, "Silver or gold I do not have, but what I do have I give you. In the name of Jesus Christ of Nazareth, walk." Taking him by the right hand, he helped him up, and instantly the man's feet and ankles became strong. He jumped to his feet and began to walk. (Acts 3:1–3, 6–8)

The change produced by the Holy Spirit becomes evident right away in the disciples, now called "apostles." As Peter and John are headed into the temple to pray, a lame beggar asks for money. These men, who—like many of us today—are accustomed to encountering "down and out" individuals, would normally pass by to get on to more important business. This time, they don't simply throw a few coins and hurriedly move on. Instead, they stop and make eye contact with the beggar, treating him as a person worthy of respect.

Then the apostles do what they have had trouble doing in the past. They heal the man in an instant, through the name and power of Jesus Christ. Just as Jesus' miracles did, this one draws a crowd, and Peter takes the opportunity to teach about the meaning of Jesus' life, death, and resurrection.

"Repent, then," Peter urges, "and turn to God, so that your sins may be wiped out, that times of refreshing may come from the Lord." Peter knows that the only hope lies in coming to God for forgiveness and freedom from the guilt of sin. Life without Jesus is a burden too great to bear. But when we come to God and repent, we find refreshment at last.

—BQ

Daily Contemplation

In what ways have you felt refreshed since coming to God?

DAY 286

Peter and John Before the Sanhedrin
Acts 4:1–31

The next day the rulers, the elders and the teachers of the law met in Jerusalem.... They had Peter and John brought before them and began to question them: "By what power or what name did you do this?" Then Peter, filled with the Holy Spirit, said to them: "Rulers and elders of the people! If we are being called to account today for an act of kindness shown to a man who was lame and are being asked how he was healed, then know this, you and all the people of Israel: It is by the name of Jesus Christ of Nazareth, whom you crucified but whom God raised from the dead, that this man stands before you healed. Jesus is

'the stone you builders rejected,
which has become the cornerstone.'

Salvation is found in no one else, for there is no other name under heaven given to mankind by which we must be saved." (Acts 4:5, 7–12)

The Jewish religious leaders continue in the same disbelief they showed when Jesus was on earth. Here we see the first of many imprisonments the apostles will endure throughout the book of Acts. Just as the Pharisees and Sadducees tried repeatedly to silence Jesus, they will now try to restrain the apostles. Yet the news about the resurrected Messiah, Jesus, continues to spread.

Even during periods of oppression, the apostles speak out more boldly than ever, empowered by the Holy Spirit. People respond, with God's Spirit drawing new Christians from all parts of the known world.

Acts records the beginnings of the Christian church. Despite periods of ongoing persecution, the church has continued to grow and spread to the most remote areas of the world in the two thousand years since Jesus came to earth.

—BQ

---- *Daily Contemplation* ----

Do you have a desire, as did Peter and John, to talk to the people in your life about the things Jesus has done for you?

DAY 287

The Gift of the Holy Spirit
Reflection

Who is the Holy Spirit, anyway? Jesus promised to send an Advocate to take his place when he left the earth. Pentecost followed soon after, and Jesus' disciples, long confused, afraid, and immature, changed nearly overnight into passionate, fearless evangelists. The Spirit made a sudden, dramatic impact on Jesus' followers.

Jesus called the Holy Spirit "the Paraclete," from the Greek word *parakletos*, which means "Comforter, Counselor, Helper, Advocate, Strengthener, Supporter." The Spirit fills these roles in a way immediately present and accessible to us.

J. I. Packer, a respected theologian, professor, and author, explains that through the Holy Spirit we have a personal relationship with Jesus, we are transformed to be more and more like him (sanctification), and we are given confidence that God loves us, has redeemed us, and has made us part of his family through Jesus.[58]

Pastor and author Francis Chan compares the change in a new believer's life to the transformation a caterpillar experiences in becoming a butterfly.

> As believers, we ought to experience this same kind of astonishment when the Holy Spirit enters our bodies. We should be stunned in disbelief over becoming a "new creation" with the Spirit living in us. As the caterpillar finds its new ability to fly, we should be thrilled over our Spirit-empowered ability to live differently and faithfully. Isn't this what the Scriptures speak of? Isn't this what we've all been longing for?
>
> It really is an astounding truth that the Spirit of Him who raised Jesus from the dead lives in you. He lives in me. I do not know what the Spirit will do or where He'll lead me each time I invite Him to guide me. But I am tired of living in a way that looks exactly like people who do not have the Holy Spirit of God living in them. I want to consistently live with an awareness of His strength. I want to be different today from what I was yesterday as the fruit of the Spirit becomes more manifest in me.[59]

When the Bible speaks of the Holy Spirit, it often uses the word *power* in the same sentence. The Spirit gives us the power we need each day to overcome temptation and live in God's strength rather than in our own weakness. The Spirit also reveals God's truth to unbelievers. Theologian John Stott stresses that the Holy Spirit acts primarily as a "missionary Spirit."[60] The entire book of Acts, he explains, tells the story of God, through his Spirit, making his plan of salvation known far and wide. Still today the Spirit enables us to introduce Jesus to others.

These qualities of the Holy Spirit apply to all believers, for we all have the Holy Spirit living in us. Do all of us, then, experience the same presence of the Spirit in our lives? Author Stormie Omartian in her book on the Holy Spirit explains, "*We* don't decide what the Spirit of God does in our lives or how He manifests Himself. We *invite* Him to do what He *wants*. But we cannot let the fear that the Holy Spirit won't do what we want cause us to shut Him out of our lives. Nor can we force Him into a mold of our own making that causes Him to resemble *us* rather than allowing Him to mold *us* into His image."[61] The Bible teaches that the Holy Spirit was alive at the creation of the world, spoke through the prophets in the Old Testament, and is alive still today. We have the challenge, then, to give the Holy Spirit the freedom to be all that God intends him to be in our lives.

Catherine Marshall writes, "For years (sometimes a lifetime) a Christian can keep the Spirit at a sub-basement level by the insistence on running one's own life. Then . . . the person consciously recognizes his divine Guest's presence, opens the hitherto closed doors into certain rooms in his being so that the Spirit can enter there too." She quotes Hannah Whitall Smith, who says that when the Spirit influences every part of us, "the real evidence . . . is neither emotion nor any single gift such as tongues, rather . . . there *must* be Christ-likeness in life and character: by fruits in the life we shall know whether or not we have the Spirit."[62]

Unfortunately, the Christian world has sometimes attached an inappropriate measure of mystery to its teaching on the Holy Spirit. Believers may be taught to seek extreme behavior as proof of the Spirit's presence. As a result, many are afraid of giving God complete control. Some fear the Holy Spirit will make them too emotional or force them to do things they don't want to do. Some fear the unknown or feel reluctant to open themselves to something that could be controversial. Yet if we know God at all, we can believe that he intends only good for us. The Holy Spirit is the presence of our loving, Almighty God, bringing comfort and continual help, transformation in our inner being, power in living and loving others, the words and ability to share the gospel, and fruit for God's kingdom that Jesus so often taught his followers to bear. Come, Holy Spirit!

—BQ

Daily Contemplation

How much do you sense the Holy Spirit's presence in your life? God wants you to know him in the fullest, most life-changing way. He desires you to have the joy and peace the Spirit offers. He wants to help you do, through his Spirit, what you can't do alone. As you pray and reflect on the Holy Spirit, watch how God moves in your life through his Spirit.

DAY 288

The Fellowship of the Believers
Acts 2:42–47; 4:32–37

> They devoted themselves to the apostles' teaching and to fellowship, to the breaking of bread and to prayer. (Acts 2:42)

On the eve of his death, Jesus prayed that believers would live in complete unity so the world would believe in him. Within a few months, his prayer seems on the way to being answered. The earliest Christians live and worship together in unity and purity of love for each other. They are unselfish, helping any among them who have needs, even selling land or houses to give to others and support the ministry of the apostles.

These early Christians achieve the delicate balance of becoming a supportive, life-giving community while staying focused on spreading the word about Jesus to those who don't know him. This was Jesus' desire: that believers would be unified, loving and caring for each other, and in so doing attract those who hunger for the same kind of fellowship.

In their time together, believers of the earliest church hold to a fourfold focus. They are committed to the apostles' teaching; to fellowship, or encouraging each other as they worship together; to the breaking of bread, or the Lord's Supper; and to prayer. These aspects of their spiritual life carry equal weight. None is neglected or reduced for the sake of the other. The earliest Christians also enjoy meals together in their homes and make a habit of living in gladness and praise to God.

We live in a different time and culture from the believers in the book of Acts, but we find here a picture of one of Jesus' last hopes realized on earth. It's a picture still possible for his followers today. Surely, the outcome of this way of life is possible as well—God adding to our numbers daily those who are being saved.

What, then, keeps us from living out such life together? What keeps us from readily sharing all we have, to help others who will live with us for eternity? What keeps us from meeting together often to joyfully worship God and enjoy each other? We battle distraction, fear, and disbelief. Yet it is through living in this very kind of Christ-centered community that we stand against these struggles, and then can have the same powerful witness the first Christians had in their day.

—BQ

Daily Contemplation

Have you observed a group of believers who resemble the first Christians in Acts?

Ananias and Sapphira; The Apostles Persecuted
Acts 5:1–42

The disciples, newly empowered with the Holy Spirit, start acting a lot like Jesus. They go to the temple and preach sermons; they heal the sick; they care for the poor. To many bystanders, the message of new life in Jesus sounds wonderful, like the first note of music to people born deaf. Five thousand men have come to believe, including some priests. The Jesus followers are soon organizing and electing officers to handle the demands of a growing church.

But problems spring up alongside the successes. The church becomes popular, an "in" place to belong. Sorcerers and magicians drop by, drawn by the reports of healings and other wonders. Wealthy people, such as Ananias (AN-uh-NI-uhs) and Sapphira (suh-FI-ruh), see the church as a place to gain applause for their benevolence. Such opportunists learn that the apostles, not to mention God, will not tolerate corruption in the fledgling church.

Before long, the focus of concern shifts away from internal problems to outside opposition. The same forces that conspired against Jesus—temple officers, the Sadducees, the high priest, the Sanhedrin, Roman guards—align themselves against the new phenomenon of the church. Every so often they haul in the leaders, but for what can they prosecute them—healing the sick? Inciting people to praise God? The Christians hardly resemble dangerous conspirators, and they usually meet openly on the temple porch.

Even so, religious leaders beat and jail the apostles on trumped-up charges. What happens next should give the establishment a clue into exactly what they are up against: The apostles respond to the beatings with praise to God for the privilege of suffering, and an angel of the Lord springs them free from jail.

Gamaliel (guh-MAY-lee-uhl), a wise old Pharisee, has perhaps the best advice of all (Acts 5:38–39): "Let them go! For if their purpose or activity is of human origin, it will fail. But if it is from God, you will not be able to stop these men." He could not have been more prophetic.

—PY

Daily Contemplation

What problems concerning the church today bother you most? Are they internal or external problems?

DAY 290

The Stoning of Stephen
Acts 6:8–8:3

> But Stephen, full of the Holy Spirit, looked up to heaven and saw the glory of God, and Jesus standing at the right hand of God. (Acts 7:55)

Opposition to the early Christians gets worse. Not only are the apostles working miracles, but now other believers are doing the same, threatening the Jewish religious establishment. The Jews can't win arguments against one of these believers, Stephen, so they resort to lying about him before the Sanhedrin. Stephen's speech so incenses the listeners that they drag him outside the city and stone him, making him the first recorded martyr of the early church.

Stephen's speech to the Jewish court reviews the history of the Israelite people from Abraham through Isaac, Jacob, Joseph, Moses, Joshua, David, and Solomon (Acts 7:6–50). Stephen notes God's promises to his people throughout the generations and the people's repeated unfaithfulness. Charged with speaking against the synagogue, Stephen reminds the Jewish leaders of God's words through Isaiah (7:49–50). All creation is God's temple, and further, Christ replaced the temple by becoming the way for all people to come to God.

Stephen's accusations prove true even in his own life. The Israelite people have a history of persecuting God's messengers, including Jesus, the Messiah. Insistent on their own agendas, they often resisted the new things God was accomplishing. Now they follow suit by stoning Stephen. Like the prophets before him, and like Jesus himself, Stephen remains fixed on God to the end, praying for those who take his life.

The church must now go underground. Believers are forced to scatter, and in doing so they bring the gospel to new places. As the church continues to grow, one of its most vengeful opponents appears on the scene, a man named Saul. With the same fervency that new believers show toward Christ, Saul seeks to imprison them and squelch the burgeoning threat to Judaism. He is intent on his mission, but God has other plans.

—BQ

Daily Contemplation

Where, other than in a church, have you been especially focused on God?

DAY 291

Philip and the Ethiopian
Acts 8:26–40

> As they traveled along the road, they came to some water and the eunuch said, "Look, here is water. What can stand in the way of my being baptized?" . . . Philip baptized him. When they came up out of the water, the Spirit of the Lord suddenly took Philip away. (Acts 8:36–39)

The early church quickly spread beyond the Jewish world. Philip and Stephen were part of a group of seven men chosen to help the apostles by caring especially for Greek believers in need. Like Stephen, Philip performed miracles of healing and exorcism of demons. Along with many other believers, he left Jerusalem after Stephen's death.

We next see Philip in Samaria, where he is continuing to preach about Christ among the people there. From Samaria an angel directs Philip to head south again and journey on a desolate road leading from Jerusalem to Gaza. The Holy Spirit guides him to an Ethiopian official, who needs help interpreting a prophetic passage from Isaiah 53. This man, a castrated African bureaucrat, may have seemed an unlikely candidate for conversion, but God had been working in him even before he and Philip met. When the two come across a source of water, the Ethiopian spontaneously suggests that Philip baptize him.

As these stories show, God has a plan for drawing all peoples to himself, and he uses his followers to carry out his plan. As Philip was led by the Holy Spirit to an unlikely person in an unlikely place, so believers today are guided by God to minister to unlikely people who need him. If we are willing to venture out and be used, God will speak through us in surprising and powerful ways.

—BQ

Daily Contemplation

When have you had the opportunity to share with someone the good news about Jesus, only to find out that God had previously prepared that person for this moment?

DAY 292

Living by the Spirit
Reflection

The book of Acts illustrates that life with the Holy Spirit adds another dimension to our faith. Our days can become unpredictably exciting, and our lives may take unexpected and miraculous turns. But life with the Spirit doesn't mean we become perfect. We will still fail, and we will not always make the right decisions.

The apostles experienced dramatic changes, but they did not become perfect. Ananias and Sapphira prove that people in Spirit-filled communities sometimes go their own way. Living in the Spirit is a growth process of continually giving over control to God.

Hannah Whitall Smith, author of *The Christian's Secret of a Happy Life*, found this to be poignantly true. Catherine Marshall tells Smith's story. Born in Philadelphia in 1832 to a Quaker family, Smith felt from a young age a great zeal for spiritual matters. Her Quaker upbringing gave her a thorough knowledge of the Bible, and she began to believe early on that Christians must know God primarily through what he says in his Word rather than through their emotions toward him. Emotions, she found, can be unreliable and deceptive.

Hannah and her husband, Robert, became part of a lively church and one summer attended a camp meeting at a woodland campsite. Here, in the woods, Robert had an emotional experience with the Holy Spirit. He felt the Spirit enter him in a way that brought joy and connection to God such as he'd never known. Soon after, he became a powerful evangelistic teacher, drawing crowds wherever he spoke. Hannah meanwhile tried repeatedly to prompt a similar experience with the Holy Spirit, but to no avail. She realized in time that her experience with God was as real as her husband's but simply different. Marshall writes, "She wanted emotions and was given conviction. She 'wanted a vision and got a fact.'"[63]

Robert's success in preaching flourished but then was suddenly cut short. Gossip began circulating about improper conduct with females, causing him to lose the respect of audiences and the support of sponsors. We don't know how much truth the gossip contained, but it seems that at some level Robert let his emotions lead him to actions the Spirit wouldn't have prompted. He never regained his passion for living or sharing Christ. Hannah meanwhile kept on in a steady faith that strengthened her and enabled her to continue letting God use her.

We learn from the Smiths' story that if we let our emotions become our primary means of connection with God, we risk moving outside of the Spirit's control. We become prone to following our own urges. Marshall sees this emotionalism as a real danger for the church today. It can happen if we allow "too great a love affair with emotion, too little grounding in Scripture, too [much] wanting in garden-variety discipline, too small an emphasis on purity, strict honesty, morality—Christ's own life living in us. What is needed, of course, is a balance: plenty of solid teaching—but plenty of joy as well."[64]

More, we need to open our lives to other believers who can see when we're moving in a dangerous direction. "We must deliberately make ourselves subject one to the other," Marshall urges, "be willing to be checked and corrected as well as encouraged and strengthened."[65]

We don't need to fear letting the Holy Spirit control our lives. He is God and we can fully trust him. However, says Francis Chan, "If you say you want the Holy Spirit, you must first honestly ask yourself if you want to do His will. Because if you do not genuinely want to know and do His will, why should you ask for His presence at all? But if you decide you do want to know His will, there will be moments when you have to let go of the fear of what that might mean—when you have to release your grip of control on your life and decide to be led, come what may."[66]

When we continue to live in God's Word and walk each day in humility with him, we can trust that the Spirit will protect us and lead us into a richer, more mature and fulfilled life with God.

—BQ

Daily Contemplation

What has been your experience with the Holy Spirit? Do you need to guard against over-emotionalism? Are you resistant to letting the Spirit take control? Ask God to help you stay open and committed to all he desires you to be through his Spirit.

DAY 293

Saul's Conversion
Acts 9:1–31

The most surprising converts often make the best crusaders. Former alcoholics can convince others of drinking's dangers; former drug addicts give the most forceful warnings against drugs. And when the book of Acts introduces the most effective Christian missionary of all time, he turns out to be a former bounty hunter of Christians.

Acts 9 shows a glimpse of the early church even before it has a name; people call its followers "the Way" or "the brothers" or "the Nazarene sect." Its members live in constant fear of arrest and persecution—if not from the Romans, then from the Jews. Already a leader named Stephen has been publicly stoned. And no one inspires more fear in the hearts of the early Christians than a man named Saul, who participated in Stephen's execution.

But then comes a miraculous turnabout on the road to Damascus. In a dramatic move, God steps in and, against all odds, selects the bounty hunter Saul to lead the young church. It doesn't take much to convince Saul: A blinding light and a voice from heaven knock him out of commission for three days and change his whole attitude toward Jesus. Such is Saul's murderous reputation, however, that the Jesus followers in Damascus and Jerusalem accept him only gradually.

Soon Saul (referred to more frequently as Paul) is on the other side of the persecutors' whips; his former colleagues are now trying to kill *him*. He proves to be as fearless in preaching Christ as he had been in working against him. In four great missionary journeys, Paul will take the news of the gospel around the shores of the Mediterranean. During those journeys he finds time to write half the books of the New Testament, and in so doing lays the groundwork for Christian theology. Paul is perhaps the most thoroughly converted man who has ever lived.

—PY

Daily Contemplation

Have you ever had an abrupt about-face?

DAY 294

Peter's Vision; Peter at Cornelius's House
Acts 10:1–48

> Then Peter began to speak: "I now realize how true it is that God does not show favoritism but accepts from every nation the one who fears him and does what is right. You know the message God sent to the people of Israel, announcing the good news of peace through Jesus Christ." . . . While Peter was still speaking these words, the Holy Spirit came on all who heard the message. The circumcised believers who had come with Peter were astonished that the gift of the Holy Spirit had been poured out even on Gentiles. For they heard them speaking in tongues and praising God. (Acts 10:34–36, 44–46)

An important step in the spread of the gospel has taken place. During his time on earth, Jesus ministered primarily to the Jewish people. Yet throughout his ministry he proclaimed salvation not only for the Jews but for all people. In his last words on earth he urged the disciples to carry his message to the ends of the earth.

Although his disciples accepted these words, in the first days of the early church they still do not change their long-held practice of associating and worshiping exclusively with other Jews. Now this practice must end. God comes to Peter when he's hungry and uses a vision of food to reveal one more characteristic of Christ's new church. God's old covenant declared certain foods—and people—unclean and commanded God's people to stay separate from them. His new covenant, heralded by Jesus the Redeemer, does away with distinctions of clean and unclean. Now all are clean through salvation in Jesus.

Overnight Peter must give up a way of life he has followed since birth, and then proceed to instruct believers everywhere to accept God's new command. Now Peter and the other apostles will preach to Gentiles as well as Jews. They will all worship together as one family.

—BQ

Daily Contemplation

What old ways of thinking did you have to give up when you became a believer?

DAY 295

Peter's Miraculous Escape from Prison
Acts 12:1–19

The night before Herod was to bring him to trial, Peter was sleeping between two soldiers, bound with two chains, and sentries stood guard at the entrance. Suddenly an angel of the Lord appeared and a light shone in the cell. He struck Peter on the side and woke him up. "Quick, get up!" he said, and the chains fell off Peter's wrists. Then the angel said to him, "Put on your clothes and sandals." And Peter did so. "Wrap your cloak around you and follow me," the angel told him. Peter followed him out of the prison, but he had no idea that what the angel was doing was really happening; he thought he was seeing a vision. . . . Then Peter came to himself and said, "Now I know without a doubt that the Lord has sent his angel and rescued me from Herod's clutches and from everything the Jewish people were hoping would happen." (Acts 12:6–9, 11)

Although Christians are being persecuted and some killed, still God's plan prevails. With further work for Peter to do, God easily removes him from a dangerous situation. God orchestrates such miraculous acts as making chains fall from a prisoner, restraining guards, and opening iron gates.

In this second prison escape, the prayers of the church play a big part in accomplishing Peter's release. Many believers have gathered in a home to pray for Peter's safety. Even they don't realize the power their prayers carry—when Peter appears at the door, they don't believe it's really him. In answer to the earnest prayers of the church, God spares Peter from further suffering and releases him to continue his work.

—BQ

Daily Contemplation

Are you praying for anything you inwardly doubt God can provide?

DAY 296

Faith or Observance of the Law
Galatians 3:1–4:7

Jesus' disciples were Jewish, as were most of the converts from the day of Pentecost. On his first missionary journey, however, Paul learns to his surprise that non-Jews are more receptive to the news about Jesus. He begins a policy that he will follow throughout his career: First he goes to the synagogue and preaches among Jews, and if they reject him, he turns to the Gentiles.

In a twist of history, Paul gains a reputation as "the Apostle to the Gentiles." Before conversion he was a Pharisee, a strict Jewish legalist. But as he sees God work among non-Jews, he becomes their champion. This letter to the churches in Galatia (guh-LAY-shuh) dates from the time of the early Jew-Gentile controversy. Paul is emotionally heated. In fact, he is downright furious at misguided attempts to shackle the church with legalism. In the first paragraph, Paul explodes with full force; he then proceeds to give a "Christian," rather than Jewish, interpretation of the Old Testament covenants with Abraham and Moses.

Legalism may seem like a rather harmless quirk of the church, but Paul can foresee the outcome of the Galatians' thinking. They will start trusting in their own human effort (keeping the law) to gain acceptance with God. Faith in Christ will become just one of many steps in salvation, not the only one. The bedrock of the gospel will crumble as they, in effect, devalue what Christ has done.

Paul's letter to the Galatians stands, then, as a protest against treason. Paul insists that faith in Christ alone, not anyone's set of laws, opens the door to acceptance by God. If a person could reach God by obeying the law, then he, the strict Pharisee, would have done it. Galatians teaches that there is nothing we can do to make God love us more or love us less. We can't "earn" God's love by feverishly following rules.

—PY

―――――――――― *Daily Contemplation* ――――――――――

The Galatians became obsessed with legalism. Others refused to follow anyone's rules. Which are you more prone to do?

· DAY 297

Faith, the Only Way
Reflection

Belonging to a Christian community can be challenging. Joining a group opens up a whole new world of voices telling us what to do, how to act, who to vote for, how to worship, what to buy or not buy, and more. Gaining a grasp of the Bible and getting to know God are merely the beginning, it often seems.

These pressures are hardly new. Since the days of the early church God has had to remind believers that only one thing matters for salvation: faith in Christ. In the apostle Paul's day, Jewish Christians, accustomed to following the letter of the law, pressured the Gentile converts in Galatia to keep particular parts of the Old Testament law in order to retain their salvation. Because the Jews knew the Scriptures and ranked several notches higher on the religious ladder, the Galatians followed their teaching.

The Jews struggled to accept that when Jesus came, he changed the requirements, fulfilling the law and making belief in himself the one and final way to new life. Emphatic about this point in his letter, Paul warned that the Galatians were allowing themselves to be "bewitched" by wrong teaching. In so doing, they had accepted an unnecessary burden and were misleading others. One who believes in Jesus, Paul declared, is saved from sin. Period. Nothing else is needed.

Paul's letter could not have been clearer. Still, each ensuing generation of believers has lost sight of his words and struggled with its own varieties of legalism, requiring certain actions or behaviors in addition to faith. Martin Luther, father of the Reformation, rediscovered the emphatic message of Galatians and helped redirect many to a more grace-filled theology. He spoke to a church that required religious routines and penance for a person to achieve salvation. Luther's teaching made Galatians the "cornerstone of the Protestant Reformation," and he was so indebted to the book that he even referred to it on occasion as his "wife."

Despite the insistence of Paul, Luther, and others who have striven to keep believers on guard, legalism (following rules prescribed by people, not God) still thrives today, with believers imposing additional burdens on one another. J. B. Phillips, a British pastor and scholar of the Anglican Church, wrote about various false gods that believers often mix with the true God. One, the god of "one hundred percent," expects perfection. This god "has led quite a number of sensitive conscientious people to what is popularly called a 'nervous breakdown.' And it has taken the joy and spontaneity out of the Christian lives of many more who dimly realize that what was meant to be a life of 'perfect freedom' has become an anxious slavery."[67]

Phillips continues: "Some of our modern enthusiastic Christians of the hearty type tend to regard Christianity as a performance. But it still is, as it was originally, a way of living, and in no sense a performance acted for the benefit of the surrounding world . . . The modern high-pressure Christian of certain circles would like to impose perfection of one hundred per cent as a set of rules to be immediately enforced, instead of as a shining ideal to be faithfully pursued."[68]

God gives guidance in the Bible about how to live. Indeed, "the secret of the easy yoke," writes Dallas Willard, "involves living as [Jesus] lived in the entirety of his life—adopting his overall lifestyle."[69] God doesn't, however, hold these standards over our heads as a prerequisite for salvation. Jesus and the Bible teach us God's true ideal. This ideal, when taken as God intended, doesn't threaten us but rather "stimulates, encourages, and produces likeness to itself," Phillips writes.[70]

As we hear the voices that would tell us how we must live, no voice should be stronger than God's Word: "Clearly no one who relies on the law is justified before God, because 'the righteous will live by faith'" (Galatians 3:11).

—BQ

Daily Contemplation

Do you worry about whether or not you measure up as a Christian? Do you get confused or frustrated by what the voices around you are telling you to do? Ask God to help you remain grounded in the message of Galatians, trusting that already and always you are saved by your faith in Jesus.

DAY 298

Lydia's Conversion; Paul and Silas in Prison
Acts 16:6–40

The book of Acts follows Paul on three distinct missionary journeys. All in all, it's a good time to travel, for by Paul's lifetime Rome has established absolute mastery over a vast territory. Language is unified, and a rare empire-wide peace, the Pax Romana, prevails. Moreover, Roman engineers have crisscrossed the empire with a network of roads (built so well that many still survive), and as a Roman citizen Paul holds a passport valid anywhere.

In his travels, Paul concentrates on the chief trade towns and capital cities of Roman colonies. From them, the gospel message can radiate outward around the globe. If a young church shows promise, Paul will stay on, sometimes as long as three years, to direct its spiritual growth. His letters glow with affection for the friends he has made in the process. On his second and third journeys Paul revisits many of the churches he has founded.

This chapter shows how one of Paul's favorite churches comes into existence. Philippi (FIL-ih-pie) is a leading city in the region of Macedonia, where a vision has directed him. A casual conversation with a woman by a river opens the way for Paul (women play a crucial role in many of the early churches). What takes place in Philippi stands almost as a pattern for Paul's never-dull missionary visits: early acceptance, violent opposition, and providential deliverance from danger.

As this account reveals, Paul does not hesitate to use the prestige and status that come with his Roman citizenship. He is escorted from the city with proper respect, but he leaves behind two transformed households: one led by a woman cloth merchant, one by a city jailer. From that unpromising combination the lively church at Philippi will grow.

—PY

Daily Contemplation

How has God used a casual conversation to bring someone or something important into your life?

DAY 299

Imitating Christ's Humility
Philippians 2:1–30

Fully a decade after founding the church, Paul writes his Philippian friends a personal letter. He has suffered much in the intervening years: beatings, imprisonment, shipwreck, hostility from jealous competitors. Surely he must have sometimes wondered, *Is it worth all the pain?* Even as he writes this letter, he is under arrest, "in chains for Christ" (Philippians 1:13). But whenever Paul's thoughts turn to Philippi, the apostle's spirits lift.

Paul declines gifts from most churches out of fear that his enemies might twist the facts and accuse him of corruption. But he trusts the Philippians. At least four separate times they sacrifice to meet his needs. Just recently, they have sent Epaphroditus (ep-af-roh-Dl-tuhs) on an arduous journey to care for Paul in prison. Paul writes the book of Philippians, in fact, mainly as a thank-you for all that his friends have done.

If someone bluntly asked the apostle, "Paul, tell me, what keeps you going through hard times?" he likely would answer with words straight out of this chapter. In Philippians 2, Paul reveals the source of his irrepressible drive. First, Paul gives the example of Jesus. In a stately, hymn-like paragraph, he marvels that Jesus gave up all the glory of heaven to take on the form of a man—and not just a man but a servant, one who pours out his life for others. Paul takes on that pattern for himself.

Then, in a seeming paradox, Paul describes a kind of teamwork with God: While God is working within, we must "work out" salvation with fear and trembling. This common formula aptly summarizes Paul's spiritual style: "I pray as if all depends on God; I work as if all depends on me."

Philippians gives an occasional glimpse of the apostle Paul's fatigue. But it also shows flashes of what keeps him from burnout. To him, the converts in Philippi shine "like stars in the sky." That kind of result, along with his joy in their progress, keeps Paul going.

—PY

Daily Contemplation

How can you "consider others better than yourself" without developing a bad self-image?

DAY 300

Paul in Thessalonica, Berea, and Athens
Acts 17:1–34

Jesus told a parable about a farmer sowing seed, some of which fell on rocky places, some among thorns, and some on fertile ground. This chapter, which reviews events from Paul's second journey, proves that he, the first foreign missionary, encountered all those responses in quick succession.

In Thessalonica (THES-uh-lah-NIE-kuh), Paul's visit sparks a riot. An angry mob chases the apostle out of town, accusing him of causing "trouble all over the world." The next town, Berea, proves far more receptive. After studying the Scriptures to test out Paul's message, many believe, both Jews and non-Jews. Yet agitators from Thessalonica soon stir up trouble there as well. Paul is often trailed by hostile opponents who seek to confute his work.

In Athens, Paul faces perhaps his most daunting missionary challenge. That city, renowned for its philosophers, subjects each new thinker to a grueling intellectual ordeal. Local philosophers, full of scorn for Paul ("this babbler"), haul him before the council of Areopagus, which oversees religion and morals.

Confident that the new faith can compete in the marketplace of ideas, Paul stands before the skeptical audience and, in a burst of eloquence, delivers the extraordinary speech contained in this chapter. Paul gains few converts among the elite Athenians, but he will next travel to the melting pot city of Corinth (KOR-inth) and found a church remarkable for its ethnic diversity.

I once heard Stuart Briscoe, a British evangelist, assess Paul's career this way: "Whenever the apostle Paul visited a city, the residents started a riot; when I visit one, they serve tea."

—PY

---- *Daily Contemplation* ----

What works best for you in starting a conversation with someone about Jesus or the gospel?

DAY 301

Finding Common Ground for the Gospel
Reflection

Charles Colson tells the story of a well-known media figure who invited him to dinner to "talk to me about God." "Tom" set the record straight from the start. He didn't believe in God but wanted to hear Colson's opinions nonetheless.

A former member of Richard Nixon's presidential staff who served a sentence for his Watergate crimes, Colson came to belief in Christ while in prison. He began to tell his story but was cut off. Nice but unconvincing, as New Age spirituality had also "worked" for another of Tom's friends.

Colson proceeded to speak of Jesus as a historical person, of the assurance of heaven, and of an afterlife. He discussed the Bible and its historical validity. Yet Tom had reasons for dismissing each argument supporting Christianity.

Straining for a new tack, Colson threw out a question. "Have you seen Woody Allen's movie *Crimes and Misdemeanors*?" The movie depicts a doctor who hires a killer to murder his mistress. Haunted by guilt, the doctor ponders justice and God's punishment. Never caught, he eases his conscience by concluding we cannot expect justice in the world. Rather, as Darwin proposed, the powerful come out on top.

"When we do wrong, is that the only choice?" Colson asked. "Either live tormented by guilt—or kill our conscience and live like beasts?" At last Tom was silent. Colson noted Leo Tolstoy's *War and Peace*, a story of a man who wrestled with his conscience, decrying his inability to do what he knew to be right. Colson spoke of writer C. S. Lewis's argument for natural law and of the teachings of Romans in the Bible on sin and conscience. Christ is the only one who can rightfully remove the guilt of sin.[71]

Though Tom didn't come to belief in Christ that evening, Colson learned something. Apart from Woody Allen, Tolstoy, and Lewis, he would not have found a connection to discuss spiritual matters. Like the Greeks of Athens in Paul's day, unbelievers today need conversation that challenges them on their level. Just as Paul spoke of the "unknown god" familiar to Athenians, we too build bridges when we talk about familiar ideas or people, discussing by starting with common ground.[72]

In today's spiritually thirsty culture, we may hear an invitation like "Talk to me about God" more frequently than we expect.

—BQ

Daily Contemplation

What personal needs first drew you to Jesus? What made the Bible relevant? Ask God to help you find common ground with people who don't know him.

DAY 302

Living to Please God
1 Thessalonians 2:17–4:12

Born in the midst of strife, the church at Thessalonica continues to meet hostility long after Paul has been chased out of town. When he hears of their troubles, the apostle writes this intimate letter, which provides clues into what makes him so effective as a "pastor." First Thessalonians, dating probably from AD 50 or 51, is our earliest record of the life of a Christian community. It provides a firsthand account of Paul's relationship with a church planted barely twenty years after Jesus' departure.

Paul reviews his pastoral style with the Thessalonians, reminding them that he had been gentle and loving among them, "as a nursing mother cares for her children" (1 Thessalonians 2:7). He writes as if he has no one else on his mind all day. He praises their strengths, fusses over their weaknesses, and continually thanks God for their spiritual progress. A recent report from Timothy has indicated they are heading down the right path, but Paul urges them to live for God and to love each other "more and more."

In this letter, Paul also answers criticisms that have been leveled against him. Is he in it for the money? Paul claims that during his sojourn with the Thessalonians he worked night and day (he supported himself as a tentmaker) to avoid becoming a financial burden. Has he abandoned them? Paul takes pains to explain the reasons behind his unavoidable absence.

Unlike some of Paul's letters, 1 Thessalonians does not major in theology. Rather, it expresses the gratitude, disappointment, and joy of a beloved missionary who can't stop thinking about the church he left behind. Surely one reason for Paul's success centers on his churches' having made as big an impression on Paul as he made on them.

—PY

Daily Contemplation

Who has been like a parent to you in your spiritual life?

DAY 303

Stand Firm
2 Thessalonians 2:1–3:13

One topic dominates 2 Thessalonians more than any other: Jesus' return to earth. Church members are disturbed by a rumor, allegedly from Paul, that the last days have already arrived. In this letter Paul denies the report and outlines what must occur before the Day of the Lord arrives.

The controversy actually traces back to a portion of Paul's first letter. Toward the end of 1 Thessalonians, he gave direct answers to questions about the afterlife. For example, will people who have already died miss out on resurrection from the dead when Jesus returns? That is more than an idle question for the Thessalonians, who live with the constant threat of persecution. On any night a knock on the door could mean imprisonment or death.

Initially, Paul allayed the Christians' fears by assuring them that people still living when Jesus returns to earth will rejoin those who have died before them. In the meantime, however, the Thessalonians have gone several steps beyond Paul's advice. Their speculation about the impending Day of the Lord, fueled by rumors, has become an obsession. Some of them have quit their jobs and simply sit around in anticipation of that day. They are becoming, in Paul's words, "idle" and "busybodies."

Paul writes 2 Thessalonians mainly to correct the imbalance. In the second chapter he tells of certain obscure events that must precede the second coming of Jesus. Some details remain unclear because Paul is expanding on teaching he gave the Thessalonians in private.

Here, as elsewhere, the Bible does not focus on the last days in an abstract, theoretical way. Rather, it makes a practical application to how we should live. Paul counsels patience and steadiness. He asks his readers to trust that Jesus' return will finally bring justice to the earth, urges them to live worthily for that day, and commands them not to tolerate idleness—a good prescription for an obsession with the future in any time period.

—PY

Daily Contemplation

How should you prepare for Jesus' second coming?

DAY 304

Paul in Corinth
Acts 18:1–28

> One night the Lord spoke to Paul in a vision: "Do not be afraid; keep on speaking, do not be silent. For I am with you, and no one is going to attack and harm you, because I have many people in this city." So Paul stayed in Corinth for a year and a half, teaching them the word of God. (Acts 18:9–11)

As a strategic center for land and sea trade, the ancient city of Corinth attracted people as well as goods from surrounding regions, making it a hub of ethnic and cultural diversity. In Paul's day Corinth had a reputation for immoral living and the worship of Aphrodite, or Venus, the goddess of love. Woven even into its religious fabric, the practice of free love was widely accepted and even encouraged. No wonder Paul enters the city in weakness, fear, and much trembling (1 Corinthians 2:1–5).

While in Corinth, Paul meets Priscilla and Aquila, a married couple who become strong partners in ministry. They establish a church in their home and ultimately risk their lives for Paul. In his absence they take an Egyptian named Apollos into their home and teach him about Jesus. Through the mentoring of Priscilla and Aquila, he too becomes an active partner in ministry, helping to further the spread of the gospel to Jews and Gentiles.

The ministry of Priscilla and Aquila displays the importance of both men and women in the early church. Paul calls Priscilla his "fellow worker" (Romans 16:3), a term he also uses to describe key male partners in ministry. Four of the six times he mentions the couple, he lists Priscilla first. Many scholars, including Chrysostom of the fourth century, believe Priscilla was the one who took the ministry lead in working with Apollos and others in Corinth, as well as in Ephesus and Rome.[73] Called by God and gifted to teach others the truths of Christ, Priscilla responds faithfully to the opportunities before her.

—BQ

Daily Contemplation

Whom would you identify as your partners, or fellow workers, in your life with God?

DAY 305

One Body, Many Parts; Love
1 Corinthians 12:1–13:13

Paul's first visit to the Grecian city of Corinth occurs during one of the most stressful times of his career. Lynch mobs had chased him out of Thessalonica and Berea. The next stop, Athens, brought on a confrontation with intellectual scoffers, and by the time Paul arrives at Corinth he is in a fragile emotional state.

Shortly, opposition springs up in Corinth, and Jewish leaders haul Paul into court. But in the midst of this crisis, God visits Paul with a strong message of comfort: "I am with you, and no one is going to attack and harm you, because I have many people in this city" (Acts 18:10).

These last words must have been startling to Paul, for in his day Corinth was known mainly for its lewdness and drunken brawling. The Corinthians worshiped the goddess of love, after all, and a temple built in her honor employed more than a thousand prostitutes. Thus Corinth seems the last place on earth to expect a church to take root. Yet that's exactly what happens. A Jewish couple has opened their home to Paul, and for the next eighteen months he stays in Corinth to nurture an eager band of converts.

Corinth serves as a melting pot for Syrians, Persians, Jews, Greeks, Egyptians, slaves, sailors, athletes, gamblers, and charioteers. And the Corinthian church reflects that same crazy-quilt pattern of diversity. When Paul writes them this letter, he searches for a way to drive home the importance of Christian unity. At last he settles on a striking analogy from the human body. By comparing members of the church of Christ to individual parts of a human body, he can neatly illustrate how *diverse* members can indeed work together in *unity*.

This analogy fits so well that it becomes Paul's favorite way of portraying the church. He will refer to "the body of Christ" more than thirty times in his various letters. Having also raised the question of how diverse people can work harmoniously in a spiritual body, he answers with a lyrical description of love, the greatest of all spiritual gifts.

—PY

Daily Contemplation

First Corinthians 13 describes the qualities of ideal love. Which of these characteristics do you need to work on?

DAY 306

What Is a Church?
Reflection

The first few chapters of 1 Corinthians show the apostle Paul struggling with a basic question: Just what is this thing called a "church"? Paul had never asked such questions about Judaism; culture, religious tradition, race, and even the worshipers' clothing established the identity of that religion. But what is a Christian church? What does God have in mind? The answer must have seemed elusive indeed in the unruly context of Corinth. Almost twenty centuries later, the answer still seems elusive.

Paul's first letter to Corinth betrays his hesitation, mainly in the way he gropes for words. You are God's field, he says in chapter 3, and proceeds to explore that metaphor for a while. On the other hand, you are more like God's building. Yes, exactly. I lay the foundation, and someone else adds the next layer. Better yet, you're a temple, a building designed to house God. Yes, indeed! Think about that: God living in you, his sacred building.

He continues in such a vein throughout the book until finally, in chapter 12, he seizes upon a metaphor that fits best: the church as God's body. The book changes tone at that point, its style elevating from that of personal correspondence to the magnificent prose of chapter 13.

What would Paul, the master of metaphor, say if he were to write 1 Corinthians today—if he were writing, say, to the First Presbyterian Church of Spokane, Washington, or to St. Mark's Episcopal Church in Atlanta, Georgia, or Flatirons Church in Lafayette, Colorado? What word pictures would best communicate to us moderns what God has in mind for the church?

I (Philip) feel secure using the image of family for the church, for it is one used within the Bible. I believe, though, that the vision of the church as a family has even more meaning today than in biblical times because of changes in society.

In an institution, status derives from performance. The business world has learned that human beings respond well to rewards of status; they can be powerful motivators. In families, however, status works differently. How does one earn status in a family? A child "earns" the family's rights solely by virtue of birth. An underachieving child is not kicked out of the family. Indeed, a sickly child, who "produces" very little, may actually receive more attention than her healthy siblings. As novelist John Updike once wrote, "Families teach us how love exists in a realm above liking or disliking, coexisting with indifference, rivalry, and even antipathy."[74]

Similarly, in God's family, we are told, "There is neither Jew nor Greek, neither slave nor free, nor is there male and female" (Galatians 3:28). All such artificial distinctions have melted under the sun of God's grace. As God's adopted children we gain the same rights, clearly undeserved, as those enjoyed by the firstborn, Jesus Christ himself—a book like Ephesians underscores that astonishing truth again and again.

For this reason, it grieves me to see local churches that run more like a business institution than a family. In his discussion of spiritual gifts, the apostle Paul warns sternly against valuing one member more highly than another (1 Corinthians 12:21–26).

In this passage Paul is drawing on his favorite metaphor for the church: the human body. And yet the best way I can visualize how these truths might play themselves out in an actual group of people is to go back to a scene of a human family gathered around a table for a holiday meal.

Every family contains some successful individuals and some miserable failures. At Thanksgiving, corporate vice-president Aunt Mary sits next to Uncle Charles, who drinks too much and has never held a job. Although some of the folks gathered around the table are clever and some dense, some are ugly and some attractive, some healthy and some with disabilities, in a family these differences become insignificant.

I sometimes think that God invented the human institution of the family as a training ground to prepare us for how we should relate within other institutions. Families work best not by papering over their differences but rather by celebrating them. A healthy family builds up the weakest members while not tearing down the strong. As John Wesley's mother put it, "Which child of mine do I love best? I love the sick one until he's well, the one away from home until she's back."

Family is the one human institution we have no choice over. We get in simply by being born, and as a result we are involuntarily thrown together with a menagerie of strange and unlike people. Church calls for another step: to voluntarily choose to band together with a strange menagerie because of a common bond in Jesus Christ. I have found that such a community has much in common with a family. Henri Nouwen once defined a community as "a place where the person you least want to live with always lives." His definition applies equally to the group that gathers each Thanksgiving and the group that congregates each Sunday morning.[75]

—PY

Daily Contemplation

Have you ever attended a church? What challenges have you encountered there? What benefits have you realized? Thank God for the ways in which the church has helped you meet him and sense his love. Ask God to help you accept the less-than-perfect aspects as just a part of the larger blessing he intends the church to be.

DAY 307

The Resurrection of Christ and the Dead
1 Corinthians 15:3–57

Some people in Paul's day are challenging the Christian belief in an afterlife. Death, they say, is the end. Throughout history, many people have taken such a position. In Jesus' day, a Jewish sect called the Sadducees denied the resurrection from the dead. Doubters persist today, including Buddhists, Marxists, and most atheists. Some New Age advocates present death as a natural part of the cycle of life. Why consider it bad at all?

The Corinthian church soon learns not to voice such an attitude around the apostle Paul. To him, belief in an afterlife is no fairy tale; it is the fulcrum of his faith. If there's no future life, he thunders, the Christian message would be a lie. He, Paul, would have no reason to continue as a minister, Christ's death would have merely wasted blood, and Christians would be the most pitiable of all people on earth.

The Bible presents a gradually developing emphasis on the afterlife. Old Testament Jews had only the vaguest conception of life after death. But as Paul points out, Jesus' resurrection from the dead changed all that. Suddenly the world had primary proof that God had the power and the will to overcome death. Chapter 15 of Paul's letter weaves together the threads of Christian belief about death. With no hesitation, Paul brands death "the enemy," the last enemy to be destroyed.

This chapter often gets read at funerals, and with good reason. As people gather around a casket, they sense as if by instinct the *unnaturalness*, the horror, of death. To such people, to all of us, this passage offers soaring words of hope. Death is not an end but a beginning.

—PY

Daily Contemplation

How does a belief in the afterlife affect your life now?

DAY 308

Treasures in Jars of Clay
2 Corinthians 4:1–5:10

Paul blasts anyone who, as the phrase goes, "is too heavenly minded to be of any earthly good." He does *not* prepare for the next life by sitting around all day waiting for it to happen. Paul works as hard as anyone, but with a new purpose: "We make it our goal to please him, whether we are at home in the body or away from it." He seeks to do God's will on earth just as it is done in heaven.

This passage shows that Paul's hope for the future keeps him motivated when the crush of life tempts him to "lose heart." He writes this letter just as an intense struggle with the Corinthian church is coming to a head, and as a result it reveals the apostle in one of his lowest, most vulnerable moments. He has, barely, survived hardships "far beyond our ability to endure, so that we despaired of life itself" (2 Corinthians 1:8). He describes his present state as "hard pressed on every side, but not crushed; perplexed, but not in despair; persecuted, but not abandoned; struck down, but not destroyed."

In typical style, Paul uses a word picture to express his inner thoughts: "Treasure in jars of clay." In his day, jars of clay are nearly as common—and as disposable—as cardboard boxes are today. Beset by difficulties, Paul feels as durable as one of those fragile jars. Yet he recognizes that God has chosen to entrust the gospel, and its good news of forgiveness and eternal life, to such ordinary people as himself.

That insight seems to give Paul renewed hope. He offers a stirring example of how a future life with God can affect a person on earth: "Therefore we do not lose heart. Though outwardly we are wasting away, yet inwardly we are being renewed day by day. For our light and momentary troubles are achieving for us an eternal glory that far outweighs them all. So we fix our eyes not on what is seen, but on what is unseen, since what is seen is temporary, but what is unseen is eternal."

—PY

Daily Contemplation

When you feel the way Paul feels in this passage, how likely are you to fix your eyes "not on what is seen, but on what is unseen"?

DAY 309

The Ministry of Reconciliation; Do Not Be Yoked with Unbelievers
2 Corinthians 5:11–6:2; 6:14–7:1

Therefore, if anyone is in Christ, the new creation has come: The old has gone, the new is here! All this is from God, who reconciled us to himself through Christ and gave us the ministry of reconciliation: that God was reconciling the world to himself in Christ, not counting people's sins against them. And he has committed to us the message of reconciliation. We are therefore Christ's ambassadors, as though God were making his appeal through us. (2 Corinthians 5:17–20)

Do not be yoked together with unbelievers. For what do righteousness and wickedness have in common? Or what fellowship can light have with darkness? . . . Or what does a believer have in common with an unbeliever? What agreement is there between the temple of God and idols? For we are the temple of the living God. (2 Corinthians 6:14–16)

These two passages may seem to contradict each other, with one encouraging a ministry of reconciliation and the other warning believers to join themselves only with other followers of Christ. Which way does Paul want it?

He is passionate about both, with good reason. Paul preaches a message of forgiveness and salvation made possible through Jesus' death and resurrection. No longer does belonging to a special group of people or adhering to a particular set of laws define acceptance by God. Now anyone can become right with God through faith in Jesus.

Some people in Corinth, however, are distorting Paul's message of the centrality of Christ. Rather than being influenced by the believers, these false teachers are enticing others away from God's truth, posing a serious threat. At the same time, the young church in Corinth is experiencing moral problems, and Paul sees a need to address both false doctrine and bad behavior.

—BQ

―――――――― *Daily Contemplation* ――――――――

Are you yoked in a relationship that is drawing you away from Jesus rather than toward him?

DAY 310

Sowing Generously
2 Corinthians 9:6–15

> Remember this: Whoever sows sparingly will also reap sparingly, and whoever sows generously will also reap generously. Each of you should give what you have decided in your heart to give, not reluctantly or under compulsion, for God loves a cheerful giver. And God is able to bless you abundantly, so that in all things at all times, having all that you need, you will abound in every good work. . . . This service that you perform is not only supplying the needs of the Lord's people but is also overflowing in many expressions of thanks to God. Because of the service by which you have proved yourselves, others will praise God for the obedience that accompanies your confession of the gospel of Christ, and for your generosity in sharing with them and with everyone else. (2 Corinthians 9:6–8, 12–13)

The Corinthian church has been collecting money for the impoverished. The collection flows out of Paul's desire that churches respond to each other with mutual aid when needs arise. This gift in particular shows that believers in Gentile areas have not forgotten the Jewish Christians in Jerusalem, where it all started.

In chapters 8 and 9, Paul sets forth his ideas on generosity as well as giving a practical example of fundraising. Some of the Corinthians worry that the money isn't all going to Jerusalem and accuse Paul of taking some for himself. Earlier Paul has defended his integrity, stating that he is "taking pains to do what is right, not only in the eyes of the Lord but also in the eyes of men" (2 Corinthians 8:21). Now he takes a broader view of the matter, reminding his readers that God is the giver. Everything we have comes from God. Furthermore, whatever we give out of a willingness of heart, God is able to give back to us in even greater measure.

Paul encourages believers to give generously and cheerfully. When we give, we'll find that we are blessed in return, both by God and by those who receive.

—BQ

Daily Contemplation

What goes through your mind when you are given an opportunity to help someone in need?

Paul Boasts About His Sufferings, His Thorn
2 Corinthians 11:16–12:10

Although the Jewish and Roman establishments treat Paul as a major threat, Paul expects their opposition. Antagonism from fellow Christians bothers him far more. Jealous competitors have infiltrated the Corinthian church, spreading rumors to undercut Paul's reputation. He isn't fully Jewish, they charge. He doesn't deserve the title "apostle" since he was a latecomer to Jesus. Worse, like other false teachers, he is in it for the money.

In his letters to the Corinthians, Paul confesses a reluctance to defend himself—"I am out of my mind to talk like this"—but their criticisms have gotten out of hand. Jewish? Paul is a strict Pharisee who has studied with the famous teacher Gamaliel. Apostle? True, Paul did not serve as one of the twelve disciples. But he met the risen Jesus on the road to Damascus and was later granted a special revelation of "inexpressible things, things that no one is permitted to tell." Exploiter? Paul has supported himself financially to avoid taking money from the church.

Paul then begins to "boast" about his weaknesses. He runs through the amazing list of beatings, imprisonments, insults, and hardships that have marked his career. And he balances his veiled reference to the special vision with a frank account of one urgent prayer that has never been answered.

Three times Paul has asked God to remove a mysterious "thorn in the flesh." Bible scholars don't agree on the precise nature of the "thorn." Some suggest a physical ailment, such as an eye disease, malaria, or epilepsy. Others interpret it as a spiritual temptation or a series of failures in his ministry. Whatever the ailment, Paul stresses that God has declined to remove the thorn, despite all his prayers for relief, in order to teach him an important lesson about humility, grace, and dependence.

Paul never seems to get over the wonder of the fact that God has chosen him, a former enemy, to bear the good news. He feels humbled and honored that even his weaknesses—*especially* his weaknesses—could be used to advance the kingdom.

—PY

Daily Contemplation

How has God spoken to you through your weaknesses?

DAY 312

Living with Thorns
Reflection

Paul's imagery is to the point—literally—when he describes the "thorn in my flesh" that was given to torment him. Although we don't know the specifics of the thorn, the metaphor makes us squirm with understanding. Whatever plagued him was a painful, ongoing trial.

When I'm worrying over some frustration with myself or my circumstances, I (Brenda) imagine my misfortune as a briar and seek comfort in Paul's, and God's, words. "'My grace is sufficient for you, for my power is made perfect in weakness.' Therefore I will boast all the more gladly about my weaknesses, so that Christ's power may rest on me. That is why, for Christ's sake, I delight in weaknesses, in insults, in hardships, in persecutions, in difficulties. For when I am weak, then I am strong" (2 Corinthians 12:9–10).

As Philip Yancey put it, "Grace, like water, flows downward."[76] When I am weakest and most desperately in need of help, God is most anxious to respond—though not always in the way I expect. Rather than removing the bad circumstances, God works something good from them. Paul is describing one of the paradoxes of life: a painful thorn bringing good? How could a weakness in me or a painful circumstance bring me delight, as Paul describes?

Author and speaker Brennan Manning found the truth of this principle after becoming an alcoholic, losing his home and job, and finally landing on the street. "Probably the moment in my own life when I was closest to the Truth who is Jesus Christ was the experience of being a hopeless derelict in the gutter in Fort Lauderdale, Florida. In his novel *The Moviegoer*, Walker Percy says: 'Only once in my life was the grip of everydayness broken: when I lay bleeding in the ditch.' Paradoxically, such an experience of powerlessness does not make one sad. It is a great relief because it makes us rely not on our own strength but on the limitless power of God. The realization that God is the main agent makes the yoke easy, the burden light, and the heart still."[77]

Each of us struggles with our own personal thorn. We can shut God out and continue to fail, or we can let his power fill the thorn-shaped wound within. When God fills our broken place, he meets us in a way that is different from when we're strong. There is no doubt it's God at work. Delight becomes possible because God is doing more in us than we could realize on our own without the thorn.

Psychologist Larry Crabb describes it this way: "We rarely learn to meaningfully depend on God when our lives are comfortable . . . The entire fabric of Scripture is woven with the thread of relationship. God longs for us to give our heart to Him. He loves us. To the degree that we embrace our thirst and realize who He is, we long for Him. There is nothing dull about the romance between our heavenly Bridegroom and His hurting but fickle bride. The more honestly we face whatever may be locked inside, the more passionately we can be drawn to the beauty of a Lover who responds consistently with all the tender strength our heart desires."[78]

—BQ

Daily Contemplation

What thorn is causing you pain? Have you asked God to remove it? Have you asked him to fill your wound with his power, to replace your weakness with his strength? Talk to him about your struggle. Ask for his help in letting go so you can let him take over.

PART 11

Paul's Legacy

DAY 313

No One Is Righteous
Romans 3:10–31

Throughout his arduous and adventurous life, the apostle Paul keeps one career goal before him: a visit to Rome. At that time, Rome stands alone, the center in every way—law, culture, power, and learning. From that capital city, a powerful empire rules over the entire Western world.

A tiny new church has formed there, stirring great excitement among other Christians. They know that in key ways the future of the church rests on what happens in Rome. If they ever expect to make a dent in the larger world, their faith will have to penetrate Rome.

Paul prays for the Roman church constantly and makes many plans to visit there. Since none of those plans have yet materialized, Paul writes this letter in preparation for his long-awaited visit.

Unlike the letters to the Corinthians, Romans contains few personal asides and emotional outbursts. Paul is addressing sophisticated, demanding readers, most of whom he has never met. In the letter he seeks to set forth the whole scope of Christian doctrine, which is still being passed along orally from town to town. The resulting book has no equal as a concise yet all-encompassing summation of the Christian faith.

Romans is a book to savor slowly and carefully. The logic of Paul's argument unfolds thought by thought from the very first chapter. He is presenting the good news about God's amazing grace: A complete cure is available to all. But people won't seek a cure until they know they are ill. Thus Romans begins with one of the darkest summaries in the Bible. "There is no one righteous, not even one," Paul concludes (Romans 3:10). The entire world is doomed to spiritual death unless a cure can be found.

Out of the mournful notes, however, comes a bright sound of wonderful news, expressed in what some have called the central theological passage in the Bible. Paul sums up the core message of the gospel in these verses (3:21–31).

—PY

Daily Contemplation

Who in your life needs to understand the message Romans presents? Pray for them now.

DAY 314

Struggling with Sin
Romans 7:1–25

One question comes up in virtually every one of Paul's letters: What good is the law? To most of Paul's readers, the word *law* stands for the huge collection of rules and rituals codified from the Old Testament. Thanks to his earlier days as a Pharisee, Paul knows those rules well. And whenever he starts talking about "the new covenant" or "freedom in Christ," the Jews want to know what he now thinks about that law.

This chapter, the most personal and autobiographical in Romans, discloses exactly what Paul thinks.

Paul never recommends throwing out the law entirely. He sees that it reveals a basic code of morality, an ideal of the kind of behavior that pleases God. The law is good for one thing: It exposes sin. "Indeed I would not have known what sin was except through the law." To Paul, such rules as the Ten Commandments are helpful, righteous, and good.

The law has one major problem, however: Although it proves how bad you are, it doesn't make you any better. As a legacy of his days of legalism, Paul has a very sensitive conscience. Yet, as he poignantly recounts, it mainly makes him feel guilty all the time. "What a wretched man I am!" he confesses. The law bares his weaknesses but cannot provide the power needed to overcome them. The law—or *any* set of rules—leads ultimately to a dead end.

Romans 7 gives a striking illustration of the struggle that ensues when an imperfect person commits himself to a perfect God. Any Christian who wonders, *How can I ever get rid of my nagging sins?* will find comfort in Paul's frank confession. In the face of God's standards, every one of us feels helpless, and that is Paul's point precisely. No set of rules can break the terrible cycle of guilt and failure. We need outside help to "serve in the new way of the Spirit, and not in the old way of the written code." Paul celebrates that help in the next chapter.

—PY

Daily Contemplation

What personal struggle makes you feel most helpless? Where do you turn?

DAY 315

Life Through the Spirit
Romans 8:1–27

The Holy Spirit is the theme of Romans 8, and in this passage Paul gives a panoramic survey of how the Spirit can make a difference in a person's life.

First, Paul sets to rest the nagging problem of sin he has just raised so forcefully. "There is now no condemnation," he announces. Jesus Christ, through his life and death, took care of the sin problem for all time.

Elsewhere (Romans 4), Paul borrows a word from banking to explain the process. God "credits" Jesus' own perfection to our accounts, so that we are judged not by our behavior but by his. Similarly, God has transferred all the punishment we deserve onto Jesus through his death on the cross. In this transaction, human beings come out the clear winners, set free at last from the curse of sin.

As always, Paul insists on the best news of all: that Jesus Christ did not stay dead. Paul marvels that the very same power that raised Christ from the dead can also "enliven" us. The Spirit is a life-giver who alone can break the gloomy, deathlike pattern described in Romans 7.

To be sure, the Spirit does not remove all problems. The very titles the Bible applies to him—Advocate, Intercessor, Helper, Counselor, Comforter—assume there will be problems. But "the God within" can do for us what we could never do for ourselves. The Spirit works alongside us as we relate to God, helping us in our weakness, even praying for us when we don't know what to ask.

The way Paul tells it, what happens inside individual believers is the central drama of history: "The creation waits in eager expectation for the children of God to be revealed." Somehow, our spiritual victories will help bring about the liberation and healing of a "groaning" creation. The apostle can hardly contain himself as he contemplates these matters. Romans 8 ends with a ringing declaration that nothing—*absolutely, positively nothing*—can ever separate us from God's love. For Paul, that is a fact worth shouting about.

—PY

Daily Contemplation

According to this passage, how can the Holy Spirit make a difference in your daily life?

DAY 316

How God Changes Us
Reflection

After we give our lives to Jesus, our thinking about ourselves changes. The self we may have once viewed as basically good begins to look hopelessly flawed. Bad behavior, wrong thoughts, hurtful words, and maybe addictions happen too frequently, and the mind constantly replays all our mistakes and regrets.

Maybe yours plays words of inner frustration like these: "I do not understand what I do. For what I want to do I do not do, but what I hate I do." (Romans 7:15). Even Paul, writer of much of the New Testament, struggled with his own self-mastery. If your thinking runs like Paul's, you have probably begun to grasp at a deeper level the holy character of God, and how far we fall short.

When I (Brenda) was a teenager, my sin presented itself most blatantly in the form of gossip. For the first time I learned about working with God on a habit that with each fresh failure seemed beyond repair. I smile now at those frustrations, yet I must admit that the failures of the tongue haven't proved less challenging as I've aged. I still find myself confessing, and confounded by, a slip of my tongue.

Is this how God intends us to live, struggling to improve, mostly unsuccessfully? Richard Foster, in his classic book *Celebration of Discipline*, writes,

> The Spiritual Disciplines are the means of God's grace for bringing about genuine personality formation. . . . When we despair of gaining inner transformation through human powers of will and determination, we are open to a wonderful new realization: inner righteousness is a gift from God to be graciously received. The needed change within us is God's work, not ours.
>
> The apostle Paul says, "he who sows to his own flesh will from the flesh reap corruption; but he who sows to the Spirit will from the Spirit reap eternal life" (Gal. 6:8). Paul's analogy is instructive. A farmer is helpless to grow grain; all he can do is provide the right conditions for the growing of the grain. He cultivates the ground, he plants the seed, he waters the plants, and then the natural forces of the earth take over and up comes the grain. This is the way it is with the Spiritual Disciplines—they are a way of sowing to the Spirit. [They] are God's way of getting us into the ground; they put us where he can work within us and transform us.[79]

What are the Spiritual Disciplines? They are the "means God uses for producing in us the needed transformation of heart and mind and soul." Foster explains,

Two distinct movements mark the Spiritual Disciplines: the *via negativa* and the *via positiva*. The *via negativa* focuses on ascetical Disciplines like meditation, fasting, simplicity, solitude, submission, and confession. These teach us life-giving ways of self-denial and letting go. The *via positiva* focuses on incarnational Disciplines like prayer, study, service, worship, guidance, and celebration. These teach us life-giving ways of growth and affirmation. Together these two movements are aimed at freeing us from soul-crushing patterns of death and creating joy-filled patterns of life.

This way of living is not confined to people in religious orders or those who have special skills in spiritual matters. No, this life is also for ordinary people. People who work in the high-pressure jobs of information technology and finance. People who are constantly dealing with the stresses of raising children and balancing the family budget. People who teach school and work in hospitals and provide social services and so much more. In short, people just like you and me.[80]

Do you struggle with sin? Do you want to draw closer to God and experience his transformation of even the most difficult parts of yourself? Do you want to experience what Paul wrote of, a "mind governed by the Spirit [bringing] life and peace" (Romans 8:6)? You *can* do something to position yourself before God so that the Spirit can shape you. You can practice Spiritual Disciplines that act as the soil for God's work in growing you.

Though the word and idea of "discipline" might strike you as stern and burden-filled, the opposite is actually true. Through these basic, intentional practices (many of which you may already be familiar with), God unites us with Jesus and his work in us. In the process, we experience an overflow of **joy**. "Joy is the keynote of all the Disciplines. The purpose of the Disciplines is liberation from the stifling slavery to self-interest and fear."[81]

"Thanks be to God, who delivers me through Jesus Christ!" (Romans 7:25)

—BQ

Daily Contemplation

How often do you regret your sin? Have you felt more despair or more hope since coming to know Jesus? Ask God which of the spiritual disciplines might help you to experience transformation regarding your inner struggles.

DAY 317

Peace and Joy; More than Conquerors
Romans 5:1–11; 8:28–39

You see, at just the right time, when we were still powerless, Christ died for the ungodly. Very rarely will anyone die for a righteous person, though for a good person someone might possibly dare to die. But God demonstrates his own love for us in this: While we were still sinners, Christ died for us. (Romans 5:6–8)

And we know that in all things God works for the good of those who love him, who have been called according to his purpose. For those God foreknew he also predestined to be conformed to the image of his Son. (Romans 8:28–29)

In all these things we are more than conquerors through him who loved us. For I am convinced that neither death nor life, neither angels nor demons, neither the present nor the future, nor any powers, neither height nor depth, nor anything else in all creation, will be able to separate us from the love of God that is in Christ Jesus our Lord. (Romans 8:37–39)

These passages focus on a part of life familiar to all of us: suffering. The moment sin entered the world through Adam and Eve, suffering became an inescapable reality. Sin brought about a separation from God and also gave evil a foothold in the world that would lead to much suffering.

The verses in Romans 5 remind us that suffering can have unexpected benefits. Paul mentions some of the qualities suffering can help develop in us: perseverance, character, and hope. He also refers to the greatest example of something that humans meant for evil being turned into good: the execution of God's Son, a day we now commemorate as *Good* Friday.

In moments when we're hurting, these words may be the last ones we want to hear. Yet in time, as we look back on difficulty, we begin to see that the principle holds true. Mature Christians almost always credit the hard times, not the easy times, as the ones that led to the most spiritual growth.

Mysteriously, God brings lasting good from what at first seems like utter ruin. Paul closes chapter 8 with a quick review of his own suffering-filled life—and ends with a soaring, triumphant conclusion.

—BQ

Daily Contemplation

What time of suffering can you look back on and see that God brought good out of pain?

DAY 318

Living Sacrifices; Love
Romans 12:1–21

Too often people view theology as stuff for hermits to think about. When there's nothing else to do, *then* is the time to ask abstract questions about God. Such a notion would have exasperated the apostle Paul. To him, theology is worthless unless it makes a difference in how people live. Thus, after laying out the most thorough, concise summary of Christian theology in the Bible, he turns his attention at the end of Romans to a down-to-earth discussion of everyday problems.

Paul's own life offers a good example of how to make theology practical. In fact, he is writing the lofty book of Romans while traveling to raise funds for famine relief. By collecting offerings from Gentile Christians for the sake of Jews in Jerusalem, Paul models the kind of unity sorely needed by both groups. (See 2 Corinthians 8 for more details of this mercy mission.)

Romans 12 needs no special commentary or study aids. The problem lies not in understanding these words but in obeying them. Paul is describing what love in action should look like. Once more he uses the analogy of the human body to illustrate how diverse parts can work together in unity.

"Offer your bodies as living sacrifices," Paul urges his readers. The Romans of his day, both Jews and Gentiles, associated the word *sacrifices* with lambs and other animals they brought to the temple for priests to kill on an altar. But Paul makes clear that God wants *living* human beings, not dead animals. A person committed to God's will is the kind of offering most pleasing to God.

—PY

Daily Contemplation

Use the second half of this passage as a kind of checklist. Which commands do you have the most trouble with? Which are the easiest?

DAY 319

Submission to Authorities; Love
Romans 13:1–14

> The commandments, "You shall not commit adultery," "You shall not murder," "You shall not steal," "You shall not covet," and whatever other command there may be, are summed up in this one command: "Love your neighbor as yourself." Love does no harm to a neighbor. Therefore love is the fulfillment of the law. (Romans 13:9–10)

Once more Paul encourages believers to keep one thing at the top of the list: love. The second half of the chapter is clear: love others and you will be following all God's commandments. Live like followers of Jesus and stop trying to find satisfaction in things that will never satisfy.

The first half of the chapter raises some questions, however. The way Paul writes, you may conclude that the authorities he mentions are good, moral leaders deserving of God's appointment. In reality, the leaders of Paul's day are scandalous pagans who regularly and openly persecute Christians. Think of emperors like Nero and Caligula. Paul knows the type, yet he tells his readers to submit. Because governing authorities are ultimately established by God, he advises us to honor, respect, and give what we owe to those in authority.

In Acts, Peter and the apostles show that a time may come when "we must obey God rather than human beings" (Acts 5:29; see also 4:19). When believers face a clear choice between following God or following a human authority, they must obey God. Jesus himself said, "Give back to Caesar what is Caesar's and to God what is God's" (Matthew 22:21). His followers have puzzled over how to apply that principle ever since.

—BQ

Daily Contemplation

How do you usually handle dissatisfaction with a leader who doesn't meet your approval?

DAY 320

The Weak and the Strong
Romans 14:1–15:13

Accept the one whose faith is weak, without quarreling over disputable matters. One person's faith allows them to eat anything, but another, whose faith is weak, eats only vegetables. The one who eats everything must not treat with contempt the one who does not, and the one who does not eat everything must not judge the one who does, for God has accepted them. . . . Let us therefore make every effort to do what leads to peace and to mutual edification. Do not destroy the work of God for the sake of food. All food is clean, but it is wrong for a person to eat anything that causes someone else to stumble. It is better not to eat meat or drink wine or to do anything else that will cause your brother or sister to fall. (Romans 14:1–3, 19–21)

Part of loving others, Paul teaches, involves accepting that we will live differently from each other. Some are weaker or less mature in their faith, and some are stronger. God may lead some to live one way, within the realm of his overall guidelines, and others to live another way. As long as all are living within God's commands in the Bible, we shouldn't insist that one way is right for all. Love calls us to let God guide each believer.

Sometimes our freedom may conflict with the weakness of a brother or sister, and these areas of disagreement change over the years. For example, in Paul's day believers differed on whether it was wrong to eat meat that had been offered to idols—not a current issue of controversy. Paul gives a guiding principle that applies in every case: "It is wrong for a person to eat anything that causes someone else to stumble. It is better not to eat meat or drink wine or to do anything else that will cause your brother or sister to fall" (Romans 14:20–21). Love demands that we take care that others aren't prone to stumble because of our choices.

—BQ

Daily Contemplation

What kinds of differences do you have with other believers that fit what Paul is talking about here? How well do you succeed at not passing judgment? How well do you do in taking care not to cause another person to stumble?

DAY 321

Spending Myself on God
Reflection

How are you spending your life?
The word *spend* may first bring to mind questions related to money—how we choose to use what we have. *Spend* also applies to time—how we use the time we have. Both issues are important to Paul as he writes to the Romans about becoming "living sacrifices" (Romans 12:1–8). In the last several chapters of his letter, Paul encourages the Christians to let their beliefs influence all they do. Their daily lives need to reflect their love for God.

Animal sacrifices are a thing of the past, merely token gifts. Now God wants people themselves, living sacrifices! And if we give ourselves, we'll begin making new choices about how we spend time, money, and everything else. "Do not conform to the pattern of this world," Paul explains (Romans 12:2). God's business is more important. Conforming to God brings God joy and in turn brings us deeper joy than our former ways.

Popular business leader and author Stephen Covey writes about managing time and personal life. "The way you spend your time is a result of the way you see your time and the way you really see your priorities," he says.[82] Although he is not speaking from a strictly spiritual perspective, Covey is in essence echoing Paul's teaching. The things most important to us will impact the choices we make in using our time, our money, our very selves. If God is most important, we'll want to spend ourselves on him.

How, then, does God want us to go about doing so?

Paul is quick to explain. How we spend ourselves will look different for each of us. Together we constitute a body of believers, and like the parts of the human body, we all have a unique function. God has made us with different strengths, or gifts. Paul's list includes the gifts of prophecy, serving, teaching, encouraging, contributing to the needs of others, leadership, and mercy. His point: God gave us a particular function within the world and the Christian community. We each have strengths, and these should bring into focus the way in which God means us to spend ourselves.

What are your strengths? What compliments have you received from others concerning your abilities? What are the ways you feel most comfortable and energized in giving to God and other people? Most likely these strengths relate directly to your gifts, and that should guide your choices. Are you gifted at encouraging? Then call a hurting friend or visit someone lonely. Are you gifted at contributing to others' needs? Then find ways to meet the real needs of other people.

In the life we live day to day, hour by hour, our love for God should impact all we do—even the way we play and rest.

Stephen Covey explains that if we're to change the way we spend our time, holding to our priorities rather than doing the things we've always done, we must have a "bigger 'yes' burning inside."[83] That yes in a believer's mind is a yes to living for God. It's a yes to worshiping him with our daily lives. It's a yes to spending what we have and who we are on God and God's kingdom.

—BQ

Daily Contemplation

Have you taken a spiritual gifts test? Ask God to help you better understand who he has made you to be. If you know your gifts, are you focused on using them? Ask God to help you worship him by using your gifts.

DAY 322

Paul Before Agrippa
Acts 25:23–26:32

Paul determines to deliver in person the relief money he has collected for the Jews in Jerusalem. Friends warn him not to go to that city, still a hotbed of persecution against the Christians. But Paul, "compelled by the Spirit" (Acts 20:22), persists. He knows that God wants him to carry his word to Rome, and nothing that might occur in Jerusalem can thwart that plan.

When Paul reaches Jerusalem, the worst happens: He is arrested on trumped-up charges. Forty Jewish fanatics vow not to eat or drink until they have killed Paul. His reputation as a Christian missionary has so aroused the conspirators that it takes a brigade of 470 Roman soldiers to protect him.

The last few chapters of Acts show Paul at his most fearless. He boldly confronts a lynch mob until Roman soldiers have to drag him into barracks for his own protection. The next day, he takes on the Jewish ruling body, the Sanhedrin, causing such a ruckus that the Roman commander fears they will tear Paul into pieces. In the midst of all this turmoil, Paul gets a comforting vision from the Lord, who says, "Take courage! As you have testified about me in Jerusalem, so you must also testify in Rome" (23:11). That is all the encouragement Paul needs.

Smuggled out of town under heavy guard and the cover of darkness, Paul arrives at last in the palace of the Roman governor. His troubles are far from over. After hearing Paul's defense, Felix sends him to prison for two years as a political favor to the Jews. Even that does not quiet the furor. The moment the new governor Festus arrives, Jewish leaders hatch yet another death plot against Paul.

Acts preserves three of the speeches delivered by Paul on trial. Roman officials, intrigued by the most talked-about prisoner in their corner of the empire, bring him out to perform like a circus sideshow. As always, Paul makes the best of his opportunities. This chapter records the impression he makes on the most distinguished judge of all, King Herod Agrippa.

As a result of the Romans' inquisitions, Paul gets his long-awaited trip to Rome—not via a missionary journey but in a Roman ship as a prisoner of the empire.

—PY

Daily Contemplation

When others oppose your belief in Christ, are you more likely to commit to pray for them or harbor anger and condemnation toward them?

DAY 323

Paul Sails for Rome; Shipwreck
Acts 27:1–44

> Just before dawn Paul urged them all to eat. "For the last fourteen days," he said, "you have been in constant suspense and have gone without food—you haven't eaten anything. Now I urge you to take some food. You need it to survive. Not one of you will lose a single hair from his head." After he said this, he took some bread and gave thanks to God in front of them all. Then he broke it and began to eat. They were all encouraged and ate some food themselves. Altogether there were 276 of us on board. (Acts 27:33–38)

After surviving assassination plots, riots, imprisonment, and a corrupt judicial system, Paul encounters a new set of obstacles on his voyage to Rome. This chapter gives an eyewitness account of an ocean storm, the once-in-a-decade kind of storm that survivors would never forget.

Luke, a passenger accompanying Paul (note the prominent "we" and "us" in this chapter), recounts the experience in vivid detail. He depicts the frenzy onboard: sailors lashing ropes around their groaning ship, the crew heaving precious food supplies and even the ship's tackle overboard, Roman soldiers with drawn swords halting the sailors' save-our-own-necks escape attempts and preparing to slash their prisoners' throats. In the midst of all this hysteria stands the apostle Paul, perfectly calm, foretelling what will happen next. God has promised he will visit Rome, a vision confirmed it, and Paul never doubts it, even when the boat breaks into pieces around him.

Once more Paul reveals himself as a man of unassailable courage. The Roman centurion surely recognizes it: He grants Paul extraordinary privileges and protection. By the end of the storm, everyone on the ship is following the advice of the strange, unflappable prisoner from Tarsus.

—PY

Daily Contemplation

How do you normally react in a crisis?

DAY 324

Ashore on Malta; Arrival at Rome
Acts 28:1–31

The future of the Gentile church depends in large measure on what happens to Paul, God's chosen apostle to the Gentiles. Thus the last few chapters of Acts portray a kind of spiritual warfare in which God turns apparent tragedy into good. Paul gets arrested; he's sent at last to Rome. The ship wrecks; they all survive. A poisonous snake bites Paul; he shakes it off and starts a healing ministry.

Paul arrives in Rome, his ultimate destination, under guard. Undoubtedly the reputation he has gained on the voyage helps convince authorities to treat him leniently. He lives by himself under a kind of "house arrest," with a soldier always present, possibly chained to the apostle. In typical fashion, Paul puts his time to good use. The very first week he calls in Jewish leaders to explain to them the Christian "sect" everyone is talking about. Over the next months and years Paul gets hours of quiet solitude to work on fond letters to the churches he has left behind.

Luke details the process of Roman justice so thoroughly that some have speculated he wrote Acts as a legal brief for Paul's defense. Is Paul intent on inciting revolt? Luke meticulously records that, no, Paul has no political ambitions and consistently works within Roman law.

Luke breaks off the story with Paul's fate still undecided. Most scholars believe that Paul, released from this imprisonment, went on to take his message to new frontiers. Luke records nothing of these journeys and nothing about Paul's trial or sentencing. He ends with a single memory, frozen in time: Paul, confined to his house, preaching to all his visitors. Paul can no longer choose his audience; they have to seek him. But boldly, in the heart of mighty Rome, he proclaims a new kingdom and a new king. Before long, some of Caesar's own household staff are converting to the new faith. Christianity has made the journey, and the transition, from Jerusalem to Rome.

Tradition records that a few years later the Emperor Nero has Paul executed. The final verse of Acts serves as a fitting epitaph of the apostle's remarkable career.

—PY

Daily Contemplation

Do you, like Paul, strive to make the best of bad situations?

Thanksgiving and Prayer; Made Alive in Christ
Ephesians 1:15–2:13

Ironically, some of the brightest, most hopeful books of the Bible—the letters to the Philippians, Colossians, and Ephesians—come out of Paul's term of house arrest in Rome. There's a good reason: Prison offers him the precious commodity of time. Paul is no longer journeying from town to town, stamping out fires set by his enemies. Settled into passably comfortable surroundings, he can devote attention to lofty thoughts about the meaning of life.

A prisoner who survived fourteen years in a Cuban jail recounted how he kept his spirits up: "The worst part was the monotony. I had no window in my cell, and so I mentally constructed one on the door. I 'saw' in my mind a beautiful scene from the mountains, with water tumbling down a ravine over rocks. It became so real to me that I would visualize it without effort every time I looked at the cell door."

The letter to Ephesians gives a hint as to what the apostle Paul "sees" when he lets his mind wander beyond the monotony of his place of confinement. First he visualizes the spiritual growth in the churches he has founded. This passage opens with a burst of thanksgiving for the vitality of the Ephesian church. Then he seeks to open "the eyes of their hearts" to even more exalted sights: the "incomparable riches" of God's grace.

Ephesians is full of staggering good news. In it, Paul asks the grandest question of all: What is God's overall purpose for this world? He raises the sights far above his own circumstances to bigger issues, cosmic issues. And when he cranks up the volume to express God's plan of love, not one low, mournful note sneaks in.

If you feel discouraged, or wonder if God really cares, or question whether the Christian life is worth the effort, Ephesians provides a great tonic. It prescribes the "riches in Christ" available to all.

—PY

Daily Contemplation

What do you find most encouraging about Paul's good-news message?

Paul the Preacher to the Gentiles; A Prayer
Ephesians 2:14–3:21

The missionary church at Ephesus (EF-eh-sus) is one of Paul's success stories. He first visited this most important city in western Asia Minor (now Turkey) on his third missionary journey. The Ephesus of his day is renowned for its religion—but not the kind of religion Paul represents. Worship of the Roman goddess Diana centers in Ephesus, and its residents take great pride in the temple devoted to her. The temple building ranks among the seven wonders of the ancient world, and inside it, hundreds of professional prostitute-priestesses "assist the worshipers."

In this unlikely place, Paul discovers a tiny Christian community already in existence. They know something about John the Baptist, not much about Jesus, and they have never even heard of the Holy Spirit. For the next two years Paul preaches to the Jews and to the Gentiles. A burgeoning church takes root, and soon word spreads throughout the entire province of Asia.

Like most early churches, the one at Ephesus struggles with Jew-Gentile differences. Believers from a Jewish background, raised on a steady diet of anti-idolatry, have huge obstacles to overcome in accepting former idol worshipers into their church. This section of Ephesians addresses the unity issues head-on.

In keeping with the spirit of this letter and the healthy state of the church, Paul maintains an upbeat tone. He presents Christ as the great destroyer of barriers, the one who demolishes walls of division. (The Jewish temple in Jerusalem had an actual wall that no Gentile could go beyond.) No early church demonstrates the miracle of new community better than the one at Ephesus. There, idol worshipers—as far from God as anyone on earth—have been "brought near," joining Jews, the chosen people, as full members of God's household.

To Paul, the new community formed of both Jews and Gentiles is one of the great mysteries of the ages, a culmination of God's original plan, kept secret for many centuries but now made known. He can hardly contain his soaring language as he marvels at God's plan being fulfilled at that moment.

—PY

Daily Contemplation

In Paul's time, Jews and Gentiles were the two factions most given to quarreling and division. From your perspective, what groups divide Christians today? Who do you struggle to accept as family in Christ?

DAY 327

Unity in the Body of Christ; Living as Children of the Light
Ephesians 4:1–5:20

Be completely humble and gentle; be patient, bearing with one another in love. Make every effort to keep the unity of the Spirit through the bond of peace. (Ephesians 4:2–3)

For you were once darkness, but now you are light in the Lord. Live as children of light (for the fruit of the light consists in all goodness, righteousness and truth) and find out what pleases the Lord. Have nothing to do with the fruitless deeds of darkness, but rather expose them. (Ephesians 5:8–11)

It is a passage we would do well to read every day. Paul continues to stress the importance of unity among believers and explains what we will look like as believers who are maturing together.

God distributes different gifts so each person can serve others. The maturing process will show in the way we live, day to day and minute by minute. "Be very careful, then, how you live," Paul implores. We are children of the light, and this shines through in our behavior.

What we talk about, the way we joke together, how we handle sexual desires, the place we give to greed, the people we choose for close companions, the way we handle anger, what we let fill our minds—all these matter because they reflect who we are. If we belong to Jesus, we want to live for him, seeking sanctification—a growing likeness to him—every day. This won't happen if we take lightly the choices we make in daily life.

As believers, we "put off [our] old self" and "put on the new self, created to be like God." When this is our prayer, God gives us the help we need to care about the way we live, and then to live as if we care.

—BQ

Daily Contemplation

How often, in the course of a day, do you consider whether your behavior is pleasing to God? Pray that with each day you would more closely resemble Jesus.

DAY 328

Fixing Broken Love
Reflection

In a day of broken families, broken relationships, and broken concepts of love, Paul's prayer for the Ephesians is one most of us today need to pray for ourselves and each other. He says in 3:14–19:

> For this reason I kneel before the Father, from whom every family in heaven and on earth derives its name. I pray that out of his glorious riches he may strengthen you with power through his Spirit in your inner being, so that Christ may dwell in your hearts through faith. And I pray that you, being rooted and established in love, may have power, together with all the Lord's holy people, to grasp how wide and long and high and deep is the love of Christ, and to know this love that surpasses knowledge—that you may be filled to the measure of all the fullness of God.
>
> Now to him who is able to do immeasurably more than all we ask or imagine, according to his power that is at work within us, to him be glory in the church and in Christ Jesus throughout all generations, for ever and ever! Amen.

English poet Samuel Taylor Coleridge called the book of Ephesians "the divinest composition of man."[84] Paul's language is so divine, in fact, that in places it can be hard to understand. One thing rings clear, though: His message is about love.

Paul writes about being rooted and established in love, a precursor to understanding Jesus' love for us. Pediatrician Dr. Frederic Burke speaks of the importance of love from an early age in enabling people to love later. "I firmly believe that early physical experience with parents' loving hands and arms is imprinted in the child's mind; and while apparently forgotten, it has a tremendous influence on the child's ego and the kind of adolescent he or she becomes."[85]

Maybe you didn't receive a lot of physical love as a child, or maybe the problem was not just physical but emotional. Maybe love was spoken to you yet was not reliable and available. Maybe you were wounded by love later in life. For love-starved people especially, a "rooted and established" love needs to come from somewhere else. We can find dependable love in community with other believers. Yet ultimately only in Jesus will we find the fullness of love we need. Paul describes the love of Jesus as "wide and long and high and deep," a love that "surpasses knowledge." When we begin to grasp this immense love of Jesus, we experience the fullness of God, and life finally satisfies.

Paul ends his prayer as he began it, referring to God's power. All hope for change may seem unlikely, even impossible, when we look at the brokenness that imperfect love has wrought. But God's power is beyond understanding. One of the best promises of the Bible lies in Paul's closing words: "To him who is able to do immeasurably more than all we ask or imagine . . ." God truly is able to fill us full of love so we don't feel hungry, hurting, or angry. He is able to heal the wounds of a broken past and give us a new future. Life-giving love can be a reality. God's power works within us to make it happen.

—BQ

---- *Daily Contemplation* ----

What brokenness have you known in the relationships of your life? Do you have doubts as to whether love—God's or people's—can be trusted? Pray Paul's prayer slowly and talk to God about the pain you feel over failed love. Ask him to help you experience the healing, life-changing love of Christ.

DAY 329

Submit to One Another; The Armor of God
Ephesians 5:21–6:20

After giving overarching guidance on how all God's people are to relate to one another, Paul gives specifics on what some of these relationships will look like among believers who are living together in unity. As a general principle, he begins, believers should "submit to one another out of reverence for Christ." Jesus lived his life on earth in an attitude of voluntary submission and service to others. In the same way we should submit to one another, serving each other as we allow Christ to live through us.

This idea of mutual submission is revolutionary in Paul's day, yet it's merely a reflection of the love and voluntary submission that Jesus modeled while living with people on earth. Jesus surrendered his rights, even to the point of death on the cross.

Paul looks first at marriage. These verses have been a source of confusion, and even resentment, for many. But when we understand them as God intends, they only reflect what Jesus taught throughout his life. Paul asks both husband and wife to sacrificially love one another. This mutual submission does not imply that one partner is subservient to the other; it means that both choose to serve the other, putting the other's needs first.

Wives are asked to submit in the way that all believers voluntarily submit to Christ. The comparison to Christ implies a voluntary service springing from a love relationship; it does not indicate a "doormat" submission. Husbands, as well, are asked to love in the way Christ himself loved believers, submitting his very life to redeem them. He could not have loved more deeply or served more humbly, and this is the character Paul asks husbands to reflect.

Paul tells children to obey and honor their parents, and fathers to raise their children to know God. Then he speaks to the slaves of his day, instructing that also for them the rule of love, submission, and respect applies. Even in the unjust reality of human enslavement, Paul calls believers to be Christlike.

Paul concludes his letter to the Ephesians by reminding them of the spiritual battle that is always a reality. We aren't merely fighting against ourselves to live like Jesus. We are fighting against "the spiritual forces of evil in the heavenly realms." It's a battle we can win in the Spirit's power, however, and Paul tells us how to fight.

—BQ

Daily Contemplation

What makes submitting to or serving the people in your life difficult? What spiritual battle are you facing, and how can this passage guide you in fighting it?

DAY 330

The Supremacy of Christ, Son of God
Colossians 1:1–2:5

The book of Colossians may sound like Ephesians, and with good reason—fully half the verses in Ephesians appear in some form in Colossians. The two cities are neighbors in Paul's day, and one of the converts from Paul's stay in Ephesus has taken the gospel over to Colossae (kuh-LAH-see). Paul himself has never visited Colossae and thus writes this book to people who know him by reputation only.

The letter opens on an optimistic note, with Paul thanking God for the Colossians' spiritual progress. Yet he also brings up for discussion a doctrinal flaw that has crept into their church. The best modern equivalent would be a sophisticated "cult," one that includes some Christian principles overlaid with many other mysterious beliefs.

First-century Colossae, situated on a major trade route from the East, was a perfect breeding ground for various pagan religious movements. Even Jews in this area worshiped angels and river spirits. Often these religious groups (like many now) did not reject Jesus Christ outright; they merely worked him into their own belief structures. Christ and simple forms of worship, they likely taught, were fine for beginners, but the "deep things of God" required some further steps.

Rather than attacking each peculiar belief point by point, Paul counters with a positive theology. "Christ is enough," he declares in this first chapter. He is God, the fullness of God, the one who made the world, the reason that everything exists. All the "mystery" and treasure and wisdom you could ask for are found in the person of Jesus Christ; there is no need to look elsewhere. The masterful summation paragraph that begins at 1:15 may have been adapted for use as a hymn by the early church.

Paul tells the Colossians the same thing he told the Ephesians: Before Christ, a mystery was kept hidden for many centuries. But when Christ came, everything broke out into the open. The fullness of God lived, died, and then reappeared after death, all in broad daylight. Why settle for counterfeits?

—PY

Daily Contemplation

Has anyone ever tried to deceive you with "fine-sounding arguments"?

DAY 331

Rules for Holy Living
Colossians 3:1–25

Since, then, you have been raised with Christ, set your hearts on things above, where Christ is, seated at the right hand of God. Set your minds on things above, not on earthly things. . . . Put to death, therefore, whatever belongs to your earthly nature: sexual immorality, impurity, lust, evil desires and greed, which is idolatry. Because of these, the wrath of God is coming. You used to walk in these ways, in the life you once lived. But now you must also rid yourselves of all such things as these: anger, rage, malice, slander, and filthy language from your lips. Do not lie to each other, since you have taken off your old self with its practices and have put on the new self, which is being renewed in knowledge in the image of its Creator. Here there is no Gentile or Jew, circumcised or uncircumcised, barbarian, Scythian, slave or free, but Christ is all, and is in all. (Colossians 3:1–2, 5–11)

Once more Paul writes a message to the Colossians that resembles the one he gave the Ephesians. He tells them how to live holy lives, as people who belong to Christ. He shortens some of his instructions and then summarizes for all believers the attitude we should have toward daily life as we work and as we strive to live the way God calls us to live: "Whatever you do, work at it with all your heart, as working for the Lord, not for human masters, since you know that you will receive an inheritance from the Lord as a reward. It is the Lord Christ you are serving."

We might read this passage slowly practicing the discipline of *meditatio*, or meditation, letting God's words descend from the mind into the heart and asking God to shape us through them.

—BQ

Daily Contemplation

In what area of your work do you especially need to remember that you are working for the Lord, not for men or women?

DAY 332

Fighting a Spiritual War
Reflection

As I (Brenda) was growing up, I often sang in Sunday school a popular hymn titled "Onward, Christian Soldiers." The first verse goes,

> *Onward, Christian soldiers, Marching as to war,*
> *With the cross of Jesus, Going on before;*
> *Christ, the royal Master, Leads against the foe;*
> *Forward into battle, See His banners go.*[86]

As a child, I had fun with the song. Sometimes we would march around the room, maybe carrying a Christian flag, envisioning ourselves in Jesus' army. That was before I knew anything of the realities of war. Back then war was an otherworldly prospect, a nebulous vision that revolved around the words of a song.

My feelings have changed toward that childhood hymn. I've become too peace-loving to sing the song with the relish I once did. Now I'd rather sing about love. I'd rather look at life through eyes that see the good, even in those with whom I disagree.

I've also come to realize, however, that a proper understanding of the hymn, and many biblical references to warfare, point to a war not so much against people as against the evil that rages out of sight in a realm beyond our world. Such evil, directed by Satan, focuses on combatting the people and things of God.

Paul never lost sight of this battle. In his letter to the Ephesians he wrote, "Put on the full armor of God, so that you can take your stand against the devil's schemes. For our struggle is not against flesh and blood, but against the rulers, against the authorities, against the powers of this dark world and against the spiritual forces of evil in the heavenly realms" (Ephesians 6:11–12). Many times we feel that the hardships we encounter, and temptations we face, stem from sin and our own weakness. We assume that only a determined outlook and strong will can help us overcome. Paul reminds us that we may have forgotten one component in the equation: the very real presence of spiritual forces opposing us. We're not merely fighting ourselves; we are fighting Satan and his agents.

After discussing the armor believers need to do battle—truth, righteousness, peace, faith, salvation, the Spirit, and the Word of God—Paul speaks of prayer, both for ourselves and for one another. When the battle rages, which is most of the time, we need frequent contact with the One on our side. We need him fighting every struggle we enter, and we need the prayers of those around us to give further strength.

Paul mentions one believer who prayed like this for the church he loved. Paul writes in his letter to the Colossians that Epaphras (eh-PAF-ruhs), though a prisoner, was "always wrestling in prayer" for them (4:12). Epaphras and Paul both faced their own enemies, on earth and in spiritual realms, yet they recognized and helped fight the battles of the ones they loved.

Those who still sing "Onward, Christian Soldiers" would do well to approach it again from a child's perspective, envisioning a battle fought not here on earth but in another realm. We should sing both for ourselves and for others, with all the fervor a child can muster. The battle is real. It is God's. And in the words of a hymn by Martin Luther, "He must win the battle."[87]

—BQ

Daily Contemplation

Do you feel ready to face the reality of spiritual warfare? Talk to God about your need for his help. Take a moment to pray for a friend or family member who may be facing a spiritual battle right now. Thank God that he is more powerful than anything that can come against us.

DAY 333

Paul's Plea for Onesimus
Philemon 1–25

The New Testament includes four of the apostle Paul's letters to individuals (1 and 2 Timothy, Titus, Philemon [fi-LEE-muhn]). Of these, Philemon is the briefest and also the most personal. Paul is writing a friend to ask a favor—a *big* favor, for a person's life hangs in the balance.

Like most well-to-do citizens of his day, Philemon owns slaves (historians estimate as many as sixty million slaves served within the Roman Empire). One of these, Onesimus (oh-NES-ih-muhs), has stolen from his master and run away to Rome. There he has met Paul and become a Christian.

As a Christian, the slave Onesimus feels the need to make restitution to his master, whom he has wronged. But the laws of the empire are merciless to runaway slaves. If Onesimus returns, his master Philemon has the legal power to sentence him to immediate execution. Or he can brand the letter *F* (for *Fugitivus*) on his forehead with a hot iron, marking him for life.

The apostle Paul agrees to use his full influence on Philemon, and this brief letter, a masterpiece of persuasion and diplomacy, is the result. Every phrase in Philemon seems crafted to produce the best possible effect. Paul appeals to Philemon's friendship, his status as a Christian leader, his sense of love and compassion. He applies blatant pressure, reminding Philemon that "you owe me your very self." He even offers to pay back Onesimus's debts.

Paul does not call for the outright abolition of slavery in this letter. Such a call would have grossly contradicted the social and economic way of life of the ancient world. In fact, slavery will endure for another eighteen hundred years after this letter is written. The tiny book of Philemon, however, shows that faith had a profound impact on slavery long before its abolition.

Onesimus, his Christian conscience troubled, will assume a grave risk by turning himself in. In Philemon, Paul asks for a second miracle, pleading with the slave's owner to "welcome him as you would welcome me." Onesimus is no longer "property" but rather a Christian brother. Such an attitude, in this culture, is social dynamite.

—PY

Daily Contemplation

Do you know of any situations in which you could be a reconciler between two estranged parties?

DAY 334

Paul Instructs Titus: Tell People to Do Good
Titus 2:1–3:8

In his early years Paul, in a whirlwind of energy, personally carried the message of the gospel to the far corners of the Near East. But age and poor health gradually have slowed him down, and he spends many of his later years locked away in prison. Increasingly he turns to loyal helpers to carry on his work.

The name Titus appears fourteen times in Paul's letters. The book of Galatians (2:1–5) introduces him as Paul's "exhibit A" proving that a Gentile can become a fully acceptable Christian. For more than a decade Paul relies on his trusted associate, who seems to specialize in crisis churches. Twice Titus is dispatched on a diplomatic mission to the rowdy church at Corinth. This letter indicates he faces an equally challenging task on Crete. Paul is writing him a set of personal instructions on how to handle a difficult assignment.

Crete, an island in the Mediterranean, had an ethnically divided population in the ancient world. Its main knowledge of the outside world came through pirates and coarse sailors. You can get an idea of the challenges Titus faced there by reading between the lines of Paul's advice. For example, Paul's advice to the older men to "be temperate, worthy of respect, self-controlled" reveals something about their normal patterns; likewise, his charge to the women "not to be slanderers or addicted to much wine." One of the island's own poets, Epimenides, described Cretans as "liars, evil brutes, lazy gluttons."

Paul always keeps in mind that the Christian church, as a new phenomenon, will attract close scrutiny from the outside world. In Titus, he gives advice on how each of the diverse groups in the church—older men, older women, younger women, younger men, slaves—can provide the best example for that watching world. The goal: "So that those who oppose you may be ashamed because they have nothing bad to say about us."

—PY

Daily Contemplation

Of the advice Paul gives to the various groups, which applies most directly to you?

DAY 335

Teaching on Church Issues, Worship, Leaders
1 Timothy 1:1–3:8

The role of women in the church, social welfare programs, fundraising techniques, a Christian's relationship to society, materialism, order of worship—the topics could reflect the agenda for a modern-day denominational convention. But the apostle Paul was already addressing these issues in the first century, just a few decades after Jesus' life on earth.

The problems discussed in 1 Timothy actually represent growth pains. For instance, out of Christian compassion believers have extended help to needy widows. But before long some members with a "welfare mentality" see the widows' list as an easy way to avoid financial responsibility for their families. In 1 Timothy, Paul outlines a form of "enrollment" to establish who is truly needy.

These and other problems are afflicting the church at Ephesus, where Timothy now serves as pastor. The church has thrived despite intense opposition from within this secular city. His earlier letter to the Ephesians was one of Paul's happiest, but now, almost ten years after his visit to Ephesus, Paul has learned of the troubles brewing. The time has come for older churches to get organized and bring some order to their worship and outreach programs. Otherwise they will drift toward endless division and disagreement.

For that thankless job, Paul turns to his trusted companion Timothy. Converted during Paul's first missionary journey, Timothy has over time gained the apostle's complete trust, despite some major differences in personality. Timothy has a reserved, timid disposition, which may contribute to his chronic stomach trouble. Given his shyness and his half-Jewish, half-Gentile ancestry, Timothy does not seem the ideal choice for a heresy fighter in a turbulent church. But Paul believes he can do the job.

"I have no one else like him," Paul once wrote of Timothy. "As a son with his father he has served with me in the work of the gospel" (Philippians 2:20, 22). Through disturbances, riots, and even into prison, Timothy has loyally accompanied the apostle. Six of Paul's letters begin with the news that Timothy is at his side. Despite a weak stomach and timid disposition, Timothy has proved his mettle to Paul in many ways, and Paul writes this letter to encourage him in a difficult task.

—PY

Daily Contemplation

Do you have any personality traits that make Christian service seem difficult?

DAY 336

Finding a Family That Works
Reflection

Many believers today look upon church involvement as optional. They may be content with a group of like-minded Christian friends. Or they are satisfied simply to work on a personal relationship with God. Gathering with other believers feels inconvenient or too messy. For Paul, the question is not whether to join a church but how to be involved. He underscores the vital importance of the family of God.

The church Titus pastored on the island of Crete had its share of difficulties. For them, to develop a personal spiritual life represented challenge enough. In his letter to Titus, Paul reminds his readers that we have something to give one another that will help, not burden, us. Participating with a diverse group of others in the church will give us a new perspective and help us grow.

Paul mentions "sound doctrine" as the first step (Titus 2:1). Beyond that, all believers need to be self-controlled, reverent, kind, and full of integrity. Differences add diversity to the body, but in areas of character we're all seeking God's way.

Church also offers the chance to learn across generations. God's people who have lived through more life experiences can act as role models and encouragers. In turn, those who are younger fill the church with energy and creativity. All ages are needed.

"But they don't understand me," we may murmur. "I can't relate to them."

Dietrich Bonhoeffer, German pastor of an underground seminary during the Nazi years, writes about the changes Jesus brings to relationships. "Christ became the Mediator and made peace with God and among men. Without Christ we should not know God, we could not call upon Him, nor come to Him. But without Christ we also would not know our brother, nor could we come to him. The way is blocked by our own ego. Christ opened up the way to God and to our brother. Now Christians can live with one another in peace; they can love and serve one another; they can become one. But they can continue to do so only by way of Jesus Christ."[88]

Unity in Jesus changes how we relate to each other. Church may still hold challenges, but when we're committed to life together as God intended, something new takes shape: the body of Christ, God's visible presence in the world.

—BQ

Daily Contemplation

What role does the church play in your life? Do you regularly interact with Christians of other generations or social, economic, or ethnic backgrounds? Pray about any struggles you may be having. Ask God to give you his vision for the church, a place where you are needed both to give and to receive.

DAY 337

Love of Money
1 Timothy 6:3–21

> But godliness with contentment is great gain. For we brought nothing into the world, and we can take nothing out of it. But if we have food and clothing, we will be content with that. Those who want to get rich fall into temptation and a trap and into many foolish and harmful desires that plunge people into ruin and destruction.
> (1 Timothy 6:6–9)

Money represents danger, Paul warns. It isn't inherently evil—we all need it to survive. But a *love* for money puts us on a destructive path, mainly because it displaces our worship of God. Satan uses money to draw our focus away from God toward material things that won't last.

Jesus spoke often about money, warning that "it is hard for someone who is rich to enter the kingdom of heaven" (Matthew 19:23) and "you cannot serve both God and money" (Matthew 6:24). More concerned about peoples' hearts than about the size of their savings, Jesus knew that money has a way of stealing away the love that should belong to God. It can bankrupt our souls, promising security, happiness, and respect but in the end leaving emptiness. Only with a heart centered on God and generosity toward his Kingdom are we truly rich.

"Life does not consist in an abundance of possessions," Jesus said (Luke 12:15). His words, and Paul's, offer loving insight. What we *have* has little to do with who we *are*. Solomon, the wisest man of his time (and one of the wealthiest), said, "Whoever loves wealth is never satisfied" (Ecclesiastes 5:10). God makes it clear: Money won't give us what we truly need. Only he can do that.

—BQ

Daily Contemplation

When have you recently been tempted to let money distract you from your life with God?

DAY 338

Encouragement to Be Faithful
2 Timothy 1:1-18

For this reason I remind you to fan into flame the gift of God, which is in you through the laying on of my hands. For the Spirit God gave us does not make us timid, but gives us power, love and self-discipline. So do not be ashamed of the testimony about our Lord or of me his prisoner. Rather, join with me in suffering for the gospel, by the power of God. He has saved us and called us to a holy life—not because of anything we have done but because of his own purpose and grace. This grace was given us in Christ Jesus before the beginning of time, but it has now been revealed through the appearing of our Savior, Christ Jesus, who has destroyed death and has brought life and immortality to light through the gospel. (2 Timothy 1:6–10)

Paul, now imprisoned for the second time in Rome, has little time left on earth. He writes to Timothy, reassuring him of the hope and conviction that yet fill him: "I know whom I have believed, and am convinced that he is able to guard what I have entrusted to him until that day" (1:12). Paul can look ahead with such confidence because of his bedrock belief in God, who has never left him and has shown himself trustworthy in so many ways.

Despite beatings, stonings, imprisonments, shipwreck, and times without food or clothing, Paul knows he can trust God. Something wonderful awaits him, and his present suffering will be redeemed. "If we endure," he tells Timothy, "we will also reign with him" (2 Timothy 2:12). Paul knows God and the love of Jesus through the Holy Spirit, a relationship that gives him strength no matter what befalls.

—BQ

Daily Contemplation

How does your relationship with God affect how you handle suffering?

DAY 339

A Workman Approved by God
2 Timothy 2:1–26

In 2 Timothy 2:9 Paul writes, "I am suffering even to the point of being chained like a criminal. But God's word is not chained." These words from Paul to Timothy sum up both Paul's personal plight and his burning desire to see his life's work continue after his death.

The second letter to Timothy contains many clues about Paul's circumstances. This time the treatment seems far harsher than his previous house arrest in Rome. Now he is being kept in chains in a cold dungeon that his friends can barely locate. Paul's spirits are sagging. He feels abandoned by "everyone in the province of Asia" (1:15).

This letter almost certainly dates from the reign of Emperor Nero around AD 66–67. By now Christianity has grown from a splinter sect of Judaism into a major force with many thousands of converts, and Nero seizes upon it as a scapegoat for the ills of the empire. He burns Rome to the ground and promptly blames the Christians for the fire. Soon the crazed emperor is torturing believers by crucifying them, by wrapping them in animal skins and turning his hunting dogs loose on them, or by burning them alive as human torches to illuminate the games in his garden.

Little wonder that Paul, imprisoned during this era, exhorts Timothy on the need for boldness in the face of suffering. Paul's own life is nearing an end, and he writes these, his last recorded words, as a legacy to pass on to Timothy and other "reliable people who will also be qualified to teach others."

Second Timothy is a moody book. Sometimes Paul makes himself vulnerable, exposing his fears and his loneliness. Other times, as in this chapter, he gives a rousing "pep talk" meant to lift Timothy's spirits—and perhaps his own. Life is closing in on the apostle, and he strings together last-minute reminders: advice on pure living, essential nuggets of theology, inspiring analogies, one-line proverbs, warnings, common sayings. There is no particular order to this book; Paul has no time for that. He is setting down a kind of spiritual "last will and testament" for his son in Christ.

Tradition teaches that in the end Rome executed Paul for his faith. But thanks to his life and the legacy he passed on to converts like Timothy, the world changed forever.

—PY

Daily Contemplation

What issues would concern you if you were facing death?

Choosing to Run or Remain
Reflection

How do we live amid people who don't know Jesus? I (Brenda) used to reason that in most cases I should stick with people who were behaving in ways I didn't condone as a Christian. Better to be a light than to leave and perhaps appear self-righteous. If I suffered or gave in to sin, the fault was mine, I felt.

I've since come to better understand Paul's admonitions to Timothy. He wrote, "Flee the evil desires of youth and pursue righteousness, faith, love and peace, along with those who call on the Lord out of a pure heart" (2 Timothy 2:22). Paul didn't counsel Timothy to remain strong in the midst of sin. He told him to run the other way.

Probably in his mid-thirties at the time, Timothy had likely come to Christ after meeting Paul and he still knew well the "evil desires of youth" or "youthful passions," as another translation words it (NRSV). Paul taught Timothy and us that in some cases, believers should remove themselves from compromising situations. Sometimes God prefers us to surround ourselves with others "who call on the Lord."

C. S. Lewis helps explain. "What makes [the] contact with wicked people so difficult is that to handle the situation successfully requires not merely good intentions, even with humility and courage thrown in; it may call for social and even intellectual talents which God has not given us. It is therefore not self-righteousness but mere prudence to avoid it when we can."[89]

Lewis and Paul understood that believers are still human. We have God's Spirit, yet we fail at times. God asks that when obvious temptations loom, we flee rather than expose ourselves to what we may not be able to handle.

We need balance, and Jesus modeled that balance for us, spending time with common sinners. Paul acknowledges to Timothy that when some oppose him, Timothy must gently instruct, "in the hope that God will grant them repentance leading them to a knowledge of the truth" (2 Timothy 2:25).

We also will spend time with people who live or believe differently than we do. God asks us to be kind, to avoid quarrels yet be honest (2 Timothy 2:24). Sometimes we need to flee, and sometimes we must speak the truth in love (Ephesians 4:15).

—BQ

Daily Contemplation

In what situations are you likely to be pulled away from God? Are you able to flee these situations? Where in your life is God asking you to stay and, kindly and gently, speak the truth? Ask for wisdom in knowing when to run and when to remain.

PART 12

Vital Letters

DAY 341

Jesus Made Superior to Angels and Fully Human
Hebrews 2:1–3:6

"Are religions all that different?" skeptics ask. "Isn't the most important thing to be sincere in whatever you believe?" Such seemingly modern questions have actually been debated for thousands of years. In fact, the book of Hebrews was written in response to people torn between the Jewish religion and the new faith of Christianity.

Some in the early church favor sticking with the familiar routine of Judaism, which has centuries-old traditions behind it. There's another advantage: The Jews of the day enjoy Rome's official protection, while Christians are subject to persecution. Is faith in Christ worth the risk?

Hebrews insists there are decisive reasons to choose Christ. The whole book revolves around the word *better*. Jesus is better than the angels or Moses or the Old Testament way—better than any real alternative.

Nevertheless, after recording a gust of grand theology from the Old Testament, the author of Hebrews (whose identity we don't know) seems to pause and reconsider. "At present we do not see everything subject to him." Could a world in which Christians are being arrested, tortured, and tossed into jail really be subject to Christ?

From there the author explores why it matters that God descended to the world and became a human being. He did not magically remove all human problems but rather *subjected himself* to the same hardships that any of us face. Hebrews goes further than any other New Testament book in explaining Jesus' human nature.

This chapter gives two powerful reasons why Jesus came to earth. First, by dying he freed us from the power of death and won for us eternal life. And second, after experiencing normal human temptations, Jesus can better help us with our own temptations.

No angel, and no God in distant heaven, could have accomplished those things. Jesus came, in effect, on a rescue mission to free humanity from slavery. Apart from Christ, we live in dread of death and in constant bondage to our failures or sins. Only Jesus can set us free. That's why he's worth the risk.

—PY

Daily Contemplation

From what fears or bondage has Jesus set you free?

DAY 342

A Call to Persevere
Hebrews 10:19–39

> Therefore, brothers and sisters, since we have confidence to enter the Most Holy Place by the blood of Jesus, by a new and living way opened for us through the curtain, that is, his body, and since we have a great priest over the house of God, let us draw near to God with a sincere heart and with the full assurance that faith brings . . . Let us hold unswervingly to the hope we profess, for he who promised is faithful. And let us consider how we may spur one another on toward love and good deeds, not giving up meeting together, as some are in the habit of doing, but encouraging one another. (Hebrews 10:19–25)

The author of Hebrews reminds readers that because of what Jesus has done for us, we can approach God with confidence. We have no need to feel afraid, unworthy, or unloved. We can come to God freely, without a guilty conscience, because of the forgiveness we've received. As we draw near to God, we can hold tightly to the hope he gives us in the Bible. God means for us to count on his promises.

The writer also encourages believers to keep meeting together, even in difficult, dangerous times. God never intended his people to walk alone. He wants us to find mutual support and encouragement from each other.

Finally, the writer answers the question of why a loving God would punish those who aren't committed to him. God gave his entire self, through Jesus, for all people. If some don't accept his gift, they are choosing to remain separate from God. If they don't respond to the Spirit of grace, they cut themselves off from God. Those who follow Jesus, however, have every reason for confidence. God is faithful, and no matter how things look in difficult times, his promises hold true.

—BQ

Daily Contemplation

Are you ever afraid to approach God? Why?

DAY 343

By Faith
Hebrews 11:1–40

The last few paragraphs of Hebrews 10 reveal much about the original readers of this letter. Converting to Christ has brought them abuse: confiscation of property, public insult, and even imprisonment. In the early days they accepted such persecution gladly, even joyfully. But as time has gone on and the trials continue, some are beginning to lose heart.

To these discouraged people, Hebrews 11 presents a stirring reminder of what constitutes "true faith." It's tempting to think of faith as a kind of magic formula: If you muster up enough of it, you'll get rich, stay healthy, and live a contented life with automatic answers to all your prayers. But the readers of Hebrews are discovering that life does not work according to such neat formulas. As proof, the author painstakingly reviews the lives of some Old Testament giants of faith. Some have dubbed Hebrews 11 the "Faith Hall of Fame."

"Without faith," Hebrews says bluntly, "it is impossible to please God." But the author uses rather pointed words in describing that faith: "persevere," "endure," "don't lose heart." As a result of their faith, some heroes triumphed; they routed armies, escaped the sword, and survived lions. But others met less happy ends; they were flogged, chained, stoned, and sawed in two. The chapter concludes, "These were all commended for their faith, yet none of them received what had been promised."

The picture of faith that emerges from this chapter does not fit into an easy formula. Sometimes faith leads to victory and triumph. Sometimes it requires a gritty determination to hang on at any cost. Hebrews 11 does not hold up one kind of faith as superior to the other. Both rest on the belief that God is in ultimate control and will indeed keep his promises—whether that happens in this life or in the next. Of such people, Hebrews says, "God is not ashamed to be called their God, for he has prepared a city for them."

—PY

Daily Contemplation

As a believer, do you more closely identify with the victorious heroes of faith or with those who hung on at any cost?

DAY 344

God Disciplines His Sons
Hebrews 12:1–28

Hebrews 12 takes up right where the previous chapter left off, only the author moves the spotlight from Old Testament history to the readers themselves. He likens faith to an athletic contest in a stadium. Those who have gone before—the giants of faith from chapter 11—are like "a great cloud of witnesses" watching the rest of us run the race of faith. Therefore, "throw off everything that hinders," Hebrews coaches, and again, "Strengthen your feeble arms and weak knees."

Evidently, the original readers of Hebrews have expected a short sprint, not a grueling marathon run. They need extra encouragement and discipline to survive a long-distance spiritual contest.

The analogy of a marathon race provides a way to think about the Christian life. Why do people punish their bodies through a twenty-six-mile course? Most runners mention a sense of personal accomplishment, combined with the many benefits of exercise. There are parallel benefits in a "spiritual marathon." Developing the discipline needed to resist temptation and to endure hardship will lead to good results: namely, strong character and a clean conscience—not to mention the eternal rewards awaiting all who finish the race.

True competitors set their sights on the lead runner, and, as might be expected, Hebrews holds up Jesus as the ultimate standard for our faith. He endured the terrible suffering of the cross for the sake of "the joy set before him." Because of Jesus, no one can complain, "God doesn't know what it's like down here." He does know, for he, too, has been here. And for anyone tempted to grow weary and lose heart, the very best cure is to "fix our eyes on Jesus, the pioneer and perfecter of our faith."

The chapter ends with a soaring passage that celebrates how much better is Christ's new covenant than the old one between God and the Israelites. The new covenant will culminate in a new creation and a new kingdom—one that can never be shaken.

—PY

―――――――――― *Daily Contemplation* ――――――――――

If maturing spiritually is like a marathon race, how far along are you?

DAY 345

The Radical Side of Faith
Reflection

The book of Hebrews devotes an entire chapter to faith. The author first gives a memorable definition—"Faith is confidence in what we hope for and assurance about what we do not see" (11:1)—and then details the many ways in which people of the Old Testament demonstrated their faith.

Some, such as Abel, exhibited faith through a simple love for God, giving him a gift that came from the heart. Others took more extreme measures, such as Isaac, Jacob, and Joseph, who believed God's promises about the future even as death seemed certain. Abraham and Moses left their homes to move to a foreign land. Noah built an ark, Abraham offered his son on an altar to God, and others accepted prison, torture, and death. Only radical faith could have enabled these people to make such sacrificial choices.

The former seminary president Vernon Grounds tells three modern-day stories of people who demonstrated great faith. Mildred Cable grew up in Great Britain and believed God had called her to a ministry in China. Before going she fell in love with a man, and the two desired to marry. However, he felt a strong call to remain in ministry in England. After much prayer and many tears, the two parted, convinced of God's will for them to live out their separate callings. Mildred went on to establish a long and fruitful ministry in China.

George Müller, a poor man with a rich love for God, built five orphanages to care for more than ten thousand orphans in England. He established Sunday schools worldwide and published two million Bible resources and three million books and tracts, all while liberally supporting missionaries in many countries. His faith enabled him to do, humanly speaking, the impossible.

Frank Laubach, in his early ministry, worked in the Philippines with people he literally despised. He felt unhappy and unproductive. One afternoon he sat alone on a hill and wept, wishing to die rather than continue with life as he knew it. Instead, his attitudes died along with his self-pity and pride. He became a different man and went on to found a global ministry that helped millions learn to read God's Word in their own language.[90]

Mildred Cable, George Müller, and Frank Laubach sacrificed their own desires, believing in faith that God had something better for them. Müller explained, "There was a day when I died, utterly died, to George Müller, his opinions, preferences, tastes, and will—died to the world, its approval or censure; died to the approval or blame even of my brethren and friends—and since then I have studied only to show myself approved to God."[91]

We are now surrounded by this cloud of witnesses—Cable, Müller, Laubach, Noah, Abraham, and so many others who gave their lives in radical faith. Let's pray that we also may have the courage to take the steps of faith God asks of us.

—BQ

Daily Contemplation

Do you desire to live out a radical faith in God if he asks you to? How do you feel about giving up your plans for God's plans? Pray about this, asking God to continue developing in you a greater longing for his way for you than for anything else.

DAY 346

Test of Faith; Listen and Act; Show No Favoritism
James 1:1–2:10

You get a sense of James's style in the first two sentences of his letter. After the sparsest greeting, he dives immediately into the topic at hand and starts dishing out advice. James lacks the education and sophistication of the apostle Paul; you won't find his letter wandering off into abstract theology. He is a simple man, a man of the soil. As such, he draws analogies from nature—ocean waves, wilted flowers, a forest fire, spring rains—and expresses his thoughts in pithy sayings almost like proverbs.

Since James's church in Jerusalem is attracting persecution in his day, his letter understandably begins with encouragement for people undergoing trials. But it quickly moves on to a variety of topics, in each case exhorting readers to live out their beliefs. *Be humble!* James orders. *Control your tongue! Stop sinning!* James is as forthright as an Old Testament prophet. His point is hard to miss.

One verse in the first chapter neatly summarizes the pervasive message of this book: "Do not merely listen to the word, and so deceive yourselves. Do what it says." James offers a very pointed illustration of exactly the kind of hypocrisy he is talking about: church members who defer to the wealthy and powerful. The message hits close to home and leaves no room for ambiguity.

The illustration of preferential treatment seems as relevant today as when James first wrote it twenty centuries ago. Modern readers face the same dilemma as the first recipients of this unsettling letter. His words are easy enough to understand, but are we doing what he says?

—PY

Daily Contemplation

To whom do you tend to show favoritism? The rich? People of your race? Those who agree with you politically? Whom do you tend to look down upon?

DAY 347

Faith and Deeds, Taming the Tongue, and Wisdom
James 2:14–3:18

What good is it, my brothers and sisters, if someone claims to have faith but has no deeds? Can such faith save them? Suppose a brother or a sister is without clothes and daily food. If one of you says to them, "Go in peace; keep warm and well fed," but does nothing about their physical needs, what good is it? In the same way, faith by itself, if it is not accompanied by action, is dead. But someone will say, "You have faith; I have deeds." Show me your faith without deeds, and I will show you my faith by my deeds. You believe that there is one God. Good! Even the demons believe that—and shudder. (James 2:14–18)

James, the author of this letter, was probably one of Jesus' brothers, and became a prominent leader in the early church. He teaches, as Jesus did, that how we live reveals the sincerity of our faith. Certainly good works do not bring us God's acceptance, but if our salvation has not changed how we live, we might well question whether we've really given our life to Christ. "Faith without deeds is dead," writes James.

As an example, James mentions a small part of the body that can pose a great danger: the tongue. It is "a restless evil, full of deadly poison," capable of causing great harm and damage (James 3:8). Yet the tongue can also be a source of healing and life. Jesus followers face an ongoing challenge in controlling their tongues. Words, both spoken and unspoken, matter.

May God's Spirit prompt and enable us to speak the words that give life and leave unspoken the words that destroy.

James also discusses wisdom and its tie with humility. God's people will do good out of pure motives. When envy and self-promotion creep in, we are no longer acting wisely but rather from our flesh. James goes so far as to call this focus—on lifting up the self—evil. We can test our motives, he explains, examining whether they are "peace-loving, considerate, submissive, full of mercy and good fruit, impartial and sincere." It is these motives that bring about a harvest of righteousness.

—BQ

Daily Contemplation

When have you recently spoken life-giving words? When have you lost control and spoken destructive words?

DAY 348

Submit Yourselves to God
James 4:1–17

Submit yourselves, then, to God. Resist the devil, and he will flee from you. Come near to God and he will come near to you. Wash your hands, you sinners, and purify your hearts, you double-minded. Grieve, mourn and wail. Change your laughter to mourning and your joy to gloom. Humble yourselves before the Lord, and he will lift you up. (James 4:7–10)

A relationship with God, like any relationship, works in two ways. The Bible assures us of God's love, reminds us of his forgiveness, and pictures his grace. We have no reason to doubt that God longs to be in relationship with us. The book of James turns the focus back on believers, reminding us that there is a right way and a wrong way to treat God. Just as in any friendship, business partnership, or marriage, a relationship with God requires that we act in specific ways to make it work.

James states bluntly that God needs our total commitment. "Double-minded" believers may try to keep one foot in the world and the other foot in God's path. Yet we can't have life both ways. James compares this attempt to unfaithfulness in marriage—we are adulterers toward God when we cheat on the covenant we've made with him.

All believers find themselves drawn back into the world at times, pulled by material things and temptations toward sex or prestige. James urges submission and humility toward God. When we fail, we can seek fresh forgiveness, knowing it's ours when we ask.

—BQ

Daily Contemplation

For what reasons do you need to come near to God today and receive cleansing?

DAY 349

Warning to Rich Oppressors; Patience in Suffering; The Prayer of Faith
James 5:1–20

Is anyone among you in trouble? Let them pray. Is anyone happy? Let them sing songs of praise. Is anyone among you sick? Let them call the elders of the church to pray over them and anoint them with oil in the name of the Lord. And the prayer offered in faith will make the sick person well; the Lord will raise them up. If they have sinned, they will be forgiven. Therefore confess your sins to each other and pray for each other so that you may be healed. The prayer of a righteous person is powerful and effective. (James 5:13–16)

James finishes his letter with practical reminders about what spiritual maturity looks like in believers. They should not hoard wealth or fail to pay what they owe their workers. Ideally they are patient in suffering, remembering all those in the past who have persevered and seen God bring victory. They should be trustworthy in what they say, following through with a yes or no. And they should pray faithfully about everything, including troubles, joys, and sickness. God hears and answers prayer and we must never underestimate the power he unleashes when we pray.

Finally, believers should remember the power they have over one another. James's words offer an important corrective in light of the "live and let live" philosophy of modern culture. We tend to mind our own business and let others live as they choose. Though perhaps preferable to judgment and legalism, this attitude is not always helpful. Among the community of believers, James stresses, we are committed to one another's spiritual growth. By caring enough to confront, we can help turn a brother or sister back to God.

—BQ

Daily Contemplation

When have you, in conviction and love, challenged another follower of Jesus to hold to his or her commitment to God?

DAY 350

Grace and Works
Reflection

I (Philip) once attended a conference at a place called New Harmony, the restored site of a century-old utopian community. As I ran my fingers over the fine workmanship of the buildings and read the plaques describing the daily lives of the true believers, I marveled at the energy that drove this movement, one of dozens spawned by American idealism and religious fervor.

Many varieties of perfectionism have grown on American soil: the offshoots of the Second Great Awakening, the Victorious Life movement, the communes of the Jesus movement. It struck me, though, that in recent times the urge to achieve perfection has nearly disappeared. Nowadays we tilt in the opposite direction, toward a kind of anti-utopianism. The recovery movement, for example, hinges on a person's self-confessed *inability* to be perfect.

I prefer this modern trend. I find it much easier to believe in human fallibility than perfectibility, and I have cast my lot with a gospel based on grace. Yet in New Harmony, Indiana, I felt an unaccountable nostalgia for the utopians: all those solemn figures in black clothes breaking rocks in the fields, devising ever-stricter rules in an attempt to rein in lust and greed. The names of the places they left behind tug at the heart: New Harmony, Peace Dale, New Hope, New Haven.

Yet most utopian communities—like the one I was standing in—survive only as museums. Perfectionism keeps running aground on the barrier reef of original sin. High ideals paradoxically lead to despair and defeatism. Despite all good efforts, human beings don't achieve a state of sinlessness, and in the end they often blame themselves (a blame encouraged by their leaders: "If it is not working, there must be something wrong with you").

Still, I admit that I sometimes feel a gentle longing for the quest itself. How can we uphold the ideal of holiness, the proper striving for life on the highest plane, while avoiding the consequences of disillusionment, pettiness, abuse of authority, spiritual pride, and exclusivism?

Or, to ask the opposite question, how can we moderns who emphasize compassion (never judgment), honesty, and introspection keep from aiming too low? An individualistic society, America stands in constant danger of freedom abuse while its churches lean toward grace abuse.

It was with these questions in mind that I read through the New Testament Epistles, charting the motives they appealed to. I read them in a different order than usual. First I read Galatians, with its magnificent charter of Christian liberty and its fiery pronouncements against petty legalism. Next I turned to James, that "right strawy epistle" that stuck in Martin Luther's throat. I read Ephesians and then 1 Corinthians, Romans and then 1 Timothy, Colossians and then 1 Peter. In every epistle without exception I found both messages: the high ideals of holiness and also the safety net of grace, reminding us that salvation does not depend on our meeting those ideals. I will not attempt to resolve the tension between grace and works because the New Testament does not. We must not try to solve the contradiction by reducing the force of either grace or morality. Grace presents a "Yes, and," not a "Yes, but."

Ephesians pulls the two strands neatly together: "For it is by *grace you have been saved*, through faith—and this not from yourselves, it is the gift of God—not by works, so that no one can boast. For we are God's handiwork, created in Christ Jesus to *do good works*, which God prepared in advance for us to do" (2:8–10, emphasis added). Philippians expresses the same dialectic: "*work out your salvation* with fear and trembling, for it is God *who works in you* to will and to act according to his good purpose" (2:12–13, emphasis added). First Peter 2:16 adds, "Live as free people, but do not use your freedom as a cover-up for evil; live as God's slaves."

I take some comfort in the fact that the church in the first century was already on a seesaw, tilting at some points toward perfectionist legalism and at other points toward raucous freedom. James wrote to one extreme; Paul often addressed the other. Each letter has a strong correcting emphasis, but all stress the dual message of the gospel. The church should be a people who strive toward holiness and yet relax in grace, who condemn themselves but not others, who depend on God and not themselves.[92]

—PY

Daily Contemplation

Do you lean more toward perfectionistic legalism or raucous freedom? Talk with God about the way you usually approach your spiritual life. Ask him to help you find the balance you need.

DAY 351

Praise to God for a Living Hope; Be Holy
1 Peter 1:1–2:3

The Gospels portray Peter cowering in the darkness the night of Jesus' trial and execution, while denying with an oath that he had ever known the man he had followed for three years. But in this letter Peter welcomes suffering as a badge of honor, proof of his commitment to Christ at any cost. Seeing the resurrected Jesus—especially in the poignant scene by a lake when Jesus reinstated him (John 21)—changed Peter forever.

Most likely, Peter is writing this letter during an outbreak of persecution under Nero. Urgent questions stir up within the embattled Christian community. Should they flee or resist? Should they tone down their outward signs of faith? Peter's readers, their lives in peril, need clear advice. Beyond that, they also want some explanation of the meaning of suffering. Why does God allow it? Does God care?

As this chapter shows, Peter's response focuses not on the *cause* of suffering—the *why?*—but rather on the *results*. He answers that suffering can "refine" faith, much as a furnace refines impure metals. Suffering shifts attention from the rewards of this world—wealth, status, power—to more permanent "imperishable" rewards in the life to come. And if Christians maintain their faith through persecution, a watching world will have to acknowledge the source of that faith, God himself.

Evidently, the early Christians heed Peter's advice. More often than not, intense persecution has led to a spurt of growth in the church. An ancient saying expresses this phenomenon: "The blood of martyrs is the seed of the church."[93] According to tradition, Peter himself dies a martyr's death, crucified head downward on a Roman cross thinking himself unworthy to die right side up like Jesus.

In this first chapter, Peter turns what could be a reason for despair into a reason for great hope. He sees the church, in all its birth pangs, as the long-awaited goal of the Old Testament prophets—indeed, the goal of all history.

—PY

Daily Contemplation

When have you recently questioned the reason for suffering in your life?

DAY 352

Suffering for Doing Good; Living for God
1 Peter 3:8–4:19

> Dear friends, do not be surprised at the fiery ordeal that has come on you to test you, as though something strange were happening to you. But rejoice inasmuch as you participate in the sufferings of Christ, so that you may be overjoyed when his glory is revealed. (1 Peter 4:12–13)

Peter teaches that believers may have to suffer for doing good, and they may even suffer for being Christians. His teaching remains foreign to many of us who, in the Western world, don't often see blatant religious persecution occurring. But oppression is a reality in other parts of our world. In some places Christians are forbidden to practice their faith. If caught they are often beaten, imprisoned, or killed.

Even in our own society, however, Christians can suffer a bad name. Stereotypes linked to politics and culture can brand us or lump us together unfairly. As a result, we may hesitate to use the label "Christian" or "Evangelical" because of the assumptions others may make.

"Do not be surprised," Peter says, in reference to persecution, "as though something strange were happening to you" (1 Peter 4:12). And "do not be ashamed, but praise God that you bear that name" (4:16). Be open about your faith, no matter what others think, and always be ready to "give the reason for the hope that you have" (3:15). "Do this with gentleness and respect," Peter adds in the same verse. Such an attitude should mark the true identity of a Christian.

Sandwiched between his verses about suffering, Peter says even more about living as a Christian. The end is near, a time when everyone will answer to God, even those who now condemn us. In the meantime, through the power of love we can hope to soften the hearts of those who misunderstand.

—BQ

Daily Contemplation

When have you been hesitant to admit you are a Christian?

DAY 353

Making One's Calling and Election Sure
2 Peter 1:1–2:3

As 1 Peter demonstrates, leaders of the New Testament church did not consider persecution a grave threat. To the contrary, they held that such trials would purify and strengthen the church by forcing true believers to come forward and exhibit their courage and faith.

The real dangers to the church come from within. Think of unity. At the Last Supper with the disciples, Jesus prayed that believers "may be one as we are one" (John 17:11). But within a generation the church had splintered into followers of Paul or his rivals, legalists, freewheelers, Judaizers, doomsdayers, and dozens of different groups.

Typically, these groups would focus on a minor doctrinal issue and waste energy on meaningless debates. This letter, for example, seems directed toward Christians obsessed with the last days. Some of them, impatient over unfulfilled predictions of Christ's second coming, are already beginning to scoff at the whole idea.

The author of 2 Peter has strong words of correction for such splinter groups. He reminds them that the gospel is no fairy tale, no collection of "cleverly devised stories." As an eyewitness on the Mount of Transfiguration, he has heard God give resounding approval to his Son, Jesus. If that God has promised a second coming, then rest assured it will take place.

As in many New Testament letters, the emphasis in 2 Peter strays back and forth between what to believe and what kind of person to be. The author lays out a progressive list of qualities—faith, goodness, knowledge, self-control, perseverance, godliness, brotherly kindness, love—that will buttress the church against any threat of disunity.

The author of this letter is an old man, soon to face death. As a final swan song, he can do no better than to remind his readers of the most basic truths of the Christian life. The answer to false knowledge is true knowledge; the answer to immoral living is moral living. As he prepares to die, the author of 2 Peter gets in one last appeal for truth.

—PY

Daily Contemplation

Of the seven qualities mentioned in 2 Peter 1:5–7, which describe your life now? Which need work?

DAY 354

Refined by Fire
Reflection

Occasionally I (Brenda) hear a Christian song that praises suffering. Does anyone, no matter how spiritual, really welcome struggle, I wonder?

I think of James's words, "Consider it pure joy, my brothers and sisters, whenever you face trials of many kinds" (1:2) and Paul's words in Romans, "We also glory in our sufferings" (5:3). They offer a similar message: Believers can and should see the positive side of suffering. Both link suffering with perseverance, and Paul adds character and hope to the list of benefits. Hard times strengthen us and also give us new eyes to see that eternity awaits us. This life and its troubles are only momentary.

Peter emphasizes that God has "an inheritance that can never perish, spoil or fade" and is "kept in heaven for you" (1 Peter 1:4). As if writing a promise in a will, God reminds us of what he has in store. I do need that reminder, and suffering can help. During the good times, it's far too easy to get comfortable with the here and now. My vision slips into a shortsightedness, focusing on short-term pleasures of life at the moment. I forget about heaven, rarely thinking of the inheritance awaiting me.

Suffering changes my awareness. As Peter says, it *refines* my faith (1 Peter 1:7), burning away all the distractions that have kept me from seeing the truth about my life with Jesus. Suffering puts me in touch—as probably nothing else can—with what matters. This gives cause for rejoicing, a reason for joy. As C. S. Lewis says, "God whispers to us in our pleasures, speaks in our conscience, but shouts in our pains."[94] During that process of refining, I can hear God more clearly. The dross that used to block my ears has now melted away.

One song on suffering I can sing with heart: "Refiner's fire, my heart's one desire is to be holy . . ." I look at times of past or present suffering, and still I can't say I'm ready for the next onslaught. Yet I can sing of a desire for God to do his good work in me when suffering comes. He has done so in the past, and I trust him to take care of me. While being refined by God may be painful, it also points ahead toward a better life that awaits me—a life with no need for songs about suffering.

—BQ

Daily Contemplation

Can you recall a hard time when God refined you, making you stronger, setting your sights on heaven? Consider the struggles you are facing now. Ask God to bring good from the pain, making you more of the person he created you to be.

DAY 355

Sin and Doom of the Ungodly; Persevere
Jude 1–25

> But you, dear friends, by building yourselves up in your most holy faith and praying in the Holy Spirit, keep yourselves in God's love as you wait for the mercy of our Lord Jesus Christ to bring you to eternal life. (Jude 20–21)

The brief letter from Jude (possibly a brother of Jesus) has much in common with 2 Peter. Both center on danger signs in the church, and the actual wording in Jude closely parallels that of 2 Peter 2. But Jude speaks with an even shriller tone. The disease has spread. If not arrested, it will infect the entire body.

In its approach, Jude resembles the scary movies against drugs and drunk driving that high schools sometimes show their students. They make viewers uncomfortable—which is precisely their purpose. Jude confesses that although he would prefer to write a more joyful letter about salvation, first he must alert them to the serious threat posed by certain troublemakers.

Jude doesn't elaborate on what the troublemakers are saying, but the early church is rife with roving teachers who claim some special word from the Lord. Often these false teachers, seeking a profit, tell audiences exactly what they want to hear: God's grace is so great that you can live however you want with no penalty. Jude leaves no doubt as to what he thinks of such ideas. He calls the impostors "spies" and urges believers to fight for the true faith.

Ironically, only one portion of Jude gets much attention today: the beautiful doxology at the end. Evidently, Jude's strong words are no easier to take today than when they were first given.

—PY

Daily Contemplation

When have you been influenced by a "spiritual" book or teacher who strayed from the central teachings of the Bible? Did you sense any danger?

DAY 356

Children of God; Love One Another
1 John 3:1–24

During World War II, the brilliant Christian thinker C. S. Lewis recorded a series of British radio broadcasts that were later edited into the book *Mere Christianity*. He covered the basics, the bare essentials of Christian belief. Yet even that slim book would seem overly long and complex to the apostle John, author of this letter. John uses the simplest language of any New Testament writer—his three letters together employ barely three hundred different Greek words—to express the gospel in its most distilled form.

An early Christian writer named Jerome tells the story of John as a very old man being carried into the church at Ephesus. The people had gathered to hear a message from the famous apostle, but he would only repeat, "Little children, love one another." When asked why, he replied, "Because it is the Lord's command, and if this is done, it is enough."[95]

That kind of single-mindedness shines through John's letters. This passage begins with wonder, astonishment even, that God has lavished his love on us. We are his children! But then John asks the obvious question: If we are God's children, why don't we act like it? Don't children of good parents naturally want to emulate them?

John is the last surviving apostle. He lives almost to the end of the first century and may be in his eighties when he writes this book. Already, elite religious groups such as the Gnostics have sprung up within the church, and Christians are hotly debating esoteric matters of theology and ethics. John dismisses these with a wave of his hand. To him, the proof of a person's faith is perfectly obvious: "If anyone has material possessions and sees a brother or sister in need but has no pity on them, how can the love of God be in that person?" His words are as piercingly direct as the words of the Sermon on the Mount. A person who loves God acts like it—it's that simple.

—PY

Daily Contemplation

If you could condense the code you live by into one sentence, what would it be?

DAY 357

Test the Spirits; God's Love and Ours
1 John 4:1–21

> Dear friends, let us love one another, for love comes from God. Everyone who loves has been born of God and knows God. Whoever does not love does not know God, because God is love. This is how God showed his love among us: He sent his one and only Son into the world that we might live through him. (1 John 4:7–9)

John begins this part of his letter with a caution that applies as much today as it did in John's day. The early church is encountering a variety of spiritual voices, some of which sound helpful and even authoritative. But believers need to realize that not all seemingly spiritual teaching is from God. Those who don't acknowledge Jesus Christ as God's Son are not inspired by God.

Frank Gaebelein, headmaster of a Christian school in New York, once wrote, "All truth is God's truth."[96] He makes the point that truth may be revealed even through those who aren't committed to God. We need to be careful, however. False teachers may present pieces of God's truth mixed in with untruth. John stresses that believers must maturely discern what is of God and what is not.

John returns in this passage to his favorite theme of love, emphasizing a few aspects of God's love for us: It came first, preceding our love for him; it compels us to love one another; and it summons no fear. All the love that we experience is a reflection of God's prior love toward us. If we have trouble loving the people around us, then we may not have fully realized God's love for us. And when we see God's love as it is, fear dissolves, for fear has no place alongside love.

Regrettably, many people today struggle to give and receive love in healthy ways due to deep wounds they received, when love did involve fear. This passage points to a promise as we seek to move out of our struggles. "No one has ever seen God; but if we love one another, God lives in us and his love is made complete in us" (1 John 4:12). His power and his own love for us can bring the healing we need. Seek the love of others who can help you to keep walking more fully into God's perfect love.

—BQ

Daily Contemplation

When have you experienced or offered a love that involved fear?

DAY 358

Faith in the Son of God
1 John 5:1–15

> Everyone who believes that Jesus is the Christ is born of God, and everyone who loves the father loves his child as well. This is how we know that we love the children of God: by loving God and carrying out his commands. In fact, this is love for God: to keep his commands. And his commands are not burdensome. (1 John 5:1–3)

John concludes his letter by finishing his discourse on love. If we know God's love for us, we'll respond by following his commands, trusting what he tells us to do. Motivated by love, we'll want to please God, and following his way won't feel like a burden. We may not obey him perfectly, but any burden we sense will come only from ourselves or from a source at odds with God.

Jesus' followers have the victory in this world, John proclaims. A popular teacher of John's day taught that Christ was human, apart from a short period of divinity between his baptism and crucifixion. John refutes this belief and affirms rather that Jesus "is the true God and eternal life" (1 John 5:20). As his followers, we partake in that eternal life.

Our love of God and the victory we're promised will become evident in our prayers. As we try to follow his ways, God promises to help. He'll answer any prayer, meeting our needs and giving us strength. True to his love, he'll never fail in his promise.

—BQ

Daily Contemplation

What are you praying for today? Are you asking for God's will to shape your desires and even your prayers?

DAY 359

When to Be Hospitable
2 John 1–13; 3 John 1–14

Most of the early churches founded by missionaries like the apostle Paul met in private homes. Later on, Paul would send out emissaries, such as Timothy and Titus, who joined the original apostles in making "the circuit" from church to church. Christians began the practice of hosting itinerant teachers in their homes, rather than making them stay in the notoriously unsafe Roman inns.

Before long, however, "false teachers" followed suit, bringing distortions of the original gospel and sowing confusion and discord. Soon religious racketeers joined in, seeking free food and lodging. The issue arose concerning what to do with the new breed of pseudo-evangelists. Should Christians offer hospitality to them too? The letters of 2 and 3 John, the shortest letters in the New Testament, deal with this very problem.

These two letters are best read together, since each gives one side of a problem facing a young church. The book of 2 John urges Christians to use discretion in testing a visitor's message and motive. It cautions against hosting visitors who do not teach the truth about Christ. True to his nickname, the Apostle of Love repeats his motto, "Love one another," even in this letter of warning.

On the other hand, 3 John praises a man named Gaius (GAY-yuhs) for warmly welcoming genuine Christian teachers. Gaius's church is dominated by a gossipy dictator who excludes all outsiders.

In a very condensed form, John's second and third letters deal with heresy and church splits, two problems that have plagued the church in every age and in every place. To defend against those dangers, John stresses the need for love and discernment. Believers must know whom to accept and support, and whom to resist.

—PY

Daily Contemplation

When have you encountered a modern deceiver or false teacher?

DAY 360

The Song of the Bible
Reflection

It's appropriate that John's letters on love fall at the end of the Bible. From the first pages of Genesis, the Bible tells a long story of God's love for humanity, and his desire for us to love him and each other. Early in the story Moses and the Israelites sang, "In your unfailing love you will lead the people you have redeemed. In your strength you will guide them to your holy dwelling" (Exodus 15:13). Without knowing it, they were singing a summary song of the entire Bible. From creation to eternity God would lead and redeem his people, bringing them finally to their true home.

Unlike Moses and the people, God knew very well what lay ahead. He described himself to Moses, proclaiming, "The LORD, the LORD, the compassionate and gracious God, slow to anger, abounding in love and faithfulness, maintaining love to thousands, and forgiving wickedness, rebellion and sin" (Exodus 34:6–7). Many of those he loved in the centuries to come would rebel, living self-indulgently rather than for him, and God would forgive again and again, never losing his love for those he'd created.

The Israelites would rebel many times in the desert with Moses, despite the miracles they saw with their own eyes. David later murdered and committed adultery despite God's clear hand in sparing his life and making him king. Solomon, in all his wisdom, ended his life reveling in wealth and women rather than in God. After Israel split into two kingdoms, both fell prey to an attraction for other nations' gods and riches. God expressed through Hosea his grief and his love for his wayward children. Eventually they did return to him, yet the pattern of waywardness would continue to the time of Christ.

Finally, God's Son came to earth to stop the cycle of sin and punishment. Living a life of love and then dying to end the power of sin, Jesus redeemed the people God so dearly loves. Christ rose again to live out his life in believers through his Spirit.

Now, after many letters of instruction to those believers who have followed Christ, John returns us again to the theme of love. "We know and rely on the love God has for us," John says. "Perfect love drives out fear" (1 John 4:16, 18). He knew that love and fear are two of the greatest motivators of the human spirit. They drove the lives of many in the Old Testament and lie at the root of humanity's fickle relationship with God. Fear often causes rebellion, but God's love has the power to conquer fear.

Henri Nouwen, writer and scholar, declared that all people live either in the "house of fear" or in the "house of love." He explained, "When St. John says that fear is driven out by perfect love, he points to a love that comes from God, a divine love . . . The home, the intimate place, the place of true belonging, is therefore not a place made by human hands. It is fashioned for us by God, who came to pitch his tent among us, invite us to his place, and prepare a room for us in his own house."[97]

We can rely on the love God has for us. He desires that we live in his love, making our homes there and acting with others out of the comfort of his love. To guide us we have the Bible, God's book about life lived both in his house of love and in the house of fear. The choice is ours. Each time we waver, we need only open the Bible and listen to its song—a love song, one the Israelites heard thousands of years ago—calling us to our true home.

—BQ

―――――― *Daily Contemplation* ――――――

Do you act more often out of fear or out of love? Is your relationship with God filled more with fear or with love? Ask God to help you move out of the house of fear and into his house of love, confidently believing the message he has given you throughout the Bible.

DAY 361

One Like a Son of Man
Revelation 1:1–20

Imagine the Bible without the book of Revelation. After the Old Testament come the four Gospels, which then lead into Acts and its account of missionary ventures, followed by the letters to the resulting churches. All fine so far, but one thing is missing. Where is history going? Where will it end up?

Jesus' disciples, all Jewish, grew up hearing about a Messiah who would overturn injustice and unrighteousness and usher in a new kingdom of peace and love and justice. Such long-awaited dreams vanished as they watched Jesus die between two thieves, but a few days later the dreams came surging back when Jesus reappeared. "Lord, are you at this time going to restore the kingdom to Israel?" were the last words on their lips (Acts 1:6) just before he left them at the ascension.

One would have to reach beyond all credibility to make a case that the prophets' promised kingdom of peace and righteousness has come about in the years since the ascension. The twentieth century included two world wars, several hundred lesser wars, two atomic bomb attacks, the Holocaust, the Gulag Archipelago, and numerous mass killings by half-crazed dictators. The twenty-first century has already seen the Twin Towers terrorist attack and major wars in Afghanistan, Iraq, Syria, Sudan, Ukraine, and Gaza. Where is the golden age of peace promised by Isaiah?

Revelation adds a two-word message: Just wait. God is not finished with this planet. The Bible stakes God's own reputation on his ability to restore this planet to its original state of perfection. Only when that happens will history have run its course.

As the book opens, the apostle John has been banished to the island of Patmos, a hard-labor colony. In that bleak setting, he receives a vision remarkably similar in style to those reported by the prophets Ezekiel and Daniel. Many details of John's vision no one can claim to understand with confidence. But this first chapter establishes why the visions were given. John presents a new picture of Jesus.

Yes, Jesus is the babe in the manger, the Good Shepherd, the teacher of disciples, the model of humanity, and the Son of God who died on a cross. But he is something else as well: He is the Creator of this world who will someday return to re-create and make new all that humankind has spoiled.

—PY

Daily Contemplation

Does your image of Jesus include the one given in this chapter?

DAY 362

To the Churches in Ephesus, Smyrna, Pergamum, and Thyatira
Revelation 2:1–29

The letters in this chapter and the next are the words of Christ to seven of the early churches. The letters appear in geographical order based on the route one would travel from the seaport town of Ephesus heading north along the coast of the Aegean Sea and then circling south and east to the four remaining cities. Jesus speaks specifically to the churches of John's time and the characteristics they displayed, but his words apply to churches and individuals in future times as well. God's words in the epistles of the New Testament are meant as guidelines for Christians of all times.

Christ commends the members of the Ephesian church for their hard work, perseverance, and hatred of evil men. He warns, though, that they've forgotten the most important thing of all. Second-generation Christians in Ephesus are living outwardly like believers yet with hearts not deeply devoted to Christ. Jesus pleads with them to return to their first love—himself.

Christians in Smyrna (SMUHR-nuh) are experiencing severe persecution and poverty. Their suffering has kept them pure, and Jesus doesn't rebuke them. Rather, he encourages them to hold to the true riches they possess and stay faithful to the end.

Pagan groups abound in Pergamum (PER-guh-mum), a wealthy city caught up in the worship of prominent Greek gods. Although sincere believers live in the city as well, some have compromised and taken on the morality of the city. They have begun imitating the lifestyle of the pagans and have allowed the world's thinking to influence their church doctrine. The church is growing corrupt, and Jesus urges repentance.

Believers in Thyatira (THIE-uh-TIE-ruh) are facing similar problems. Although Christ commends their love, faith, service, and perseverance, he rebukes many for tolerating Jezebel, a prophetess who leads others into sexual immorality and the eating of food sacrificed to idols. This tolerance will carry a cost, Jesus says: intense suffering. To those believers who have not been drawn into Jezebel's web, Jesus encourages perseverance until he comes again.

—BQ

Daily Contemplation

Which of Jesus' rebukes in this chapter hits closest to home with you? Which encouragement speaks to you?

DAY 363

To the Churches in Sardis, Philadelphia, and Laodicea
Revelation 3:1–21

This chapter contains the last three of Christ's letters to seven early churches. To Sardis (SAR-dis), he gives the stern declaration that although they may appear alive, they are dead. Sardis in John's time is a wealthy city located on an important trade route. A center of pagan worship, it also contains a Christian church. Some scholars feel this letter applies to churches of today that build elaborate buildings and attract crowds but lack evidence of genuine life in Christ.

Jesus encourages faithful believers in Philadelphia to endure patiently. Jews who oppose their Christian beliefs are currently oppressing them, but Christ promises that one day the same people will fall down and acknowledge him and his love for his own.

To the church at Laodicea (LAY-uh-dih-SEE-uh) Jesus gives his harshest rebuke. Christians in this prospering city live content with their wealth and blind to their spiritual poverty. Jesus may be referencing a custom of the day to drink liquids either hot or cold, never lukewarm. He makes a strong spiritual application: The Laodiceans are lukewarm and unacceptable in his eyes. The city's wealth stems from its wool industry, notably black garments made out of black wool. But its people take pride in the wrong product. They need to be clothed instead in the white of right relationship with God. Similarly, a Laodicean medical school offers a special salve for eye problems, yet what the people really need is spiritual sight.

All who are blind to the riches of God's kingdom need to open their eyes and repent. Out of love, Jesus rebukes Laodicea and believers of today. He wants us, his people, to walk in the fullness of relationship with himself, seeing through God's eyes rather than our own.

—BQ

Daily Contemplation

When did you first become conscious of your own spiritual poverty? Where were your eyes focused before they caught sight of God?

DAY 364

The Woman and the Dragon
Revelation 12:1–17

In this passage from Revelation John uses bizarre, cosmic symbols: a pregnant woman clothed with the sun; a seven-headed red dragon so enormous that its tail sweeps a third of the stars from the sky; a flight into the desert; a war in heaven. Despite its many interpretations, almost all agree that this chapter has something to do with Jesus' birth and its effect on the universe. When a baby was born, the universe shuddered.

In a sense, Revelation 12 presents Christmas from a cosmic perspective, adding a new set of images to the familiar scenes of manger and shepherds and the slaughter of the innocents. What was visible on earth represented ripples on the surface; underneath, massive disruptions were shaking the foundations of the universe. Even as King Herod was trying to kill all male babies in Judea, cosmic forces were at war behind the scenes. From God's viewpoint—and Satan's—Christmas was far more than the birth of a baby; it was an invasion, the decisive advance in the great struggle for the cosmos. Revelation depicts this struggle as a murderous dragon opposing the forces of good.

Which is the "true" picture of Christmas: the account in Matthew and Luke or that in Revelation? They are the same picture, told from two different points of view. This view of Christ's birth in Revelation 12 typifies the pattern of the entire book, in which John fuses things seen with things normally not seen. In daily life, two parallel histories occur at the same time: one on earth and one in heaven. Revelation, by parting the curtain, allows us to view them together. It leaves the unmistakable impression that as we make everyday choices between good and evil, those choices are having an impact on the supernatural universe we cannot see.

Revelation portrays history through sharply contrasting images: good versus evil, the Lamb versus the Dragon, Jerusalem versus Babylon, the bride versus the prostitute. But it also insists that, no matter how it appears from our limited perspective, God maintains firm control over all history. Ultimately, even the despots will end up fulfilling the plan mapped out for them by God. Pontius Pilate and his Roman soldiers demonstrated that truth. They thought they were getting rid of Jesus by crucifying him. Instead, they made possible the salvation of the world.

—PY

Daily Contemplation

When have you ever felt part of a spiritual battle?

DAY 365

The New Jerusalem; The River of Life
Revelation 21:1–22:5

In its "plot," the Bible ends up very much where it began. The broken relationship between God and human beings has healed over at last, and the curse of Genesis 3 is lifted. Borrowing images from Eden, Revelation pictures a river and a tree of life. But this time a great city replaces the garden setting—a city filled with worshipers of God. Nothing will pollute that city; no death or sadness will ever darken that scene. There will be no crying or pain. For the first time since Eden, the world as it is will finally match the world as God wants it.

John sees heaven as the fulfillment of every Jewish dream: Jerusalem restored, with walls of jasper and streets of gleaming gold. For someone else—say, a refugee in the developing world today—heaven may represent a family reunited, a home abundant with food and fresh drinking water. Heaven stands for the fulfillment of every true longing. As C. S. Lewis has said, all the beauty and joy on planet Earth represent "only the scent of a flower we have not found, the echo of a tune we have not heard, news from a country we have never yet visited."[98]

Revelation promises that our longings are not mere fantasies. They will come true. When we awake in the new heaven and new earth, we will have at last whatever we have longed for. Somehow, from out of all the bad news in a book like Revelation, good news emerges—spectacular Good News. A promise of goodness without a catch in it anywhere. There is a happy ending after all.

In the Bible, heaven is not an afterthought or optional belief. It is the final justification of all creation. The Bible never belittles human tragedy and disappointment—is any book more painfully honest?—but it does add one key word: *temporary*. What we feel now, we will not always feel. The time for re-creation will come.

For people who feel trapped in pain or in a broken home, in economic misery or in fear—for all those people, for all of us, heaven promises a future time, far longer and more substantial than the time we spend on earth, a time of health and wholeness and pleasure and peace. The Bible began with that promise in the book of Genesis. And the Bible ends with that same promise, a guarantee of future reality. The end will be a beginning.

—PY

Daily Contemplation

What do you long for in the re-created earth?

DAY 366

Confidence in the Future
Reflection

For many years as a Christian I (Brenda) avoided the book of Revelation. I didn't understand it, and worse, it scared me. I'd heard lots of interpretations of the book—everything from predictions of who the Antichrist might be and how Christians could soon expect to be tattooed with a number to the belief that the entire book is merely symbolic, describing events in the spiritual realm that will never be seen on earth. How was a person to know the truth about such a fantastical book?

I felt it better to concentrate on the rest of the Bible, doing my best to embrace God's straightforward teaching and invest my time in what I understood. Why flounder with what would remain mere speculation and would likely cause me to live in fear rather than passion for God?

When finally I did study Revelation as part of a writing project, my view changed unexpectedly. Questions remained, but a whole new vision of the future took hold in me. Not only is God wise and loving and compassionate; he is powerful in a sense I'd never grasped as clearly through any other book. Not only is Jesus the God who walked the earth and whose Spirit now lives in believers; he is the one who will reign forever with full strength and authority over every other power. The images of Revelation make that startlingly real. As a believer, this future lies ahead for me, and knowing it is coming impacts everything about my life here and now.

Philosopher and scholar Dallas Willard, writing about heaven and eternity, says, "You are never going to cease existing, and there is nothing you can do about it."[99] If this is true and God indeed commands all that happens after this life on earth, our perspectives should radically shift. Life now is just a foretaste, a preparation for something inconceivable ahead.

The Bible supplies just a few scattered passages and a colorful vision of how eternity will come about. Our minds now can handle no more. Yet what lies ahead will become clear. "When we pass through what we call death," Willard says, "we do not lose the world. Indeed we see it for the first time as it really is . . . We will not disappear into an eternal fog bank or dead storage, or exist in a state of isolation or suspended animation, as many seem to suppose. God has a much better use of us than that."[100] It will feel like waking up from a dream rather than falling asleep. Everything we've learned of God in this life will take on a striking new dimension. It will appear as vivid as the images we find in Revelation, yet without confusion or unfamiliarity.

The book of Revelation is the flag God waves at the end of the Bible, motioning us to the exciting finish of his story. Don't miss this, he alerts us. This is what you've been waiting for, the goal of the Book, the culmination of all you've invested in the life you're living. Surely, Revelation is the one book of the Bible that we should feel compelled to read out of turn. It's the ending we can't resist discovering.

I don't know what lies ahead in my lifetime concerning the end of life on this earth. I don't know whether I'll be called to suffer as I see the unfolding of the events Revelation heralds. I may be seeing some of them now, or they may await my children or several generations to follow. Yet I do know that the book of Revelation is for me. Without it I would be left hanging, left without a powerful word of assurance to ground me and guide me in all the decisions I make. This life is vital for me because it is the life I'll carry into eternity. God has prepared something fantastic and wondrous, and for those who know him the future is not a bit scary.

—BQ

Daily Contemplation

How do you react to the book of Revelation? Do you fear the future? Consider spending more time in Revelation, praying as you read that God would give you his perspective on what lies ahead. You belong to him, and he has magnificent things in store for you.

Notes

1. "Global Christianity Surges Beyond Projections in 2024," Frontier Partners International, March 15, 2024, https://www.frontierpartners.org/global-christianity-surges.
2. Adapted from Philip Yancey, *Disappointment with God* (Zondervan, 1988), 63–65.
3. Julian of Norwich, *Showings,* quoted in Richard J. Foster and James Bryan Smith, eds., *Devotional Classics* (HarperSanFrancisco, 1990), 71.
4. Lewis B. Smedes, *The Art of Forgiving* (Moorings, 1996), 5–7.
5. Simone Weil, *Gravity and Grace* (Routledge, 1972), 9.
6. Pat Ashworth "Solzhenitsyn, Taught to Pray in the Gulag, Dies, 89," Church Times, August 6, 2008, https://www.churchtimes.co.uk/articles/2008/8-august/news/uk/solzhenitsyn-taught-to-pray-in-the-gulag-dies-89.
7. Gary Smalley and John Trent, *Love Is a Decision* (Word, 1989), 8.
8. Nijay K. Gupta, *Tell Her Story* (InterVarsity Press, 2023), 14.
9. John Maxwell, *Developing the Leader Within You* (Nelson, 1993), 146.
10. Tom Wolfe, *The Right Stuff* (Farrar, Straus and Giroux, 1979), 122.
11. Frederick Buechner, *Peculiar Treasures* (Harper & Row, 1979), 24.
12. Thaddeus Williams, *Don't Follow Your Heart* (Zondervan, 2023), 77.
13. Williams, *Don't Follow Your Heart*, 76.
14. Brother Lawrence, *The Practice of the Presence of God*, quoted in Richard J. Foster and James Bryan Smith, eds., *Devotional Classics* (HarperSanFrancisco, 1990), 82–83.
15. Hannah Whitall Smith, *The Christian's Secret of a Happy Life* (1870; repr., Revell, 1942), 67.
16. Smith, *Christian's Secret*, 68.
17. Smith, *Christian's Secret*, 69.
18. Smith, *Christian's Secret*, 73–74.
19. Jim Cymbala and Dean Merrill, *Fresh Wind, Fresh Fire* (Zondervan, 1997), 16–17.
20. Robert Frost, *A Masque of Mercy*, as quoted in *The Atlantic*, November 1947, 70.
21. Corrie ten Boom, *He Cares for You* (Revell, 1978), 189–93.
22. Frederick Buechner, *Wishful Thinking: A Theological ABC* (Harper & Row, 1973), 95.
23. Richard Foster, *Celebration of Discipline* (Hodder & Stoughton, 1978), 122.
24. Eugene Peterson, *A Long Obedience in the Same Direction* (InterVarsity, 1980), 11–13.
25. Peterson, *Long Obedience*, 11–13.
26. Richard J. Mouw, *Uncommon Decency* (InterVarsity, 1992), 41–42.
27. Mouw, *Uncommon Decency*, 11.
28. Flannery O'Connor, *Mystery and Manners* (Farrar, Straus and Giroux, 1961), 34.
29. Brent Curtis and John Eldredge, *The Sacred Romance* (Nelson, 1997), 145.
30. Curtis and Eldredge, *Sacred Romance*, 147–48.
31. Curtis and Eldredge, *Sacred Romance*, 196.
32. Ted W. Engstrom, *The Pursuit of Excellence* (Zondervan, 1982), 20.
33. Engstrom, *Pursuit of Excellence*, 24.
34. Excerpted from Philip Yancey, *Where Is God When It Hurts?* (Zondervan, 1977, 1990), 81–84.

35. Tom Sine, *Wild Hope* (Word, 1991), 212.
36. Sine, *Wild Hope*, 218.
37. Sine, *Wild Hope*, 213, 226.
38. Philip Yancey, *What's So Amazing About Grace?: Revised and Updated* (Zondervan Books, 2023), 35.
39. Adapted from Philip Yancey, *The Jesus I Never Knew* (Zondervan, 1995), 72–82.
40. Richard E. Eby, *Caught Up into Paradise* (Revell, 1978), 91–101.
41. Mother Teresa, *A Simple Path* (Ballantine, 1995), 80–81.
42. Mother Teresa, *Simple Path*, xxx–xxxi.
43. Catherine Marshall, *Meeting God at Every Turn* (Bantam, 1980), 59–60.
44. Marshall, *Meeting God at Every Turn*, 71.
45. Marshall, *Meeting God at Every Turn*, 84.
46. Adapted from Yancey, *The Jesus I Never Knew*, 105–44.
47. "Rabbi Yosef Yitchak Schneerson of Lubavitch," *Tzakikim*, February 8, 2025, https://dailyzohar.com/tzadikim/238-Rabbi-Yosef-Yitchak-Schneerson-of-Lubavitch.
48. John Muir, *The Wilderness World of John Muir*, ed. Edwin Way Teale (1954; repr., Houghton Mifflin, 1982), 103.
49. Muir, *Wilderness World*, 70.
50. Muir, *Wilderness World*, xvi.
51. Eugene H. Peterson, *Eat This Book* (Wm. B. Eerdmans Publishing Co., 2006), 69.
52. Peterson, *Eat This Book*, 70–71.
53. Peterson, *Eat This Book,* 71–72.
54. Augustine, *The Confessions of St. Augustine* (Outler, Wikisource), Book 1, Chapter 1.
55. Blaise Pascal, *Pensees* (Penguin Group, 1995), 45.
56. Macrina Wiederkehr, *Seasons of Your Heart: Prayers and Reflections*, rev. ed. (HarperSanFrancisco, 1991), 58.
57. Oswald Chambers, *My Utmost for His Highest* (Dodd, Mead & Co., 1963), 39.
58. J. I. Packer, *Keep in Step with the Spirit* (Revell, 1984), 9–49.
59. Francis Chan, *Forgotten God* (David C. Cook, 2009), 37.
60. John Stott, *The Contemporary Christian* (InterVarsity, 1992), 329–30.
61. Stormie Omartian, *Lead Me, Holy Spirit* (Harvest House Publishers, 2012), 13.
62. Catherine Marshall, *Something More* (Chosen Books, 1974), 276.
63. Marshall, *Something More*, 279.
64. Marshall, *Something More*, 281.
65. Marshall, *Something More*, 281.
66. Chan, *Forgotten God*, 51.
67. J. B. Phillips, *Your God Is Too Small* (Simon & Schuster, 1997), 30.
68. Phillips, *Your God Is Too Small*, 31–32.
69. Dallas Willard, *The Spirit of the Disciplines* (Harper & Row, 1988), 5.
70. Phillips, *Your God Is Too Small*, 32, 55.
71. Charles Colson, "Reaching the Pagan Mind," *Christianity Today* (November 9, 1992), 112.
72. Colson, "Reaching the Pagan Mind," 112.
73. Terran Williams, *How God Sees Women* (The Spiritual Bakery Publications, 2022), 240.

74. John Updike, "Brother Grasshopper" in *The Afterlife: And Other Stories* (Random House, 2012), 44.
75. Adapted from Philip Yancey, *Church: Why Bother?* (Zondervan, 1998), 45–47, 61–65.
76. Philip Yancey, *What Good Is God?* (Faith Words, 2010), 79.
77. Brennan Manning, *The Signature of Jesus* (Revell, 1988), 110.
78. Larry Crabb, *Inside Out* (NavPress, 1988), 86, 102.
79. Richard Foster, *Celebration of Discipline*, 4th ed. (HarperOne, 2018), xiii, 6–7.
80. Foster, *Celebration of Discipline*, xv–xvii.
81. Foster, *Celebration of Discipline*, 2.
82. Stephen R. Covey, *The Seven Habits of Highly Effective People* (Simon & Schuster, 1989), 158.
83. Covey, *Seven Habits*, 158.
84. William Barclay, *The Letters to the Galatians and Ephesians* (The Westminster Press, 1976), 61.
85. Elisa Morgan and Carol Kuykendall, *What Every Child Needs* (Zondervan, 1997), 25–26.
86. Sabine Baring-Gould, 1865, *Psalter Hymnal, Onward Christian Soldiers* (Publication Committee of the Christian Reformed Church, Inc., 1959), Hymn 466, p. 542.
87. Martin Luther ,1529, *Psalter Hymnal, A Mighty Fortress Is Our God*, Hymn 444, p. 517.
88. Dietrich Bonhoeffer, *Life Together* (Harper & Row, 1954), 23–24.
89. C. S. Lewis, *Reflections on the Psalms* (Harcourt, 1958), 74.
90. Vernon Grounds, *Radical Commitment* (Multnomah, 1984), 42–45.
91. Grounds, *Radical Commitment*, 44.
92. Excerpted from Philip Yancey and Brenda Quinn, *What's So Amazing About Grace? Study Guide* (Zondervan, 1998), 119–21.
93. Tertullian, *Apology*, chap. 50, in *Ante-Nicene Fathers*, vol. 3, ed. Alexander Roberts and James Donaldson (Christian Literature Publishing Co., 1885).
94. C. S. Lewis, *The Problem of Pain* (Macmillan, 1962), 93.
95. From Jerome's Commentary on Galatians 6:10.
96. Frank Gaebelein, "Towards a Christian Philosophy of Education," *Grace Journal*, Fall 1962, 12.
97. Henri J. M. Nouwen, *Lifesigns* (Doubleday, 1986), 36.
98. C. S. Lewis, *The Weight of Glory and Other Addresses* (The Macmillan Company, 1965), 5.
99. Dallas Willard, *The Divine Conspiracy* (HarperCollins, 1998), 391–92.
100. Willard, *Divine Conspiracy*, 395.

About the Authors

Philip Yancey previously served as editor-at-large for *Christianity Today* magazine. He has written thirteen Gold Medallion Award–winning books and won two ECPA Book of the Year awards for *What's So Amazing About Grace?* and *The Jesus I Never Knew*. Four of his books have sold over one million copies. He lives with his wife in Colorado. Learn more at philipyancey.com.

Brenda Quinn currently serves as a pastor of Spiritual Formation. She wrote reflections on Bible characters in Renovaré's *Life with God Bible* and has written study guides for several of Philip Yancey's books. She lives in Colorado with her husband and has three grown sons.

Acknowledgments

We are grateful to John Sloan and Bob Hudson, who edited the first version of this book, titled *Meet the Bible*. Stephanie Newton and Kristen Parrish provided faithful leadership for this revised edition, *The Bible Revealed*. Blake Jurgens and JoLeigh Buchanan spent many hours in tedious and skillful editing, and we thank them and also the design team for their rounds of creative work.

In addition, we're deeply grateful for Joannie Barth, who adopted this project as her own. And we thank our spouses, Janet and Mike, and our families for all of their faithful support.

All thanks to our God for Your divine inspiration of the Bible, and to Jesus Christ, our Living Word.